PENSIONS *IN* DEVELOPMENT

For our pensioner parents

Elsa W.B. Charlton, May McKinnon and Iain McKinnon

As far as conversational no-go areas are concerned, genital warts and crabs are right down there along with pensions ...

Jordan, 1999

In ... all the 365 days of the year are Rulers' Days, whether the ruler is a political party or the military, and it is decent of them to lend some of them to the United Nations for occasions like Children's Day and Women's Day and the altogether unnecessary Senior Citizen's Day. I call it unnecessary because the rulers may be doing something for women and children in their own way, but the Senior Citizen's Day obliges them to tell lies, make silly promises and use up all their stock of cliches. ... All said and done, the senior citizens stuff in ... is good fiction, if not bad farce.

Rahman, 2000

Pensions *in* Development

ROGER CHARLTON
School of Social Sciences, Glasgow Caledonian University

RODDY MCKINNON
Division of Risk, Glasgow Caledonian University

ASHGATE

Published by
Ashgate Publishing Limited
Gower House
Croft Road
Aldershot
Hants
GU11 3HR
England

Ashgate Publishing Company
Suite 420
101 Cherry Street
Burlington, VT 05401-4405
USA

Ashgate website: http://www.ashgate.com

British Library Cataloguing in Publication Data
Charlton, Roger
  Pensions in development
  1. Pensions
  I. Title II. McKinnon, Roddy
  331.2'52

Library of Congress Control Number: 2001089783

Reprinted 2003

ISBN 1 84014 560 9

Printed in Great Britain by Biddles Limited,
Guildford and King's Lynn.

Contents

List of Figures

List of Tables

List of Maps

About the Authors

ROGER CHARLTON is a Reader in the School of Social Sciences, Glasgow Caledonian University, Scotland.

Roger Charlton has published extensively in the fields of African politics, development studies, and international political economy. He has held research fellowships at Birkbeck College, University of London and at the University of Botswana. His recent research and consultancy has focused on Botswana and Uganda.

RODDY McKINNON is a Research Fellow in the Division of Risk, Caledonian Business School, Glasgow Caledonian University, Scotland.

Roddy McKinnon, formerly of the UK Benefits Agency, has published in the fields of the international political economy of old age pension systems and social security reform but also ranging more widely across the field of development studies, with a particular focus on developments in francophone Africa.

Preface

This volume has had a lengthy gestation. For Roddy McKinnon, its origins date precisely to 1987 when he completed an undergraduate dissertation on the developmental states of East and Southeast Asia, leading to research focused on the Malaysian EPF (McKinnon, 1996). For Roger Charlton, origins are more diffuse but crystallised in the early 1990s in work on the importance of the financial bases of 'autonomy' in the 'developmental' state (Charlton, 1993; Charlton and Donald, 1995). We worked jointly from 1995, initially on the political economy of the NPFs of Southeast Asia, moving inexorably into the consideration of wider issues relating to pension system development and reform, as we responded in a somewhat piecemeal fashion to the World Bank's highly successful attempt to define a global pension reform agenda. Building on publications that have ranged widely across pension reform issues in transition states and developing countries, this book represents our consolidated, albeit still developing, perspectives on key 'developmental' issues relating to old age/retirement pensions provision.

Pensions provision, reform and restructuring present the researcher with a classic set of 'comparative' problems, raising the complex set of methodological issues associated with a limited number of cases and a multitude of variables - too many to be easily encompassed and enforcing selectivity. In turn, approaches to pension systems are framed by wider considerations relating to what, until comparatively recently, was called social security and more recently has been termed social protection, an increasingly encompassing term incorporating both social insurance and social assistance approaches. Currently, this area of study and policy aspires to be designated additionally, and sometimes alternatively, as involving problems of 'social risk management' (Holzmann and Jørgensen, 1999, 2000; Lund and Srinivas, 2000). In relation to this expanding universe of concepts and practice, our findings are tentative and our suggestions provisional. We define our work as falling within the parameters of a specific approach - pensions *in* development (PID) - to the relationships between pension systems and socio-economic development, widely defined. In contrast to the 'radical' PID approach, exemplified in World Bank publications, our more 'moderate' approach seeks to balance welfare aims and economic development agendas more evenly. Our primary interest, reflected in the final and longest part of this volume, is, first, in the problems and policy needs of low income countries, particularly those in sub-Saharan Africa and, second, in those of middle income countries. In pursuing this developing country (DC) focused agenda, the book is structured as follows:

- Part I overviews and critiques the on-going tendency towards the crystallisation of a global pensions reform *monologue*;
- debates the welfare and developmental implications of currently dominant and fashionable reform agendas and proposals;
- concentrates on central but problematic elements within the currently dominant 'radical PID' approach to pension system reform and restructuring, particularly questions relating to state management versus pensions privatisation, and introduces issues relevant to the problems posed by pensions funding options.

- Part II outlines and evaluates regional trends in pension reform implementation, seeking to distil appropriate reform lessons, both positive and negative;
- using examples, predominantly from middle and low income countries (MICs; LICs), seeks to build greater flexibility into fashionable 'pillared' proposals, specifically advocating the continuing relevance of public management.

- Part III, presents pension system options for LICs and MICs with a particular focus on the identification of mechanisms and instruments for achieving universality in coverage and for providing at least a minimal cash income on a regular basis to the elderly;
- proposes an expanded consideration of additional and alternative instruments for, and approaches to, the provision of financial support in old age in DCs;
- examines the record of funded systems, both public and private, and their respective impacts on savings, investment and financial system development.

In Chapter 9 we conclude this volume with a summary of the key policy implications of our moderate version of the PID approach. Our analysis and interpretation of the policy implications of the developments and proposals considered below leads to the following contentions:

- Our first contention is the particular salience of the retention of state control over the management and disposal of pension funds to enhanced prospects for the effective mobilisation and strategic utilisation of long term savings for the achievement of economically and socially coherent developmental impacts with welfare enhancing outcomes, even, or perhaps especially, in low income economies.

- Our second contention is that the central focus - defined contribution funded systems - of recent work on pension provision, including our own, must, in the current circumstances of burgeoning non-formal sectors among DCs and transition states, be defined as of tangential rather than of direct importance precisely to those, many many million, citizens of the Third World most clearly in urgent need of enhanced income support, the elderly poor.

- Our third contention is that a policy priority for DCs should be to provide regular, even if small, cash incomes, preferably on an individual, not simply a household, basis, universally to all the elderly, including, especially, the 'hard to reach' elderly poor.

- Our fourth contention is that the currently fashionable, and currently dominant, rather hard-nosed economic growth-oriented version of the PID approach to pension system design and reform espoused by the World Bank should be softened and appropriately adjusted to more clearly and comprehensively incorporate those aspects of the earlier, welfare orientated, pensions *and* development (PAD) approach that have continuing validity and relevance.

- Our fifth contention is that the neoliberal assault on existing social and welfare policy has been too easily accepted. In relation to pension reform this neoliberal agenda has prioritised growth orientations over poverty alleviation objectives, hence largely neglecting possibilities for pension systems designed actively to pursue growth and welfare objectives more equally.

- Our sixth contention is that pensions policy and pension system design for DCs should, and can, actively contribute to the pursuit of the dual goals of growth and equality - a potentiality that neoliberal impacts on

DCs over the last two decades have both deliberately and accidentally, or incidentally, made more difficult.

- Our seventh contention is that the Bank model of pillared pension provision - never likely to be particularly appropriate for the great bulk of DCs, including the MICs for which the model was originally designed - has become even less appropriate as a model for developing and transition economies as a direct consequence of the outcome of the cumulative impacts of the World Bank's own policies.

- Our eighth contention is that the assumption, underpinning the World Bank's pensions reform agenda, that savings grow best when they are placed in the hands of private sector fund management 'professionals' is at least ill-judged and at worst highly risky for the life-savings of the citizens of DCs who can ill afford the potential consequences even of poor returns on their investments, let alone the consequences of total loss.

- Our ninth contention is that for DCs in general, but for small and poor DCs in particular, there is significant, as yet largely unconsidered and untapped, potentiality in the public management of the investment function of pension funds.

- Our tenth and final contention advocates a more organisationally inclusive, hence less policy didactic, international advisory regime, actively pursuing dialogue rather than in engaging in a policy advice monologue. Positively, what is required is an advisory regime that is more overtly sensitive to the needs and views of DCs on appropriate measures for addressing, in the short term, the welfare problems of the elderly and for developing, in the medium and long term, fiscally sound and sustainable systems of income provision for the old.

Acknowledgements

The authors are grateful to the International Labour Office and the Secretariat of the International Social Security Association for having provided access to their respective archives in Geneva. Thanks are also due to the many individuals within these two organisations for finding the time to impart to us important insights into, and to share with us their considerable knowledge about, recent international and national developments in old age pension provision. Similarly, we would like to thank the many individuals who have refereed, both knowingly and anonymously, earlier published work which has contributed to this volume. Appreciative acknowledgement is due to the British Academy (SG-29783) and to the Carnegie Trust for providing grant funding for archival research essential to the completion of this book. The authors are also grateful for research funding awarded to Roddy McKinnon by the Division of Risk and the Caledonian Business School Research Committee. Our thanks are also expressed to colleagues forming our informal 'pensions *in* development' network, Armando Barrientos, Łukasz Konopielko, Katharina Müller, and Andràs Simonovits. Thanks for more specific forms of assistance are due to Frank Lynch, Michael Tribe, Roy May and Ian Livingstone. Finally, these acknowledgements would not be complete without a mention for our 'nearest and dearest' to whom we are indebted for being so patient and understanding while we have completed this volume. Thank you Jackie, David, Pascale and Ségolène.

List of Acronyms

ADB	Asian Development Bank
AFP	Administradoras de Fondos de Pensiones
AIDS	Acquired Immune Deficiency Syndrome
BRO	Baltic States, Russia and Other Former Soviet Union Countries
BWI	Bretton Woods Institutions
CDF	Comprehensive Development Framework
CEE	The Countries of Central and Eastern Europe and the Baltic States
CIS	Commonwealth of Independent States of the Former Soviet Union
CPF	Central Provident Fund (Singapore)
DB	Defined Benefit
DC	Developing Country
DRC	Democratic Republic of the Congo (formerly Zaire)
EBRD	European Bank for Reconstruction and Development
EC	European Commission
EMU	Economic and Monetary Union
EPF	Employees' Provident Fund (Malaysia)
EU	European Union
FDI	Foreign Direct Investment
FNPF	Fiji National Provident Fund
FSU	Former Soviet Union
FYR	Former Yuglosav Republic
GDP	Gross Domestic Product
GNP	Gross National Product
HAI	HelpAge International
HIC	High Income Country
HIV	Human Immunodeficiency Virus
HKSAR	Hong Kong Special Administrative Region
HPAE	High Performing Asian Economy

IBRD	International Bank for Reconstruction and Development
IDA	International Development Association
IFC	International Financial Corporation
IFI	International Financial Institution
IFPSES	InFocus Programme on Socio-Economic Security (ILO)
IGO	Intergovernmental Organisation
II	Institutional Investor
IIF	Institute of International Finance
ILO	International Labour Organisation
IMF	International Monetary Fund
IO	International Organisation
IPD	Implicit Pension Debt
IPO	Initial Public Offering
ISSA	International Social Security Association
KIA	Kuwait Investment Authority
LDC	Least Developed Country
LIC	Low Income Country
MAS	Monetary Authority of Singapore
MAT	Multidisciplinary Advisory Team (ILO)
MIC	Middle Income Country
MPF	Mandatory Provident Fund
NBFI	Non-Bank Financial Intermediary
NDC	Notional Defined Contribution
NIS/FSU	Newly Independent States of the Former Soviet Union
NPF	National Provident Fund
NSAP	National Social Assistance Programme (India)
NSPF	Non-State Pension Fund
OECD	Organisation for Economic Cooperation and Development
OPSSR	Office of the Government Plenipotentiary for Social Security Reform (Poland)
PAD	Pensions and Development
PAP	Peoples' Action Party (Singapore)
PASIS	Pensiones Asistenciales (Assistance Pensions, Chile)

PAYG	Pay-As-You-Go
PID	Pensions in Development
PNG	Papua New Guinea
PRC	Peoples' Republic of China
SAF	State Accumulation Fund (Kazakhstan)
SAMAT	Southern African Multidisciplinary Advisory Team (ILO)
SAP	Structural Adjustment Programme
SIPS	Social Insurance Pension System
SOE	State-Owned Enterprise
SPF	Supplementary Pension Fund
SRM	Social Risk Management
SSA	Sub-Saharan Africa
SSHFC	Social Security and Housing Finance Corporation (The Gambia)
STEP	Strategies and Tools against Social Exclusion and Poverty (ILO)
UN	United Nations
UNCTAD	United Nations Conference on Trade and Development
UNDP	United Nations Development Programme
UNRISD	United Nations Research into Social Development
USSR	Union of Soviet Socialist Republics
USSSA	United States Social Security Administration
UT	Union Territory (India)
VNPF	Vanuatu National Provident Fund
VNSPF	Voluntary Non-State Pension Fund
VSPF	Voluntary Supplementary Pension Fund
ZNPF	Zambian National Provident Fund
ZUS	Zaklad Ubezpieczen Spolecznych (Poland)

Part I

Global Perspectives and Issues

1 Introduction

An optimally designed old age pension system should fulfil the dual purpose of protecting the old from income insecurity and being an engine of economic growth.

Georges Heinrich, 1997

Pensions policy is a central element within most national social security and social protection policy strategies. Despite the rather earlier institution of national work injury programmes in many states - a fact which rendered these schemes, as recently as 1990, the most common benefit type within social security systems - there are now a larger number of schemes providing old age benefits than there are providing any other benefit contingency. According to US Social Security Administration's (USSSA) biennially published survey of *Social Security Programs Throughout the World* (1999), one hundred and sixty seven countries, theoretically, currently provide some form of social security benefit to meet the contingencies associated with old age. At the end of 1999, and largely predictably in relation to their characteristic problems of poverty, violence, state repression and instability, only the Asian country of Myanmar (Burma) and the African countries of Angola, Comoros, Eritrea, Ethiopia, Guinea Bissau, Lesotho, Malawi, Sierra Leone, Somalia and, even more unsurprisingly, Western Sahara,[1] are either listed as not yet providing an old age benefit within their respective national social security provisions or not listed at all in the USSSA's compendium. Notwithstanding these least developed country (LDC) exceptions,[2] the global expansion of national systems for the provision of old age protection is rightly considered by the ILO as 'one of the great social developments' (Gillion, 1999, p.1) of the 20th century. Nevertheless, this social policy success story should not distract attention from remaining problematic issues of great current and potential significance, not least the problems raised by demographic ageing. World Bank cost projections based upon likely future global demographic ageing

3

levels suggest that 'public spending on old age security will escalate sharply in all regions over the next fifty years' (World Bank, 1994, p.6). These mounting costs are portrayed as likely to be most acutely felt in OECD economies in particular, followed by the transition economies of central and eastern Europe, with average pension costs in relation to GDP within these two groups of economies reaching double digit figures in the first and the second decade of the new millennium respectively. Similarly, in China the demographic situation looks set to deteriorate markedly after 2020. In contrast, in sub-Saharan Africa (SSA) pension spending, as projected by the World Bank, is expected to remain fairly stable, continuing to average less than one percent of GDP for the next twenty years (1994, p.7, Fig. 2). This projection, in turn, reflects SSA's status as 'both the "youngest" continent and the one where the population is ageing most slowly' (Fultz, 1997, p.3).

As these predicted regional variations in the future cost of pension provision suggest, the demographic context within which the global pension system reform debate occurs will become differentially problematic, with obvious implications for both analysis and practice. Currently, the fashionable focus on the problems posed by demographic ageing to established pension systems has often tended to obscure many wider, and much more immediately problematic, issues of serious concern to a very large percentage of the world's older persons, defined for the purposes of this volume, following the UN, as those aged 60 years and above. Nevertheless, three discernible strands can be identified within contemporary pension reform debates. First, responding to demographic projections, one strand of debate relates to a growing concern regarding the projected longer term affordability of old age benefit provision within predominantly the high, and some middle income, economies. This book is largely unconcerned with the specifics of this debate since ageing of populations does not yet constitute a key issue for most low income countries (LICs). In particular, 'Africa will remain young well into the 21st century. The predicament of social security financing that ageing populations pose is thus not on the immediate horizon' (Fultz, 1997, p.4). Nevertheless, as Maps 1.1 and 1.2 underline, Africa is only *relatively* unaffected by demographic ageing. 'The older population of Africa, currently estimated to be slightly over 38 million, is projected to reach 212 million by 2050. Thus Africa's older population will increase six-fold in five decades' (HelpAge International, 2000, p.3).

Map 1.1 Global Population 60+ 1999

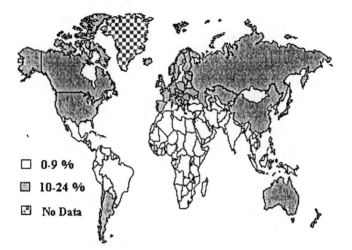

Source: UNDP Population Division

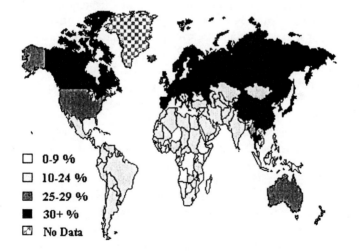

Map 1.2 Global Population 60+ 2050

Source: UNDP Population Division

A second policy debate relates to the general, albeit not universal, inadequacy of old age benefits across the transition economies of central and eastern Europe (CEE) and the newly independent states of the former Soviet Union (NIS/FSU). Although our central concerns lie elsewhere, this volume deals with those transition economy pension policy developments and issues of wider relevance to the low and middle income developing countries on which we primarily focus in this book. Our reasons for this choice of focus are straightforward. Today, 61 percent of the world's over-60s live in developing countries (DCs). By 2025, 70 percent will do so. Moreover, as Colin Gillion, former Director of the ILO's Social Security Department has stated, soberingly, 'the vast majority of the world's population is still without some form of income security in old age' (1999, p.1). Current figures suggest that only around 40 percent of the world's working population, and just over 30 percent of the world's elderly, 'are covered by formal arrangements for old age' (World Bank, 1994, p.6). In response, a third pensions policy debate, to which this volume seeks to contribute, relates primarily to pensions problems predominantly associated with the DCs of the Third World: specifically, their characteristic problems of poor formal system coverage and benefit inadequacy.[3] However, in dealing with these DC-specific issues below in Chapters 6 and 7 we have been conscious of Amanda Heslop's stricture that '[t]oo often development of formal pension and social security programmes is taken as the single reform agenda for older people' (1999, p.27). With almost 70 percent of the world's elderly, on the Bank's estimate, relying on 'informal' means of support, we have sought to respond positively to this reality and to tailor our proposals for LICs, presented in Chapter 7, appropriately.

The 'Global' Pension Reform Debate: Content versus Context

Currently, there is a rather obvious mismatch between the contents of much of the ongoing pensions reform debates and the contexts within which 'radical' pension reform is mainly occurring on the ground as policy. In practice, it is somewhat ironic that the so-called 'radical' pension reform proposals championed by the World Bank, involving an agenda centred on private rather than public provision, has, to date, been largely ignored by the high income countries to whose problems the Bank's proposals are largely addressed. Responding to the views of both the International

Monetary Fund (IMF) and the European Commission (EC) regarding significant negative costs associated with the wholesale abandonment of mature unfunded public pension systems and conversion to a system based mainly on funded private provision, many high income countries (HICs) have preferred to implement cost-cutting, or parametric, reforms as their mechanism for controlling the cost of public pension provision (Espina, 1996, p.204; EC, 1998a, section 2.3.1). As a result, in practice, as considered in Chapters 3 and 4 of this volume, it is middle income countries (MICs) that have implemented pension system reforms modelled upon, or at least significantly influenced by, the World Bank's 'radical' agenda of pension privatisation. Nevertheless, as we argue below in Chapter 6, the 'radical' reform agenda is now targeting even sub-Saharan Africa, previously considered to be too poor and to possess insufficiently developed financial sectors to be included in the debate on pension privatisation. It is the widening scope of this agenda that has given rise to, what may now more appropriately be referred to as, a 'global' pension system reform debate.

For better or for worse, and again reflecting the mismatch between the content and the context of debate described above, contemporary discussions of appropriate pension system reform agendas for developing countries and transition economies are focusing on an increasingly narrow range of options, notably preferencing fully funded over unfunded, pay-as-you-go (PAYG) schemes, and, among the former, aggressively asserting the advantages of private provision over public management. Accordingly, the not inconsiderable welfare merits of unfunded, PAYG, state pension schemes operated on social insurance principles are largely ignored (as are the enormous, unavoidable, short-term administrative and medium-term transition costs involved in either reforming and restructuring, or abolishing, established, mature, systems) in much of the burgeoning literature on appropriate pension reform strategies for low and middle income economies. Central to the case against existing unfunded PAYG systems, which, prior to recent, increasingly global, waves of pension reform, monopolised retirement provision in Latin America, Eastern Europe and the former Soviet Union (FSU), and, so far, continue to predominate in East Asia, the Middle East and francophone Africa, is their irrelevance to financial system development. As Dimitri Vittas and Roland Michelitsch of the World Bank bluntly put it, these 'pay-as-you-go social pension systems ... make little or no contribution to the accumulation of financial assets' (1996, p.264) in total contrast to their funded counterparts' observed capacities to drive financial sector development and their increasingly accepted capacities as important elements in wider economic growth sequences.

The correct choice of pensions funding, management and delivery systems is increasingly perceived as central to the functioning and healthy development of national economies in free market systems. Not only is 'the organization of a country's pension system ... a major determinant of the structure of the financial system' (Vittas, 1992, p.2; see also Vittas and Michelitsch, 1996, p.262), but financial system deepening is seen as crucial to the achievement of sustainable economic development. As the 1997 *World Development Report* summarises: 'Our understanding of financial sector development has changed dramatically over the past decade. We now know that the depth of a country's financial sector is a powerful predictor and driver of development' (1997, p.65). Among the key assumptions made by the advocates of the current pension reform orthodoxy are that the widening and deepening of national financial markets associated with the process of pension fund privatisation should create more opportunities not only for the government to restructure fiscal debt and other liabilities but should also serve to facilitate national economic development more widely. In the light of the comparative evidence available not only from Malaysia and Singapore, our two main counter-examples, but also from Chile, the Bank's model reformer, we demonstrate below in Chapter 8 that current pension reform prescriptions, based on the model proposed by the World Bank, are not fully appropriate for developing countries even in these limited respects.

In principle, stimulating the development of private pensions sectors and other forms of contractual savings, most rapidly and most comprehensively achieved through making pensions saving mandatory, can aid the development of capital markets. In practice, the capital market benefits of such pension system reform may have been oversold. In some cases the exercise may well prove self-defeating. Wide-ranging financial system underdevelopment combined with a relatively small volume of assets held by each of a number of contractual savings institutions all competing with each other for customers, are likely, in the short to medium term, to undermine the achievement of such goals. Initial set up costs combined with administration expenses and commercial costs suggest, moreover, that it may take several decades for even the best run private funds to build assets to a level significant enough to make an identifiable impact upon financial sectors and systems, let alone on the wider economy. More widely, in this book we seek to question whether pension reform models which demand a significant role for private defined contribution pension funds provide DCs with the most appropriate means for serving the twin purposes of Georges Heinrich's optimum pension system – providing social welfare for the old in the form of adequate incomes and forming an engine of economic development.

The History of Pension System Diffusion

The history of the development and diffusion of pension systems, originally within Europe and then outwards from Europe to Latin America and beyond, has been frequently and exhaustively chronicled and will not be reiterated here in any great empirical detail. Our interest in these historical developments is essentially analytical and conceptual, seeking to identify the balance between international and domestic forces in earlier examples of pension system adoption and reform in order to place the more recent and on-going developments, with which this volume is mainly concerned, in perspective: our focus in Chapter 2. All that needs to be underlined at this point, therefore, is that the historical evolution of social security policy in general, and of pension policy in particular, demonstrates that international, and inter-state, influences on the policy and institutional choices of individual states, far from constituting novel departures, have a very long pedigree. As chronicled below, events occurring earlier in the 20th century anticipated recent developments in a number of very significant respects.

　　As a large number of analysts, across a range of disciplines, have separately concluded, the history of national developments in welfare and social security policy has long been intimately bound up with the trajectory of the complex of international economic developments and interactions that are encapsulated in the term 'globalisation'. At the highest level of generality, for example, the close correlation between a country's economic openness to international trade and the early adoption of comprehensive social security systems is striking, indicating the logic of utilising the promise of social protection as a form of domestic policy insurance against the vagaries of international competition. Social security, therefore, becomes a policy carrot offered by states to its workers in order to buy-off their likely opposition to free trade (Rodrik, 1997). In turn, the fundamental similarities in policy format and content between national social security programmes, as well as the close coincidences in the timing of first adoption among groups of similarly situated states, have generated assumptions of more immediate and direct inter-state influences at work. Consequently, emphasis on the significance of the inter-state diffusion of policy innovations has been a hallmark of research on the spread of social security programmes around the world for some decades. Rather than recording a simple series of independent national inventions in response to similar problems, such as the threats of international openness, an established literature records the specificities of the impact of cross-national pressures and influences in the construction of national social security policies. For example, in a seminal paper published a quarter of a century ago, Collier and Messick demonstrated how, from 1920, standardised social security policy packages, centred on the adoption of social insurance programmes, spread swiftly from the early adopters in Europe to the Americas and beyond, diffusing rapidly down a hierarchy of modernisation to cover the developing countries of South and central America by the early 1940s (Collier and Messick, 1975).

In practice, therefore, it has long been acknowledged that 'national' policy, not least social policy, is not formulated in isolation. The relevant processes were well summarised by Rose Spalding two decades ago in framing an insightful case study of the complex interactions occurring between domestic and non-domestic forces shaping the adoption and evolution of welfare policy in Mexico. Specifically, 'nations do not exist in a vacuum, devising social policies in a wholly independent fashion, oblivious to programs and decisions being formed elsewhere. Instead, internal policy developments are influenced by similar developments occurring in other areas. Thus, the worldwide spread of social security programs is not simply the result of nations independently responding in a similar fashion to similar problems, but at least in part, [is] the product of the diffusion of models and concepts from innovative centers to other nations throughout the world' (Spalding, 1980, p.421). Moreover, as Spalding underlines, the processes of social security diffusion identified in this well-established analytical literature were not exclusively or simply state-to-state or directly region-to-region but also, from the establishment of the League of Nations institutions, most relevantly the ILO in 1919, progressively involved Deacon's 'international organisations' (Deacon, 1997) as crucial players in these diffusion processes and patterns. Importantly, Spalding was able, in 1980, to refer to 'numerous works that emphasize the role of international organizations and transgovernmental networks in the transferral of information and development of international standards' (1980, p.421), thereby significantly facilitating and reinforcing the international diffusion of social security instruments and programmes from the 1920s.

Considered separately the two processes of diffusion identified above explain much about the specifics of the impact of inter-state influences and international factors in determining substantial policy and programme convergence in the social security sphere among those states, both developed and developing, that were independent prior to the Second World War. Considered together, and viewed as operating in tandem, the two processes explain much more. For example, Mexico adopted its first national social security programme in 1943, comparatively late for central America's most industrialised state. By then, 'the proliferation of social security policies in Latin American countries and ... the increasing association of this policy with progressive government' meant that 'the continuing lack of a program became a source of some embarrassment to Mexican leaders. This fact, combined with the ability of ILO officials to supply technical assistance and encouragement, allowed diffusion influences to play a notable role' in programme definition and formulation (Spalding, 1980, pp.426-427). Diffusion, however, at least in the Mexican case, was not a sufficient condition for welfare policy adoption. 'In the final analysis ... the crucial impetus emerged from within the regime itself. Acting in a relatively autonomous and entrepreneurial fashion, key decisional elites formulated this policy in order to achieve central state- and nation-building objectives' (Spalding, 1980, p.427).

Nor should we find this assertion of the importance of domestic factors in the formation of pensions policy in a developing country particularly surprising. Conventional interpretations, significantly influenced by Collier and Messick, of the mainsprings of developments within and relationships between successively adopting states over the decades from the invention of the principle of social insurance in Bismarck's Germany to the emergence of fully developed 'welfare states' in Europe and elsewhere among the wealthy OECD states, rightly emphasise the importance of the inter-state diffusion of policy lessons and the standard-setting impact of organisational influences on an international scale. In other cases, however, particularly in relation to some early adoptions within Europe, neither the timing nor the content of initial social security policy adoption can parsimoniously be explained by diffusion models, suggesting that diffusion may not even have been a necessary condition in pensions policy initiation.

Accordingly, our analysis, in focusing on the undeniable, and currently still increasing, dominance of the global pension policy reform agenda by the World Bank, also seeks to question both the achieved and the prospective impact of this 'global', international organisation-based, agenda on the ground in actually defining, or in redefining, national pension policies and systems. To the contrary, we find considerable evidence both of the continuing importance of domestic, intra-state, influences in defining national pension policy choices in general and comparable evidence of the particular, enduring, impact of domestic, in-country, factors on possibilities for significant pension policy innovation and for the achievement of major pension reforms. We also argue for the salience of regional inter-state impacts in spreading, by a process we would define as 'adaptive diffusion', reform innovations from one national pension system to those of near neighbours, essentially suggesting that the impacts of international organisations - even the impact of such a dominant and powerful international organisations as the World Bank - on national policy choices are likely to remain limited to the reinforcement of pre-existing reform trends and to the further encouragement of reform contagion, most obviously on an inter-regional basis.

The World Bank and Pension Reform: Towards Monologue

In asserting the likely continuing importance of domestic and regional factors over international ones in defining which pensions policy options are chosen by specific groups of states as well as when and how chosen options are implemented, it is important to be clear about what options are immediately available and on offer. In this respect the crucial point, explained in greater historical detail below in Chapter 2, is the increasingly restricted range of pensions policy and system options that are effectively on the table and available for adoption and implementation. With the increasing concentration of control over pensions policy expertise and technical advice in the hands of the World Bank, and with the achievement of the effective marginalisation of the previously significant Geneva institutions, the ILO and the ISSA, the outcome is, in effect a monologue in favour of an increasingly narrow neoliberal version of an appropriate pension system. This orthodox, and restrictive, version of the three-pillared system that was more expansively and more flexibly outlined in the Bank's seminal work of synthesis *Averting the Old Age Crisis* has been frequently, extensively, and, we would argue, effectively critiqued by a wide range of scholars and practitioners, including, most recently, the former Chief Economist at the World Bank, Joseph Stiglitz. Significantly, the ILO's recently released riposte to the Bank orthodoxy, *Social Security Pensions: Development and Reform* (Gillion *et al.*, 2000) received comparatively little publicity, despite its importance in restating the ILO's increasingly flexible and encompassing four-tier approach to pension system design, underlining both the limited financial resources available to the members of the UN family of institutions and the ILO's traditional preference for quiet, behind-the-scenes, discussions with interested governments.

Nevertheless, despite its critics and irrespective of alternative approaches, the Bank's influence on the trajectory of pensions policy reform continues to rise. The World Bank now occupies centre stage in the field of pension system choice and reform, effectively monopolising agenda-setting, and, increasingly, controlling supply of the provision of advice and technical assistance on pensions to interested governments through the selective mobilisation of its financial resources. Moreover, with the possibility of funding in support of the implementation of approved reform packages the Bank offers powerful and attractive incentives to DC and transition states to conform to its pensions policy preferences. Accordingly, whilst nominally remaining a *dialogue* between the Bank, other interested international organisations, such as the ILO, the ISSA and the IMF, and interested governments, the reality is an increasingly Bank-dominated *monologue* on global pensions policy.

In line with the Bank's growing interest during the 1990s in building financial systems and sectors as key elements in its 'post-Washington consensus' focus on the development of self-sustaining liberalised market economies, came a focus on pension systems as, potentially, key saving and investment instruments in financial intermediation, specifically with the capacity to underpin and stabilise capital market development through their theoretically long investment horizons (for a summary of central policy elements within both the 'Washington consensus' and the 'post-Washington consensus', see Appendix Figs. A1.1, A1.2). This view of pension systems was clearly antipathetic to the existing state-managed, social insurance-based, tax-financed PAYG systems traditionally championed and defended by the ILO and characteristic of the high income economies of the OECD, but also substantially replicated at lower income levels in Latin America and across what had become the transition economies of CEE and the FSU/NIS. The Bank's chosen point of attack on this welfare state model of pension provision was to indicate looming fiscal unsustainability due to the impact of demographic ageing as the numbers of the pension-dependent retired rose and as the size of the pension-supporting workforce shrank (see above, Maps 1.1, 1.2). In the USA and the UK, already well attuned to neoliberal and neoconservative assumptions, it was commonly accepted that the welfare state had become a drain on limited fiscal resources, a bottomless pit essentially diverting revenue from potentially more productive uses.

In theory, a pensions policy based primarily on the privatisation of previously state-run provision, replacing collective systems of tax-financing with individual accounts managed on a contractual savings basis, offered obvious advantages in meeting, on a sustainable basis, the fiscal challenges posed by the rapid greying of populations and in transparently and creatively linking life-time savings from earnings to pensions. In this context it is unsurprising that

> [t]he World Bank's approach, with its argument for the primacy of the market ... , its assumption that most people are able to save for their old age, and its belief that the key determinant of older people's welfare is the performance of the whole economy, has had a powerful influence on governments.
>
> Gorman, 1999b, p.6

In practice, however, reliance on such a system is feasible only in high-wage economies with permanently full employment; a fortuitous combination of circumstances which no longer prevails even among the high income economies of the OECD. Even more limited reliance on such a system becomes problematic when employment histories are increasingly discontinuous due to changing employment patterns, when incomes are permanently or even temporarily low affecting the capacity to save, and when family and domestic commitments preclude waged employment for significant portions of time.

Nevertheless, despite the significant welfare disadvantages of a privatised pension system and the specific threats presented to the more vulnerable sections of the population that welfare states had, ironically, been inaugurated to protect through systems of collective insurance providing universal benefits, no fully convincing cost-effective alternative to the Bank model of pension provision was available. To the contrary, as described here in relation to the German case, to the extent that western welfare state models of social protection continued to be based on traditional social insurance principles, they must remain 'oriented towards the dependent worker, the full time job, the stable one-earner family, and standard life courses. Contribution-financed social insurance systems relying heavily on the equivalence principle protect primarily the middle classes against standard risks and leave growing numbers dependent on less reliable tax-financed and often means-tested assistance programmes' (Hauser, 1995, p.53). In many high income countries (HICs) such trends towards selective rather than universal provisioning are further reinforced by on-going attempts to remove any remaining residually redistributive elements from social insurance systems, with the aim of leaving any such redistributive responsibilities entirely in the hands of tax financed social assistance 'safety nets'.

For DCs, therefore, most of which had spent the 1980s implementing IMF and World Bank mandated economic stabilisation and structural adjustment programmes in which strict expenditure control over 'unnecessary' or 'inefficient' government programmes had frequently extended to social and welfare commitments, no fully convincing social policy answers to the charge that most existing 'welfare' expenditures constituted a drain on scarce financial resources diverting the latter from more productive uses, were forthcoming. On the surface this was not perhaps particularly important in terms of any immediate impact on the great mass of the elderly in the South since the demographic structure of DCs had determined that it was the young, not old, who had been the main target for formal social policy interventions in the post-colonial era. In the light of limited resources available for state welfare expenditures in poor countries, the low visibility of the elderly and their relatively low numbers in less developed regions combined to determine their low priority as expenditure targets (see Appendix Tables A1.1, A1.2). Bluntly, '[a]geing issues have not been a major concern of leaders in developing nations of the world ... ' (Schulz, 1999, p.87). For example, as a recently published article in a Pakistani newspaper complained,

> Actually there are some fields of welfare activity in which no government in Pakistan would do anything off its own bat. It's only when the subject is adopted by the United Nations as one of its welfare objectives that the government feels obliged to make a show of interest so that it may be counted among the civilised, and should not appear to lag behind the rest of the world. The Senior Citizens' Day is one of those things.
>
> Rahman, 2000

Across the developing world, care for the old has, for the most part, remained only marginal to government welfare programmes, and is widely left mainly or even exclusively in the hands of family and community. Such family or community-based provision, commonly termed 'traditional', 'informal' or 'non-formal' in the literature, is expected to show sufficient resilience to provide, on a continuing basis, for the majority of the needs of the elderly poor, essentially the great majority of the old in most DCs.[4] However, despite the often remarkable resilience and adaptability demonstrated by such family and community-based systems, frequently in the face of combinations of shocks, not least those associated with global economic recession and the imposition of structural adjustment programmes, the inevitable reality, at least from the early 1980s onwards, was that the essential bases for such non-formal provision were significantly undermined rather widely across the South, with no realistic prospect of any significant additional or alternative forms of support for the elderly poor on the horizon. Again, the Pakistani case is illustrative, both underlining the continuing resilience of family-based support and the increasing incapacity of the poorest families to match commitments to declining resources.

> Fortunately the average family in Pakistan still cares for its aged members, and I have heard people scorning the government's promises to help. "We can look after our *buzurgs* [older people]", they say. Of course at the poorest level the story is different and heart-rending. Their lot will only improve when the lot of the common man improves.
>
> Rahman, 2000

Beyond these non-state forms of support, various forms of formal old age and 'retirement' pension provision had also developed over time, albeit on a substantially *ad hoc* basis, across the developing world, but nowhere, except in the communist states, prior to the 1980s, even seriously aspiring to, let alone achieving, universality of coverage. By the 1970s almost all DCs, including the poorest among them, had established some form of 'pension' provision, typically generously provided on a non-contributory, tax-financed, basis to senior civil servants and officers of the armed forces, in some cases extended, albeit often only on a contributory 'provident fund' basis, more widely both within the state bureaucracies that dominated formal sector employment and beyond into aspirant, but characteristically small, private sectors. However, inevitably, given large informal sectors and economies dominated by self employment in subsistence agriculture, the population coverage achieved under such formal schemes remained generally low across the South. Ironically, it was precisely in the developing states with the most expansive systems of formal pension provision, specifically those in Latin America with Chile as the region's most 'successful' example of widely extended coverage, that the practical limits of welfare state models of social insurance pensions were most comprehensively and damningly exhibited. As a large critical literature, mainly emanating from within Latin America and epitomised by the work of Carmelo Mesa-Lago, underlined, not only did the increasingly PAYG source of pensions funding in the region effectively guarantee their 'ascent to bankruptcy' (1989) as available tax revenue increasingly failed to cover expenditure, but the social insurance basis of the system also continued to ensure that pension provision was highly regressive, disproportionately favouring elite groupings within formal sectors and among the latter favouring state elites in particular.

More widely important for other DCs, what Latin American experience most conclusively confirmed was, as Mesa-Lago (1991a) in particular had underlined repeatedly, 'that coverage of the informal sector cannot be accomplished within the confines of the model of social insurance introduced by Bismarck in Germany' (Sherraden, 1995, pp.184-185). Since one of the major impacts of the structural adjustment programmes instituted across Latin America by the International Financial Institutions (IFIs) in the aftermath of the economic chaos following the debt crisis was a significant fall in formal sector employment, and a consequent rise in both the size and economic importance of informal sector employment, the substantial redundancy of existing Latin American pension systems either as welfare instruments, or as potential welfare models for other DCs, was already firmly established well before the World Bank was to take a major interest in pension policy in DCs.

From Pensions *and* Development to Pensions *in* Development

In the light of the huge volume of work published on pension systems and, in particular, on their reform over the last decade it is easy to forget that current perceptions of the central importance of pension systems in financial and economic development are both recent and novel. Quite rightly, development studies has been forced to take cognisance of issues surrounding the specifics of pension system design that had previously been regarded as substantially peripheral to its central concerns. Previously, the bulk of published work had tended to focus on the wider issues of social security, both formally and informally provided, in DCs or, much more commonly, and even more widely, to focus on the issues of social welfare and/or poverty alleviation rather than specifically on pensions *per se*. In what is characterised here as the earlier 'pensions *and* development' (PAD) perspective and approach there was comparatively little interest in the issue of old age pensions in DCs because of two widespread assumptions centred on the importance of developmental 'thresholds', namely:

- that pensions and the other elements of formal social security provision are essentially dependent variables in relation to the stage of development reached by a particular state - that developmental prerequisites are necessary before public pension provision becomes feasible and sustainable.

- that the pension elements within formal systems of social security (welfare states) are both very costly and administratively complex rendering them of almost no relevance to low income countries (LICs) and of only limited relevance to middle income countries (MICs).

In short, PAD perspectives are based on the assumption that the appropriate analytical approach is to view the effects of development on possibilities for pension provision as the key issue - the key questions being whether appropriate prerequisites are in place and appropriate developmental thresholds have been reached in order to sustainably support the considerable fiscal costs and associated administrative burdens involved in providing pensions to the old. In contrast, the more recent and currently predominant 'pensions *in* development' (PID) perspectives view pensions as independent variables in relation to development, specifically suggesting significant potential for achieving positive impacts on developmental outcomes through appropriately structured pension and 'retirement' provision systems. Here the essence of the argument is that pension systems, when appropriately designed, financed and managed, can have important developmental impacts with direct and indirect growth-enhancing effects spreading well beyond straightforward outcomes relating to welfare enhancement.

There is much in such PID perspectives with which we concur. However, we depart from the currently predominant version of the PID approach, specifically the 'radical' version developed and promulgated by the World Bank, in a number of specific and significant respects. First, it is central to our argument that pension, and related retirement savings, systems are not 'magic bullets' either within a country's financial system or, more widely, in relation to the achievement of positive economic growth sequences. Much has been made of the crucial importance of financial system development to wider prospects for national economic development in recent years, contrasting starkly to the earlier tendency to neglect financial systems and sectors within developing economies. Much is to be welcomed in this change of focus, and of fashion, within development studies, but much remains unproven, not least in relation to the precise impacts of pension systems within financial systems and beyond. Specifically, it is a central theme of this volume that the evidence directly linking (appropriately designed and managed) pension systems to financial system deepening, via a lengthening of investment horizons within expanding capital markets, is far from overwhelming and, consequently, that the potentialities of pension systems in these respects have been overstated by pension 'reform' enthusiasts.

A second, related, theme pursued below is that the case for private rather than public management of pension systems - a case that is itself central to the World Bank version of the PID perspective - is heavily dependent on the claimed positive financial market impacts flowing from pensions privatisation. If this impact is absent, or even unclear, the case for mainly private provision of pensions in DCs weakens significantly, essentially disappearing for LICs. Accordingly, and positively, the defence of and continuing justification for public provision and management of retirement pensions within DCs is a key theme pursued below. A crucial factor in our justification of (mainly) public over private management in relation to retirement provision in DCs, and one largely neglected in the extreme version of the PID approach, is the vital, but all too often potential, importance of 'pensions' as welfare instruments in poor countries. Although we accept much of the PID case for pensions funding over PAYG provision we do not regard funded pensions as the only feasible answer either to the problems of the fiscal sustainability of existing and well established public pension systems in high income countries (HICs) or to the development of fiscally sound systems in DCs.

More importantly, the narrow focus on the virtues of full pre-funding that characterises the Bank version of the PID approach leads to a view of pensions as closed 'savings' systems within which the crucial test of system adequacy is the achievement of a long-term balance between revenue and expenditure elements for each and every individual affiliate. In this search for fiscal neatness the implications for, and potential impact on, the individuals that technically fall inside the system but have only limited capacities to save on a regular basis, as well as on those falling outside, are too easily brushed aside as of secondary concern. Specifically, in itself funding neither guarantees adequacy of provision for those encompassed by the system but making limited contributions based on low incomes, nor, crucially, will it solve problems of coverage, further marginalising those who, lacking identifiable 'incomes', cannot make regular contributions. For LICs and most MICs, in practice, funding, whether privately or publicly managed, simply guarantees small pensions for a significant, probably very significant, percentage of affiliates and limited, often very limited, coverage of total populations. It is our case that coverage, in particular, is inherently problematic under private management, and is especially problematic in DCs with their large informal sectors. Since inadequate or even non-existent coverage is the key problem facing most DCs, including all LICs with their problems of chronic poverty and the many MICs with large agricultural sectors and significant informalisation of employment, our approach and proposals focus specifically on the goal of universality of old age provision in all countries.

A third theme is that the dominant 'Washington' version of the PID perspective increasingly presents a largely undifferentiated approach to pension system design; involving an approach essentially fully relevant only to HICs with full, or close to full, employment, but, paradoxically viewed by its advocates as applicable immediately and *in toto* to MICs, and increasingly, it appears, to LICs also. Our view, developed below, is that pension system design issues are, or should be, substantially different for MICs, and substantially different again for LICs. Ironically, the Bank version of the PID approach has not so far found favour with the governments of HICs, the latter largely preferring parametric tinkering to systemic reform as their preferred mechanism for *'Averting the Old Age Crisis'*. Consequently, systemic reform on the basis of the Bank version of the PID thesis, has been undertaken mainly in the MICs of, first Latin America and, more recently, among the transition economies of CEE and the FSU - states where the continuing need for external financial support on a concessionary basis, *i.e.* foreign aid, has given the Washington institutions significant leverage over chosen development strategies and policy choices.

Unsurprisingly and predictably, as argued at various points in this volume, implementation of the Bank model has not been unproblematic, providing due warnings of the inherent limitations of the radical PID strategy advocated by the Bank. Our theme is that these inherent limitations increase as implementing country income falls. To date, however, despite a very large and rapidly growing PID literature on the fashionable and high-profile subject of pension system reform in both HICs and MICs comparatively little of this recent work has been focused directly on the subject of, and particularly the significant issues and problems involved in, developing appropriate pension and old age support systems for LICs. In such countries, in which, by definition, poverty is widespread and deep-seated, informality of employment prevails [see Table 1.1] and subsistence agriculture supports a majority of the population,[5] in which markets, including not least financial markets, are poorly developed, and states are chronically weak, both fiscally and administratively, the design of appropriate old age support presents specific challenges. Moreover, these challenges are arguably quite different, particularly in degree but also to some extent in kind, from those facing even the poorer of the MICs with which the Bank has so far mainly been dealing in relation to pension reform issues. These poor and poorest country issues are the central focus of Chapter 7.

Table 1.1 Estimated Regional Trends in Informal Employment*

Regions	1980s	1990s
North Africa	38.8 (1)	43.4 (1)
Sub-Saharan Africa	66.5 (1)	73.7 (1) (2)
Latin America	52.3 (1)	56.9 (1)
Asia	53.0	62.6

* As % of non-agricultural employment
Notes: (1) Non-weighted arithmetical means. (2) Excluding South Africa
Source: Adapted from Charmes, 2000, p.63, Table 1

Exactly why we stress the importance of the inauguration of old age 'pensions', in the form of a guaranteed minimum cash payment provided on an universal, demogrant, basis, as an immediate policy priority even, indeed especially, for the poorest countries is more fully justified below. However, it is important to introduce and to provide a provisional justification for this key proposal at this early stage, not least since our approach runs directly contrary to the ILO's general view that cost considerations preclude early implementation of universality among DCs. For example, a recent ILO/SAMAT *Discussion Paper* argues specifically that the costs involved in providing universal old age provision determine that this aim 'can only be a long term goal for most Southern African countries' (Fultz and Pieris, 1999, p.50). Quite simply, we would argue that in relation to costs the potential benefits from such cash transfers to the elderly are disproportionately substantial. First, the elderly in DCs generally face both increased needs for cash and declining opportunities for obtaining it. Again, the views of an elderly Pakistani are representative and informative, particularly in underlining the importance of cash incomes in lending dignity to survival into old age in the face of continuing government indifference.

> What ... successive governments have failed to realise is that old people need financial assistance most of all. If they can be self-sufficient to a reasonable extent, dignity and respect will come automatically.
>
> Rahman, 2000

Second, cash transfers to the elderly are potentially key elements in wider poverty alleviation and reduction strategies, not least because the available evidence confirms that these benefits, in providing incomes to many of the most vulnerable households, are also highly significant vectors for diffusing positive impacts widely across family groupings. Accordingly, as the ILO's own researchers have argued in relation to the lessons provided by recent southern African experience, cash transfers to the old are very effective in avoiding many of the problems associated with attempting to target the specific needs of the poorest and most vulnerable individuals in low income countries. Bluntly, 'in countries with large populations of poor people' targeting does not work, and, as southern African 'regional experience suggests ... it is simply not possible to direct protection narrowly at particular needs. Instead the extended family channels protection provided for one contingency (e.g. old age) to members who face other problems (e.g. underemployment or orphanhood), creating a broad ripple effect' (Fultz and Pieris, 1999, p.34). As Lund and Srinivas rightly conclude on the basis of the long list of the ripple effects associated with South Africa's social pension, such programmes have the clear potential to enhance 'the ability of ... households to plan for integrated risk management' (2000, p.107).

In turn, this crucial point provides us with a response to the World Bank's recent adoption of a social risk management (SRM) approach to the provision of social protection. Whilst we welcome the Bank's concern to encompass the needs of what they term the critically poor in DCs, we are concerned by the overt linkage of the Bank's SRM agenda to its ongoing pension reform activities. Indeed, Holzmann and Jørgensen reveal the strength of the linkage between these two separate strands of Bank work by concluding their jointly-authored *Social Protection Discussion Paper* with an affirmation that the social risk management framework approach to social protection 'also provides an additional support for a multi-pillar pension reform approach proposed by the Bank' (2000, p.27). It must be stressed that our reservations about the Bank's SRM approach particularly relate to its implications for the elderly. In relation to the working age poor, there is much common sense in the Bank's adoption of sustainable 'basic livelihoods' perspectives and approaches, just as there is much that is challenging in the Bank's proposals to support the poor in engaging in productive activities that involve a combination of *potentially* higher risks and *potentially* higher returns.

In the long term, if appropriately designed and structured in programme or project form, such initiatives would provide clear possibilities for gradually pulling critically poor households out of poverty. However, as a short and medium term strategy such approaches are irrelevant to the current needs of the elderly poor, given their limited physical capacities to support the productive activities of household groupings. Similarly, the elderly poor, whose energies are necessarily more likely to be directed towards strategies for risk coping, can hardly be expected to engage in risky activities, however well underpinned and 'insured'. It is the specific needs of this current age cohort that we seek to address. In doing so, we are at one with the Bank in arguing that tax-financed schemes delivered on a universal basis remain too expensive to cater for *all* the needs of *all* the poor in the world's poorest economies (Holzmann and Jørgensen, 2000). However, as suggested above, cash incomes paid as pensions to the old provide a strategic intervention, targeting a particularly vulnerable section of the poor but also offering significant poverty alleviating potentialities for many of the South's poorest households. Southern African experience is once again instructive in this regard.

> In rural South Africa where there are large numbers of unemployed and more than a third of the population lives in poverty, the social pension is a significant source of income for both immediate and extended families .... In Namibia and Botswana, the combination of urbanisation and AIDS mortalities is fueling a similar phenomenon, with growing numbers of elderly using their pension for food, clothing, and school fees for grandchildren left in their care.
>
> Fultz and Pieris, 1999, p.23

More generally, the Bank's formal adoption of a 'modular' SRM approach (World Bank, 2000) provides further evidence of changing institutional agendas in relation to the evolution of more cooperative and responsive attitudes both towards the interests and perspectives of the other IOs involved in social protection and welfare issues and to the concerns and opinions of previously simply 'recipient' DC governments. Crystallised in the Bank's recent promise to pursue the reform of 'development cooperation to attack poverty', these are distinctly encouraging indications. The Bank's development of what it terms a 'Comprehensive Development Framework' (CDF) (World Bank 2000, pp.194-195; Pender, 2000) has increasingly placed the 'attack' on poverty at the centre of its policy agenda, thereby placing the overt priorities of the wealthy Washington institutions significantly closer to those of their less well endowed Geneva counterparts.

Although these evolutionary developments are to be welcomed as indicative of possibly substantial positive adjustments in an advisory and donor assistance regime that had previously been characterised by monologue rather than dialogue, we also note the quite different signals emanating from the Bank's continued assertion of an unchanged approach to its on-going pension system reform agenda. In Chapter 2 we present historical perspectives on the present conjuncture: namely the Bank's increasing dominance of the pension reform agenda and its progressive monopolisation of reform options. These historical perspectives offer some bad news and some good. On the one hand, the evidence from the long period of ILO dominance of the international 'social security' agenda suggests that, once in place, the impact of a frozen and change-resistant policy regime may be very long lasting, precluding change over many years. Nevertheless, as chronicled more fully below, the lessons to be drawn from the more recent displacement of the ILO by the World Bank as the lead international advisory institution in the pensions policy field can also be read in a more positive light; specifically, that such dominance is inherently self-limiting. Accordingly, this book should be seen as a small contribution to wider efforts to ensure both plurality and responsiveness in framing the policy advice provided to DCs. We return to the institutional implications of this aspect of our Pensions *in* Development approach in our final chapter.

Notes

1. Western Sahara is here presented as a sovereign independent territory. The UN has stated openly its support for a referendum on self-determination for the people of Western Sahara.
2. Throughout this book, we use the term 'developing country' (DC) much as the World Bank uses the related term, developing economies, 'for convenience; it does not imply that all such economies [countries] are experiencing similar development or that other economies [countries] have reached a preferred or

final stage of development' (World Bank, 2000, p.335). The UN's *Least Developed Countries 2000 Report* (UNCTAD, 2000b) identifies forty eight LDCs. The criteria used to identify these countries are: a) a low income, as measured by GDP per capita; b) weak human resources as measured by a composite index based on indicators of life expectancy at birth, per capita calorie intake, combined primary and secondary school enrolment, and adult literacy; c) a low level of economic diversification, as measured by a composite index based on the share of manufacturing in GDP, the share of the labour force in industry, annual per capita commercial energy consumption, and UNCTAD's merchandise export concentration index. The forty eight designated countries are: Afghanistan, Angola, Bangladesh, Benin, Bhutan, Burkina Faso, Burundi, Cambodia, Cape Verde, Central African Republic, Chad, Comoros, Democratic Republic of Congo, Djibouti, Equatorial Guinea, Eritrea, Ethiopia, Gambia, Guinea, Guinea Bissau, Haiti, Kiribati, Lao People's Democratic Republic, Lesotho, Liberia, Madagascar, Malawi, Maldives, Mali, Mauritania, Mozambique, Myanmar, Nepal, Niger, Rwanda, Samoa, Sao Tome and Principe, Sierra Leone, Solomon Islands, Somalia, Sudan, Togo, Tuvalu, Uganda, United Republic of Tanzania, Vanuatu, Yemen, and Zambia.

3. In this volume, for convenience in discriminating between different categories of developing countries we largely follow the World Bank (2000) criterion of gross national product (GNP) per capita for classifying economies, but, also for convenience, refer generally to MICs rather than distinguishing between lower and upper echelons within this category. As the World Bank underlines, 'classification by income [does not] necessarily reflect development status' (World Bank, 2000, p.335).
    Low-income economies are those with a GNP per capita of $755 or less in 1999.
    Middle-income economies are those with more than $755 but less than $9,266 in 1999. A further division at $2,995 is made between *lower-middle-income economies* and *upper-middle-income economies*.
    High-income economies are those with a GNP per capita of $9,266 or more in 1999.

4. This literature is succinctly and expertly summarised by Jeffery Nugent in a chapter on 'Informal Arrangements' in the World Bank's *Averting* (1994, Chapter 2).

5. We use the blanket term 'non-formal' employment throughout this book to denote and cover employment in both the informal sector and self-employment (mainly in agriculture), paralleling our use of 'non-formal' to denote both 'traditional' and 'informal' systems of social protection introduced at footnote 4 above. Our use of the term 'non-formal' also denotes recognition of the importance of the distinction between the 'informal' and 'underground'

economies (see Appendix Fig. A6.1. for expanded definitions of these terms). In SSA, excluding South Africa, informal employment currently accounts for only 18.4 percent of total employment (Charmes, 2000, p.64, Table 2), underlining the dominance of subsistence agriculture in largely low income economies. As a quick visual comparison between the countries listed in footnote 2 and the Bank's Classification of Economies by Income and Region 2000 (World Bank, 2000, pp.334-335) reveals, there is a rough correspondence between the UN's LDCs and the Bank's LICs. Similarly, as Table 1.1 indicates, informal sector employment levels and trends underline differences between, broadly, middle income Latin America and low income/LIC Africa. Asian figures, covering both low income South Asia with high informality of employment and middle income East and Southeast Asia with often falling levels of informal employment, are less discriminating.

2 International Organisations and Pension System Reform

Introduction

What the historical evolution of social security policy in general, and of pension policy in particular, underlines is that intergovernmental organisations (IGOs) have a long record of significant impacts on the policy and institutional choices of individual states. These impacts often operate alongside, but are analytically and empirically separate from, specific and direct inter-state diffusionary influences. As Strang and Chang summarised, an established tradition of historically-focused 'research on the adoption of welfare programs suggests the importance of global models and transnational linkages' (Strang and Chang, 1993, p.238). Prior to the First World War, welfare programme innovation, adoption and adaptation was largely confined to Europe, indicating the predominance of state-to-state impacts in an era characterised by relatively few IGOs. However, following the war, reflecting the 'League of Nations' era's aspirations toward globalised governance and standard-setting, a more internationally encompassing welfare regime emerged. 'In the postwar period social welfare policy was integrated into prevailing conceptions of enlightened labor relations, intelligent fiscal policy, and basic human rights. The rapid and universal spread of welfare programs suggests change in global norms rather than isolated national events' (Strang and Chang, 1993, pp.238-239). These, aspirant, global welfare policy norms were further reinforced, following the Second World War, by the emergence of increasingly comprehensive 'welfare state' models in Europe and by subsequent adoptions more widely across the wealthy states of the OECD. Thus, from widest possible dissemination of the principles underlying the Bismarckian social insurance model (Ritter, 1983, pp.6-7), through the International Labour Organisation's (ILO) advisory, training and technical support activities during the inter-war years in support of the widest possible diffusion of social insurance pension systems among those independent states able and prepared to commit the requisite financial resources, to the post-war spread of the 'welfare state' as both policy model and normative standard, a pattern of IGO-defined and driven international welfare norms, operating parallel to, and frequently in tandem with, inter-state policy influences, was exhibited on an increasingly 'global' scale, clearly anticipating current developments in a number of significant respects.[1]

Accordingly, far from constituting a significant departure from previously prevailing norms of significantly greater national policy independence, the contemporary conjuncture is rather reminiscent of earlier episodes in the development of social security systems and the emergence of welfare states. Specifically, the current substantial international, putatively global, convergence on one specific normative and practical model of pension provision increasingly under the auspices of reform programmes coordinated and financially and technically supported by the Washington institutions, notably the World Bank, largely reproduces an earlier pattern of the international diffusion of specific policy norms in relation to social security, including retirement pension provision as an integral element, prevailing prior to the Second World War and further reinforced in the post-war era. In this earlier process of establishing international norms for social security, the ILO was a key institutional 'locus of diffusion' for a specific 'welfare regime', involving 'notions of appropriate state policy' based on the norms of social insurance. These norms were, in turn, disseminated and distilled into national policies through the ILO's core institutional activities, notably 'the formulation of international standards; the collection of cross-national statistics; the dissemination of information on working conditions; technical assistance; and promotional and educational activities' (Strang and Chang, 1993, pp.239-241; for a detailed outline of the benchmark ILO 'Minimum Standards' for social security provision, see Appendix Fig. A2.1).

Direct assistance to states provided by the ILO in support of the inauguration and development of social security programmes went well beyond the international standard-setting activity that is characteristically viewed as its key function.[2] From an early period in its history the ILO offered states support for policy formulation and implementation, commonly providing 'technical experts [to] help write national laws and design administrative structures', becoming the locus for 'an international community of policy technocrats that support program developments in areas like social security' (Strang and Chang, 1993, p.242). As Giovanni Tamburi, the Chief of the Social Security Branch of the ILO, noted in 1969, in celebrating the fiftieth anniversary of that organisation, not only was it important 'to emphasise the influence of the standard-setting activities of the ILO on the concept of social security in the different countries and on its generalisation', but also to underline the long-standing, but less public, importance of '[t]he practical activities of the Organisation as concerns technical co-operation' (Tamburi, 1969, p.480). As Tamburi was at pains to emphasise, citing specific examples of advice and assistance to Greece, Venezuela and Turkey on social insurance policy from the 1930s, 'the ILO was already putting technical co-operation into practice as concerns social security, long before the United Nations era' (1969, p.481).

The ILO and Standard Setting

A defining characteristic of the ILO's role in this pre-war period was that 'the technical assistance of the International Labour Office *was mainly designed to help Member States to understand and develop social insurance and its techniques* in a period of economic crisis and in spite of the vicissitudes arising from a generally disturbed political situation' (Tamburi, 1969, p.482, emphasis added). It is, in particular, this specific normative focus of ILO policy advice and technical assistance on the social insurance model in the economically and politically troubled context of the 1920s and 1930s that has such strong contemporary resonances, largely mirroring both the specificity and the normative basis of recent World Bank advice and assistance for pension reform in developing and transition economies. Specifically, Peter Orszag and Joseph Stiglitz have rightly pointed out in a recently presented, 'deliberately provocative' (Orszag and Stiglitz, 1999, p.3) conference paper, how, 'in practice, the "World Bank" model of best practice' pension reform 'has been interpreted as involving one particular constellation of ... pillars', centring on 'the inclusion of a *privately managed, defined contribution* component' as the central element in the envisaged reform scheme (Orszag and Stiglitz, 1999, p.4, emphasis in original). Ironically, the key policy shift advocated by the Bank involves supporting states in moving away from precisely the publicly managed, largely social insurance based, defined benefit (DB) pension schemes that the ILO had so strongly advocated and that had been so successfully diffused in the pre-war era, thereby substantially rejecting the policy norms and undermining the ILO's social security standards that had remained the international pension policy norm for more than a century following Bismarck's original reforms. 'Over the past decade, following the seminal reforms in Chile in the early 1980s, *and with support from the World Bank*, many nations have moved away from a public defined benefit pension system and toward a private defined contribution one' (Orszag and Stiglitz, 1999, p.4, emphasis added), indicating the altered balance of power among international organisations both, specifically, in the provision of policy advice and, more broadly, in social security standard setting.

By the 1990s the ILO had largely surrendered the initiative that it had held for six decades in standard setting in relation to social security as it stubbornly maintained the global validity of its social insurance model of welfare in the face of the mounting tide of opinion arguing the model's substantial irrelevance to meeting the needs of the mass of the population, the poor, in typical middle and low income states with, respectively, large urban informal sectors and high levels of employment in subsistence agriculture. Comparably overwhelming arguments underlined the inappropriateness of social insurance programmes to DCs, responding negatively to the hypothesised impacts of their reputed organisational complexity, thereby rendering both initial implementation and subsequent management problematic, and their potential cost implications, thereby making the task of ensuring sustainability *per se* impossible. 'Most of the case material on developing countries describes ILO standards on social security as too demanding, given organizational and fiscal constraints' (Strang and Chang, 1993, p.256). As Strang and Chang bluntly point out, the findings of their detailed statistical study of relevant developments between 1960 and 1980, are clear-cut. 'ILO standard setting does not seem ... to contribute to the growth of welfare programs in the developing world ... LDCs tend not to ratify ILO standards on social security, and spending does not markedly increase when they do ratify them ... The Western voices that dominate the ILO are involved in a difficult bootstrapping operation, using the existing prestige of the western welfare state to promote its further realization' in poor DCs 'where such policies face severe fiscal and organisational constraints' (Strang and Chang, 1993, pp.250-259).

Essentially, by continuing to base its social security standards on Bismarckian social insurance principles, the ILO increasingly, from the 1960s, priced itself out of the global standard setting market in relation to welfare instruments in general. What remained important to the ILO, and comparably important to the increasing number of states overtly associated with its work, was its on-going programme of technical assistance, in which policy advice on retirement provision and pension systems continued to be an important element. The rapid increase in the number of states as colonies became independent was reflected, albeit more slowly, in the number of countries reporting annually on their welfare expenditure to the ILO, in turn providing a useful indicator of the ILO's increasingly global customer base. In 1960 only sixty-one states reported to the ILO on their welfare expenditure profiles, increasing steadily to reach seventy-eight countries by 1970, and progressing to one hundred and six a decade later. As decolonisation reached its African climax in the early 1960s, the number of developing states seeking the ILO's practical assistance in relation to welfare policy in general, and retirement policy in particular, also rose rapidly. From 1960, if not before, it had become clear that the ILO's 'most concrete relation to nonindustrialized countries works through technical assistance, not standard setting' (Strang and Chang, 1993, p.259). In one sense this pattern of ILO activity and its related influence profile pertains today: a significant number of DCs continued during the 1980s and 1990s to seek the technical assistance of the ILO in relation to welfare instruments, including pensions.

However, in another sense the direct outcomes of the Third World debt crisis, notably the rise of the Washington institutions, the IMF and the World Bank, as effective policy makers for the South from the early 1980s in an era, first, of economic stabilisation and, second, of structural adjustment programmes, ensured that the balance of advisory and standard-setting power in relation to social security and welfare policy would increasingly shift from Geneva to Washington. Among DCs the 1980s at once signalled the marginalisation of the UN and its Geneva institutions, including the ILO, as policy advisers and the marginalisation of social policy as a policy priority for 'adjusting' states facing the imposition of strict fiscal conditionality rules and tight expenditure ceilings. Significantly, when, from the mid- to late 1980s, it became increasingly apparent that countries operating under SAP conditionalities were experiencing severely negative social consequences, thereby forcing social policy back onto the policy agendas of low and middle income countries across the Third World, it was to continue to be mainly the Washington IFIs, not the Geneva institutions, which called the tune and defined that agenda.

Supplanting the ILO

What remains to explained is exactly why the ILO's recent eclipse and displacement by the World Bank as the lead international organisation in the social policy field has been most comprehensive in relation to pensions. This outcome is particularly ironic in that the meteoric rise of the Bank's pension policy profile was occurring at precisely the time that pension reform began to emerge as a major item on national political agendas. Moreover, these two developments are organically related. Simply stated, the swift process of displacement of the ILO by the World Bank as the lead international organisation in researching pension systems and as the repository and provider of advice, finance and technical assistance for approved pension system reforms in selected states, has centred on the deliberate, and substantially successful, attempt by the Bank to raise the political profile and salience of the pension reform issue both nationally and internationally. The effect of the Bank's intervention has been to turn what the ILO had traditionally treated as essentially low-key technical questions appropriate for private negotiations within and between national and international governmental institutions into high profile policy issues centred on the impending global threat of an 'old age crisis'. In its seminal 1994 publication dramatically titled, *Averting the Old Age Crisis*, the Bank sought to both identify the key problem likely to stem from demographic ageing, namely the fiscal unsustainability of existing, increasingly pay-as-you-go or unfunded, state pension systems, and to provide a solution to the sustainability problem. That solution, came in the form of the privately managed, but also mandatory, defined contribution schemes involving individual savings accounts based on the pioneering Chilean model. The Bank sought to address the long term fiscal sustainability issue by advocating the desirability of progressively moving away from the single pillar 'welfare state' model of tax-financed pensions towards a 'multipillar' system in which individual pensions were to be substantially pre-funded via accrued savings and investments based directly on dedicated worker and employer contributions with tax financed pensions fading into the background as a residual safety net.

In practice, there was little that was really novel in the individual empirical and analytical elements that collectively comprised the *Averting* compendium, including its focus on demographic ageing as the problem and privately managed defined contribution schemes as the solution. Rather, it was a superb, but selective, synthesis of existing work; work substantially undertaken by non-Bank staff and organisations, including the ILO. What the Bank's large and talented research team produced was a final product in which the whole comfortably exceeded the sum of its parts, and which, in particular, convincingly identified an impending crisis of unfunded, PAYG, state pension provision demanding radical policy change where others, not least the ILO, had identified the same emerging problems but had interpreted them as requiring substantial, but mainly parametric, adjustments to existing mechanisms of management and delivery and to existing entitlements to provision.

For example, in a volume published, with the ILO's usual minimal publicity, five years before *Averting*, the ILO had itself highlighted the fact that 'the population of Europe is ageing, in so far as the proportion of older people - whatever the definition applied - is growing steadily and, in many cases, spectacularly', referring, in turn, to a large body of work confirming 'that the unfavourable effect on social security of the ageing of European populations ... has been statistically perceivable and predictable since the 1950s' (ILO, 1989, p.1, p.85).[3] Nevertheless, as the ILO noted, expert 'concern about demographic trends was not reflected in subsequent government policy on pensions', underlining widespread politician unwillingness to deal with problems that, in the 1950s, lay half a century and more into the future (ILO, 1989, p.85). From the mid-1970s, however, the onset of economic recession shook European complacency, ensuring that '[t]he threat posed by the ageing of the population in practically all European countries was analysed more systematically by governments and the social partners. Public opinion thus became aware of the implications of demography on the financing of pensions in future years' (ILO, 1989, p.1, p.86). By the 1980s, ageing, combined with a steady drop in European birthrates, and occurring in a continuing context of chronic economic stagnation which effectively precluded the possibility of recourse to the large-scale encouragement of foreign immigration as a remedial policy strategy, added up to a significant forthcoming problem for existing state pension systems which forced the issue onto the political agenda for the first time. 'This combination of adverse factors cannot fail to raise doubts as to the very future of the social security schemes developed over the years in Europe ...' (ILO, 1989, p.1).

Unsurprisingly, in response to these challenges, and with ILO prompting, 'a number of Western European countries ... in the 1980s embarked upon *major reforms* of their pension systems' (ILO, 1989, p.1, p.86, emphasis added). In relation to its own role in these developments the ILO argued, somewhat defensively, that 'it may be useful to recall that the ILO did not fail to draw attention to the emerging issues and to contribute from an international viewpoint to the current debate on pension policy and the position of the elderly'. The claimed outcome of the ILO's largely low key, largely behind the scenes, activities was that 'several governments and the social partners were led to reassess the financial outlook of the pension system and to consider the adoption of possible remedial measures ...', developments occurring in a general climate of 'awareness that pension policy should be reassessed without further delay' (ILO, 1989, p.1, p.85).

Global Reform Models: From Switzerland to Chile

Nevertheless, the changes actually achieved in European pension systems in the 1980s, for the most part hardly merited the collective epithet of 'major reforms' accorded by the ILO at the end of the decade, and quoted above. In practice, as the ILO recognised, the resulting changes in funding formulae or sources or in the range of or eligibility for benefits, for the most part, only added up to parametric reforms of established systems. In summarising both the actual substance of a series of national reform achievements across Europe and what the ILO termed the available reform 'policy options', the final conclusion was that 'all the measures referred to ... are essentially adjustments of existing systems', rather than more radical 'solutions, of wider scope, aimed at redefining the role or even the very nature of general pension schemes' (ILO, 1989, p.113). Justification for the ILO's continuing commitment to its advocacy of parametric adjustments to existing PAYG social insurance pension systems rather than radical reforms requiring fundamental changes to the existing balance between state and market in pension provision, therefore, came from its reading of European, essentially Western European reforms. Crucially, despite the widespread adoption in the post-war period of what the ILO by 1989 already referred to as 'second-tier' pension programmes, offered variously either on a 'complementary' or an 'occupational' basis, among Europe's states, the ILO was at pains to stress that it was only in Switzerland that 'the establishment, at the level of individual enterprises, of a complementary pension arrangement for employees has actually been made compulsory by ... legislation' (ILO, 1989, p.79).

Significantly, even in case of the Swiss reform the process of change was very long drawn out, underlining the caution with which Europe's governments approached the pension reform issue. Implementation of the Swiss mandatory occupational pension proposals, having been approved in principle via a referendum in 1972 and subsequent constitutional amendment, followed only in 1985 when the law on professional pensions was enacted. Thus, cautious, slow and, mainly, limited reforms of the existing pension systems on the ground across Europe, in turn, enabled the ILO largely to avoid discussion of those 'very sensitive' issues, such as pension system privatisation or state withdrawal from provision, whose 'importance' it recognised but with which it remained uncomfortable as potential 'policy options' (ILO, 1989, p.113). No doubt there was some circularity in the influence flows involved in cementing these positions as the ILO and the representatives of the major European welfare states sought mutual reinforcement of their long-standing and deeply held commitments to existing models of social security. The major OECD states, after all, both 'play a leading role in the ILO and may be thought of as "carriers" of the welfare state model' (Strang and Chang, 1993, p.246). In contrast, the World Bank, with no pre-existing commitments to existing pension delivery models, had no comparable reservations either concerning the available radical reform options or in relation to potential reform modalities. Unencumbered by past commitments either to 'social security' in general or to social insurance in particular, the Bank was at once ideologically comfortable with the principle of privatisation, and, by the early 1990s, acutely aware that political commitment to the implementation of the comprehensive privatisation programmes favoured by the Bank was often lacking among developing and transition economies. Accordingly, the idea of mandatory privatisation of pension provision, anathema to the ILO, to the extent that such a system is likely to engender 'risks' unacceptable to the satisfactory fulfilment of the 'criteria embodied in the ILO's international labour standards' (Gillion and Bonilla, 1992, p.190), received an increasingly sympathetic reception in the Bank.

One operational model of the requisite combination of privatisation and compulsion, indicated above, was to be found in the Swiss reform of 1985 which made occupational pensions mandatory for the waged and voluntary for the self-employed. As Dimitri Vittas, reflecting Bank thinking prior to the full development of its preferred model in *Averting*, pointed out: 'In Britain and the US less than half of private sector employees are covered by company pension schemes, against 100 percent in Switzerland' (Vittas, 1993, p.3). However, in practice, the impact of the Swiss system on the evolution of the Bank's pension reform thinking was, in the end, less significant than the impact of the earlier, and substantially more radical, Chilean reform. On the one hand, the Bank was happy to adopt the broad principle of a 'three-pillar' pension system from common Swiss usage to characterise its own preferred format for a 'multi-pillar' system.[4] On the other hand, *Averting's* focus on the overriding importance of a specific variant of the second pillar to pension reform strategies for developing, transitional and developed economies alike, meant that the Swiss model faded increasingly into the background.

First, the Swiss pension system *in toto* was not easily packaged as a simple model. As Vittas underlined, '[t]he Swiss system, like those of most OECD countries, is extremely complex and opaque ... The complexity of the system makes it difficult to measure its cost or to assess the investment performance of the funded components of the system' (Vittas, 1993, p.3). As Queisser and Vittas (2000, p.2 fn.3) outline, the Swiss system is only nominally a three-pillar model;

> In reality, the Swiss system has six components: the public pillar is supported by the offer of noncontributory supplementary benefits; the private pillar can be divided into the legally required benefits and the super-obligatory benefits, which continue to play a large role in the private pillar; and the third pillar comprises "tied individual savings" that benefit from tax incentives and other personal savings.

By 1988 a total of 108 first pillar institutions and more than 18,000 second pillar administrative units were operational (Vittas and Skully, 1991, p.54).[5] Second, some of the specific features of the Swiss model that initially found favour, at least among the more traditionalist and Eurocentric of the Bank's pension researchers, had become more negatively perceived by the time *Averting* was published. Specifically, the fact that the Swiss 'first pillar ... appears to achieve well its redistributive and insurance objectives and does not seem to be exceedingly costly', had led Dimitri Vittas - in his almost universally well-received pre-*Averting* proposals for a 'Bank' model of 'multi-pillar' provision - to argue that the first pillar 'would follow the approach of the Swiss first pillar' (Vittas, 1993, p.9, p.20, see Appendix Fig. A2.2). However, whilst the intentionally redistributive aims, in favour of low-income workers, of the Swiss 'first pillar' social insurance scheme continued to be endorsed in *Averting*, Vittas' proposal for a two-part structure following the Swiss combination of 'a flat-rate full-career minimum pension; and an earnings-related pension' had been abandoned. By 1994 the search for a public 'first' pillar that was to be 'modest in size', in line with its 'unambiguous and limited objective' to alleviate old age poverty, meant that the idea of retaining an earnings-related element had lost favour with the Bank's pension research team who defined the retention of such Bismarckian differential benefits as constituting 'a poor choice for the public pillar' (World Bank, 1994, p.16, p.17, see Appendix Fig. A2.3).

More important still in ensuring the priority of Chile over Switzerland in the crystallisation of the format of the crucial 'second', but never secondary, element in the Bank's preferred multipillar model, was the perceived undesirability of basing the central mandatory private pillar on Swiss-style occupational schemes. In this respect, in particular, there is a strong thread of continuity running from Dimitri Vittas' *Swiss Chilanpore*, through *Averting*, to the current Bank proposals on optimal pension reform. The '[t]wo points that should be stressed' concerning the design of the original multi-pillar system that Vittas proposed, were that it involved 'a continuing, though reduced, role for a public pension pillar and *a much reduced role for company-based pension schemes*' (Vittas, 1993, p.25, emphasis added). Bluntly, occupationally-based pension schemes were inconsistent with the need for maximal portability of pensions in the development of the flexible labour markets that were, and remain, so central to the Bank's economic liberalisation creed. Vittas makes this point with characteristic precision and balance, considering distributional as well as labour market impacts. 'The much reduced role of occupational pension schemes can be justified on two grounds. First, occupational pension schemes ... [t]o the extent that they are used as a personnel management tool, ... are bound to penalize some workers more than others. Eliminating these shortcomings, by appropriate regulations ... would weaken the incentive of employers to continue sponsoring such plans. The second argument is that, with declining stability in employment patterns, company-based schemes would become exceedingly unsuitable for providing employment-based social benefits such as pension and health insurance' (Vittas, 1993, pp.25-26). Or, as *Averting* succinctly put it, '[o]ccupational plans ... may impede the smooth functioning of labor markets' (World Bank, 1994, p.14). Conversely, 'coverage under personal savings plans can be broad, and benefits are fully portable. Because of these distributional and labor market effects, personal savings plans are probably preferable to occupational plans for the funded pillar ...' (World Bank, 1994, p.18).

The Crystallisation of the Bank's Pillared Model

In the absence of alternative operational models that satisfied the Bank's 'second pillar' requirements for mandatory private pensions provided on the basis of individual savings accounts, it was Chile's 'AFP system', operational from 1981, that provided, first, *Swiss Chilanpore* and then *Averting* with both the conceptual inspiration and the empirical justification for their central and most novel proposals. Simply stated, it was the only available model. 'Until 1994, Chile was the only country that had fully replaced an existing public pay-as-you-go pension scheme with a mandatory saving scheme. Chile was also the only country whose mandatory saving program is privately and competitively managed ... Because Chile's is the only fully implemented decentralized scheme at this point, the discussion here draws heavily on its experience', the authors of *Averting* explained, by way of justification for that volume's heavy reliance on Chilean evidence in support of its key themes of mandatory privatisation via individual capitalisation accounts (World Bank, 1994, p.204). Crucially, Chile provided the Bank with a working example of the apparently successful rebalancing of pension provision towards the private sector and away from the public sector, and did so, moreover, in the context of a middle income developing state, with all the obvious implications for, and, in many cases, potentially direct relevance to, the many other similarly placed DCs and transition economies with which the Bank was dealing.

However, in one important respect the Bank approach to both pension system privatisation and the Chilean model exhibited a significant change over the year that separated *Swiss Chilanpore* from *Averting*. In the earlier work Dimitri Vittas had argued, in line with the *Averting* approach, that '[t]he second pillar would be very similar in structure and regulation to the Chilean system ...', but had immediately qualified this statement, inserting the phrase '*except in one very important respect*' (Vittas, 1993, p.22, emphasis added). This qualification related to what Vittas termed 'the apparently excessive level of operating costs' that were generally acknowledged as a key downside of the AFP system. To avoid these costs, Vittas proposed an alternative to the decentralised, competitive, administration that characterised the Chilean model; an alternative that was based on lessons learned from 'the ruthless efficiency of Singapore' (Vittas, 1993, p.2). Accordingly, *Swiss Chilanpore*, deliberately blending the best elements of the pension systems of the three countries, looked to Singapore's National Provident Fund (NPF), the Central Provident Fund (CPF), characterised by its 'high efficiency and low running costs', to provide the appropriate model of cost-effective administrative efficiency required to manage the second pillar effectively (Vittas, 1993, p.11). Thus, efficiency and economy aims required that 'a central agency ... be responsible for record keeping, collecting contributions, paying pensions and sending out financial statements', rather than relying, as in the Chilean system, on the separate administrative systems of the competing private companies that were to be entrusted with the responsibility of investing the collected funds. As in the case of the Singaporean CPF, '[t]he central agency could be a public body or it could be jointly owned by all the private companies that would be allowed to participate in the investment management of the pension funds' (Vittas, 1993, p.22).

Interestingly, in an earlier paper, co-authored with Michael Skully, Vittas had advanced an even stronger case for the centralised and state-led management of a three pillar, mixed, public and private, pension system, based on the Swiss model of centralised administration of an otherwise highly decentralised system. In the Swiss system one state agency collates information on individual affiliates across all three pension pillars, namely for the public social insurance system of first pillar, the mandatory private occupational pensions of the second pillar, and the additional, voluntary, personal savings plans of the third pillar, which has the important additional function of covering the self-employed and others not included in second pillar occupational schemes. Across this administratively and managerially complex and highly institutionally diverse system, '[o]perating costs are contained by the use of joint administration for all institutions through the Central Equalisation Office, which keeps all individual records and also administers an equalisation fund' (Vittas and Skully, 1991, p.54). Overall, Vittas and Skully conclude that centralised administration is preferable in DCs, not simply due to the 'benefit from lower operating and marketing costs' but also, crucially, because of the likely greater disadvantages of decentralised private administration. 'Such centralized institutions may suffer from lack of autonomy and administrative inefficiencies, but in countries with weak regulatory frameworks, a decentralised system of private providers of contractual savings facilities would probably suffer from greater weaknesses, such as the potential opportunistic behavior of private suppliers' (Vittas and Skully, 1991, p.54). In *Averting*, in marked contrast, the general case made by Vittas, and Vittas and Skully, for centralised control over record keeping and general administration is simply ignored, whilst centralised public management is dismissed as typically leading to 'compulsory monopolies [that] may have little incentive to operate efficiently ... Decentralized competitive plans, by contrast, face market pressures to operate efficiently ...' (World Bank, 1994, p.208).

In essence, therefore, the encompassing aims of *Swiss Chilanpore*, to devise 'a pension reform strategy that combines the best features of each country, while avoiding their weaknesses' (Vittas, 1993, p.19), were deliberately abandoned in *Averting*, in favour of an approach that focused more narrowly on generalising the Chilean AFP system, whilst, at the same time, marginalising the Swiss elements and totally abandoning the Singaporean dimension of the earlier model. The inappropriateness of this strategic selectivity, both in relation to the ignored virtues and potentialities of what we term the 'NPF model' and in relation to the exaggerated advantages and unsustainable expectations heaped upon the Chilean 'AFP system', are the subjects dealt with, albeit to different degrees and within different contexts, in Chapters 4, 5 and 8. Here, our focus is on outlining the background to, and identifying the mainsprings of, these key strategic choices, seeking to situate the evolution of Bank thinking on pension reform in a wider context of national and international developments.

'A privately managed mandatory personal saving scheme was pioneered in Chile and is now being incorporated into new systems in

Argentina, Colombia, and Peru', *Averting* pointed out, summarising the pension reform situation in Latin America in 1994 (World Bank, 1994, p.18). In these developments, as Robert Holzmann, currently Director, Social Protection at the Bank, has recently underlined, the role of the World Bank was essentially one of reinforcement of (selected) pre-existing reform trends and of support for would-be reformers through its research resources, through publicity and communication of findings and through policy advice and technical assistance. In practice, 'when Averting the Old Age Crisis was published in 1994, a global shift in pension provision was already unfolding ... The World Bank did not create the current trends, but it has taken a leading role in providing advice and technical assistance to a growing number of our client countries who are interested in pension reform' (Holzmann, 1999, pp.1-2; see Appendix Map A2.1). Prior to the initiation, in the early 1990s, of the massive research exercise that was to lead to the publication of *Averting the Old Age Crisis* less than three years later, the Bank's 'knowledge' profile, covering both research and consultancy dimensions, in relation to retirement pensions was minimal, overshadowed in this field not only by its Geneva rival, the ILO, but also by its sister Washington institution, the IMF. In practice, the comparatively limited Bank work undertaken on pensions-related issues prior to the watershed change in focus initiated when 'Lawrence Summers, then Chief Economist of the World Bank, launched a major study of global pension provision' (Holzmann, 1999, p.1) in 1992, was considerably less 'mainstream' and considerably less prominent than that undertaken during the 1980s and early 1990s by its sister Washington institution, the IMF. Yet, by 1999, Richard Hemming, Head of the Fiscal Analysis Division of the IMF, was stating categorically that: 'The World Bank is *primarily responsible for advice* from the Bretton Woods institutions on the structure of public pension schemes' (Hemming, 1999, p.6, emphasis added).

This outcome clearly demands explanation, since, as Richard Hemming is at pains to underline, albeit obliquely, the Bank, despite its vast human, organisational and financial resources, appears to have added little to what was already known in the late 1980s about the problems of established and maturing public pension systems, and, more importantly, has similarly contributed little to the design of alternative, superior, arrangements. Hemming is more specific about the sources of research on public pension systems prior to the 1990s. Significantly, no mention is made of any Bank contribution. 'Much of the work which highlighted the financial strain that pay-as-you-go (PAYG) public pension systems in industrial countries would inevitably face was done during the 1980s. This work', Hemming continues, 'included cross-country studies of industrial countries undertaken by the OECD and the IMF, as well as individual country studies' (Hemming, 1999, p.3). In line with the ILO's summary of the problems facing Europe's pension systems previously outlined, '[t]wo sources of financial strain were identified in these studies. The first was generous pension benefits ... The second, more important, source of financial strain was prospective population ageing ...'. The standard policy response, widely proposed but less widely implemented, was, again as outlined above, parametric reform. 'With projected contribution rates in most industrial countries looking set to reach unsustainably high levels around the end of the first quarter of the 21st century, the required policy response was almost unanimously judged to be a scaling back of pension benefits, and to varying degrees this is what happened in those countries that have faced up to the financial problems of their public pension systems'. However, as Hemming points out, the identification of what was *not* discussed or proposed in the 1980s pension reform debate has, in retrospect, become of equal, if not greater, significance. 'During the 1980s, relatively little attention was paid to the possibility of changing the way in which public pensions were financed, *and specifically to switching from PAYG to funding*' (Hemming, 1999, pp.3-4, emphasis added).

'Move on to the mid-1990s and all the talk is about a switch to funding. *What has happened to explain the emphasis now placed on funding?*' (Hemming, 1999, p.4, emphasis in original). The question is in fact largely rhetorical, since the answer, in effect is: not much, and certainly not enough to justify the current stress placed on full pre-funding as the appropriate and desirable basis for any and all pension systems. Certainly, in the intervening period no significantly new research findings had appeared to justify this fundamental shift in policy strategy or to underpin such a radical change in policy advice. On the one hand, it is notable that there has 'been no significant intellectual debate in the interim that has produced a widely accepted conclusion that funding is inherently superior to PAYG'. On the other hand, as confirmed by the IMF's own on-going comparative studies, given both appropriate and sufficiently far-reaching parametric adjustments, it is clear that 'PAYG pension finances can be placed on a sustainable path' even in mature systems, always provided that there is sufficient political commitment to reform (Hemming, 1994, p.4).

Unsurprisingly, there has been little 'fault ... found in the approach some industrial countries have taken to scaling back pensions', confirming that, in practice, even seemingly 'unsustainable public pension finances can be addressed through bold parametric reform' in the IMF's view (Hemming, 1999, p.4, p.7). Moreover, as confirmed in IMF studies and as reflected in that institution's standard policy advice, there are large and lasting additional costs involved in comprehensively abandoning an existing pension system and moving to an alternative system. In this context it is important to underline the IMF's related finding that these unavoidable reform costs also vary directly with the comprehensiveness of the reform contemplated. Where, as 'in Pillar 2 of the World Bank three-pillar pension system, [the move to] funding goes hand in hand with a switch from defined-benefit to defined-contribution pensions and ... privatization of public pensions' (Hemming, 1999, p.20. We have omitted the word 'limited' since, as discussed fully below, we, following the general view, agree with the standard interpretation the Bank model as advocating substantial, not limited, privatisation of existing systems, the costs involved will be very large indeed).[6]

As Hemming summarises, on the basis of a detailed overview of both the theoretical issues and the available empirical evidence, the choice between funding and PAYG is far from straightforward and clear-cut, whether envisaged in principle or met in practice. Overall, 'if funding has an edge over PAYG ... it is not an overwhelming one ... Nevertheless, despite the absence of a strong case for funding, the momentum for shifting from PAYG to funding remains'. Why, then, has this puzzling, paradoxical and largely irrational, outcome occurred? Hemming's answer to this question, which we explore in more detail below with specific focus on the origins, genesis and subsequent impact of the reform model, can be simply summarised: Chile.

> If there is a single explanation for the attention now being paid to funding public pensions, it is most likely to be the success of pension reform in Chile, where some have claimed that the changeover to a funded system in 1981 has not only put in place a lower-cost, more secure pension system but also spurred the country's subsequent impressive savings, investment and growth performance.
>
> Hemming, 1999, p.4

The Evolution of Bank Interest in Pension Systems

The clear, and, we would suggest, clearly intended, implication to be drawn from this argument is that the role of the World Bank in both the development of the current 'funding' orthodoxy and in the subsequent, on-going, processes of dissemination and implementation of funding-based reforms, has been of secondary, rather than primary, significance. Significantly, this 'outsider' interpretation does not differ significantly in substance from the 'insider' interpretation provided by Robert Holzmann and quoted above. The World Bank neither initiated the current reform agenda nor influenced the early processes of dissemination of the reform fashion within Latin America, although currently, as the lead BWI in this field, it now presides over and guides on-going reform developments with care. The publication of *Averting* in 1994, therefore, constituted a double watershed, at once announcing the emergence of the Bank as a major new force in the pensions research field and providing both justification and agenda for the rapid expansion of the Bank's technical assistance activities in this field, most obviously in the transition economies of CEE and the NIS/FSU.

Supporting evidence for such an explanation is provided by the Bank's short research and publication pedigree in pension-related fields. Specifically, the Bank's comparatively limited portfolio of pensions-related work prior to the initiation of the major programme of work underpinning *Averting* programme, can, in turn, best be characterised, initially at least, as an incidental offshoot of its general financial sector work in DCs, remaining mainly associated with analyses of the development and operation of contractual savings institutions in general rather than specifically focused on pension systems. Millard Long, in an EDI seminar paper presented in 1990 and published in 1991, provides a succinct summary of the Bank's rising interest in financial sector issues from the 1980s and of the rising importance of finance-related dimensions in its country-level work in developing countries.

> Twenty, or even ten years ago, the World Bank used financial institutions, primarily development finance institutions, to onlend the Bank's funds ... But aside from the operations of the institutions funded, the Bank paid little heed to the remainder of the financial sector. In terms of sector work, in the years prior to 1980, the Bank had done studies of the financial system in only three countries. In the 1980s the Bank undertook studies of

the financial system in most countries in which it had operations. Financial issues have become a key element in the policy dialogue between countries and the World Bank. The Bank made 13 policy based loans in the last 3 years to improve conditions in the financial system, and has another half dozen under preparation.

Long, 1991, p.159

This extended quotation neatly underlines the rapidly growing importance of financial sector work in Bank operations during the 1980s. The focus of the bulk of this financial sector work was on macroeconomic policy issues relating to liberalisation, and was not, therefore, primarily institutional, and where it was institutional the focus was mainly on banking issues rather than on those relating to non-bank financial intermediaries such as contractual savings institutions, including NPFs and pension systems, both public and private. As Vittas and Skully summarise, up to the early 1990s, '[f]or understandable reasons, given the pervasiveness of financial repression and the precarious position of banking systems in many countries, the World Bank, in line with other multilateral lenders, has focused its financial sector work on macropolicy reforms and banking restructurings' (Vittas and Skully, 1991, p.3). Accordingly, the Bank came only belatedly into financial sector work and even more belatedly into work on non-bank financial intermediaries (NBFIs), including that on contractual savings institutions.

Long duly provides an equally succinct explanation of the basis for the emergence of the Bank's interest in pension and retirement savings institutions and systems within the developing trajectory of its wider financial sector analyses. Initially, the Bank's focus was on the broad front development of non-bank financial intermediaries and capital markets in the bank-based, but thin and weak, financial systems widely characteristic of DCs in the 1980s. As Long argued, '[b]uilding nonbank financial intermediaries and capital markets as alternatives to banks will increase competition and efficiency and provide for more extensive service'. Giving as his illustrative example the problematic issue of the shortage of long term finance for investment, Long, who was addressing a largely African audience, underlined the potential importance to DCs of contractual savings institutions as a source of term money for investment purposes.

In most developed countries, contractual savings institutions, that is, life insurance, pension programs, and so on, are the major sources of term finance. With the changes in demographics and living conditions, developing countries also have an opportunity to develop these sources of term finance. For example, in Singapore the pension assets are now equivalent to 65 percent of GNP. In Chile a reformed pension system grew to 18 percent of GNP in 8 years ... If a market for sound financial assets can be developed to give ... investments liquidity and a reasonable degree of stability, some of the resources collected by pension programs and insurance companies could be invested in private securities and become a genuine source of term finance, just as they have in many developed countries.

Long, 1991, p.168

The Bank, therefore, was encouraged to focus more precisely on the potential developmental roles of specific types of non-bank financial intermediaries due to the growing, and increasingly widely recognised, impact of contractual savings institutions, both public, in the form of NPFs and private, in the form of personal pensions, in acknowledged national success stories among DCs.

The picture deliberately painted by the Bank researchers, as exemplified by Long and Vittas and Skully respectively, was that Bank research on DC contractual savings sectors, with its increasingly positive analysis of achieved and potential economic growth impacts, was essentially reactive and decidedly retrospective. 'The visible financial and economic success of such countries as Singapore, Malaysia, Korea and Chile, in combination with the growing financial pressures confronting most social pension insurance systems, have induced policymakers in many countries to examine the case for reforming their contractual savings industries and to pay a closer look at their potential contribution to economic development' (Vittas and Skully, 1991, p.3), clearly indicating little or no interest in these questions prior to the 1980s. Institutional memory, in this case, is not entirely reliable, since researchers in the Public and Private Finance Division of the Development Economics Department of the Bank had, in fact, published several seminal papers during the 1970s, in the then highly influential 'Studies in Domestic Finance' series, on the achieved and potential developmental impacts of contractual savings, or social security, sectors - the terms were used interchangeably (see, particularly, Shome, 1977). This Bank work, in turn, was simply continuing a line of analysis and thinking initiated by IMF staff in the 1960s on issues relating to the potentials of social security institutions and contractual savings sectors, particularly provident funds, as generators of savings that might underpin economic growth (see, Reviglio, 1967a, 1967b and Joshi, 1972).

Overall, however, particularly in comparison to the volume of research on pension systems, and prospective pension system problems, in HICs, research on contractual savings institutions in DCs, even if defined to include social insurance pension systems, can best be termed limited in both quantity and in scope, largely as Vittas and Skully claimed. In its essentials their summary of what had been achieved in volume terms by 1991 was not inaccurate. 'Relatively little work has been done on the state of the contractual savings industry in developing countries and on the policies that are required to assist its development', specifically pointing out that a 1990 Bank research consultancy 'report on the contractual savings industry in Mexico represents one of the first comprehensive studies of the industry in a developing country' (Vittas and Skully, 1991, p.3, p.4). Vittas and Skully are less reliable in their depiction of the intra-sectoral scope and institutional focus of the work previously undertaken on contractual savings institutions in DCs. In particular, their listing of 'various studies' produced by '[o]ther international bodies' - citing items from the IMF, the OECD, the ILO, the ISSA and UNCTAD, 'on particular sectors of the contractual savings industry, such as social security systems and life insurance companies' - is most notable for its failure to mention NPFs as a specific subject of research (Vittas and Skully, 1991, p.3, p 4).

As indicated above, this rather curious lapse of institutional memory may simply be that, but it is more plausible that the omission indicates a disinclination to discuss the wider issues raised by the sea changes that had occurred in the Bank's view of the potential developmental roles of, and of appropriate promotional or supportive policies towards, contractual savings institutions in general, and NPFs in particular, between the 1970s and the 1990s. Specifically, as the Bank moved from its 1970s position as a funder of projects in DCs to its 1980s focus on policy-based lending in support of structural adjustment programmes, an earlier, largely positive view of the developmental capacities of the state was replaced by an increasingly negative perception of an entity largely inimical to development. Thus, Shome's 1977 'preliminary survey' of the role of contractual savings institutions in resource mobilisation in DCs records that it was still 'sometimes assumed that if savings are lent to the state, then they will automatically be channelled for development together with providing security and optimum yield'. Although Shome was at pains to qualify this assumption of automaticity, his corrective was mild, arguing that 'even though loans to the state are usually secure, they may not always be used for developmental purposes, going instead towards current expenditures of non-developmental types' (Shome, 1977, p.28).

Moreover, in direct contrast to current Bank thinking, which favours a liberalisation of the international investment restrictions still widely imposed on contractual savings institutions in DCs, Shome advocated in-country investment as developmentally preferable, despite the potential security and yield advantages offered by diversified portfolios of international securities. 'A clearly non-developmental channel is investing in foreign securities ... An investment in the State is clearly a better alternative for development. Indeed even though channelling the funds through the State may not be a guarantee towards development, the funds may increase the pool available to the government, which can then be utilised for different purposes in the private or public sector according to national priorities in a way that will increase productivity and taxable capacity ...' (Shome, 1977, p.29). V.V. Bhatt, in his Preface to Shome's survey, underlines where this line of reasoning on the potentially welfare enhancing effects of investments made on the basis of contractual savings might lead, and, bluntly, why the Bank might now prefer that this early example of its work on contractual savings sectors/social security institutions is quietly forgotten. 'Since they [*i.e.* contractual savings sectors/social security institutions] have been one of the principal sources for medium and long term finance, and hence one of the major investors in long-term financial assets, they seem to have reduced the degree of concentration in the distribution of wealth and incomes. The term "Pension Fund Socialism" in a way describes this phenomenon' (Shome, 1977, Preface p.ii). Unsurprisingly, in the context of the 1980s, an era of development thinking and policies increasingly unfriendly to socialism of any sort and in any guise, V.V. Bhatt's view that 'it should be one of the major objectives of financial policies in the LDCs to promote the growth of social security institutions', was unlikely to fall on fertile ground within the Bank (Shome, 1977, Preface p.ii).

The Bank and Pension Reform: From Interest to Involvement

More widely, in a Washington context progressively bound up in the liberalisation agenda and in the post-debt crisis construction of policy conditionalities focused largely on macroeconomic dimensions within stabilisation and structural adjustment programmes, the microeconomics of the financial sector and its organisational and institutional basis was inevitably sidelined as a policy issue. As outlined above, the Bank's developing interest in financial sectors during the 1980s was primarily an interest in the macropolicy dimensions of liberalisation, with institutional dimensions impinging largely due to the need to address banking crises and the widespread problems of bank insolvency. Non-bank financial intermediaries were, for the most part, off the Bank policy agenda during the 1980s, largely ensuring that it would be a 'lost decade' not only for social policy within DCs but also for social security and contractual savings institutions as well. Not unreasonably, in relation to the sum total of previously published work in this field, Vittas and Skully define their 1991 *Overview of Contractual Savings Institutions* as 'an attempt to offer a comprehensive survey of contractual savings institutions in different countries', immediately adding the qualification that this aim 'is handicapped by the limited availability of up-to-date statistics on a consistent basis' (Vittas and Skully, 1991, p.4).

In practice, despite the efforts of Vittas and Skully to redress this institutional imbalance within the Bank's portfolio of contractual savings research, NPFs have remained comparatively neglected, just as, for reasons that we explain elsewhere in Chapter 5 of this book, NPFs received little attention as retirement savings systems compared to that accorded to social insurance pension systems. Significantly, in this regard, Vittas and Skully, are at pains to point out that '[s]ome work has been carried out on social pension insurance systems' by Bank researchers during the 1980s, citing five publications, mainly from 1988 and 1989, but with one from as early as 1983. Interestingly, this last paper, by Christine Wallich, was on Chile. However, despite the date of publication, two years after the inauguration of the AFP system in 1981, and despite its tantalising title, 'Savings Mobilization through Social Security', its focus was not on the newly privatised system but on the savings and fiscal performance of its disregarded social insurance predecessor between 1916 and 1977 (Vittas and Skully, 1991, pp.3-4).

Although Vittas and Skully's short list of Bank publications on pension systems during the 1980s is certainly not exhaustive - for example a Bank paper specifically on the Chilean pension reform circulated in 1987 - it is certainly indicative of the low priority that pensions-related work had within the Bank prior to the crash research programme launched in 1992. As of 1991 the Chilean AFP model appeared to be of less interest to the Bank than it was to other DCs, although even Chile's Latin American neighbours at that time appeared in no hurry to emulate Chile's system of personal pension plans, remaining particularly reluctant to adopt the system on a mandatorily privatised basis as a direct replacement of existing public social insurance schemes. 'Following the Chilean lead, other developing countries, especially in Latin America, have also considered the introduction of such plans and have enacted measures to promote their use alongside existing social security and company-based schemes'. Crucially, however, as Vittas and Skully underlined, 'no country appears to have made much progress in this regard ...' (Vittas and Skully, 1991, p.48). This absence of progress on the pension reform front in the 1980s is unsurprising given the very different sets of policy priorities that dominated the 1980s in comparison to both the 1970s and the 1990s. The contrast between the more state-centric, expenditure oriented and social security friendly 1970s, and the more expenditure-constrained and welfare-antipathetic 1980s is clear-cut and obvious.

Less obviously explicable, but in its own way equally clear-cut, is the contrast between the largely pension system-ignoring 1980s and the increasingly pension reform-focused 1990s, despite the shared basis in liberal or neoliberal thinking that underpins the Bank's policy agendas across the two decades. In short, whereas the 'Washington consensus' of the 1980s had found no place for pension reform, even on the distinctly market-friendly Chilean AFP basis, in its policy agenda, the 'post-Washington consensus' of the 1990s has placed pension system pillarisation and restructuring through privatisation increasingly at the centre of the Bank's research interests and at the heart of its policy reform programmes. Thus, John Williamson's classic, 1990, account of what he termed the 'Washington consensus' or the 'Washington agenda', relating to his identification of the '9 or 10 policy areas in which "Washington" could muster something like a consensus on what countries ought to be doing ...', contained nothing of significance on pension system reform (Williamson, 1990, p.1). Whilst Williamson's discussion of fiscal deficits - 'Washington believes in fiscal discipline' (Williamson, 1990, p.8) - referred critically to the fact that '[t]he buildup of future liabilities of the social security system is not included in budget outlays' was one of the 'questionable practices [that] seem to involve understatement of the true deficit', no further lessons or implications are drawn from this example (Williamson, 1990, p.10, p.9). Significantly, Williamson's discussion of the specific policy instruments involved in *'What Washington means by Policy Reform'* did not mention financial system reform as such, but focused specifically on interest rates, whilst the short section on privatization reminds us that this was a policy instrument that was only added to the IFIs' agenda after 1985 (Williamson, 1990, p.13, p.16).

Accordingly, although on the one hand, as Stanley Fischer's comment on Williamson's listing of instruments underlines, financial system issues were already, by 1990, looming larger than the former had suggested, Williamson's silence was, also, on the other hand, a fair reflection of the limited, indeed substantially negative, impact that the Chilean pension system privatization had on Washington during the 1980s. Consequently, whilst it was clear by 1990 that 'Washington's emphasis on financial sector reform goes well beyond a concern with real interest rates, to the notion that the banking system and the financial sector in many developing countries need fundamental restructuring' (Fischer, 1990, p.26), it was still very far from clear that Chile offered the appropriate role model in respect of pension system restructuring. The picture of the outcome and long term impact of the 1981 Chilean pension reform that was emerging from Santiago by 1990 was, to say the least, mixed and substantially ambiguous overall, and, indeed, distinctly problematic in some significant respects, of which one, the impact on public finances, was of very direct interest to Washington. As Patricio Meller put it in his overview of the Chilean model of adjustment in the Williamson volume, '[t]he social security reform of 1981 transformed most of the state-administered pay-as-you-go civil pension fund into a system of privately administered and capitalized pension funds, financed by a 10 percent compulsory tax on wages and salaries, revenues from which are transferred directly to the funds. In this way, the public sector has kept the current pension obligations while losing most of the contributions' (Meller, 1990, p.78). Given, Washington's 1980s overriding predilection for maintaining strict 'fiscal discipline', it is unsurprising that Meller cites a 1987 World Bank report as his source in underlining that the pension 'reform has generated an additional annual fiscal deficit of 3 percent to 4 percent of GDP, which will start declining only in the year 2000' (Meller, 1990, p.78, citing World Bank, 1987).

Averting the Old Age Crisis: Impact and Legacy

What the Bank's programme of '[e]xtensive research revealed [was] the widespread failure of public, defined benefit schemes to protect the old. Politicians made pension promises that could not be kept so that defined benefits often turned out to be quite the opposite ... At the same time, the distortions caused by these schemes and the fiscal burden of unfunded liabilities threatened the economic future of pensioners and workers alike' (Holzmann, 1999, p.1), particularly in the middle income DCs of Latin America and among the transition economies of CEE and the FSU/NIS where existing tax-financed systems were already in fiscal crisis. As Holzmann rightly stresses, '[t]hese findings and their implications were not new to reformers in many countries', citing the 'growing popularity' of the type of multipillar system advocated by the Bank (Holzmann, 1999, p.1) with several adoptions already in process of implementation prior to the release of *Averting*. This particular 'multipillar' system involved the introduction of 'mandatory, funded and privately managed components or second pillars alongside the tax financed and publicly-managed first pillar. The third pillar consisted of voluntary retirement savings. By the time *Averting* was released, countries as diverse as Australia and Argentina had already customized this approach to their own circumstances' (Holzmann, 1999, p.1). Nonetheless, not only did the pace of reform accelerate markedly following the release of *Averting* but the profile of pension reform rose exponentially, rapidly becoming a 'global' issue of major policy salience from the mid-1990s. 'In the last five years, a dozen more countries have introduced multipillar schemes. In many more, it is one of the options being seriously considered' (Holzmann, 1999, p.1).

However, the most important trend that has characterised the development of the pension reform agenda over the years that have passed since *Averting* appeared, has been the effective narrowing of multipillar options. Instead of generating a constructive and wide-ranging international debate in the manner of its sister 'World Bank Policy Research Report' analysing *The East Asian Miracle*, the impact of *Averting* served rather to obviate the need for debate by dint of increasingly narrowing the multipillar options discussed as potential policy reform options. These multipillar possibilities, although already, as presented in *Averting*, less encompassing than those envisaged in a number of Bank research publications published before 1994, but especially Vittas' *Swiss Chilanpore* (1993), were still sufficiently widely delineated to indicate some possibility of flexibility in the balance between the private and the public elements within the Bank's overall multipillar framework. As the World Bank's former Chief Economist, Joseph Stiglitz, underlined in a co-authored conference paper delivered shortly before his premature resignation, the key issues do not relate to the multipillar proposals presented within *Averting* itself but rather to the subsequent restatements of these proposals both by academic commentators, and, more importantly, by the Bank's key pensions researchers themselves. 'In principle, the "three pillars" delineated in *Averting the Old Age Crisis* are expansive enough to reflect any potential combination of policy measures - especially if the second (funded) pillar incorporates both privately and publicly managed systems' (Orszag and Stiglitz, 1999, p.4). In practice, the resultant 'popular interpretation' (Orszag and Stiglitz, 1999, p.4, fn.5) of the Bank's preferred model invariably focuses on the need for the crucial second pillar to be both fully funded and privately managed. 'That interpretation - especially the inclusion of a *privately managed, defined contribution* component - is common among policymakers and pension analysts, regardless of whether it fully reflects the nuances of *Averting the Old Age Crisis* itself', and is now correctly defined as forming the current 'conventional wisdom' of pension system reform and restructuring (Orszag and Stiglitz, 1999, p.4, p.39). Moreover, it is precisely this narrow interpretation that is constantly restated and reinforced in the writings of the Bank's own pension researchers.[7]

The main problems stemming from *Averting*, therefore, do not relate to its research findings, despite their combination of selectiveness and sensationalism, nor even to its central policy proposals, provided the latter are broadly conceived rather than narrowly interpreted, but rather to the foreclosing of policy options and the constraining of debate that has followed its publication. Orszag and Stiglitz' differential judgements, positive on the importance and timeliness of *Averting*, but negative in relation to the subsequent interpretation of its key thesis and its consequential and continuing policy impacts, are both sound and balanced. 'Underfunded public pension systems represent a potential threat to the fiscal soundness - and, more broadly, economic stability of many developing countries. The World Bank's study, *Averting the Old Age Crisis*, provided an invaluable service in drawing attention to this problem and in discussing specific policy changes to address the issue. Unfortunately, as often happens, the suggestions have come to be viewed narrowly - focusing on a second pillar limited to a private, non-redistributive, defined contribution pension plan' (Orszag and Stiglitz, 1999, p.39). The outcome, in practice, has been an increasing tendency to assume that one pension system reform model will, effectively, fit all countries largely irrespective of their stage of economic development, or of the state of their economies. This view reflects an universalist assumption paralleling, but clearly in its encompassing global reform aspirations going well beyond, the ILO's pre-war assumption that social insurance-based state pensions were the appropriate model for all countries to aspire to, albeit only once a particular level of economic affluence had been achieved.

Accordingly, the legacy of *Averting* is particularly problematic in respect of the tendency to underestimate the complexity of the pensions reform problem, to assume that there is one best reform model, and in its self-confidence that the suggested reform package has general validity, that the one best model fits all countries and cases. Conversely, we would propose an approach to reform that is more nuanced in its attention to the importance of national, and regional variations, to the significance of historical legacies and past institutional and policy choices, and in its sensitivity to the institutional and policy constraints imposed by wide disparities in national income levels and associated disparities in organisational and institutional assets. In these respects we share the reservations regarding the Bank reform model expressed by Orszag and Stiglitz. 'The complexity of optimal pension policy should caution us against believing that a similar set of recommendations would be appropriate in countries ranging from Argentina to Azerbaijan, from China to Costa Rica, from Sierra Leone to Sweden' (Orszag and Stiglitz, 1999, p.3). Inevitably, with these considerations in mind, our approach is less narrowly focused on the virtues of the expansion of the private sector in pension management and delivery and less self-confident concerning the general superiority of the private over the public sector. Specifically, for example, Orszag and Stiglitz are clearly correct in their view that '[t]he debate over pension reform would benefit substantially from a more expansive view of the optimal second pillar ... A privately managed second pillar is not always optimal. A more expansive perspective would allow policy-makers to weigh appropriately all the tradeoffs they face ...' (Orszag and Stiglitz, 1999, p.39).

However, the immediacy, and the directness, of the Bank's response to the 1999 Orszag and Stiglitz conference paper itself underlines how entrenched in that institution's thinking the narrow, selective, approach to multipillar options has become in the years since *Averting* appeared. Both the content and the tone of the response demonstrate how important defending the validity of that approach is to the Bank, and how intolerant even of constructive criticism and antagonistic to alternative reform proposals it remains, particularly when that criticism is internal and the alternative approaches suggested would undermine the Bank's on-going, and expanding, advisory and policy consultancy work. As Robert Holzmann (1999, p.2), writing as a member of the World Bank Pension Team and registering the Bank's negative response, explains,

> [t]he World Bank recently held a research conference entitled, New Ideas in Pension Reform ... Most of the conference addressed key challenges facing pension reformers ... One paper received disproportionate attention, however. This is partly due to the fact that one of the authors is the current Chief Economist of the World Bank, Joseph Stiglitz, known for his provocative positions in many areas.

As Holzmann continues,

> the authors claim there are 10 myths about social security systems that, if properly understood would lead to different conclusions about pension reform. The list of myths is somewhat puzzling. Most of the myths are not commonly held beliefs in the pension reform community and therefore required no debunking ... Myths aside, the authors alternative to the multipillar reform was not really clear.

However, the key points are contained in Holzmann's final paragraph - the Bank's newly won analytical pre-eminence and burgeoning policy influence in the pensions reform field was under threat. Accordingly, the Bank must respond swiftly and directly to reassert its position as the lead institution in the pension reform field and to reassure its clients and potential clients that it remains the repository of appropriate knowledge and the purveyor of sound policy advice. 'Over the last five years, the World

Bank has established itself as a leader in pension reform issues in a world that is rapidly ageing. The reality is that we are experiencing a historic shift in the way the world provides for old age. We will continue to learn from our experiences to ensure that we can provide the quality advice our clients expect and deserve' (Holzmann, 1999, p.3). Our alternative proposals for a more encompassing advisory regime are contained in Chapter 9, whilst the intervening Chapters can be read as an extended commentary on the Bank's approach.

Notes

1. As noted by Dimitri Vittas of the World Bank in a nicely ironic, and significantly heretical, formulation detailing the main short-term beneficiaries of recent radical pension reforms, '[e]xperience from Latin America shows that the first beneficiaries are the various *"consultores"*, all those who advise government about the need and implications of pension reform. ... This includes not only the numerous Chilean economists that have become popular travelers in Latin America and other parts of the world, but also the growing army of actuaries, economists and pension specialists in North America and Europe, not to mention those working for multilateral institutions, such as the World Bank and the OECD' (Vittas, 2000, p.18).
2. The present International Labour Organisation was founded in 1919 under the auspices of the Treaty of Versailles as a League of Nations entity, although a precursor institution, the International Labour Office, was created in 1901. From 1945 the ILO became the first specialised agency of the United Nations.
3. The ILO's definition of 'Europe' was an encompassing one, covering both Western Europe and what was still, in 1989, referred to as Eastern Europe and the USSR.
4. In 1963, Switzerland was the 'first country that articulated publicly the benefits of a multi-pillar pension system ...' (Queisser and Vittas, 2000, p.2, citing Helbling, 1991, p.23).
5. In 2000 there were 105 first pillar funds and around 11,600 second pillar funds in operation in Switzerland, see Queisser and Vittas, 2000, p.26; p.31.
6. We have been precluded by the twin pressures of time and space from dealing with IMF thinking and advice more fully in this volume. However, analysis and explanation of the IMF's changed, and recently much reduced, role in the on-going global pension reform process is clearly needed. Specifically, over many years, the constrained and limited Bank interest in pension systems

research described in this chapter, contrasted markedly, up to the early 1990s, with the IMF's increasingly wide-ranging interest in the savings and investment dimensions and implications of specific types of public expenditure instruments, including pensions. The IMF's long-standing interest in pension systems as a key global expenditure item increasingly influencing the fiscal balance negatively in many of its client states, notably, during the 1980s, those in Latin America, and, from the end of that decade, the transition economies of CEE and the FSU/NIS, is readily explicable. The more important, and as yet unanswered, question relates to how and why the IMF has come to be displaced as the lead BWI in the pensions field.

7. In particular, Orszag and Stiglitz (1999, p.4, fn.5) argue that 'the Bank's leading pensions scholars', such as Robert Holzmann and Estelle James, could be 'misinterpreted as advocating' this narrow interpretation. Bluntly, as we show in Chapter 3, they do advocate it, unequivocally. See also, Appendix Fig. 3.3.

3 Public-Private Partnerships in Pillared Pension Provision

Introduction: An Historical Partnership

As Chapters 1 and 2 of this volume underline, the positive potential for creating developmental synergies between national pension systems and national economies is increasingly appreciated. In turn, the development of effective synergies within financial systems are seen as crucial in ensuring that financial system development leads to wider economic impacts (Vittas, 1998). Increasingly, for both developed and developing countries, it is accepted that financial sector development requires a rebalancing of retirement support from public to private sectors if positive growth potentials are to be realised (World Bank, 1994). In response to the somewhat recent forays of the World Bank into the realms of social policy, an important focus of this chapter will be the policy influence and wider implications of the Bank's proposals for pension system reform. It is our contention that the Bank-dominated approach essentially prioritising financial sector issues over social welfare considerations in pensions reform is problematic in two respects. First, it is insecure in its increasingly dogmatic prioritisation of private over public sectors. Second, it is shortsighted in its implicit assumption that historical patterns of retirement provision have failed to consider the importance of the public-private interface in financial sector development in general, and pension provision in particular. This chapter deals with both issues but is primarily concerned with the second. It examines current systemic pension reform agendas with a critical eye and with the aim of reconceptualising the problem of pension reform as a public-private partnership issue with a long pedigree rather than as a new problematic stemming from existing or anticipated state failures.

We would suggest that the novelty, and contentiousness, of current pension reform proposals does not derive from the fact that such reform models advocate a rebalancing of public-private roles in the provision of national pensions. In practice, the history of retirement provision has exhibited periodic changes in the relative importance of public and private elements in pension delivery. Consequently, what is now required is a wider appreciation of the often overlooked fact that the principle of public-private symbiosis in the management and delivery of national pension provision is neither a new nor radical concept. The long historical tradition of, in contemporary terminology, public-private partnerships in national pension provision has produced a very rich mixture of the public and the private in pensions management and delivery with significant variations in approach both over time and between countries. Unsurprisingly, therefore, despite the clearly neoliberal inspired, anti-state, sentiments which pervade much of the current lively debate on pensions provision led by the World Bank, the positive potentialities which arise from public-private sector synergy in pensions provision remain widely but quietly acknowledged, particularly within the 'Geneva institutions' that have both traditionally defined perspectives on social protection and have a long term perspective on evolutionary trends. For example, Tamburi and Mouton of the International Labour Organisation (ILO) cite Bismarck's historically influential 'achievement' in the late 19th century of 'merg(ing) into a public system the private mutual benefit movement and the technique of private insurance. The two ingredients were combined to produce the policy of compulsory pension insurance, which became increasingly widespread throughout the first half of the 20th century' (Tamburi and Mouton, 1987, p.30). Moreover, the issue of public-private partnership in pensions delivery was deemed suitably important for the International Social Security Association (ISSA) to publish an edited monograph, tellingly entitled *Conjugating Public and Private: The Case of Pensions*, on the topic of comparative as well as historical variations in the public-private mix (ISSA, 1987).

The problematic element in the current reform proposals from the World Bank is its advocacy of a significant departure in the required future balance of power within the 'public-private' relationship. Specifically, whilst public and private sectors have 'long existed side by side (albeit) to different degrees and in different ways according to the particular system, the country and the period' (Tamburi and Mouton, 1987, p.29), the current debate on pension system reform differs from its antecedents in significant ways. In particular, a judgemental value has been applied to the relative and different institutional capacities of the public and private sectors which assumes that the former lacks the capacity sustainably to supply adequate national retirement provision.

The current context of national pension system reform can be largely characterised as one advocating an expanding role for mandatory privately managed defined contribution financed pension funds operating in conjunction with restructured and correspondingly downsized state mandated pensions provision. Significantly, the World Bank has presented the reform model of 'pillared' pension provision - involving separate pillars for the redistributive and savings functions, and with a major emphasis upon the importance of the latter - as a universal prescription which will allow for the possibility of both significant regional variations in the institutional architecture of multipillar provision and in the timing of reform implementation. Nevertheless, to reiterate, it is conspicuous that no developed high-income country has 'quickly' been persuaded to radically reform existing provision in a manner consistent the Bank's approach. To date, 'radical' pension system reform approaching a kind advocated by the World Bank has been limited to middle income countries of Latin America and, more recently, has now gained a foothold amongst the transition economies of central and eastern Europe and the Baltic states (CEEs) and the newly-independent states of the former Soviet Union (NIS/FSU). This reform pattern contrasts markedly to the earlier diffusionary expansion of social security practices and standards which largely exhibited a movement down a hierarchy of modernisation from rich to middle-income countries.

Emergence and Evolution of the Pillared Pension Programme

Recent prioritisation of the importance and relevance of the concept of pillared pensions stemmed directly from a growing recognition of the potential advantages, and wider relevance to the emerging needs of other countries, of the Swiss pensions reform legislation of 1982 and the later implementation, on 1 January 1985, in that country of what 'is typically', albeit somewhat misleadingly, 'described as a three-pillar system' (Vittas, 1993, p.4). As outlined in Chapter 2, with all three of its pillars fragmented, the Swiss system of pension and retirement provision is more accurately described as consisting of six components. Negotiation over the institutional framework eventually enacted in Switzerland evolved slowly (see Chapter 2 footnote 3) with national discussion and debate occurring from the early 1970s. The coherent strategy to create pillared provision in Switzerland is indicative of a legislative process which, arguably, is untypical of the rather messier reality in pensions policy found amongst other OECD countries. Interestingly, the outcome as a three pillared, or tiered, pension system was deliberately conceived as an attempt to provide a 'judicious balance between types of financing (pay-as-you-go versus capitalisation), compulsory and voluntary schemes, public and private insurance, and the collective and the individual' (Roduit, 1993, p.76).

Significantly, and albeit retrospectively simplified for export purposes into three elements, the Swiss model has proved enormously influential in framing the institutional parameters of recent global pension reform agendas. This simplified export model defines the Swiss system as comprising a first pillar in the form of a pay-as-you-go (PAYG) basic state pension. This state-provided element is, in turn, balanced by a varied array of occupational schemes forming the mandatory second pillar. The system is completed by supplementary individual savings funded retirement schemes and personal arrangements collectively providing a voluntary or optional third pillar. Later national variants on this institutional template, exhibiting the patterns of international diffusion of useful innovations characteristic of the earlier spread of pension systems from the late 19th century and of modern welfare states in the post-war period, tended to be characterised by rather less pragmatic adaptation and more planning, hence some degree of institutional standardisation, than was evident in the original Swiss model.

Even before 1993, for example, when the ILO recorded that '[i]n recent years pensions systems in the developed countries appear to be moving towards a three-tier structure' (ILO, 1993, p.58) there was already a wider appreciation amongst the Geneva institutions of the influence of the Swiss model. As the ILO's Director-General noted, this institutional convergence reflected 'attempts to amalgamate the best elements of the different possibilities' for pension system reform and restructuring currently available. Similarly, in relation to developments within the EU, MISSOC noted in 1994 that 'a real convergence of policies in European social protection ministries' had occurred, adding that even 'more wide ranging measures appeared imminent, given the number of studies and reviews of the different social security systems which were afoot' (EC, 1995, p.11). Nevertheless, at least in relation to the World Bank's criteria, it can still be argued that the pillared pension agenda has, as yet, been implemented only to a relatively limited degree even in the advanced industrial states. 'Most OECD countries do not have well-developed multipillar systems, since, until recently only the public pillar has been mandatory'. Conversely, it is the Bank's view that this dominance of the public PAYG pillar has ensured that what remain largely 'voluntary occupational and personal savings plans have developed on an uneven basis' (World Bank, 1994, p.249), essentially regarding public pension provision as responsible for stunting the growth of private sector, market-based, instruments.

Accordingly, as explored below, pillared pensions provision can now be recognised as denoting a relatively clearly defined set of institutional arrangements for providing retirement protection and income replacement in old age, but, so far, these arrangements remain unevenly and incompletely implemented. Hence, in practice, the impact of the currently fashionable pensions pillarisation agenda is perhaps still best defined less in terms of the proposed implementation of an increasingly settled and precise institutional content than in terms of its relationship to a rather distinct ideology of welfare provision. Specifically, the predilection to pillarise pension regimes denotes three important political perspectives. First, a widespread dissatisfaction with the efficiency and effectiveness of a system of welfare provision predominantly financed from general taxation. Second, a clear loss of confidence in the capacity of state provided pensions to secure adequate retirement provision. Third, a generalised assumption that the state should reduce its responsibility for the provision of welfare. Increasingly, the previously predominant principles of social solidarity and collective societal responsibility underlying the provision of state welfare are themselves being questioned. In particular, the now negatively perceived 'paternalistic' (Marsland, 1992, pp.144-150) nature of the Western welfare state has been widely criticised for creating a disincentive to independence from the 'nanny' state and, conversely, for stifling incentives to practice the virtues of self-help and self-enhancement. This has inevitably led to calls for a move away from the hegemony of omniscient state welfare provision and, albeit more imprecisely, for a move towards what has been termed, at least by its critics, a 'post welfare agenda' (Bennett, 1990).

Although announcements of the death of the welfare state may prove to be premature,[1] and delineations of an emerging post-welfare era may, so far, appear somewhat artificial and contrived, it is nonetheless also becoming clear that some major, possibly irreversible, changes to the existing patterns of welfare provision are emerging. Specifically, although occurring in gradual increments and as yet lacking any clearly defining moment, recent and proposed developments in pension provision arrangements collectively reverse, or at least seek to reverse, an earlier trend towards the increasing assumption of state responsibility for welfare that characterised European and later world history since the industrial revolution, trends that may be said to have culminated in the institutionalisation of the welfare state in the post-war era. From this long term perspective, therefore, the principal driving force behind the inauguration of state pension provision was an acceptance of government responsibility for market failures in, or substantial market irrelevance to, the provision of income support in old age. In significant respects the pensions pillarisation agenda and reform project, particularly in the version currently being driven by the World Bank, reverses this proposition by focusing attention on incipient problems of state and government failure in pensions provision, specifically seeking redress from these looming crises by recourse to the market and private provision.

We accept that there is substantial validity in the contemporary questioning of the medium and long term financial viability or at least the continuing political acceptability of existing patterns of state-dominated welfare provision; a questioning significantly now converging from left and right alike on the specific issue of funding sustainability. Nevertheless, we suggest that the currently fashionable reform agenda simply provides an essentially short term, largely palliative, response to existing problems that is itself inherently flawed and limited in its appropriateness, leaving unaddressed the fundamental weakness of all existing contributions-financed pension systems, public and private alike - their inseparability from waged employment. From this perspective the focus of the pillared pensions agenda on the need to rebalance the roles of state and market in pension provision is accepted as timely, but also as inherently limited by the same market weaknesses that led so logically to the establishment of welfare states.

Proposed Models of Pillared Pension Provision

Currently, the debate over appropriate welfare provision for retirement purposes now centres on the when and how of introducing pillared pension provision with its explicit intent to reduce the role of the state. The ascendance of multipillared provision is comprehensively indicated by the endorsement of versions of a pillared pensions system by both the World Bank and, albeit less didactically, by the ILO. Unsurprisingly, given the explicitly anti-state agenda underlying many, indeed most, of the current welfare reform proposals, it is the World Bank that has made most of the running in its pursuit of its pillared pensions project. Nevertheless, it is important to stress that this policy agenda has led the Bank to enter into a field of social policy, pensions reform, which had hitherto lain beyond the boundaries of its established remit as well as into an equally unprecedented involvement in policy issues relating to developed countries in general; developments which can collectively be termed 'historically novel and remarkable' (Tamburi, 1992, p.7).

This emerging Bank interest in the pension reform agenda, and its attendant commitment to the pillared pension project, developed gradually, but also with what seems, retrospectively at least, inexorable logic, throughout the 1990s. Specifically, the Bank's enthusiasm for pillared pension systems developed logically from its well publicised support for competing privately managed fully funded defined contribution retirement schemes as favoured alternatives to, and, preferably, as replacements for ailing state PAYG system. Specifically, the Bank's original advocacy of the desirability of replacing existing state-run defined benefit social insurance schemes comprehensively with privately run funded schemes based on defined contributions, as, largely, occurred in the creation of the Chilean AFP system, has steadily evolved into a significantly more rigid and less nuanced policy strategy. As stated originally in *Averting*, this policy strategy allowed for the possibility of both significant regional variations in the internal architecture of multipillar provision and in the timing of reform implementation. 'The right mix of pillars is not the same at all times and places ... Middle- and high-income countries should move in this direction quickly, whereas low-income countries should see it as a long-term goal' (World Bank, 1994, p.254). Paradoxically, as reform horizons have widened the continued presentation of pillared provision as a universal prescription has crowded out the earlier promise of flexibility.

Driven by the Bank's involvement, the debate over pension reform strategies has moved beyond the relatively precise requirements of reformulating pension provision in already bankrupt Latin American welfare states to incorporate the specific problems and varying requirements of all other regions and economies, developed, developing and transitional. Yet the Bank's pillarisation agenda increasingly overlooks significant regional variations, not least in relation to the capacities exhibited by both state and market in differing types of economy and across different regions. Nevertheless, flexibility became a practical necessity during reform implementation. Pension reform does not occur in a vacuum. Wholesale abandonment and liquidation, other than for reasons of total bankruptcy, of existing state-run pensions systems, however inefficient these may be, is in practice unrealistic, given the prohibitive costs to governments that such comprehensive transformations involve. In the Chilean case the state assumed the explicit debts of the existing social insurance scheme, whilst also retaining responsibility for the continuing 'implicit' debts incurred on behalf of those, notably the armed forces as an institution, who opted to remain in the old system. Conversely, the adoption of pillared solutions as a policy strategy neatly spreads the risks associated with each and every mono-pillar system, whether fully funded or social insurance based, whilst simultaneously avoiding some of the costs, both economic and political, associated with the complete abandonment and institutional liquidation of existing pensions systems, however inefficient.

The Bank's insistence that fully funded pension schemes will contribute more effectively than social insurance schemes to the growth and deepening of national capital markets and wider financial systems, thereby fostering sustainable economic growth more securely is not, as we demonstrate below in Chapters 4 and 8, empirically well founded. As the rapid collapse and subsequent state-funded recapitalisation of a vast portion of the newly created Chilean AFP schemes, in the wake of a banking crisis in the early 1980s, indicates (Bitran and Sáez, 1994, p.339), establishing private pension funds, arguably, may be a necessary condition, but is not in itself a sufficient condition, for achieving stable stock market growth and sustained capital market expansion. Similarly, there are sound sociological, and therefore political, reasons for retaining existing state social insurance schemes. In particular, fully funded privatised pension schemes, passing all risks on to the individual, are devoid of all aspects of social solidarity, without providing any compensating guarantee that they will adequately meet all the retirement income needs of affiliates in respect either of longevity or in relation to inflationary episodes.

Hence the World Bank's current acceptance of the desirability, or at least the inevitability, of maintaining a basic PAYG pillar, allowing for the retention of at least residual elements of existing welfare states within restructured and rebalanced pension delivery systems. These, however, will now operate alongside mandatory privately run funded savings schemes or alongside mandatory occupational plans - the former modelled on the experiences of Chile and Argentina, and the latter following Switzerland, the Netherlands and Australia - as intrinsic elements in the Bank's proposed, all-purpose and global, 'multipillar' system of social security provision. This comprises three central institutional elements or pillars, involving, first, '[a] mandatory tax-financed public pillar designed to alleviate poverty', second, '[a] mandatory, funded, privately managed pillar (based on personal accounts or occupational plans) to handle people's savings', and, third '[a] supplementary voluntary pillar (again based on personal saving or occupational plans) for people who want more protection' (World Bank, 1994, p.292, see Appendix Fig. A2.3). Although the public pillar is mentioned first, it is important to stress that the Washington view is that 'it should be modest in size, to allow ample room for other pillars ...' and to keep tax burdens low. Similarly, it 'would have the limited object of alleviating old age poverty and coinsuring against a multitude of risks'. These 'limited objectives' would, nonetheless and not insignificantly, both provide for a modicum of redistribution of income to the poor, and, exploiting the advantages of finance out of current taxation, would also allow for a hedge 'against long spells of low investment returns, recession, inflation, and private market failure', that would otherwise undermine the effectiveness of the market-based and privately provided second and third pillars. The Bank's expectations, however, are more up-beat: 'a successful second pillar should reduce the demands on the first pillar' (World Bank, 1994, p.16).

It is instructive to compare and contrast this 'radical' World Bank model of pillared pensions with the more nuanced, significantly more tentative and markedly less market-didactic formulation for pillared or, in alternative terminology, 'tiered' pensions advanced by the International Labour Organisation. Importantly, the ILO outline two structural issues which are to be considered when addressing the issue of pensions provision. First, the ILO have been careful to highlight the more extensive possibilities available for the more developed economies. Specifically, the 'best approach for advanced countries can be characterised as a four tier system' (Turner, 1997, p.6). In contrast, the less advanced countries should seek progressively to develop three tier pension systems. Second, tiered pension provisions should be understood not as an empirical statement about the way retirement income systems actually are but as a statement about how they should be structured.

Specifically, and in its most comprehensive form, the ILO propose for the first public tier a social safety-net in the form of a 'government-provided anti-poverty benefit' (a crucial proposal, and dealt with in Chapter 7). The second public tier is a 'mandatory unfunded defined benefit scheme or notional defined contribution scheme provided through the government social security system'.[2] This second PAYG tier 'provides social insurance for workers against some economic risks by spreading the effects of risks across the population'. The third tier comprises 'funded benefits provided by the government or by private sector entities', either on a voluntary or mandatory basis. This third tier has the potential to 'be combined with the second tier as a single partially funded plan'. Finally, the ILO propose 'a voluntary and supplementary tier'. This fourth tier 'includes private savings, voluntary occupational pension schemes, voluntary individual pension accounts, labour earnings, support from family members, and charity' (Turner, 1997, p.7, see Appendix Fig. A3.1).

The Contemporary Context of Pension System Reform

The increasingly mediatised topic of pension system reform indicates that the provision of retirement income for old age is now emerging as a public policy issue of global relevance. The underlying logics driving the increasingly global interest in national pension system reforms are complex. For instance, and although the issue of demographic ageing is already, or is soon to be, a reality for many nations, it is oversimplistic to suggest that the so-called demographic 'time-bomb' (see Maps 1.1, 1.2; see Appendix Fig. A3.2) is the only important factor shaping demands for pension system reform. Moreover, it should be stressed that the global demographic 'time-bomb' will, in practice, strike different regions at different times and, significantly, to different degrees. No less important to shaping the demands for pension system reform are fundamental issues such as changing work and employment patterns and evolving political attitudes regarding the perceived appropriateness and limitations of state action in social policy. For most national pension systems, but in particular those of the Western welfare states, three major underlying problems are said collectively to denote an impending funding and sustainability crisis. First, there is an apparently insatiable demand for improvements in health care leading to 'chronic' expenditure problems. Second, levels of unemployment are now perceived as presenting an increasingly 'acute' problem undermining state income and expenditure alike. Third, a global old age crisis is now looming, presenting an 'impending' element to the underfunding equation (EC, 1995, p.11).

In addition to the underlying problems raised by the 'three overlapping crises' (EC, 1995, p.11) specified above, current underfunding problems have been, and are likely to continue to be, further aggravated by a number of trends and policy preferences espoused by many industrial states over recent years. These policy choices include deliberate fiscal restraint, as most recently in attempts across Europe to meet the exacting Maastricht criteria for currency integration under EMU, inappropriate allocation which has prioritised certain benefits above others, often for party political, and not welfare, ends and, not insignificantly, those practices which have consistently favoured early retirement as a mechanism for solving a variety of problems associated with youth unemployment and poor skills among older workers. These policy choices have, in turn, added to or accelerated the impact of the structural changes already clearly felt in Western societies, in terms of both negative demographic trends and contracting employment opportunities.

Collectively, the impact of these trends has already had marked, and largely deleterious, effects on perceived welfare outcomes achieved through existing contributory, non-means tested, instruments as well as through the expanding array of state means tested, 'safety net', provision. Welfare outcomes emanating from the operation of existing welfare states, as defined in terms of poverty reduction, are therefore, no longer perceived as capable of compensating for market failures but, essentially, are perhaps better defined as reflections of that failure in terms of a growing incapacity to match welfare supply to emerging welfare needs. Despite their previously widely, if briefly, apotheosised status, the institutions of the Western welfare state and, in global terms, state social security provision more generally, are increasingly coming to be viewed, from all sides of the political spectrum, as no longer effective nor efficient as instruments of poverty alleviation either in terms of the real value or even of the nominal level of benefits offered (Field, 1995).

In particular, state pension provision is increasingly, and more widely, being placed under a critical spotlight. Specifically, the growing perception of the inefficiency and ineffectiveness of existing pension provision is defined largely as a function of the, predominantly, PAYG nature of these schemes. The long term economic feasibility of PAYG schemes ultimately depends largely upon sustained economic growth and full employment. While adequate funding is a necessary prerequisite for the efficient and effective functioning of all pension and retirement schemes, the nature of national PAYG social insurance schemes has conferred upon the state the collective liability of the insured risk. In times of economic growth and full employment, as pertained during the long post-war boom up to the late 1970s, this state assumption of collective responsibility was not viewed as problematic. However, as underlined by the present focus on the 'unsustainable' (Kane and Palaçios, 1996, p.37) nature of Western welfare states, these conditions no longer prevail, and, crucially, are not expected to return even in the longer term. Apparently increasingly endemic conditions of relative economic stagnation, as evidenced by sustained levels of 'acute' unemployment in the Western developed economies, operating in conjunction with the 'impending' global crisis of demographic ageing and the 'chronic' (EC, 1995, p.11) growth in health care expenditure, have now collectively conspired to increase the demands upon existing state-guaranteed welfare systems to the point that the potential levels of debiting are widely, but somewhat imprecisely, perceived as threatening to exceed the acceptable levels of personal taxation, thereby undermining, at least in the long term, systemic viability and sustainability.

The funding problems underlying existing state-run, taxation-based, social insurance schemes are, therefore, rightly, perceived to be of universal concern to all states, currently forming the central problem facing policy-makers charged with defining the future evolution of national retirement pension systems. Nevertheless, in practice, open discussion, and deeper analysis, of the evolving problems of public pension funding are likely to lead rather quickly towards less widely generalised, and in some cases markedly less pessimistic, conclusions regarding the sustainability of existing systems of public pension provision. The pessimistic scenario appears to be particularly inappropriate in the case of the United Kingdom (Mullan, 2000). The UK faces what Will Hutton - using OECD projections of future public pension costs for the world's major economies based on existing policies and demographic forecasts - rightly calls 'negligible' future state pensions obligations. This contrasts starkly with the predicted Japanese expenditure on social security which is 'set to mushroom' (Hutton, 1996, p.15), with similar problems facing Italy and Germany too. In the case of all three countries the OECD projects pension costs increasing by 7-10 percent of GDP over the next half century, compared with the projected UK maximum increase of 1 per cent in 2035. Canada, France, and the USA face intermediate rises of 3 or 4 per cent of GDP over the same time scale. Although the OECD figures - as with all other projections of future pension burdens - should be, as John Hills nicely puts it, 'handled with some caution' (Hills, 1995, p.39), it is clearly erroneous to tar all the industrial country welfare states with the same pessimistic brush. Specifically, as Hills rightly emphasises, the OECD figures 'serve to emphasise the fallacy of the argument that because' some 'countries may require drastic measures in "averting the old age crisis" of public finances' all countries must therefore face 'identical problems' (Hills, 1995, p.39). Similar points can be made regarding assumptions of across-the-board necessity of pension reform for developing and transition economies given equally wide variations in demographic profiles and socio-economic contexts and capacities both among developing regions and between specific states.

Policy Debates and Responses

Despite a recognition of national specificities in the problems variably affecting national pension systems, the pension reform debate, nonetheless, has largely been dominated by the World Bank's proposals. As has already been more fully explained in the previous chapter, the ILO, historically the most actively involved and influential multilateral body engaged in the field of social security policy and the main institutional proponent of social insurance financed social security, has found its traditional vanguard position in social security policy, and old age pension policy in particular, increasingly eroded by the Bank.

Although differing widely both in terms of institutional architecture and in terms of their operational and developmental priorities, it is clearly the intention of both the Bank and the ILO to confront what is fashionably perceived to be an unsatisfactory over-dependence on state-run social insurance PAYG schemes. Accordingly, both the Bank and the ILO proposals can be seen as indicative of the widely held desire to reduce the traditional dominance of the social insurance pillar. In particular the ILO, like the Bank, is now convinced that existing mono- or unipillar systems are insufficient to address current needs and inadequate to meet future demands. As the Director-General summarises, the advantages of a multi-tier model are that '[s]uch a proposal might provide the flexibility that is missing in current schemes or in reliance on a single type of pension scheme' (ILO, 1995, p.68). Similarly, it is not insignificant that both organisations are now suggesting an expanded role for, as the ILO would have it, 'non-public', provision. Importantly, reflecting its own institutional history, the ILO's nuanced interpretation of non-public infers a continuing inclusive role for social partnerships in pension provision incorporating organised labour and employers alongside the private financial service sector in support of its role in the operation and delivery of voluntary and occupational pension schemes. Overall, the message conveyed by both institutions is clear. The institutional dominance of the state in pension provision worldwide, characteristic of post World War Two welfare states, is now portrayed as increasingly problematic for the delivery of adequate social security provision, requiring supplementation by private providers in the ILO formulation and a more comprehensive substitution in the more didactic World Bank version.

Importantly, despite some apparent schematic similarities, the two proposals are significantly different in their estimation of the implications of this expansion of private pension provision for states, not simply in relation to likely costs but more importantly in relation to obligations. In particular, and in significant contrast to the World Bank's optimism that, despite the enhanced need for state regulation under privatisation, private delivery expansion will reduce state financial burdens across the board, the distinguishing feature of the ILO model is its overt expectation of consequent increases in the scope and the scale of state involvement in the pensions recipe. As the ILO acknowledges, and willingly accepts, all multi-tiered or multipillar proposals involve costs above those involved in single element systems. In relation to existing pension systems, as a 1995 report by the ILO Director-General pointed out, a multi-tier system would both 'be more costly and require a more elaborate and intricate involvement by the

State, which would have to be responsible for the regulation and monitoring of the activities of private (fully funded) complementary schemes' (ILO, 1995, p.68). In essence, the ILO's formula exhibits an explicit conception of the partnership between public and private sectors required by envisaged reforms that is, deliberately, missing from the World Bank approach.

Promoting Partnership: The State and the Market

Significantly, assessments of the wider policy implications of the systemic pension reforms modelled upon World Bank proposals, including their social welfare implications, are often portrayed as a zero-sum reform game. It is suggested that any excess client demand for pensions provision created by state retrenchment in this field will be met through the market by an expanded supply of private sector provision. It is our view that this essentially neo-classical economic interpretation of likely institutional and individual responses to current proposals for systemic pension reform is disingenuous. Such an interpretation clearly fails to address the increased potential for market failure, both in terms of population coverage and retirement benefit adequacy, that would result from a shift towards an enhanced use of private sector delivery mechanisms. In addition, this view makes a generalised implicit assumption about the prior existence of healthy financial service sectors which have the capacity to deliver value-for-money and welfare adequate mandatory private pension products. To put this point another way, this interpretation seriously underestimates the value of the traditional role played by state pension provision. In particular, this view neglects the crucial role of state pension provision in providing retirement income for those individuals without ready and affordable access to private or occupational pension provision.

Indeed, the perceived positive potentialities of private sector pension provision have been reinforced by the subsequent reordering and reprioritisation of the World Bank's model for pillared pension provision outlined in *Averting the Old age Crisis* in 1994. Further refinements of the Bank's multipillar model by its core researchers have significantly reinforced the market-friendly, or neoliberal, emphasis of that document. In particular Bank staff now tend to publicly present the two mandatory pillars in reverse order, with the first savings-oriented pillar now formed by privately managed personal savings schemes or occupational plans. This primary private pillar is also billed specifically, if somewhat artificially, as novel and innovative, providing an option that would 'differ dramatically from most existing systems ...' (James, 1995, p.6). The public, redistributive, pillar is, therefore, deliberately presented second, thereby more consistently reflecting its essentially supportive role as 'a social safety net for the old, particularly the old whose lifetime incomes were low or whose investments in the saving pillar had failed' (James, 1995, p.6). This reordered and reprioritised multipillar blueprint is, therefore, even more overtly centred on the private provision of 'a mandatory fully funded, defined-contribution pillar, through which *individuals* could save to provide income for when they are retired or unable to work' (see Appendix Fig. A3.3). Specifically, the all-important mandatory public savings pillar is now defined as, ideally, simply to be 'supplemented by a public pension system, much smaller than the current one[s]' (Demirgüç-Kunt and Schwarz, 1996, p.46, emphasis added). Significantly, this process of 'restructuring the system to create a multipillar old-age-security system' is explicitly designated as constituting a 'radical reform' option, in deliberate contrast to what Bank staff now define as 'limited reform, which would involve keeping the present system intact but making minor changes to make it both more financially sustainable in the near term and more equitable' (Demirgüç-Kunt and Schwarz, 1996, p.45).

In practice, we would suggest that any radicalism in the World Bank's proposals should be identified as relating not to the construction of pillars *per se* but to the much greater overall emphasis being placed upon the role of private sector provision within national pension systems, to the zero-sum interpretation of this process, and to the rather rigid division of functions between public and private pillars. The earlier perception among policy makers of the positive complementarities between public and private provision highlighted by Tamburi and Mouton is missing from the Bank approach. An older emphasis on the importance of social solidarity has been replaced by a stress on individual responsibility for provision, undermining previous conceptions of pension systems as social partnerships. Tamburi and Mouton argue that '(p)ublic and private pension schemes, in particular, are not so radically at odds as one might be tempted to think, provided that by 'private' schemes we mean collective pension arrangements covering the employees of an enterprise or the broader community' (Tamburi and Mouton, 1987, p.29). Current trends, as evidenced by the Bank's proposals, would suggests that this earlier depiction of a creative public-private partnership in the provision of mandatory pension provision is no longer representative of current reality. In place of the mind-set which once recognised that public and private pensions components were capable of mutually complementing one another in a variety of ways within a system of national provision, the current trend in pensions policy has been influenced by the belief that the state's dominant role in national pension provision should be challenged and, largely, removed. Interestingly, it is worthy of note that the current environment of pension system reform is not only witnessing an evolving mind-set with regard to the validity of the public-private partnership but that this change is clearly reflected in the evolving language used by some of the major institutional interlocutors engaged within this debate. It is highly significant, and by no means accidental, that the World Bank have chosen to convey their vision of the public-private partnership in pensions provision by adopting the imagery of 'pillars'. The imagery provided by the World Bank of distinct and separate pillars rooted apart, a use of imagery which invoke notions of parallel opposition, contrasts neatly with the ILO's more traditional and all-inclusive vision of a system of 'tiers' which, like the union symbolised by a wedding cake, combine as a whole to complement one another (see Appendix Fig. A3.1).

Accordingly, the policy logic which once valued complementarity in pensions provision is now being challenged by an oppositional approach to policy making which seeks to portray the state as having little choice other than having to develop a more 'business-like' approach in order to compete with the private sector to retain its 'market share'. There is a double paradox here. First, it is likely that this competition will be unequal to the extent that affiliation to private provision is to be legally mandated. Second, the state is likely to be disadvantaged to the extent that even large and well established private pensions providers are likely to continue to require continued subsidisation through favourable taxation regimes. The sad irony of this evolving situation, and especially so when one considers, internationally, the increased role of state mandated retirement pension provision and, more generally, the creation of the post World War Two 'welfare states', is that a reduced or devalued role for the state will impact most negatively upon those individuals for whom the expansion of state provision was originally designed. Specifically, the expansion of state provision and its formal 'conjugation' with private pension delivery mechanisms was designed to aid the poorer, and also often self-employed, sections of society who previously had little or no access to affordable 'insurance' for old age. Accordingly, the Bank's proposed model of reform, in advocating a significant role for private defined contribution 'personal' pension funds, threatens to set the clock back for the relatively, and the absolutely, poor by undermining the scope and value of social redistribution and ignoring the economies of scale inherent in state control over social insurance. Simply stated, as a consequence of placing the emphasis within the World Bank's proposed pillared pension system on increasingly promoting the role of the private sector, public sector provision of retirement pension coverage is likely to be reduced to a safety-net role concerned predominantly with residual poverty alleviation.[3]

'Radical' Pension Reform: Latin America and Beyond

Despite claims that many countries will increasingly experience financing difficulties in maintaining even present levels of state pension provision, recent national pension system reforms enacted worldwide can be more readily characterised as being concerned with parametric tinkering rather than the much more difficult task of radical systemic reform. Globally, radical systemic pension reform still remains the policy exception rather than the rule. Only in Latin America, where a total of eight countries have downsized their PAYG systems, has there been a widespread process of systemic pension reform (see Map 3.1). However, even in Latin America where there has been a strengthening trend towards the introduction of privately managed defined contribution pension funds during the 1990s, there continues to be, nonetheless, an important degree of national diversity in the institutional structures of reformed national pension systems.

Following the 'radical' pension system reform enacted by the Pinochet regime in 1981, Chile is widely credited as providing the ideological and institutional impetus for all other subsequent attempts involving radical pension system reform in Latin American. Introduced by the Pinochet regime in 1981 under Decree Law No.3500 (Nigh and Wever, 1996, pp.2-5), the Chilean AFP system replaced an ailing state-run social insurance system with administratively decentralised, privately managed and competing retirement .funds. Managed by private pension fund management companies called *Administradoras de Fondos de Pensiones*

(AFPs), the system is monitored, and regulation enforced by, over one hundred officials within the Santiago-based superintendency of AFPs.

At the time of inception in 1981 there were 12 AFPs in operation At one stage this figure rose to as many as 23 competing AFPs. However recent market consolidation has meant that, as of May 1999, there wer only 8 AFPs (Rodriguez, 1999), with the 4 largest of these accounting fc more than 80 percent of total assets (Vittas, 2000, p.16).[4] The introductic of AFP accounts in Chile has, for the most part, replaced social insuran provision. The contribution rate for all affiliates to the AFP system is set 10 percent of monthly income. In addition, a further contribution equatii to around 3 percent of monthly income, although variable between AFPs, paid to meet the AFP administration costs and to enable the purchase o premium to cater for disability and survivors' benefits provision. The opti of paying additional voluntary contributions, set at a ceiling of 10 perc of monthly income, is open to all affiliates. All employers' contributii were dissolved when the AFP scheme was instituted. Under A regulations, affiliates can choose the manner in which they wish to rece their retirement income:

- the purchase of a life annuity with prescribed survivor benefits (60 percen the spouse or parent and 15 percent for each child) from an insur company;
- the withdrawal of an annually predetermined monthly amount from the dependent on the life expectancy of the participant, the family compositi the time and the accumulated balance of the account;
- a combination of the first two options.

Nigh and Wever,199

Membership of the new AFP system was made mandatory f workers entering the labour force after 31 December 1982, witl exception of the military who retained social insurance financed cov and the self employed, for whom membership of the new systen voluntary. In addition, '(a)pproximately 85 percent to 90 percent of w covered under the old system switched to the new system' (Santa 1992, p.41). Significantly, however, poor levels of coverage under th system remains a serious problem. In the mid-1990s, after a decade half of operation, at least one third of the total Chilean labour comprising 'part-time workers, seasonal or farm workers, tem workers and the disabled' (Jamieson, 1996, p.26) remained exclude

Map 3.1 Pensions 'Privatisation' in Latin America

the new system and dependent upon social assistance for income in old age. In addition, the Chilean system suffers from a serious problem with regards to lapsed contributions from a significant number of registered affiliates (Queisser, 1995, p.29).

Despite the expansion of Chilean-inspired pension system reforms throughout the 1990s, it is notable that no other country in the region has replicated the Chilean model in its entirety. Of the reforms introduced across Latin America, in Peru (1993), Argentina (1994), Colombia (1994), Uruguay (1996), Mexico (1996), Bolivia (1996) and El Salvador (1998), the Peruvian reforms have come closest to resembling those of Chile.[5] However, even in the Peruvian case, which initially aimed to replace its social insurance pension system with mandatory private pension funds, the reform package was diluted in order to permit affiliates the option of selecting between the parallel public and private systems (Mesa-Lago, 1997). Except for Chile, in all the other Latin American countries where mandatory private pension funds have been introduced, a role for the state in pensions provision has been retained. Significantly, in all the Latin American examples, including Chile, the state continues to provide some form of a minimum income guaranteed safety-net for the old.

Driven largely by the World Bank, the debate over pension reform strategies has moved progressively to incorporate the specific problems and varying requirements of other regions and economies, and particularly the transition states of CEE and NIS/FSU. Indeed, radical pension system reform in a format shaped by the World Bank formula has already been enacted in Hungary, Kazakhstan, and Poland. Again, and similar to the case of Latin America, these 'transition' examples testify to a trend towards diversity in the institutional structure of the newly reformed national pension systems, albeit within a set of parameters defined by the common denominator of a reduction in the relative importance of state provision within pension systems. Conversely, these national pension system reforms are characterised in most cases by the introduction of private mandatory defined contribution pension funds.

We would regard as positive the assertions of national diversity imposed on World Bank blueprints, notably as, at least minimally, indicating the consciousness of policy makers that the design of national pension systems requires careful adjustment to the specifics of particular states. In some cases there are additional indications that reform agendas are at least partially based on aspirations to achieve some degree of synergy between public and private elements. What is missing, however, is any real self-confidence in the capacity of states to define the essential parameters of pension systems without enhanced inputs from non-state or private sources. The converse of this is a heightened anticipation of the likely positive impacts of expanded private provision on the development of financial sectors in market economies. The *ex post* role of institutional investors, not least pension funds, in capital market development in the anglo-American systems is obvious. *Ex ante* roles for defined contribution pension funds in financial sector development and in wider economic growth sequences are currently anticipated. In practice this may be optimistic, not least because of the zero-sum strategy of a reform agenda that threatens to undermine and fragment existing state capacities in pension management. Specifically, the weakening of state capacity will be detrimental to policy linkages essential to guaranteeing synergies between public and private elements in pension provision and for securing their interaction in performing their essential functions of providing welfare and contributing to financial sector and wider economic developments.

The problem can be illustrated most readily by developments in CEE and NIS/FSU. As we explain more fully in Chapter 4, the move in the transition economies from a policy climate of 'permission for' to one of 'promotion of' private pension funds indicates the development of a cumulative reform momentum comparable to the earlier, but also continuing, wave of pension reform sweeping Latin America. In the transition states earlier 'outgrowing' policy strategies permitting private pension funds, generally with some tax incentives in place, to operate alongside the continuing public system as main provider in what we have defined as 'pluralised' systems, have had limited impacts on state predominance in retirement provision. Active pension reform promotion strategies, mandating private provision for those entering the workforce within a newly pillarised system, are increasingly seen as the logical reform strategy. We do not share this enthusiasm, noting both the irony inherent in making market provision statutory and legally mandatory and the paradox involved in the need for hefty state subsidies and incentives, in the form of liberal tax advantages, to make this mandatory private provision attractive. Unsurprisingly, such reform agendas have left state pension institutions, some of which are amongst the most dedicated and efficient elements in admittedly administratively weak, public sectors, demoralised as well as underfunded and increasingly isolated from key decision making processes.

Conclusion: Toward Alternative Reform Options

Even as nationally adjusted policy strategies, current pension agendas are clearly limited in their appreciation of the essentials of the operation of a mutually beneficial partnership between public and private elements. The dominance of the World Bank in current agendas is problematic in a number of respects, not least in relation to its tendency towards enthusiasms and fashions that are by definition transient. This situation is particularly ironic given that the World Bank's pension reform agenda is already out of tune with wider World Bank thinking on the need for an enhanced, if not necessarily expanded, role for states in transitional and developing economies. Accordingly, the time is right for a more realistic appreciation of the potentialities of both states and markets in retirement provision in low and middle income states. In particular, the agenda needs to encompass alternative reform options which actively foster a mutually beneficial symbiosis between public and private elements in national pensions provision. The displacement of the ILO as the major institutional supporter and mentor of national pension administrations, described fully in Chapter 2, removed a key element of continuity from international pensions policy and specifically reduces the scope for restating the importance of social welfare issues.

From this perspective, it becomes clear why it is crucially important that an institution such as the International Labour Organisation should be acting more forcibly to redirect the current debate on pensions provision away from the hegemony of financial market development dimensions towards a more balanced perspective which more adequately addresses social welfare issues. Unfortunately for this important, but currently one-sided, debate, the evolutionary development of the ILO's thinking beyond its traditional emphasis on contributions-financed social insurance has, in part, been constrained by its lack of financial resources, a result of its status as a United Nations Specialist Agency. These are important issues which we will return to in Chapters 6 and 9. In the absence of the traditionally strong voice of the ILO, notably its concerns with 'social justice' and poverty alleviation, the overall inability of non-aligned academics adequately to counter the force of the dogmatic arguments in favour of private defined contribution pension funds threatens to contribute to the growing propensity for the adoption of inappropriate, unbalanced and incomplete reform policies for transition and developing countries.

Currently, discussions underway across the transition economies that should be focusing upon the reform of the social insurance system *in toto* have, to date, been focused almost exclusively on the narrow issue of pension system reform, thereby largely by-passing issues of medical care, invalidity, employment injury and unemployment. Similarly, the wider systematic considerations of the reform of government activity that should frame both pension reform and the restructuring of other elements that would traditionally have fallen under the umbrella of social insurance, has been universally avoided in the transition economies (Theißen, 1998, p.36). In particular, expenditure and revenue reforms should be coordinated closely, requiring simultaneous taxation and social insurance reform which, in turn, specifically requires balancing the inputs of the Washington institutions, IMF and World Bank, with their experience on the revenue side with the inputs of the Geneva institutions, the ILO and the ISSA, with their experience on the expenditure side.

Widening the debate with a particular focus on problems of 'social justice' and searching for policy and institutional initiatives with significant potential for public-private symbiosis would allow for alternative reform possibilities to emerge. These possibilities should be as realistic about the limitations of the market in transitional and developing economies as they are currently about the limitations of the state. Realism would allow for a more balanced assessment of the potentialities of developing country initiatives in retirement provision. In Part Two and Part Three of this volume we will address in detail some of the possible alternatives available to transitional and developing countries which until recently had been largely ignored or unreasonably dismissed by the World Bank and ILO pension reform models. Specifically, what the experience of DCs, including the transition economies, underlines is the continuing importance, hence policy salience, of non-formal or informal family and community based support systems in providing at least some modicum of security for the elderly, even where formal provision exists. Consequently, in line with our knowledge of non-'formal' support systems, discussed below in Chapters 6 and 7, a DC focus further reminds us that old age support 'should always be viewed as a joint process among partners - the individual, the family, employers, and the government' (Schulz, 1999, p.95).

Notes

1. Despite benefit cut-backs and tighter eligibility criteria being introduced into most welfare state systems, the policy signals regarding the future of the 'welfare state' approach are far from unidirectional. Most notably, the German Social Dependency Insurance (SDI) scheme for long-term health care coverage enacted in 1994 has extended the benefit types which the ILO Minimum Standards (see also Appendix Fig. A2.1) suggest a social security system should ideally provide beyond the nine contingencies of medical care, sickness benefit, maternity benefit, employment injury benefit, old age benefit, invalidity benefit, survivors' benefit, unemployment benefit and family benefit. The recent, increasingly, widespread development of welfare-to-work programmes, although sometimes interpreted as an attack on previous benefit entitlements and 'rights', provides clear evidence of an additional level of paternalism consistent with earlier patterns of 'welfare state' social protection (Standing, 1999a, p.334).

2. NDC schemes aim to modify existing PAYG schemes through tying more closely individual benefit entitlement to individual contributions. As of 2000, NDC schemes have been introduced in Latvia, Sweden, the Kyrgyz Republic, Estonia, Moldova and Poland (Müller 2000c, pp.27-28).

3. For a detailed outline of the evolution of both World Bank and ILO thinking regarding the appropriate content and format of pillared and tiered pension models, see Appendix Figures A3.4 and A3.5.

4. The 8 AFPs currently in operation are Aporta, Cuprum, Habitat, Magister, Planvital, Provida, Santa María and Summa Bansander (Rodriguez, 1999).

5. In 1999, the Nicaraguan government announced plans to transform the current pension system, based on pay-as-you-go principles, into a funded scheme, with individual savings accounts managed by private pension funds (ISSA, 1999, p.7). However, the direction of pension reform in Latin America is far from unidirectional. In 2000, Venezuela decided against implementing wideranging plans developed in 1998 to privatise social security provision, including pensions (ISSA, 2000b, p.7).

Part II

Regional Responses: Distilling Lessons from Pension Reform

4 From 'Outgrowing' to 'In-Built' Strategies: Pension Reform in the Transition Economies

Introduction: The Early Years of Transition

The following two chapters highlight important pension system reform policy lessons that may be derived from recent international practice and experience. The second of these chapters considers the National Provident Fund (NPF) model, a simple institutional form of social security provision weakly regarded by both the World Bank and the ILO. Chapter 5 challenges this widely held perspective, in particular by highlighting the largely discounted development and welfare enhancing potential of pillared pension provision involving a hybrid NPF. In so doing, our aim is to attempt to bring balance to a debate which largely, as Part I highlights, has been shaped by the highly selective agendas of international organisations. First, however, we will address some of the important policy lessons to be derived from the experience of pension system reform in Central and Eastern Europe and the Baltic States (CEE) and the newly independent states of the former Soviet Union (NIS/FSU).

As the World Bank's definitional contortions throughout the 1996 World Development Report *From Plan to Market* underline, it was, and remains, far from easy adequately to define and assess the progress of this unprecedented and unparalleled transition involving about thirty countries and one third of world population. 'Each transition country is at a different stage in the reform process' both in relation to the decisiveness of the break with central planning and in relation to the 'even greater challenge ahead, that of consolidating the basis for a thriving market economy' (World Bank, 1996, p.5) by building appropriate market-supporting institutions and adopting market-friendly policies. Similarly, in the absence of any blueprint ransition priorities have tended, particularly initially, to be defined and adjusted on a necessarily *ad hoc* basis. Over time, there developed significant elements of both policy learning and policy sharing. Due attention was also paid to the outcomes and implications, albeit necessarily of only indirect, limited and partial wider relevance, of the swift and comprehensive 'instant' transition that merged the German Democratic Republic into the Federal Republic of Germany.

Of these lessons gained from the experience with what is colloquially referred to as the 'big bang with big brother', probably the most important, and certainly the most widely relevant across the transition states, was the knowledge gained about the importance, indeed cruciality, of social policy in underpinning successful transition. As Winfried Schmähl stresses in his balanced distillation of the conclusions and wider implications to be drawn from the integration of the two countries' pension systems, essentially by comprehensive absorption into the West German pension scheme in 1992, these events highlighted the 'general lesson ... that social policy plays the central role in the transformation process of making the transition socially acceptable'. Specifically, it was recognised quickly in Germany that early plans to prioritise production increases and attend to associated economic and monetary issues well ahead of social security reconstruction would have to be abandoned, since '[s]uch a strategy would have been devastating for social peace in Germany' (Schmähl, 1992, p.52). Political necessity demanded this abandonment in favour of an approach that explicitly balanced economic and social policy, production and distribution, and specifically prioritised pension reforms.

This chapter focuses on one dimension, albeit, arguably - and particularly so in the long run - the most important dimension of social security and social policy reconstruction in all the transition economies of the countries of Central and Eastern Europe and the Baltic States (CEE) and the newly independent states of the former Soviet Union (NIS/FSU), pension reform. As a major component element of the post-communist restructuring process, whether defined economically, politically or sociologically, the public pension system has been singled out as being of primary importance in underpinning transitions to sustainable market economies, particularly in relation to consolidating and securing economic transformations viewed in medium and long term perspective.

Yet, at the same time, the political economy of pension reform in the transition economies is inevitably complicated by short term considerations and by the often divergent logics that undermine 'rational' policy making in the real world of existing entitlements, burgeoning demand and limited funding. In particular, the quest for long term economic rationality is inevitably qualified, if not exactly compromised, by problems of political feasibility in the short term which tend to constrain what governments *should do* by limiting their options to what they *can do*. At one level, therefore, the issue of pension reform may be seen as a series of technical and essentially quantitative problems in which objective actuarial considerations of pension funding sustainability define pension delivery options and benefit provision limits. At another, more politically encompassing level, such an approach ignores important, and immediate, political limitations on available reform choices, and particularly those policy choices that require either, or both, additional funding or reduced benefits. Unsurprisingly, in practice and on the ground, it was the short term realities of politically-defined policy agendas, centred largely on the survival strategies of incumbent post-communist political regimes, that tended initially to overwhelm longer-term perspectives on the importance of fundamental and comprehensive pension reform, despite the fact that the latter were driven by the highly influential Washington IFIs.

The outcome was, as one commentator rightly termed it, 'deadlock in public pension reform in the transition economies' (Holzmann, 1994, p.184), as the irresistible force of IFI-driven policy advice met the immovable object of political elites acutely conscious of the fragile legitimacy of, and limited public trust in, transition regimes and their political leaders. On the one hand, therefore, at least in theory, both the unsustainability of the existing financing mechanisms and the over-ambitious scope and rising delivery commitments of the pension systems inherited from communism, left no alternative other than for these systems to be restructured, particularly given their limited and declining capacity adequately to service and financially support their existing beneficiaries. On the other hand, the widely held desire to reduce the 'omnipotence' (Stanovnik and Kukar, 1995, p.36) of the inherited social insurance system raised significant political problems as existing entitlements were threatened. Economic and political logics increasingly diverged, pulling policy-makers in confusingly divergent directions. As the ILO noted (1995b, p.2),

> If expenditures swing too far in the direction of social support, investment and economic recovery will be jeopardised, but if insufficient social

protection is afforded to those most in need, the political consensus for transition may not be sustained.

Currently, there are increasing signs that this pensions reform policy deadlock so characteristic of the transition economies in the mid-1990s, has broken down as the *status quo* is assaulted on two fronts simultaneously, namely both domestically and externally. Domestically, the declining importance of existing pension entitlements to individual and societal survival strategies has been underlined by inflation or hyper-inflationary episodes across the CEE and FSU, and additionally reinforced, particularly in the latter group of states, by growing problems of short term payment incapacity widely defined by pensioners as indicative of effective system bankruptcy. In most transition economies, voter resistance to fundamental pension reform based on fear of losing existing pension entitlements has been significantly eroded by the growing practical irrelevance of existing pensions as mechanisms for adequate income replacement. It is important, however, not to overstate this point, given the scarcity of cash in the poorer transition economies. For example, with one out of four Russians a pensioner, a total of 35 million people, a formidable constituency in support of existing pensions has developed, particularly since '[f]or many, pensions are the primary, and in many cases the sole, source of cash income' (Gupta and Hagemann, 1998, p.218). Moreover, in a very few countries pension benefits actually improved in relative terms in the years following 1989. As Kudat and Youssef have reported, in Poland and the Czech Republic the 'status of the elderly relatively improved' due to 'explicitly designed pensions adjustments' (1999, p.30, fn.20, citing Torrey *et al.*).

Externally, the IFIs have maintained, and in the case of the World Bank, have significantly reinforced, their pressure on political elites to respond positively to their market-friendly, privatisation-based, pension reform agenda, but now with their targeted political and administrative elites increasingly receptive to their policy proposals, particularly those that promise a linkage between comprehensive pension reform and sustainable economic growth in restructured marketised economies. In short, pension reform, often comprehensive pension reform, has increasingly become prioritised within both the restructuring/economic and the reform/political agendas across the CEE and the FSU.

Pension Problems and Contested Reform Strategies

For the CEE states and, to an even greater extent, for many of the states of the FSU the maintenance of civil stability in the period of unprecedented economic upheaval following the collapse of communist regimes was, to restate the obvious, never going to be anything but challenging. Retrospectively, it is now equally obvious that the early optimism over possibilities for quick transitions from failed socialism to working capitalism omitted to make full allowance for the difficulties of building market economies under chronic conditions of economic collapse and acute political dislocation. Progressive acceptance of the reality of transition as an inherently long-haul problem increasingly focused the attention of post-communist regimes on the importance of existing social security systems in maintaining at least minimal public support for restructuring programmes now widely defined in terms of decades rather than viewed on a year-by-year basis. Paradoxically, therefore, significant additional weight and policy responsibility was placed on the on-going role of existing, pre-transition, social security regimes in managing the political fallout from painful economic transitions. In itself this choice, in a context of growing revenue shortfalls, inevitably and directly limited options for fundamental economic reconstruction within increasingly constrained budgetary frameworks. In turn, the reform of existing welfare provision was made doubly difficult by the inevitably increasing demands being made on social security systems already struggling to cope with on-going obligations and commitments. Irony was added to paradox in that increased burdens were thereby placed on existing social welfare institutions and instruments; welfare regimes which were themselves in urgent need of fundamental reconstruction and realignment.

As Robert Holzmann has rightly underlined, early, and widespread, western perceptions of the essentials of the welfare-related problems facing the states of CEE and the FSU tended, sometimes rather comprehensively, to miss the point, particularly in their stress on the need for the establishment of 'safety net' welfare provisions in the transition economies. 'In contrast to the often repeated call for a social safety net in the countries in transition, suggesting a barely developed system of social benefits, almost the contrary is true' (Holzmann, 1994, p.184). In practice, as Holzmann, among others, correctly underlined, socialist central planning had inaugurated and maintained 'a rather comprehensive system of social benefits ...', albeit omitting unemployment support; benefit systems which their post-communist successor regimes naturally inherited (Holzmann, 1994, p.184). These systems were not lacking in identifiable strengths, not least the comprehensiveness of their coverage of eligible individuals. In contrast, for example, to the public pension systems of Latin America which, bluntly, 'pay a lot to the rich and little to the poor', those in the CEE and the states of the FSU more closely resemble their counterparts in the OECD countries in terms of both population coverage and benefit provision, providing 'public pensions [that] are effective means of delivering retirement income to the entire population' (Johnson, 1996, p.16).

The resultant reform issues and policy problems, however, were complex and multifaceted. From a state-centric perspective, the central issue was the high, and often rapidly rising, share of GDP committed to these benefit systems in general and to their pensions component in particular, with the latter universally swallowing up 'the lion's share' of welfare expenditure throughout CEE and the FSU, and facing rising numbers of beneficiaries (Holzmann, 1994, p.184) as transition economies increasingly addressed the problems of enterprise restructuring. Inevitably, with increasing numbers of beneficiaries, and, by definition, falling numbers of tax paying contributors, existing entitlements could not easily be maintained, ensuring that the central issue and key problem from a societal perspective was the fact that benefit levels are low, yet apparently also unsustainable even at present low levels.

Unsurprisingly, therefore, more recent western perspectives, often directly influenced by World Bank thinking and the increasingly World Bank driven Washington 'consensus' on both transition problems and transition solutions, have increasingly focused on the importance of pensions and pension reform as a key element in reform strategies. Crucially, and somewhat confusingly, pensions have become widely defined and prioritised as of dual significance in defining the developmental trajectories of transition economies, simultaneously forming both an existing reform problem and, albeit suitably and fundamentally restructured, offered as potential reform solution. Specifically, on the one hand, it is now universally argued that 'pension reform is required for fiscal, social and efficiency reasons' and, on the other hand, it is increasingly commonly accepted, at least in principle, 'that pension reform, economic restructuring, and the growth options for these countries are closely related ...' (Holzmann, 1994, p.184). The latter point relates to the growing body of empirical evidence, and associated theoretical arguments, underlining the importance of the linkages between financial liberalisation and the achievement of sustainable economic growth in market economies. In turn, the importance of pensions, and choice of pensions management and delivery systems, has increasingly come to be perceived as crucial to the functioning and healthy development of the national economy in free market systems. Specifically, by grace of the potential value of their assets and/or the potential cost of their liabilities, pension systems occupy an exalted position in relation to other elements of social security and social welfare regimes. These assets and/or liabilities give pension systems economic and political potentialities which extend significantly beyond their direct and overt social welfare role (Vittas, 1992, p.2).

Accordingly, any proposal for the fundamental reform of national pensions intrinsically implies a commensurate potential opportunity for a parallel restructuring of the country's entire financial system. Nevertheless, the converse also applies: the structure and limitations of existing financial systems and related market and state-based governance institutions provide important constraints on the prospects for successfully implementing pension reform, particularly if reform proposals are of a radical nature. Simply stated, healthy financial markets, supported by effective regulatory bodies, must be in place to enable healthy private pension fund sectors to develop. Otherwise, as in the weaker and poorer economies across CEE and the FSU, the effective absence of such markets implies the absence of a necessary precondition for the development of a secure system of long-term savings. Contrastingly, it has been argued that the creation of fully funded systems of pension provision, with individual savings accounts tying benefits directly and strictly to contributions made, will, in itself and particularly so if these schemes are privately delivered, stimulate financial system development, thereby expanding capital market capabilities and providing for the deepening and strengthening of financial sectors so necessary for sustained economic development in a market economy. Nevertheless, if internal, market-based, and external, state-based, monitoring, control and governance mechanisms remain weak, such regulatory limitations render savings at considerable risk from both inefficient institutions and unscrupulous individuals as well as from the vagaries of market forces.

Nor, as indicated already, is financial system underdevelopment the sole, or perhaps even the main, constraint on possibilities for successful development of private pensions provision across CEE and the FSU. As Paul Johnson puts it, it is the combination, prevailing across many of the transition economies, of 'primitive capital markets, [with] loosely defined property rights, unstable and/or corrupt governments, inadequate or non-existent regulatory systems, and little experience of personal financial management' (1996, p.15) that collectively indicate the problems of inaugurating successful private pension provision and the potential dangers to savers if instituted. Consequently, therefore, the absence of 'an adequate regulatory system, an efficient capital market, and a well-trained cadre of managers and administrators' (IMF, 1994, p.303) among the states in CEE and the FSU, at best, constitute important constraints on the possibilities for implementing radical solutions to the problems of reforming existing state-run pay-as-you-go (PAYG) pension systems, either by replacement or supplementation through private provision of funded schemes, however actuarially secure the latter may appear in principle. At worst, for the poorest states of the FSU and in CEE, 'where almost none of the necessary preconditions exist for secure long-term saving, private pensions at present are ... an enormous gamble rather than a way of ensuring old age security' (Johnson, 1996, p.15).

Social Security Provision: Forward to the Past

During the immediate post-World War Two era there had been an universal communist restructuring of all the existing national social insurance systems in the CEEs. It is important to note that no comparable process took place in the ex-USSR which had no pre-communist tradition of social insurance financed social security. Within the CEEs, this radical restructuring centred on the 'suppression of the employee contribution and direct assumption of financial responsibility for the scheme by the State' (Rys, 1993, p.165). This had the effect of removing the link between entitlement to benefits and the concept of social insurance. As a consequence of the abandonment of the system of a dedicated social security fund all social security came to be financed out of the general central government budget without any identifiable link to individual contributors. A somewhat perverse outcome of the removal of the employee element from the social insurance equation was the transformation of 'a system of social protection into an instrument of work incentives and rewards for services rendered to the political leadership of the society' (Rys, 1993, p.166).

Chronically inefficient economic performance under state planning systems, and with political economies further undermined by the global economic recession of the 1980s and by the direct effects of the debt crisis in particular, ensured that the welfare system became an increasingly unsustainable economic burden. Yet, both anticipating and directly paralleling continuing political obstacles to welfare system reform post-communism, there was a widespread and understandable reluctance among communist leaderships to substantially reduce actuarially over-generous benefit levels for fear that it would be politically destabilising. The collapse of the communist regimes and the consequent, if sometimes only temporary discrediting, of the policy instruments and strategies most closely associated with the rejected system, allowed welfare and social security reform to appear on the feasible political agenda. As a consequence the restitution of dedicated individual employee social insurance contributions and the separation of the social security fund from the general central government budget were targeted, thereby restoring welfare systems to pre-communist operating principles. These initial adjustments were characteristically defined and presented as essential prerequisites to any more fundamental or radical longer-term reforms of the social security system.

Nevertheless, despite widespread early post-communist calls for comprehensive and radical social security reforms it rapidly became apparent, not simply due to mounting macroeconomic pressures and the operational inertia of the existing social security institutions, but also, and increasingly, due to growing politician appreciation of the potential costs in lost political support, that implementing such reforms would be inappropriate or at least inadvisable. Inevitably, major emphasis in early proposals had fallen on possibilities for moving away from both state monopoly inaugurating fully funded and privatised schemes for pension provision based on the free market principles of competitive delivery then best exemplified by the Chilean *Administradoras de Fondos de Pensiones* (AFP) system.

Unsurprisingly, radical social security reforms to the degree envisaged did not materialise until after nearly a full decade of transition, and, to date, in only a very limited number of countries. In the course of the early 1990s, reform priorities consequently shifted towards more modest ambitions centred on changes needed to allow the former communist social security systems, which had largely been created from Bismarckian social insurance schemes, to be stabilised and restructured as PAYG social insurance schemes.

As the process of transition within the CEE and NIS/FSU has made amply clear, the building of market economies cannot be achieved either rapidly or without incurring significant economic and social costs. The fall in industrial output that has been such a significant feature of the economics of transition in the CEE and NIS/FSU has been an unavoidable consequence of the collapse of the centrally planned economies. More importantly, the rationalisation of state and formerly state owned industries under the ensuing privatisation programmes has further aggravated the situation. The outcome has been significantly higher unemployment - previously unrecognised as a concept under the former communist regimes, and somewhat transparently 'hidden' in underemployment - and equally significantly increased levels of poverty and social inequality. Market liberalisation and state retrenchment have also precipitated increasing levels of official corruption and further stimulated the growth of the informal and underground economies, reinforcing trends already firmly entrenched under state socialism. Although the prospect of moving towards welfare residualism as, for example, was at one time anticipated even for the Czech Republic, has now receded in general, the continuing problems of inadequate welfare provision and limited reform options remain daunting.

Governments in the CEE and NIS/FSU therefore continue to find themselves in an unenviable and vulnerable position, simultaneously faced by substantially declining government revenues and significantly increased demands for state welfare provision. External funding sources then become crucial not simply to sustain investments and fund development budgets but also to meet recurrent costs and routine expenditures, not least in relation to pension commitments. In turn, the domestic political impact of what has increasingly been perceived as unwarranted multilateral interference in sovereign domains had been influential in stimulating populist support for the, conservative, former communist establishment advocating 'a systematic defence of rights and privileges acquired under the communist system' (Rys, 1993, p.163). The highly significant social and welfare policy implications of these trends have, equally, stimulated anxious reflection amongst a new generation of 'democrats' who, simultaneously, view any opposition to the transition process as retrograde but who are also equally wary of the political implications of a populist backlash for reform prospects in the short and medium term (Greskovits, 1995, pp.91-106).

The Growth of Non-State Private Pension Funds

To date, state elites and the International Financial Institutions (IFIs) have tended to converge on a pension reform strategy that has prioritised theoretically cost cutting adjustments to the parameters of the existing PAYG systems in the short term, whilst seeking progressively to adopt and to implement a medium to long run programme, over 15 to 20 years, of more fundamental reforms designed to ensure actuarial sustainability in the face of worsening system dependency ratios. The medium to long term aim envisages increasingly overt pension system demonopolisation, involving both a significant expansion of scope for private provision and eventual movement towards the fullest possible pre-funding of pensions, public and private alike.

Across the transition economies and in relation to almost all business and industrial sectors, it has been the 'entry of new firms (which) has been the driving force behind private sector development' (World Bank, 1996, p.106) rather than SOE (state-owned enterprise) privatisations. Parallel tendencies can be observed in the social sectors of the transition states. 'Private sector provision of education increases largely through growth of a nascent private sector, not through privatisation. Health care is increasingly quasi-private, usually through the rise of corruption rather than as a result of privatisation' (Murrell, 1996, p.35). So too, in the specific case of pension industry developments, state pension systems in the transition economies have, so far, shrunk in prominence and priority only in relative, not in absolute, terms as private pension providers have been progressively legitimated and increasingly encouraged to supplement existing state PAYG provision across an increasing number of the CEE states and, albeit to a lesser extent, in the states on NIS/FSU. We define this process as the 'pluralisation' of pensions provision. Accordingly, the development of voluntary private pension sectors is now increasingly widespread, in particular across CEE. Towards the end of the 1990s, this somewhat haphazard process of non-state pension fund (NSPF) expansion, or 'outgrowing' (World Bank, 1995, p.71), had taken place in Albania, Bulgaria, Croatia, the Czech Republic, Estonia, Georgia, Hungary, Latvia, Lithuania, Moldova, Poland, Russia, the Slovak Republic, Slovenia, Ukraine and even as far afield as Kyrgyzstan (EBRD, 1999, pp.181-285; Müller, 2000c, p.25). In some cases, notably Russia and the Ukraine, the legal and statutory basis for NSPF development is missing and across the FSU/NIS regulatory arrangements are limited to say the least.

Profiles of emergent supplementary voluntary private pension funds in three selected countries are provided below. As far as possible, these profiles are presented in a uniform format to facilitate inter-country comparisons. Accordingly, the profiles cover both the relevant contextual arrangements framing sectoral operations, namely the legal status of pension funds, governance and regulatory issues, and their fiscal treatment, and also provide an overview of sectoral activity and key developmental features and trends. The countries covered in this analysis are the Russian Federation, Hungary and the Czech Republic.

Russian Federation

Authorised by Presidential Decree, Russian private sector, or nonstate, pension funds date from 1992. Russian NSPFs continue to develop in a manner which typifies more generally many of the recognised 'institutional weaknesses' (Hanson, 1997, p.27) of Russian capitalism. As Vittas and Michelitsch suggest, they operate largely in a 'regulatory vacuum' (Vittas and Michelitsch, 1996, p.258). While most funds are defined contribution schemes operating with individual capitalisation accounts, some NSPFs operate, at least in theory, as defined benefit schemes. Behind the often-cited problems facing the Russian NSPF sector lies a lack of consensus over appropriate regulatory and governance frameworks resulting in a legal vacuum and, inevitably, continuing controversy concerning most aspects of their development. One outcome of this regulatory shortfall is a limited degree of standardisation in the operational practices and behaviour of the NSPF sector as a whole. Similar variability in the portfolio and investment strategies of different pension funds is also characteristic of this rather shambolic element of the Russian financial services sector. It is reported that the smaller pension funds invest mainly in bank deposits and seek to give a rate of return which, at worst, is no less than the rate offered for savings deposits by the state savings bank, *Sberbank*. Other NSPFs, which have more diversified investment portfolios, also place investments in bonds and, to a lesser degree, equities. In general most NSPFs are obliged to invest exclusively in the domestic market. Funds may only invest overseas if the management company has a foreign currency licence. At present the non-state pension funds operate without any favourable tax treatment. In fact the future expansion and development of NSPFs is, in part, tied to the removal of the present onerous fiscal regime of 'triple taxation'. Specifically, not only are contributions to NSPFs not tax deductible but both investment income accruing within the fund and pension entitlements are taxed.

Despite the lack of regulation, membership of the around 1000 nonstate pension funds, which are largely located in Moscow and St Petersburg, has increased to 2 million individuals. The large number of nonstate pension funds in Russia can be explained, as can their relatively small average size, in terms of both membership and asset value, by the nature of the pension provision mandate. This is mostly employer-based leading to the present fund proliferation. One reported estimate suggests that the average value of individual private pension fund assets is currently equivalent to a mere US$0.50! (Thornhill, 1998). In turn, as Vladimir Mikhalev, drily puts it, 'non-state pension funds generally cooperate with industrial enterprises which opt for supplementary pension schemes for their employees, paying part of their profits as insurance contributions. Individual membership of private pension funds is much less widespread' (Mikhalev, 1996, p.23). The low rate of individual NSPF membership, which can not be disassociated from a more general and widespread lack of trust in Russian financial institutions, is likely to be one factor which has contributed to the growth of an 'estimated $20bn of idle savings' which are reputed to be kept 'stuffed under mattresses' (Thornhill, 1998, p.32). One result of the combined impact of the employer-based operational mandate and the lack of regulation, is that these inherently small funds commonly operate, from a membership perspective, 'more like savings banks than long-term pension funds' (Vittas and Michelitsch, 1996, p.258). For instance, it is not uncommon for members to be permitted to make withdrawals from their 'pension' accounts when unemployed. Inevitably, therefore, with funds operating with low or very low levels of accumulated capital and mainly making short-term investments, there is very limited evidence of the development of a sectoral capacity to provide the type of long-term investment funding stability required to underpin their theoretical role as pension providers. In general, Vladimir Mikhalev's claim that the Russian NSPFs 'mainly function as small-scale investment companies' is apt (Mikhalev, 1996, p.23).

Hungary

The legislative Act on Voluntary Mutual Insurance Funds permitting the introduction of voluntary supplementary pension funds (VSPFs) in Hungary was passed in December 1993. The Hungarian VSPFs, which can be either of a defined benefit or defined contribution nature, are predominantly of the latter form and based on individual capitalisation accounts. Within the 1998 pension reform legislation, which, most significantly, introduced mandatory second pillar individual pension funds, the VSPFs have been assigned the role of third pillar providers. Regulatory supervision of the VSPFs is provided through an elected board of directors and a control committee. A state instituted body which is supervised by the Ministry of Finance, the Fund Supervisory Authority (FSA) (Borish *et al.*, 1996, p.126), is responsible for issuing operational licences and for supervising the funds. Investments of fund assets must follow guidelines to avoid conflicts of interest and to reduce portfolio risk. Due to the fact that no more than 20 percent of fund assets may be invested in publicly quoted shares and bonds, while investments in non-quoted companies are limited under a ceiling of 10 percent, it must be assumed that government bonds and state guaranteed securities remain significantly important as investment options. In terms of tax treatment, both employee and employer contributions and investment income are tax deductible. Contributions are also exempt from social security taxes. The favourable tax treatment, which is meant to encourage the development of VSPFs, is effectively regressive since these schemes will not attract workers on lower incomes. Moreover, concern has been raised that the nature of the VSPF system, not only in terms of its permissive tax regime but also in respect of its largely employer-based organisation, is detrimental to the long-term financial sustainability of the state pension scheme which is dependent on payroll tax receipts from enterprises. Specifically, the tax deductibility of employer contributions has encouraged the expansion of the indirect payment of wages in the form of employers contributions to voluntary pension funds (Simonovits, 1998, p.11).

The mandate for VSPFs in Hungary lies not with the individual but with 'a common employer or on a profession, sector or region' (Vittas and Michelitsch, 1996, p.256). In 1998 there were around 300 VSPFs in operation. Despite the growing number of pension funds, this disguises the fact that the average size of fund membership has remained, for the most part, small. The average size of fund membership in Hungary stands at around 1,000. Nationally, the total membership for the VSPFs in Hungary is reported to be approaching 850,000 (Deutsch, 1997b, p.54) which approximates to 20 percent of the labour force. The withdrawal conditions in Hungary are relatively restrictive. Unless retirement age is reached, the combined total of contributions and accrued investment interest may not be withdrawn within a period of ten years. Withdrawals can be in the form of either annuity or lump sum. Both of these options are subject to income tax. Concern has been raised over the current lack of regulation pertaining to transfer rights permitting the movement of savings from one pension fund to another. At present, VSPFs frequently appear to be acting arbitrarily, and sometimes against the wishes of their members, with regards to this important issue.

Czech Republic

The existing system of voluntary supplementary pension funds (SPFs) in the Czech Republic was legally sanctioned in 1994. While these schemes may be either of a defined benefit or of a defined contribution type, they predominantly take the latter form. Operational transparency, in principle, is maintained by management and supervisory boards, but in practice relatively little is known about sectoral trends in investment behaviour within the legally-defined investment parameters under which the funds are obliged to operate, namely government and bank bonds, blue-chip equity holdings in Czech companies and property. Investment strategies, which are generally accepted as predominantly anchored upon securities traded on public stock exchanges, must, however, be disclosed to scheme members. Nevertheless, current information on the investment strategies, and on the investment returns, of the individual SPFs remains sparse.

Despite the voluntary nature of these schemes, the SPFs receive a degree of subsidisation from the central government that is frequently described as generous. These sectoral subsidies were expected to rise until 1997, reaching CSK3.25 billion, and to decline thereafter. Specifically, to encourage participation and to 'wean people off state pensions' (Economist, 1994, p.122), the SPFs operate under a system of tax credits that were designed to appear attractive to workers. This option was perceived as more progressive than the 'regressive' alternative system of tax exemptions. For monthly contributions which equate to CSK500, which is around 8 percent of the average monthly salary, tax credits amounting to 24 percent of contributions are awarded. As a result of contributions being voluntary, it has been suggested that, overall, the funds' assets are likely to be kept artificially low by contributors placing sums with the aim of qualifying for the tax credit rather than systematically contributing an amount based upon a standard percentage of income. Nonetheless, in 1995 the total value of SPFs fund assets had reached CSK4 billion, or equivalent to 0.14 of GDP.

This is indicative of contribution levels running far short of initial government predictions of annual fund incomes totalling CSK12.5 billion by 1997. This pattern places an early question mark over the expectation that fund totals would reach CSK250 billion by 2015.

The mandate for the voluntary Czech SPFs lies with the individual. This factor is significant in limiting the expansion of the number of operational pension funds. By 1996, there were 44 SPFs, significantly up in number from the three domestic funds initially granted Finance Ministry pension-fund licenses by October 1994, but very much in line with the initial 40 applicants, domestic and foreign awaiting finance Ministry clearance. About 1.2 million people were contributing to private pensions by the beginning of 1996. This figure had grown to around 1.4 million by 1999, equating to approximately 35 percent of the Czech labour force. Interestingly this figure is now approaching initial government predictions. These predictions projected that, by the end of 1997, 40 percent of the adult Czech population would be contributing to private pension funds (Economist, 1994, p.122). Currently, the average size of fund membership stands at around 30,000. Fund members may voluntarily terminate their contract with a specific pension fund and transfer their contributions to a competing fund - a law which has been perceived as being important for the development of efficient operational practices in the Czech financial services sector. The main disadvantage of this provision is that this freedom to move accounts has contributed to high administration costs in the sector, not least because of the obvious temptation to advertise heavily to attract affiliates from other funds. Honesty may also be sacrificed. Early fund advertising promised higher rates of return to fund contributors than were internally anticipated by fund managements. If a scheme member so wishes, the total value of pension account savings, including government tax credits and accrued interest on investments, may be cashed in completely. While this may act as an anti-poverty measure during periods of unemployment, there is wider concern over the adequacy of the pensions provided by the SPFs. Considering the tight fiscal constraint which transition has imposed upon the Czech government, there is a further issue concerning the value for money afforded by tax credits, especially if the adequacy of supplementary pension entitlements is questionable.

From 'Outgrowing' to 'In-Built' Pension Reform Strategies

Despite the large degree of institutional variation and the divergencies in the operational success achieved by the NSPF sectors in different countries, two common factors were influential in shaping the nature of development of private pensions provision. First, was the 'idea that pension funds will provide a rich source of savings for investment', thereby providing necessary motivation for any subsequent governmental 'drive for private pensions'. Second, was the fact that 'most of the countries in the region will wish to see the development of such schemes take place on a voluntary basis' (Iyer, 1993b, p.61). Collectively these two ultimately mutually contradictory principles, on the one hand, constitute the basis of the 'outgrowing' strategy of pluralised provision described above and, on the other hand, define its inherent limitations. These 'outgrowing' strategy limitations constrain prospects in relation to the specifics of pensions reform as well as restricting pension system potential for acting as a stimulative mechanism for savings/investment enhancement and, ultimately, for developing an interactive synergy between contractual savings institutions and the wider economy. The current, overall, state of the infant voluntary private pension fund sector across the countries of CEE, and more widely across the FSU, has been succinctly summarised by Igor Filatochev. 'As far as pension funds are concerned, these organisations are still at the rudimentary stage of development, even in the advanced Visegrad countries' (Filatochev, 1997, p.504).[1] As Filatochev rightly notes most of these private funds remain under capitalised. Clearly, the citizens of most transition economies simply do not yet have the surplus economic resources available to drive the development of a viable long-term private savings sector. Only in the Czech Republic and, to a lesser extent, in Hungary are significant percentages of labour forces covered by voluntary private pensions (Gillion *et al.*, 2000, p.567).

Moreover, widespread financial sector scandals, and frequent bankruptcies of financial services providers, have further undermined public confidence in private pension funds, as has uncontrolled and unregulated free market-driven competition both among private pension funds and between these funds and their sectoral rivals, notably commercial banks, for scarce cash-surplus customers. This largely unregulated competition, inevitably, both pushes up the administrative costs of individual firms who must sustain heavy advertising and promotional costs if they are simply to sustain their market share. Unrestrained competition, it must be added, also encourages sectoral dishonesty and, consequently, further undermines public credibility, as inflated claims of the prospect of high rates of return on investments made further underlines public perceptions of a sectoral absence of probity.[2] Such competition also encourages short-termism as fund managers desperately seek high returns through risky investment strategies, again further undermining confidence in the stability and viability of funds and the competence of fund managers. Nevertheless, despite these widely accepted financial sector problems, the current policy emphasis across the countries of CEE and NIS/FSU is moving increasingly towards the mandatory development of private pension sectors.

The development of mandatory private pension sectors is progressively seen as the key element in current pension reform strategies, even if only by default, as the only plausible mechanism to ease pressure on failing state pension systems. The developments in voluntary private pension provision outlined above can increasingly be contrasted to the more strategically focused and politically concerted reform packages, either enacted or envisaged, to create pillared pension provision in a number of transition states. Significantly, in contrast to the earlier trend of largely unplanned and market-driven pensions provision pluralisation associated with the 'outgrowing' approach, recent developments in a number of states can be increasingly clearly defined in terms of a trend towards a more overtly planned reform strategy dedicated to pension system pillarisation and incorporating the introduction of private pension funds as an 'in-built' mandatory element within this restructuring process.

Overall, and despite the fact that national pension systems exhibit some, often significant, structural variations, a developing trend in the states of CEE towards the active development of pillared pension systems, with mandatory roles for private pension funds, is evidenced by pension reform in Hungary (1998) and Poland (1999). Further, promised, reforms both in the Baltic states and in the Balkans have not yet materialised. For example, the proposed introduction of mandatory private pension funds in Croatia appears to have been put in abeyance until 2002, not least as a consequence of political changes made necessary by the death of President Franjo Tujdman. Despite widespread discussions of the Chilean model, reforms proposed and implemented in CEE to date are more in line with the format of the less iconoclastic Argentinean pillared variant. The Argentinean model comprises a 'first pillar' basic universal pension and a 'second pillar' offering affiliates a choice between membership of either a private defined contribution pension fund or a state-run defined benefit scheme (Vittas, 1997). In contrast, in the FSU state of Kazakhstan, the 1998 reforms are more reminiscent of the Chilean reforms in that the PAYG scheme has been replaced by mandatory pension funds.[3]

Generally, it is worth noting that an increasing number of countries in CEE and the NIS/FSU, and not excluding some of the least developed among them, are now, albeit to varying degrees and at differing rates, pursuing, at least in principle, reform of state pension systems (see Table 4.1). Albania, for example, prior to the recent pyramid savings schemes débâcle, had agreed the principle of adopting a three pillar pension scheme, whilst, more plausibly, Slovenia has been seriously considering the enactment of a similar three pillar system for several years. However, the Slovenian government has been obliged as a consequence of massive public protests to 'abandon, for now' (Marsh, 1998, p.3) specific aspects within the pension reform proposals. In particular there remains, at least in the short term, a significant degree of opposition from trade unions and the general public to the introduction of a mandatory funded second pillar scheme in Slovenia. Similarly, the Romanian government's plan for the introduction of pillared pension provision is facing severe political opposition from the trade union movement (Müller, 2000b, p.32). More recently, and despite the general weakness of the financial sector, Bulgaria began a reform of the pension system in 1998 envisaging the introduced of a three pillar system on a phased basis with private NSPFs operating by 2000/2001. Indications suggest that Latvia will institute a three pillar pension system in 2001. Estonia has also committed itself to implementing a three pillar system for the year 2001. The International Social Security Association (ISSA) has reported that Macedonia is also planning the introduction of a three pillar pension system (ISSA, 2000a, p.18). Significantly, and a decision which, arguably, has been influenced more by Asian-style proposals than by those from neighbouring economies within CEE, the Macedonian proposals have opted to avoid a greater degree of pensions privatisation by retaining state control over the fully pre-funded second pillar. Clearly, this decision is equally reflective of the important constraints imposed by domestic financial sector weaknesses.

Table 4.1 Systemic Pension Reforms in CEE and NIS/FSU

Country	Pluralised	Pillared
Albania	Operational	Proposed
Armenia	Proposed	----
Azerbaijan	----	----
Belarus	----	----
Bosnia and Herzegovina	----	----
Bulgaria	Operational	Proposed
Croatia	Operational	Proposed
Czech Rep.	Operational	----
Estonia[1]	Operational	Proposed
Georgia	Operational	----
Hungary	Operational	3 Pillars
Kazakhstan [2]	Operational	Parallel
Kyrgyz Rep.	Operational	Proposed
Latvia [3]	Operational	Proposed
Lithuania	Operational	----
Macedonia (FYR)	Proposed	Proposed
Moldova	Operational	----
Poland	Operational	3 Pillars
Romania	Proposed	Proposed
Russian Federation	Operational	----
Slovak Rep.	Legislated	----
Slovenia[4]	Operational	2 Pillars
Tajikistan	Proposed	----
Turkmenistan	----	----
Ukraine	Operational	Proposed
Uzbekistan	----	----

1. Estonia had planned to pluralise its pension system and institute a three pillar pension system by 2001.
2. It is envisaged new pension system will operate in parallel with the old system for the interim transition period.
3. A three pillar pension system is to be instituted by 2001.
4. The introduction of a mandatory private second pillar has been abandoned for now.

Sources: EBRD, 1996, pp.136-184; EBRD, 1997, pp.148-213; Impavido, 1997, pp.101-135; ISSA, 1998, pp.9-12.

The Transitional Costs of Systemic Pension Reform

Crucially, pension system privatisation through the active promotion of private pensions via the introduction of a compulsory element in the form of a new mandatory private pillar, and its logical corollary, the downgrading of existing public provision, entail significant short-term costs. These are costs which cannot be evaded and must be carefully weighed against the more uncertain prospect of the medium and long-term gains likely to accrue to the individual from fully pre-funded pension provision based on individual contribution accounts managed, invested, and delivered privately as well as by the state. 'The reforms envisage a gradual switch from an unfunded pay-as-you-go system to a funded system which will initially bring a fall in budgetary revenues but eventually create a growing flow of savings for investment' (Bobinski, 1997a, p.4). Where, as was the case in Poland in 1997, an election is scheduled it may become prudent to put pension reform proposals into temporary abeyance even if, as was again the case in Poland, there was both substantial inter-party consensus on the need for significant changes in existing arrangements and substantial amounts of relevant legislation had already been passed. Concerns over the cost pitfalls in Poland, for example, were such that postponement occurred despite World Bank guarantees of 'an adjustment credit to cover the cost of moving towards private pension funds' (Carnegie Group, 1997, p.1).

Clearly, systemic reforms involving the creation of mandatory private pension funds will have an immediate and negative impact upon social security receipts. With the introduction in 1999 of the new Polish three pillar system, involving the allocation of one third of employer and employee contributions to new mandatory private pension funds, the net income of ZUS (*Zaklad Ubezpieczen Spolecznych*), the state social security agency responsible for existing provisions, has been cut at a stroke, without any compensating reduction in public pension system outgoings. Official estimates, made by the Office of the Government Plenipotentiary for Social Security Reform (OPSSR), are that major transition costs will occur for at least five to seven years into the reform programme, at which point the effects of the rationalisation of the state pension system will begin to be reflected in reduced budgetary burdens. However, as the higher than expected first year deficit of the Hungarian pillared system illustrates, official estimates of both the fiscal cost of reform and time duration of the transitional period are likely to be understated. Significantly, the 1999

Hungarian budget law had to freeze the scheduled increase in the contribution rate to the mandatory second pillar NSPFs in order to counter-balance spiralling fiscal deficits stemming from unfunded state pension provision. Envisaged as a temporary slowdown to create short-term fiscal savings it is significant that the freeze on contributions was extended quickly into 2000 without any indication from the government as to when reform would recommence (EBRD, 1999, p.227).

In the case of Poland, it is envisaged that the expected budgetary shortfall of the state pension system, conservatively estimated at more than $1 billion annually, will lead to an acceleration of the privatisation process as the government is obliged to sell state assets to fund the transitional costs of the pension reform programme. Far from being controversial, this knock-on effect in the acceleration and reinvigoration of privatisation is presented as a desirable and positive outcome of pension reform in the government's blueprint document for reform. Specifically, it is anticipated that pension 'reform will contribute to the increase in privatisation income through the increase in the demand for equity' engendered by the new pension funds (OPSSR, 1997, p.81). 'Rapid privatisation also will promote higher economic growth and, in consequence, higher tax revenues and decreased specific social expenditures' (OPSSR, 1997, p.82).

This optimistic official scenario, therefore, envisages the emergence of a virtuous circularity with pension reform both accelerating and maximising returns from the privatisation process in a mutually reinforcing sequence. Nevertheless, the anticipated acceleration of the privatisation of state owned assets - even if, as currently proposed, it encompasses the most attractive and profitable of them - will not, in itself, provide revenues sufficient to cover the budget deficits automatically created as significant portions of payroll tax are channelled into the new private pension funds. Indeed, official optimism over transition funding may seem significantly misplaced given the limited funds generated for budgetary support through the medium of earlier privatisations across the transition economies. Significantly, Polish budgetary estimates for privatisation receipts for the financial year 1998 were US$830 million, albeit well up on the US$600 million raised from privatisation in the previous year, but still falling substantially short of the US$1 billion or more required annually well into the future to fill the budgetary hole left by the pillared system transition and the introduction of mandatory private funded pension funds in 1999. Prudently, therefore, it is officially accepted 'that additional privatisation income probably will not cover [the] increased

... ZUS subsidies' that will be needed. 'These subsidies will have to be financed partly from an increase in public debt' (OPSSR, 1997, p.81). If less conservative estimates of likely revenue shortfalls are utilised, for example in line with forecasts that in the first year of operation the new mandatory private pension funds may attract up to US$3 billion in contributions, all of which will be reflected in a loss of net revenue to ZUS, then it becomes clear that income from the sale of privatisation assets will have to be significantly supplemented by debt instruments such as government bonds if the government's immediate funding gap is to be bridged.

Linking Pension Reform and Enterprise Privatisation

The September 1997 enactment of the Polish law legitimating the utilisation of privatisation assets in the process of reforming the state pension system and in building a parallel mandatory private pension sector, formally links these two key economic transition elements to an extent previously regularly envisaged but never seriously implemented. The manner of linkage presented has also evolved significantly, moving from the earlier, rather crude, emphasis on direct funding of private pensions through allocations of privatisation assets to a more indirect, but also more creative, approach. Specifically, contrary to earlier expectations, it has been decided that '(p)rivatised Treasury property will not be used to fund private pension funds ...' directly through share allocations (OPSSR 1997, p.84). Under the terms of the new law, '(p)roperty of the privatised enterprises will reach the pension funds through the capital market, but only after it has been appropriately selected and valued' (OPSSR 1997, p.85). As the pension reform blueprint document argues, whilst 'it is important to create a mechanism combining privatisation and social insurance reform ... (b)oth of these processes must *independently* advance *as soon as possible*, and privatisation assets must be used for social insurance reforms', rather than for direct support of private pension funds (OPSSR, 1997, p.82, emphasis in original).

The 1997 law also provided for the creation of an 'Industrial Fund' as the intermediary instrument intended for this purpose (EC, 1997, p.14). The Industrial Fund operates by selling privatisation bonds on behalf of the state; a process best described as 'yet another form of mass privatisation', but one specifically designed to provide the state with financial resources for meeting some of the costs inherent in pension reform (EC, 1997, p.14). This mechanism supersedes earlier proposals, widely mooted and widely supported, to supplement and strengthen the capital basis of the new Polish mandatory private pension funds through a direct allocation of shares, probably minority stakes, in selected, sound-performing, companies scheduled for privatisation in a process paralleling the Bolivian 'collective capitalisation' programme (EBRD, 1996, pp.99-100). This Latin American variant of the 'voucher' privatisations of CEE and NIS/FSU states, utilised shares from the privatisation of the country's leading SOEs to fund two privately managed pension funds. These private funds, in turn, were mandated to utilise dividend income to provide initial small pensions for all Bolivians and to establish individual savings and investment accounts for future expanded pension provision (Bowen, 1996, p.9).

Both the Bolivian capitalisation programme and its Polish offshoots are themselves indirect descendants of proposals linking privatisation to pension reform that have been 'on the table' in the transition economies since the early 1990s, all previously involving the idea of allocating to newly created private sector pension funds what János Kornai termed 'valuable, truly income-generating portfolios of securities during the privatisation of the state-owned firms, as a free contribution to their initial capitalisation' (Kornai, 1992, p.17). As Frydman, Gray and Rapaczynski point out in their overview of developments up to the mid-1990s, 'Very little has been done to realise these proposals so far, although some countries are still reserving some assets for this purpose' (1996a, p.11). Comparable proposals linking the privatisation process to the restructuring of public PAYG pensions and their reformulation as fully funded systems had circulated widely among the transition economies from an early date. For example, a 1990 Polish plan suggested possibilities for the partial capitalisation of the state pension fund on the basis of voucher allocations from large enterprise privatisation and involving the transfer of 20 percent of state owned enterprise (SOE) assets (Frydman and Rapaczynski, 1994, p.63; Holzmann, 1994, p.201). Parallel proposals in Hungary envisaged that 10 percent of state assets would be transferred to the pensions administration by 1994. Like its private sector counterparts, outlined above, this brand of proposal, envisaging the funding via capitalisation of state pension systems through privatisation proceeds, was only rarely pursued with any degree of commitment, and then only, as in the Hungarian case, implemented in a strictly limited fashion, although the outcome is that the state pension fund administration currently holds significant blocks of shares in a number of major national enterprises.

The thinking behind such ideas is straightforward, based on views of the unsustainability of existing state PAYG systems currently funded through swingeing, unpopular and easily evaded payroll taxes on workforces. Pension reform, however, will turn existing, implicit, pension debt - the net value of existing pension obligations less future contributions to the state system - into an explicit debt since 'government revenues will fall sharply as contributions are diverted to the new system while the call on government pension expenditures will only gradually decline' (Reisen, 1997, p.1179). Original estimates suggested that this implicit pension debt (IPD), in the form of the present and potential claims of pensioners and workers on current and future governments (Kane and Palaçios, 1996, p.36), was very large indeed in relation to GDP across the transition countries, perhaps reaching almost 500 percent of GDP overall in CEE, and even higher than that in individual 'worst-case' states such as Poland and Hungary (Holzmann, 1994, pp.199-200). More recent estimates have been considerably lower, indicating, for example, an average IPD of 150 percent of GDP in the CEE states, albeit still underlining the point that 'the pension debt is large' (Fox, 1995, p.36).

The key point is that any transition from a PAYG system to a funded system automatically makes previously 'implicit' pension debt explicit as the payroll taxes that formerly paid existing pensioners are diverted into a fund and earmarked for future, not present, pensions. Consequently, hypothetical privatisation proceeds, in the form of potentially realisable or transferable state assets - interestingly, if very tentatively, estimated by Robert Holzmann as 'worth' between 0.25 and 1.4 times GDP for the CEE countries - present a theoretically attractive mechanism for supporting a transition to a funded public pension system, potentially compensating for at least a portion of the tax revenue automatically unavailable to governments still committed to supporting existing pension commitments on an on-going basis. Even if the potential values of state assets are prudently estimated - thereby accepting Holzmann's argument 'that only a relatively small portion of current public pension obligations could be exchanged even if major parts of socialized enterprises are handed over to pension funds' (Holzmann, 1994, p.201) - it is clear that a linkage between reform of public pension systems and privatisation programmes could potentially have had a significant effect on the former and, at least hypothetically, an even larger impact on the latter.

Significantly, however, despite the clear potential for providing portions, possibly even substantial proportions, of the capital underpinnings required to support the costs of transitions from PAYG systems toward sustainable funded systems through privatisation programmes, outwith Poland, no comprehensive linkage between pension reform and privatisation agendas has been seriously attempted in the transition economies. In part, at least, the fact that enterprise privatisation and pension reform remain parallel projects, rather than forming closely integrated elements in on-going policy strategies, can be accounted for by the mutual exclusivity of competing proposals for pension reform priorities. These either strenuously advocate the utilisation of privatisation assets for capitalising private pensions as an alternative rather than as a supplement to state provision (Jenkins, 1992a), or strongly press the case for the continued exclusivity of the public pension system, albeit to be provided on a fully funded basis when feasible (Johnson, 1993), perhaps involving the medium term retention of existing PAYG schemes until positive real rates of return in excess of population growth can underpin the transition to funded schemes (Ahmad, 1993, p.11). Since these alternatives reflect the comparable mutual exclusivity of much detailed pension reform advice, polarised between a New World enthusiasm for the private sector and Old World acceptance of a continued need for state provision, transition state elites may be viewed as sensible in steering cautiously between rocks and hard places essentially by avoiding the comprehensive reforms that would require firm and final choices to be made between public and private alternatives, particularly if these involve the totality of Chilean-style zero-sum alternatives.

There is, however, another important issue to be addressed. Arguably, the wider failure to creatively link the enterprise privatisation and pension reform agendas is due to the fact that the problem has been mainly approached from the wrong direction. Specifically, interest in linking these policy agendas has generally been pursued in terms of a perceived potential for facilitating pension reform via privatisation asset allocations, with surprisingly little interest shown in the possibilities for achieving significantly enhanced programmes of enterprise restructuring through the utilisation of pension funds for targeted investment purposes. The EBRD, for example, considers proposals for privatisation asset allocation simply as an additional, highly desirable, instrument for building pension fund investment portfolios, potentially forming an integral element in the step by step build-up of contractual savings sectors and, thereby, as contributing importantly to the strengthening of financial sectors and to the deepening of financial systems (EBRD, 1996, pp.99-100). Georges Heinrich, similarly, finds such proposals interesting as an alternative to the expansion of government debt otherwise required to support the transition from unfunded PAYG schemes to fully funded pensions (Heinrich, 1997, p.52). Iain Batty, straightforwardly, views the utilisation of privatisation proceeds in support of the expenses inherent in the transition to pension pre-funding as 'a way of dealing with such costs' (Batty, 1997b, p.2).

Nevertheless, as indicated above in relation to the Polish case, even utilising optimistic official estimates, allocations of privatisation assets can only be expected to offset limited portions of pension debt, realistically forming an addition, rather than an alternative, to funding derived from an expansion of debt instruments such as sales of government bonds. As Helmut Reisen summarises, 'It is ... unrealistic to assume that debt financing of at least an important share of the implicit PAYG debt can be avoided: a lack of marketable public enterprises will usually preclude financing PAYG debt totally through privatisation' (Reisen, 1997, p.1180). In a worst case scenario, as the East German example underlines, privatisation proceeds, taken as an aggregate across a whole economy, may actually turn out to be negative. The *Treuhandanstalt*, charged with the task of privatising the German Democratic Republic's economy rapidly but also given the responsibility of securing enterprise viability post-privatisation, disposed of 13,000 state-owned enterprises (SOEs) between 1990 and 1995, taking in US$50 billion but also spending US$243 billion in the course of the privatisation process. Although the East German transition is unique, the underlying point is clear: there are relatively limited prospects for supporting pension reform through privatisation asset allocation in most transition economies. Iain Batty, a consultant closely involved in the Polish pension reform process, provides a realistic summary of prospects in that country. 'Privatisation proceeds can ... *help* meet any shortfall caused by people paying less to the existing pay-as-you-go system' (Batty, 1997b, p.2, emphasis added), but will still leave the bulk of the funding shortfalls to be met by governments through other means. As Helmut Reisen underlines, '(t)he implicit PAYG debt is usually massive' (Reisen, 1997, p.1180). For Chile, now entering its third decade of operating its 'model' reformed pension system, estimates of its present value vary between 80 percent and 126 percent of GDP. Since tax financed transitions from PAYG systems to fully funded schemes in the CEE states are out of the question, reforming governments will, therefore, have to depend primarily on borrowing and an expansion of government debt instruments.

Pension Reform and Privatisation: Opportunities Lost

Policy makers across the transition economies have often looked with interest at the Chilean model of pensions reform, particularly noting, with envy, how 'the Chilean government found a way out of the virtual bankruptcy of the public finances that might originate from insolvency of the pension system' (Mikhalev, 1996, p.21) through far-reaching pensions privatisation. Sensibly, however, CEE state elites have so far studiously eschewed Chilean-style solutions to their own Latin American-style pension financing and sustainability problems. First, it has long been recognised that it was Chile's uniquely large budgetary surpluses that initially bankrolled, and the authoritarian Pinochet regime that drove, that country's successful transition from a state PAYG pension regime to its present system of fully funded mandatory private provision. Second, it is still unclear as to whether the successes commonly credited to the often vaunted Chilean private pension funds, the AFPs - notably a spectacular rise in the rate of savings and comparably rapid development of the stock market - are actually the cause or simply an effect of economic growth in general and of financial system deepening in particular.

It is now rather widely argued that the rise in aggregate savings was not simply the outcome of pension reform, but was also crucially dependent on the general soundness of the government's fiscal policies (Heinrich, 1997, p.41). More specifically, a 1996 report from Merrill Lynch fundamentally questioned the previously accepted wisdom that the AFPs had been central to the virtual doubling of Chile's savings rate that occurred between the early 1980s and the mid-1990s. In practice, the report argued, high corporate savings combined with consistently high economic growth rates accounted for the great bulk of the 13 percent rise in domestic savings recorded to 1995, leaving the AFPs responsible for a mere 2 percent of the savings rate increase (Mark, 1996, p.6). In short growth caused savings, rather than pension savings causing growth, as had previously often been assumed. Similarly, it is important to put the role of the AFPs in the development of Chilean capital markets into a comparably revisionist perspective. Once again it is clear that causal sequences are far from straightforwardly unidirectional, indicating that the parallel upward developmental trajectories of the AFPs and the Chilean stock market clearly involves considerable causal circularity. The same point pertains in relation to bond markets dominated by government paper.

In essence, financial system development appears to have driven AFP development at least as clearly as pension fund expansion has contributed to financial system deepening. Of particular significance to the transition economies is the place of Chilean equities in AFP portfolios. After almost a decade and a half of mandatory pension fund operation stocks comprised less than 30 percent of AFP investment portfolios whilst government bonds continued to form slightly over 40 percent of fund holdings. Moreover, almost 70 percent of equity investment remained concentrated in 5 electric power and telecommunications companies. This situation underlines not only the centrality of initial privatisation offerings to AFP equity investment expansion but also the very limited diversification of investment holdings that had occurred, leaving AFPs highly vulnerable to the inevitable market downturns of 1995-1996 that followed thirteen years of high returns.

Other worrying features are consistently high administrative costs and what has been termed the increasingly 'spotty coverage' of a system theoretically incorporating virtually all workers. Marketing costs alone are running at 15 percent of total AFP costs on some estimates, encouraging what has been termed 'a phenomenal turnover rate' of almost 25 percent of customers annually, yet without significant impact on the more than 40 percent of the 5 million fund affiliates who are in arrears, including 1.5 million who have made no contributions for over a year. Adding these factors to the evaluative equation helps to explain why Imogen Mark describes the AFPs as 'fêted abroad' but 'maligned at home', and, crucially, why most Chileans trust neither the AFPs nor the free market thinking that justifies them too unquestioningly. As opinion surveys underline, the AFPs are ranked by Chileans 'well below banks, public notaries and even stockbrokers on a scale of well-thought of institutions' (Mark, 1996, p.6). The one clear implication of the Chilean case of radical pension reform, therefore, is that it exhibits few unambiguously positive lessons for policy makers across the transition states.

Furthermore, excessive donor and policy-maker attention focused on Latin American models of private sector-led pension reform may have been one contributory factor in explaining why significant opportunities for effectively maximising the strategic possibilities for synergy between privatisation and pension restructuring agendas have so far largely been missed. Given the deep-seated and widespread political resistance across the transition states to proposals for the type of fundamental pension system restructuring required to move towards Latin American style private provider dominant, fully funded, pension systems, whether in its original, Chilean, guise or in the modified, Argentinean, format, the prioritisation and sequencing of enterprise privatisation ahead of pension reform was, in practice, made inevitable. In turn, the prioritised sequencing of enterprise privatisation ahead of enterprise restructuring became similarly inevitable in the context of very limited sources and comparably constrained amounts of investment funding available to transition governments. Although there were debates in the transition states over the sequencing of the privatisation process, the option of rehabilitation prior to privatisation was not considered feasible. In practice, 'given the past failures of state ownership and the large number of firms to be privatised, the usual decision was to try to sell the firms quickly, even with antiquated capital, redundant workers and poor financial prospects' (Brada, 1996, p.70).

Nor was the option of rehabilitation prior to privatisation deemed particularly desirable: 'In the early 1990s, many observers argued that the state-owned enterprises that dominated industry ... could not be reformed save through privatisation' (Brada, 1996, p.79). Consequently, in contrast to privatisations undertaken in the UK and elsewhere, 'Eastern European governments decided to privatize firms before restructuring them and to let the new, private owners lead the process of structural change' (Matesova, 1995, p.368). Current World Bank thinking turns this choice into a preferred policy sequence, overtly recommending that enterprise restructuring should follow rather than precede privatisation and placing explicit faith in the capacities of private sectors, not least financial intermediaries such as pension funds, to provide, alongside foreign investors, requisite investment funding.

In turn, this strategy for policy sequencing reflects the World Bank's continuing faith in its assumption that financial intermediaries, notably mandatory private pension funds, have been an important independent variable both in Chilean financial sector strengthening and in overall economic growth sequences. However, there is certainly no evidence from the transition economies that prospects for either financial sector deepening or post-privatisation enterprise restructuring have been enhanced by the activities of existing, admittedly limited in size and scope and predominantly voluntary in form, private pension sectors. The current situation, as defined by the EBRD, is that capital markets and their supporting institutions are only weakly developed and are characteristically poorly regulated across the transition states, whilst banking systems tend to remain at 'an intermediate stage of development' (EBRD, 1996, p.99), thereby imposing strict contextual limitations on the scope and potential for the development of contractual savings institutions such as private pension funds. Accordingly, the present position in relation to both financial system development and to the restructuring of enterprises across the countries of CEE is empirically clear-cut, if not exactly uniform between states: both remain highly problematic 'second-generation issues in transition'. Specifically, it is now conventional wisdom to acknowledge 'how deeply the problems in the financial sector affected transition' (Bruno, 1995, p.383), just as it is universally acknowledged that 'the restructuring of state-owned and formerly state-owned enterprises is one of the most important steps in economic transition' (Matesova, 1995, p.367).

Progress across both issues remains painfully slow in most of the economies of CEE. Despite the rapid march of privatisation across a few of the transition states, notably the Czech Republic, and despite the widespread emergence of private financial intermediaries, including, in a number of countries, private pension funds, relatively limited restructuring of individual enterprises, let alone of industrial sectors or whole economies, has occurred to date. Interestingly, and contrary to expectations, restructuring has not progressed much faster among already privatised entities than in their state-owned counterparts. In practice, 'especially in former Czechoslovakia, Hungary and Poland, after some initial hesitation, many state-owned enterprises have responded quite flexibly' to the demands and challenges of market economies (Brada, 1996, p.79), showing adaptive capacities not originally anticipated. Unexpectedly, there is now identifiable evidence of some autonomous 'restructuring by state-owned enterprises' in the major CEE states, underlining Josef Brada's finding that 'systematic differences between privatized and unprivatized state-owned enterprises are difficult to uncover' (Brada, 1996, p.81). However, progress on all remaining economic transition fronts is far from rapid. As Stanley Fischer summarises succinctly: 'It is surprising how slowly privatization has advanced in most economies, and how slowly restructuring has taken place in the Czech Republic' (Fischer, 1996, p.382).

The consequences of the reform prioritisation and sequencing choices outlined above - prioritising the privatisation of industry ahead of pension reform and sequencing privatisation ahead of enterprise rehabilitation and restructuring - are not insignificant in terms of the policy options that have been excluded. In particular, potential opportunities provided by partial or full transitions to fully funded pension systems for financially underpinning strategically planned programmes of infrastructural, sectoral or enterprise restructuring via carefully targeted investments - surely integral elements in any comprehensive privatisation process - have so far been pre-empted and most of the key issues involved have largely been ignored. 'Contractual savings have received relatively little attention so far in the discussion of the transition towards market economies', the EBRD points out, despite their 'significant potential to contribute both directly and indirectly to progress in transition', not least in relation 'to the development of local capital markets and the institutions which support them' (1996, p.100).

Specifically, all mandatory fully funded pension systems, whether publicly or privately managed, generate huge quantities of savings very quickly, potentially capable of amassing funds at a rate of 2 percent of GDP per annum (Reisen, 1997, p.1181), thereby supplying vast amounts of investment capital albeit with variable consequential growth impacts dependent on investment efficiency. Either or both privately and publicly managed contractual savings institutions may invest these huge sums efficiently and effectively, just as both public and private fund managers will be constrained by their requirements for efficient financial sectors and developed financial market institutional infrastructures to ensure productive channelling, and subsequent oversight, of invested funds (Heinrich, 1997, pp.41-42). In this sense, at least, the EBRD is right in advocating caution in actively promoting private contractual savings sectors. 'A significant role for contractual savings belongs to more advanced stages of transition rather than earlier ones', the EBRD suggests (1996, p.100) with considerable logical force.

In the absence of 'an adequate regulatory system, an efficient capital market, and a well-trained cadre of managers and administrators' - the IMF's 'preconditions for a revamping of the pension system' (IMF Survey, 1994, p.303) - it is also prudent to be comparably cautious about the prospects for successful public or state management of funded pension systems among a number of the states in CEE. For example, such a stated degree of caution would appear highly appropriate in relation to the proposed Macedonian reforms. The limited administrative capacities of many of the existing national social security institutions, not least their complete unfamiliarity with the complex issues related to the effective management of funded provision, at best, constitute important constraints on the possibilities for implementing successful transitions from PAYG schemes. Nevertheless, a sound case can be still be made for the initial prioritisation of publicly managed schemes, particularly if democratic accountability can temporarily substitute as regulatory arrangements are developed. This case mainly rests on the overriding investment needs of the transition states. Specifically, the public management of contractual savings, involving possibilities for exercising direct control over very large investment programmes, offers potentially significant advantages to transition states, if the obvious problems related to successful fund management can be circumvented. Creatively exercised, state control over both strategic investment priorities and specific targets provides at least some prospect, if no firm guarantee, of focusing financial resources on the type of fundamental economic restructuring currently required across the transition economies. From this perspective, and if implemented as envisaged, the proposals for pension reform involving the retention of state control over the funded second pillar in Macedonia will deserve close attention.

Furthermore, the state, at least in principle, has a particular incentive to evaluate the social impacts and potential wider implications of major investment decisions. In this respect the state has a potential comparative advantage over private financial intermediaries in terms of the capacity to balance requirements to meet economic targets and maximise investment returns against the equally pressing need to pay attention to the social goals and wider impacts of large-scale investment programmes. Conversely, if economic restructuring through targeted investment strategies is to serve social as well as economic purposes, it is important to underline the inherent limitations of private provision, as underlined by the Chilean case.[4] 'While some foreign observers tout the Chilean example as a perfect and finished model, many Chilean employees are looking for qualitative transformations in its *modus operandi* aimed at promoting social goals and spreading benefits more evenly' (Fazio and Riesco, 1997, p.100). Such Latin American examples, centred on the investment performance of private pension funds in a rapidly growing economy, simply underline the unclear and uncertain economic restructuring potentialities of mandatory private contractual savings schemes operating in quite different economic, political and social contexts. Indeed, in the search for appropriate examples of infrastructural, enterprise and sectoral restructuring, funded by mandatory retirement savings schemes and achieved within strategically conceived, effectively targeted and socially responsive investment programmes, Southeast Asian institutional and policy precedents, based firmly on state control and management of mandatory contractual savings sectors, are, in practice, far more directly relevant.

As policy-makers in potentially the largest transition economy of all, China, have already recognised, the significant possibilities offered by continued state control over strategic investment programmes are lost if pensions systems are funded but privately provided. This explains the close interest taken by Chinese policy-makers in two well established Southeast Asian cases of administratively simple and inexpensive, yet also state-controlled and fully pre-funded, savings and retirement provision systems, the National Provident Funds (NPFs) of Malaysia and Singapore. Specifically it is the proven capacity of these NPFs, the Employees' Provident Fund (EPF) of Malaysia and the Central Provident Fund (CPF) of Singapore, to provide funding for a creative combination of economically and socially targeted state projects which has cemented this Southeast Asian mechanism for mandatory savings and retirement provision into integral elements of successful developmental states characterised by high levels of trust in government.

In turn, it is this successful pedigree, not least the apparent capacity of NPFs to continue simultaneously to meet governmental investment requirements and to satisfy a cultural preference for flexibility in retirement savings provision, which both explains continued Chinese interest and warrants wider policy-maker consideration across the other transition states. Accordingly, these are important issues which demand greater analysis, issues which we will address in detail in Chapter 5. To cite Georges Heinrich, once more, '[a]n optimally designed old age pension system should fulfil the dual purpose of protecting the old from income insecurity and being an engine of economic growth' (Heinrich, 1997, p.56). Funded systems, private and public alike, will, if properly managed, serve both purposes adequately. Only public management, however, offers the potential for achieving truly creative synergy between them, particularly in the twin contexts, typical of the transition states, of weak financial sectors and pressing needs for large investment programmes to serve both economic and social purposes.

Conclusion: Towards Realism?

It is increasingly clear that renewed interest in the overt linkage of SOE privatisation strategies with private pensions promotion policies and/or with smoothing the transition towards full pre-funding of existing state PAYG schemes, does not indicate any real evidence of, or even prospects for, the emergence of a more strategic approach to achieving implementational synergy between pension system restructuring and enterprise reform programmes. In practice, as evidenced by the Polish pension reforms discussed above, the linkages between pensions reform and privatisation can best be defined in terms of an essentially tactical marriage of convenience. In turn, this policy linkage can be viewed, from a World Bank perspective, as a chance to make up for previously 'missed opportunities for pension reform' (Fox, 1995, p.36), or, from a policy-maker perspective, as largely designed and intended primarily to speed up the unfinished business of pensions reform.

Moreover, even when renewed policy-maker interest in exploiting the potentialities and opportunities for interaction between private pension provision and accelerated SOE privatisations represents genuinely strategic thinking, current policy sequencing and implementational priorities seem significantly misplaced, most particularly in their focus on the prioritised stimulation of the private pensions sector; a strategy now increasingly involving mandatory allocations of significant percentages of payroll tax revenues to mainly inexperienced, previously under-capitalised, and widely under-regulated private pension providers. Yet, as outlined above, the available evidence in favour of this strategic choice, largely based on the Chilean case, is far from clear-cut in its implications. In practice, as argued above, it is realistic to anticipate that even mandatory requirements for worker affiliation to private pension schemes may neither prove to be the magic ingredient for ensuring rapid financial system deepening nor provide the guaranteed impetus to coherent private sector development that is expected.

Although the World Bank continues to remain publicly bullish about its model of 'pillared' pension reform, it is already obvious that implementation has been much slower than the Bank would have wished. Where implementation has occurred, it is already obvious that expected positive synergies have not been forthcoming. As a recently published Bank paper underlined in relation to post-reform developments across the ten or so countries in Latin America and among the transition states that implemented 'radical' pension reforms in the 1990s, the performance of private pension funds has been particularly disappointing in terms of their equity market impacts.

> Although the reform programs are promising and pension funds are growing fast in all reforming countries, their total assets are mostly less than 5 percent of GDP and their quantitative impact on the development of equity markets is small.
>
> Vittas, 2000, p.9

Bluntly, as noted recently by the EBRD, and addressed below in greater detail in Chapter 8, governments have been the primary beneficiaries of any improved financial intermediation stemming from the development of either mandatory or voluntary NSPF sectors (EBRD, 1999, pp.93-94). This development is not simply unsurprising but essentially inevitable given existing weaknesses in capital markets in CEE and NIS/FSU. In this respect, the Chilean precedent should have provided advanced warning that, in the short to medium term, pension fund privatisations do not stimulate equity markets, even when, as in the Chilean case discussed above, initial public offerings (IPOs) of privatised utilities are allocated to pension funds. In the specific CEE and NIS/FSU context of fiscal imbalance, the process of mandatory privatisation of pensions leads inexorably towards government security issues to fund transitional costs.

Equally inevitably, in a context of low stock market liquidity and high market volatility the privatised funds will actively seek to buy government paper, responding both to typical institutional herding instincts and to government expectations. Overall, stimulation of NSPF sectors, either on a voluntary or mandatory basis, will not rapidly or easily lead to the anticipated goal of financial sector deepening via equity market development. In practice, financial sector development requires prior attention to banking sector weaknesses and the acceptance that existing bank-based financial systems are here to stay. Implicitly, at least, financial institutions such as the EBRD are coming to terms with this fact, as indicated by the disinterest of the decennial *Transition Report* in non-bank financial intermediaries (EBRD, 1999).

Both the 'outgrowing' and the 'in-built' strategies described above may therefore be seen as inherently self-limiting. Where funds remain voluntary, even in the 'best case' of the Czech Republic, the take up of private pensions is limited by generally low incomes across the transition economies. Even exceptionally generous government subsidisation of NSPF sectors via favourable tax provisions leads only to limited commitment of funds spread thinly across many contributors. As of 1999, Czech funds equated to only 1.3 percent of GDP, despite achieving labour force coverage approaching 40 percent (EBRD, 1999, p.211). This leads to a wider problem since low income workers must continue to rely primarily on state benefits for old age retirement provision.

Similarly, where NSPFs have been mandatorily implemented, the continuing importance of the existing state system of pension provision has been underlined by the immediate fiscal impact of reduced contributions to state schemes that must continue to support the bulk of old age pensioners into the foreseeable future. The fiscal deficits that resulted in the partial suspension of the Hungarian pension reform described above underline the point that radical programmes of mandatory pensions privatisations cannot easily be implemented rapidly even in the stronger economies of CEE under present fiscal circumstances. As such, Poland constitutes a special case where pre-pension reform fiscal deficits were comparatively modest and where financial liquidity is sufficient to envisage a successful pensions privatisation in line with 'Chilean' expectations. Finally, even in Poland, inflation currently running into double digits threatens to undermine returns to NSPF investments, further underlining the point that success is likely to remain relative. From this perspective, therefore, might these currently dominant responses to the unfinished business of pensions reform and enterprise restructuring be more appropriately viewed as indicative of 'opportunities lost', not least in relation to their likely limitations as mechanisms for stimulating some strategic synergy between these key elements within on-going economic reform programmes?

In terms of the wider concerns of this book, and in relation to the key lessons to be drawn from the experience of the transition economies, what is perhaps most marked is the seemingly poor, better partial, use to which available comparative evidence has been put by the Bank and others who have espoused the pensions privatisation agenda. As indicated above, and as further underlined in Chaper 8, Latin American, especially Chilean, 'lessons' have been overstated and substantially misused in support of the 'in-built' strategy of mandatory privatisation within pillared systems. Comparably useful perspectives on the inherent limitations of 'outgrowing' strategies of voluntary pension system pluralisation in DCs, based on the seminal, and highly instructive, case of South Africa were also available and well known to the Bank but appear to have been little utilised in forming its approaches to pension system restructuring in transition economies. Further empirical information and analytical perspectives on the South(ern) African case(s) are contained in Chapters 6, 7 and 8 below.

At this point it is important simply to indicate that, on the one hand, the South African case, confirms that large, socially responsible, well managed, often highly innovative and appropriately regulated private pensions sectors with a heavy equity bias can emerge and develop in a DC, albeit a significantly atypical one, even without the legal impetus of mandatory status. Nevertheless, on the other hand, the evolution of the private contractual savings sector in South Africa provides no really clear evidence of the type of immediate stimulative capital market and financial sector development impacts anticipated by the Bank, rather underlining the value of large domestic institutional investors as a stabilising force within financial systems and the wider economy over the longer term. In performing this function under the apartheid regime, South Africa's private pension funds were clearly crucial elements in government economic strategies, albeit with their state-determined 'buy and hold' domestic equity focus as strategic investors leading inexorably to 'a less than stellar investment performance' (Vittas, 2000, p.14). Overall, what the South African case highlighted, and more recent 'radical' pension reforms continue to reaffirm, is that 'pension reform and the development of pension funds and other institutional investors is one of the longest of "long cuts" in development. The benefits for workers and the economy take long to materialize ...' (Vittas, 2000, p.18). In Chapter 5 we look in more detail at the welfare and developmental impacts of 'mandatory' or 'forced' contractual savings systems operated, as NPFs, under state management.

Notes

1. The Visegrad countries are the Czech Republic, Poland, Hungary, and the Slovak Republic.
2. As the pension mis-selling scandal in the United Kingdom amply demonstrates, a lack of popular trust in financial service sectors, and in private pension providers in particular, is not a problem restricted to emerging markets but may also occur in developed and, purportedly, well regulated markets as well. The cost of the pension mis-selling scandal in the UK, has been variably estimated at somewhere between £15 and £20 billion.
3. The Kazakhstan system is of interest due to the existence of a publicly-run defined contribution pension fund, the State Accumulation Fund (SAF), which operates alongside privately-run funds as part of the reformed pension system. Initially, 85 percent of contributors to the reformed Kazakh system 'opted' to remain in the public fund in preference to private alternatives (see Orenstein, 1999, as cited in Müller, 2000c, p.29). Currently, 53.1 percent of contributors remain in the SAF (Andrews, 2000, p.28). The *Financial Times* reported that the value of assets held by the Kazakhstan pension system in 2000 equated to 4 percent of GDP (Stern, 2000).
4. Legislation enacted in 2000 has sought to improve the *modus operandi* of the Chilean system by seeking to reduce the high degree of investment risk borne by individual AFP members. The ISSA has reported that, from March 2000, new 'Second Funds' are available for Chilean AFP affiliates. These 'Second Funds' have been designed, in particular, for scheme members approaching retirement. The investment of these 'Second Funds' will be permitted only in fixed interest securities. The rationale underlying this development is clearly to protect the retirement savings of individuals approaching retirement from the potentially deleterious impact of severe market volatility (ISSA, 2000b, p.5).

5 The National Provident Fund Model: Epitaph or Evolution?

Introduction: Restating the NPF Model

Within the burgeoning literature on pension reform, with its emphasis upon perceived global problems and its assumption of the need for global solutions, evaluation of the potential relevance of the National Provident Fund (NPF) remains a significantly under-researched element. Moreover, despite the relatively large bibliography directly and indirectly addressing many of the crucial aspects of the comparative political economy of the NPF over its roughly half century of history from gestation to its current degree of maturity, this absence of recent attention is consistent with earlier tendencies towards somewhat patchy and often partial coverage of this topic. This incomplete picture of the NPF model has, as suggested briefly in the introduction to Chapter 4, often focused on the comparative institutional and welfare weaknesses of this particular form of old age social security provision; a perspective leading to its generalised characterisation as the 'enfant terrible of social security' (Dixon, 1989b).

A full explanation of the somewhat curious gaps in our knowledge of this still-important, if also inherently limited, mode of retirement provision would require an essay in the sociology of knowledge that itself remains unwritten and will not be attempted here. However, it is important to preface this more defined study by stressing the point that successively fashionable and dominant analytical perspectives on appropriate modes of delivering retirement provision have tended to underestimate, often to denigrate, the importance of the NPF model by consistently ignoring the welfare relevance of its wider, albeit indirectly achieved, potentialities as a development finance institution. Indeed, assessments of the NPF tend to remain essentially frozen in their time-frame, largely viewing the model as, first, a crude predecessor of social insurance, providing its affiliates with a

129

simple lump-sum payment on reaching the age of retirement, and largely ignoring more recently exhibited capacities to deliver annuities as well as established capacities to provide for the financing of housing, health, education, insurance and for the purchase of an increasingly wide range of financial assets. Second, NPFs are widely accepted as 'important financial institutions ... for mobilising savings' (Dixon, 1982, p.325) without any significant appreciation of the extent to which such savings can, within overall state developmental strategies, add significantly to welfare outcomes and avoid the need for excessive, and unpopular, tax burdens. What is also missing from the picture is the appreciation that the evolving essence of the NPF model relates to the potential for significant synergy between its twin elements, leading in the medium term to a capacity for achieving enhanced welfare outcomes that, as a totality, are far more significant than the simple sum of the NPF's two 'parts' might superficially indicate.

The NPF model, therefore, can be seen as dynamic, albeit still based on the two elements identified above; namely an administratively uncomplicated mechanism for delivering a limited range of retirement provision and a savings institution with significant potential for indirect utilisation in pursuit of welfare-enhancing outcomes. Unsurprisingly, this model has continued simultaneously to prosper in practice, albeit in a limited number of states, at the same time as it has been marginalised in pensions/retirement system theory. Bluntly, full analytical consideration and appreciation of the potentialities of NPFs in appropriate political economies has tended to be precluded largely *a priori*, by virtue of their apparently perennial failure to achieve 'politically correct' status within the lexicon of best practice in the organisation and delivery of retirement provision.

Accordingly, without any pretensions of comprehensiveness and with due recognition of the many gaps in the historical and contemporary record that remain to be filled, this chapter seeks to identify and to highlight some key elements in the comparative, and historical, political economy of the NPF in order more appropriately to define the place of this model of retirement provision in both comparative pensions practice and in its wider role in relation to broader welfare efforts and outcomes. This analysis is undertaken in order to serve two specific purposes. First, the chapter seeks to establish why organisations for retirement provision defined initially as temporary stop-gaps have remained the preferred choice of a number of the most economically dynamic states in the contemporary world. Second, the chapter seeks, albeit tentatively, to indicate the wider relevance of the NPF model for other middle income countries (MICs) with pension systems in transition. Currently, such countries tend to be offered, what is commonly referred to as, pillared options for pension/retirement provision that include, as one potential pillar, the principle of fully funded defined contribution systems provided on a provident fund basis, but, ironically, also tend to exclude the idea of state management of, or public monopoly over, such schemes.

Diffusion and the Process of Social Security Adoption

Diffusion from one country, or from one group of countries, to another has tended to play as significant a part in the global spread of the component elements of social security systems as have more strictly internal, intrastate, factors and pressures. Similarly important inter-state dimensions and influences were of crucial relevance in securing the initial inauguration, and often in determining the subsequent fate, of NPFs. Equally clearly, it is unproductive, as well as frequently technically impossible, to fully penetrate the interactions of internal and external elements in terms of precisely determining their respective roles and effects within causal and developmental sequences. For example, in the case of the spread of social security systems based on insurance principles, and leading into modern welfare states, it is clear that it was a complex combination of internal developments and external influences that determined both form and timing of institutional innovations, rather than a simple case of 'prerequisites versus diffusion' (Collier and Messick, 1975, pp.1299-1315).

Specifically, the initial inauguration of social security institutions based on social insurance principles in successive countries followed a clear-cut pattern from their initial development in the late 19th century and early 20th century up to the watershed of the Second World War. This involved diffusion down a hierarchy of modernisation: spreading from the richer states of Europe downwards, in relation to the international distribution of wealth and industrial development, as well as geographically outwards to reach the South via the Latin American states. In this diffusion sequence the role of the International Labour Organisation (ILO) was, from its foundation, clearly crucial in establishing institutional and behavioural norms and standards and in securing their international dissemination through a two stage process aptly described as 'international standardisation and technical assistance' by Vladimir Rys. The ILO, on the one hand, defined the establishment of international standards 'as one of its foremost tasks', and, on the other hand, significantly influenced the implementation of these standards through its technical assistance programmes which themselves contained 'a strong element of standardisation' (Rys, 1964, p.30).

Further diffusion of social security institutions, however, was effectively precluded until well into the post-war era by the colonial status of the rest of the countries of the South, and, crucially, by the widely accepted view that the absence of industrial development across most of the developing countries (DCs) made the inauguration of insurance based social security systems economically and administratively unfeasible. In short, an absence of the requisite developmental preconditions was deemed to preclude the possibility for the early inauguration of western-style welfare states, tax financed with defined benefits, across the rest of the South in the immediate post-war period. Nevertheless, in an era of late colonialism in which, as today, the concept of 'good government' was overtly espoused it became increasingly obvious that social welfare and social development issues had been seriously neglected in pre-war colonial policy. Accordingly, initially, for the UK at least, in relation to its South and Southeast Asian colonies scheduled for early, or relatively early, post-war independence, the immediate problem became one of providing, within existing very tight budgetary constraints, at least minimal standards of welfare provision, particularly on retirement, for workers, especially civil servants, facing an increasingly uncertain future.

The Institutional Development and Early Evolution of the NPF Model

It was as a direct result of this reassessment of social policy in the late colonial period that the NPF evolved and spread in a process that parallels that of other retirement systems in its combination of internal elements and external dimensions (see Table 5.1). Although many key documents relevant to the early historical evolution of the NPF remain largely unexamined both in the archives of the Colonial Office and in other relevant national archives, the broad outlines, and some significant details, of the key decision processes, can be found in the available secondary literature. These are most conveniently, and comprehensively, summarised in Alec Parrott's *The Iron Road to Social Security* (1985). At the same time,

Table 5.1 Chronology and Evolution of the NPF Model

Country	Commenced	Terminated	Replacement
Malaysia	1951	-	-
Indonesia	1951	-	-
India	1952	-	-
Singapore	1953	-	-
Egypt	1955	1959	SIPS
Iraq	1956	1971	SIPS
Thailand	1956	Enacted not	but Implemented
Sri Lanka	1958	-	-
Nigeria	1961	1994	SIPS
Nepal	1962	-	-
Tanzania	1964	1997	SIPS
Kenya	1965	-	-
Zambia	1965	2000	SIPS
Ghana	1965	1991	SIPS
Fiji	1966	-	-
Uganda	1967	-	-
St Kitts and Nevis	1968	1977	SIPS
Grenada	1969	1983	SIPS
St Lucia	1970	1978	SIPS
Antigua	1970	1972	SIPS
Seychelles	1971	1979	SIPS
Dominica	1971	1975	SIPS
Samoa	1972	-	-
St Vincent and Grenadines	1972	1986	SIPS
Montserrat	1972	1986	SIPS
Solomon Islands	1973	-	-
Swaziland	1974	-	-
Kiribati	1976	-	-
Tuvalu	1979	-	-
Papua New Guinea	1980	-	-
Gambia	1981	-	-
Vanuatu	1986	-	-
Yemen	1987	-	-

Key: SIPS: Social Insurance Pension System

Parrott's assertion that there was no conclusive evidence of an actively 'co-ordinated policy' (Parrott, 1985, p.136) strategy pursued by the British colonial authorities in favour of the inauguration of NPFs in appropriate colonies, is, if technically correct, at least somewhat misleading over the importance of the forces pushing for this system of retirement protection from within, and between, British colonial administrations.

In particular, what the rather patchy distribution of National Provident Funds across the UK's colonies, later ex-colonies, indicates rather nicely is the significantly decentralised nature of Colonial Office policy-making. This, in distinct contrast to the highly centralised processes characteristic of French colonialism, allowed considerable discretion to local administrators as individuals and considerable policy making autonomy to local administrations as collective entities. This autonomy, in turn, led both to inter and intra-regional variations in policy emphasis over social welfare provision. As Parrott rightly asserts, '[p]rovident funds on a national scale ... originated in Asia', rather than in Whitehall. No centrally determined policy was involved and assumptions 'that the British exported the system from their own domestic legislation' would be completely misleading - the Friendly and Mutual Assistance Societies of the mid-19th century were in terminal decline by the end of the Second World War (Parrott, 1968, pp.530-557). Regional diffusion, however, was correspondingly vital, and the widespread vitality of private provident funds in the colonies themselves, notably India and Malaya, was a further predisposing factor, as was, it must be stressed, pressure from London to avoid the expense and administrative complexity of establishing social insurance schemes *ab initio*.

Accordingly, the inauguration and patterning of NPFs exhibits a distinctly different type of inter-colony diffusion than, for example, that exemplified by the adoption of social insurance schemes across the board in the francophone colonies. Thus, from the mid-1960s the UK's larger West Indian colonies were allowed to opt directly for social insurance schemes leaving the smaller colonies with NPFs, if only 'as a first step towards the eventual introduction of schemes based on social insurance' (Jenkins, 1981, p.633). Similarly, in spite of the fact that it was initially debates over appropriate retirement provision for Indian workers that led to the original enthusiasm for the inauguration of compulsory provident funds as an affordable, second-best, solution for the Southeast Asian and Pacific colonies, the actual implementation of the NPF model in India, fragmented in form and far from comprehensive in reach, differed significantly from the highly centralised systems, singular in form and genuinely national in scope, adopted elsewhere in the region.

Most important, whilst the international diffusion of the social insurance model exhibited the important standardising effects of welfare norms driven by an international institution, the ILO, the more limited, originally distinctly UK colony focused, spread of the NPF model reflected the important impact of individual experts, initially in the form of Colonial Office administrators and advisors, in both inaugurating initial adoptions and ensuring subsequent convergent trends. Malaysian legislation, at one level, shaped the NPFs of Fiji and Singapore, but, at a deeper level, it was the movement of managerial and advisory personnel between the Funds in their early years that ensured further continuities and commonalities in administrative practice. Institutionalised originally in the form of the ISSA's Committee on Provident Funds, and subsequently renamed in 1998 the Technical Commission for Provident Funds and Allied Schemes, what Rys terms 'the international co-operation factor' has remained of crucial importance not simply to the survival but also to the adaptive development of the NPF model. Defined by Rys as playing a key role in the 'international co-operation of institutions and bodies charged with ... administration at the national level' (Rys, 1964, p.31) of all types of social security regime, the ISSA has had a specific impact in crystallising NPF administrations into coherent professional organisations with distinct identities and aims; not the least of which is a mutual interest in acting as national and international pressure groups dedicated to the defence of the NPF model.

International solidarity among NPF administrators has been particularly important given the continuing, if often rather implicit antipathy of the ILO to the NPF model as an immature and inadequate form of social security for retirement. Crystallised into the adoption of ILO Social Security (Minimum Standards) Convention No. 102 in 1952, this hostility centred on the fundamental inconsistency between a lump sum payment and the central requirement of pension insurance, namely to ensure that 'the benefits specified shall be granted throughout the contingency'. As Parrott rightly underlines, '[o]ne very influential factor' in ensuring the comparatively restricted distribution of NPFs across Asia into the 1980s and beyond, 'has been the discouraging attitude of the ILO' (Parrott, 1985, p.143). Similar conclusions can be drawn from the abandonment of the NPF model by many of its original adopters, comprehensively and collectively in the Caribbean, and increasingly among African states.

Nevertheless, ILO hostility in principle has always been tempered by realism in practice, based on the recognition that the financial problems that precluded the initial establishment of tax-financed social insurance in India and Malaya were both reproduced, and further compounded by, serious administrative weaknesses in, for example, many of the African colonies. As a result the fact that the NPF model, initially, in terms of the collection and allocation of contributions to individual accounts, 'involves simple mechanics' ensured implicit, sometimes explicit, ILO recognition of the continuing need, originally accepted in the Indian case, for realism to override desirability in many specific cases. For example, it was an ILO mission to Tanzania, newly independent in 1961, that concluded that 'general conditions ... ruled out any thought of even establishing a simplified social insurance program' (Rohrlich, 1968, p.195), explicitly opting for an NPF on the grounds that 'a true social insurance program ... entails a far greater administrative and financial engagement than does a program of the pre-insurance type, such as a provident fund' (Rohrlich, 1968, pp.194-195). Appropriately it was a 1990 report compiled by ILO officials which ultimately set in motion the recent transformation of the Tanzanian NPF into a social insurance scheme.

For the majority of NPFs the ILO's scepticism about the worth of the model as a form of retirement provision has proved to be prescient, a point enlarged upon in Chapter 6 below. Continuing administrative weaknesses, widespread political manipulation and simple corruption remain characteristic of at least some of the still operating African examples, as the World Bank was at considerable pains to demonstrate in *Averting*, using, somewhat self-servingly and selectively, the example of the Zambian NPF prior to its recent reform. Macroeconomic circumstances of high inflation have compounded politico-administrative inefficiency and predation. Consequently, even where affiliates' cumulative funds remain substantially intact in nominal terms their real value is often negligible. The ILO's alternative, however, has, in practice fared little better in recent years in a context of widespread global depression and ideological fashions that have become distinctly anti-welfare. As the case of the similarly bankrupted Latin American social insurance schemes has amply underlined, macroeconomic, particularly inflationary, pressures very quickly undermine first funded and then pay-as-you-go (PAYG) social insurance systems as government budgets come under increasing pressure.

In a wider, global, perspective the World Bank's demographically-focused identification of an incipient 'old age crisis' has similarly suggested the long-term unsustainability of unreformed PAYG social insurance systems even among the wealthy states of the OECD as their implicit pensions debt, already high as a result of welfare state entitlements and benefit expansion, mounts exponentially with an ageing population.

Pension Systems and Economic Growth

As the World Bank rightly emphasises, what the burgeoning global pensions funding 'crisis' underlines is the simple fact that all pensions systems, advanced and complex or crude and simple, are ultimately dependent on the health and growth of the wider economy to sustain them. 'Over the long haul the only way to reduce poverty is to foster economic growth ...' (World Bank, 1996, p.84). Consequently, what Drèze and Sen defined as two alternative strategies for the provision (the necessarily largely public provision in both cases, it must be stressed, according to Drèze and Sen) of social security, 'growth-mediated' on the one hand, and 'support-led' on the other, can both be seen as conditional on some guarantee of continued economic growth. Although they define the key difference between the two approaches as lying 'in the fact that the countries that have made substantial use of the strategy of support-led security have not waited to grow rich before resorting to large-scale public support to guarantee certain basic capabilities', it is clear that realism and the economic bottom line demands an appreciation of the underlying, and ultimate, 'complementarities' between the two emphases if pension expenditure is to stay within appropriate, affordable, budgetary limits (Drèze and Sen, 1989, p.39). Specifically - extending an argument made recently by the World Bank in relation to the 'transition economies' of the central and eastern European (CEE) and the newly independent states (NIS) formed following the collapse of the USSR - '[t]he first and central element of pension reform ... is ensuring that public pension spending is compatible with economic growth' (World Bank, 1996, p.82).

    This focus on the importance of economic growth, in turn, forms a significant element in the increasingly 'common vision' adopted by the Bretton Woods institutions on the one hand, and the ILO·on the other (Gopinath, 1994, p.695). 'There appears to be growing similarity, though not identity, of fundamental objectives. Thus, the IMF speaks of 'high-quality growth'; the Bank refers to 'sustainable growth'; and the ILO urges 'equitable growth" (Gopinath, 1994, p.699). Significantly, despite these 'differences of nuance' the practical outcome has been an interesting convergence of advice from the multilateral institutions, World Bank and the ILO alike, on the desirability of 'pillared' or 'tiered' systems of pension provision, thereby spreading the risks of supporting the growing numbers of those in retirement among a variety of institutionalised arrangements, funded and unfunded, defined benefit and defined contribution, and, in the case of the ILO, at least, potentially to be delivered either by public or private mechanisms. In long term perspective, of course, such pillared systems suffer from the inherent limitation of all existing mechanisms - however funded and however benefits are defined and delivered - for providing pensions: their ultimate dependence on (preferably full) formal sector employment for providing sustainable funding. Into the medium term, however, the palliative relevance of what the Bank terms the 'multipillar' approach is undeniable.

The crucial short and medium term issue becomes, therefore, the decision as to precisely what form pillared or multipillar pension provision should take for particular countries or groups of countries. Here the most significant point is that options available in principle can be excluded from reform discussions and agendas if they fall outside the purview of the Geneva and Washington institutions that collectively act as gatekeepers in brokering reform proposals into reform programmes. This, in practice, is the fate of the NPF, exemplified by the effective exclusion of the NPF model form the World Bank's developed version of its global multipillar future presented in *Averting the Old Age Crisis* (World Bank, 1994), as well as from its even more recent consideration of appropriate pension delivery options for the 'transition' states (World Bank, 1996). Here the preferred model remains the Chilean AFP system; provident funds, but not NPFs, which are privately managed on a competitive and decentralised basis. Significantly, as highlighted in Chapter 2, the earlier more balanced Bank approach, exemplified by Dimitri Vittas' advocacy of *Swiss Chilanpore*, has now disappeared (Vittas, 1993a). Aiming to combine the strengths, while at the same time avoiding the weaknesses, of the Swiss, Chilean and Singaporean pension systems, Vittas' proposed model placed heavy reliance on fully funded defined contribution schemes based on provident fund principles, but without excluding the administrative economies of scale only achievable through direct state control.

As Vittas argued elsewhere, in a formulation of pension reform options for Tunisia, the most desirable form of management for savings schemes based on individual capitalisation accounts is one that involves a 'minimisation of operating costs and a maximisation of investment returns'. These aims, in turn, mandate 'a public agency for registering affiliates, collecting contributions and paying pensions' in order to maximise administrative efficiency and effectiveness whilst retaining operational economy. Growth of fund assets, in turn, does not demand, the World Bank's later assumptions, privatisation or the abandonment of the NPF principle. On the contrary it may simply involve 'farming out the investment of accumulated funds to professional fund managers subject to clearly set out rules and guidelines' (Vittas, 1993b, p.31). as, significantly, has since been acknowledged, and is progressively to be implemented, by the Singaporean Central Provident Fund (CPF), and the Malaysian Employees' Provident Fund (EPF), and which more recently has also been 'accepted in principle' by the Government of India (Singh, 2000, p.31). Moreover, the Bank's continuing across-the-board insistence on the virtues of private sector fund managers fails to acknowledge a growing professionalism amongst public servants in fund management, competencies which will act to complement the role played by, and enhance capacities for quality control over, outside fund managers (Ghaffar, 2000, pp.99-100).

Unquestionably, binding investment restrictions, originally common to all NPFs, leading to an excessive accumulation of government instruments is, arguably, a disincentive to balanced capital market development. Financial deepening, in the form of private financial sector expansion, is, albeit again arguably, similarly discouraged by the crowding out effect of a very large NPF. At the same time it is important to remember that government securities are characteristically bought in very large quantities by private provident funds, as, for example, in the case of the Chilean AFPs. The regulations in Chile stipulate that investment in government securities should not be less than 35 percent and no more than 50 percent. However, current figures suggest that at present these account, on average, for a total of about 40 percent of AFP investments. In most cases private provident funds are statutorily obliged to purchase large quantities of government stock. Botswana's provident funds are in principle committed, for example, to the principle of investing up to 55 percent of their affiliates' contributions in government securities if ministerially required so to do.

Accordingly, the most important investment relaxation, at least from the perspective of the NPF's affiliates and ultimate beneficiaries, is the capacity to invest at least minimally offshore; a capacity now conceded for Singapore and Malaysia and long recognised, although, in practice, limited to the protection of funds during the immediate aftermath of the 1987 military coup, by Fiji. In fact, until the end of 1997, the 'entire investment portfolio' of the Fiji NPF (FNPF) 'was invested in the local economy' and around three quarters of all assets were placed in government or quasi-government securities (ISSA, 1999c, p.48). Since 1997, only a minimal figure of around 2 percent of FNPF assets have been placed with offshore investment funds. In Vanuatu a combination of factors, such as a weak domestic economy, a shortage of suitable domestic investment opportunities and widespread public dissatisfaction with the operational performance of the fund, have encouraged moves which may lead to the investment of VNPF assets outwith the country. A similar set of circumstances in Papua New Guinea (PNG) may lead the government towards similar policy conclusions, including the likelihood of the introduction of 'competitive management' for the PNG NPF (Holzmann *et al.*, 2000, Annex B8, p.3).

As in many other respects, it is the CPF, although indirectly, which provides the clearest case of the creative utilisation of the capacity to invest offshore, albeit with the returns from these investments accruing mainly to the Government of Singapore rather than to individual affiliates. As Vittas and Michelitsch explain,

> the government of Singapore has refrained from investing all the funds in local development projects but has accumulated a substantial pool of foreign exchange reserves, which has grown to exceed the total balances of the CPF. Thus, the CPF effectively operates as a compulsory national mutual fund, investing indirectly in foreign assets through the government of Singapore Investment Corporation and the Monetary Authority of Singapore (including equities and direct investments in large mining and other projects) on behalf of Singaporean households.
>
> 1996, pp.268-269

The trend towards at least some degree of offshore investment is likely to strengthen into the future as NPFs share good practice in making risk-spreading investment decisions. It is important also to underline the validity of the often-used accusation against NPFs that investment rationality via portfolio diversification can be and often is undermined by politically motivated investment strategies. Nevertheless, there is growing evidence that it is becoming both more difficult and more dangerous for states to try to hide either poor management or corrupt behaviour within NPFs. Specifically, governments across the developing countries are finding it increasingly difficult to hide problematic NPFs from public view. For example, in recent years, the Ugandan NPF has been an almost continuous object of press speculation, leading to parliamentary investigations, legal cases and on-going investigation by the Inspector General of Government. Similarly, the Vanuatu NPF is struggling at present to rebuild some semblance of credibility in the eyes of its own membership. As a consequence of a recent report by the Ombudsman, which confirmed the fact that there had been political interference in the creation, and then allocation, of housing loans disbursed by the VNPF, an ensuing riot resulted in the complete destruction of the VNPF building on 12 January 1998.

Moreover, the capacity to invest abroad only partly addresses the anomaly, particularly glaring in the case of Singapore, of low real rates of interest paid to beneficiaries (averaging 2.02 percent for the CPF 1960-1990, but climbing more recently to around 4 percent) when the government bonds placed with the Monetary Authority of Singapore (MAS) and the Government of Singapore Investment Corporation - the institutions that took the 'investment decisions that matter' - were earning far higher real rates of return from investment in foreign equities (Vittas, 1993a, pp.9-13). The crucial additional requirement becomes an increasing degree of transparency in disclosing the investment strategies and outcomes for individual NPFs. In this respect Singapore is highly atypical in the degree to which the government has been able to control both information and public reactions. Nevertheless, even in this unusual case it is noticeable that, as indicated above, interest paid on CPF accounts has quietly doubled over the last decade as the government has responded cannily to the dissatisfaction recorded by academic researchers who provided survey evidence that broad satisfaction with the CPF as principle and institution existed alongside significant dissatisfaction with the low rates of return earned on CPF accounts (Chen, Wong, and Chiang, 1997, pp.1-16). Even in Singapore, in the wake of the recent financial turmoil, the Peoples' Action Party (PAP) government has faced increased calls for greater transparency in government decision making and policy over issues affecting those on low incomes including policy relating to CPF contributions. Unsurprisingly, across states with considerably less capacity to control either information or dissent than Singapore's, further positive trends can be observed, often from countries with previously disastrous investment records. Such trends are particularly noticeable in SSA as NPFs respond to pressures for transparency engendered by moves towards democratisation and liberalisation of economies. Inevitably, progress is slow and problematic given the high inflation rates that have further undermined already poor investment performance by SSA NPFs. The Quarterly Journal of the Tanzanian NSSF (NSSF, 1998, p.4) puts the point across carefully;

> Even though the funds contributed to the Provident Fund were to be invested prudentially so as to ensure payment of high interest, in an inflationary situation they lose much of their purchasing power before they ultimately emerge as benefits.

Nevertheless, where structural adjustment programmes (SAPs) have allowed specific SSA countries to address the problems of poor investment strategies and high inflation, improved performance from NPFs is clearly feasible, allowing more easily for transparency. The best example here has been set by the Gambia, albeit with an NPF established only in 1981 thereby avoiding some of the many years of penal inflation that have plagued other SSA NPFs established in the post-independence years. As the Board Secretary of the Social Security and Housing Finance Corporation of The Gambia has claimed,

> There is nothing more desirable in the operations of a social security scheme than transparency. Workers' funds must be managed in the most transparent manner. SSHFC has put in place public relations techniques to ensure transparency in all its operations.
>
> Gaye, 1994

Importantly, in the Gambian case 'statements of account are issued to members on an annual basis' (Gaye, 1994, p.9). Similar highlighting of the centrality of transparency is exhibited in the Tanzanian case, albeit accompanying an organisational restructuring from an NPF system to one based upon social insurance principles. In Tanzania the National Social Security Fund has taken a keen interest in publicising itself and its investment strategies across a wide range of media and involving a detailed public listing of investments and performance.

The NPF Model: Welfare and Economic Outcomes

The case for incorporating the NPF model into multipillar options, however, cannot simply rest on their universally acknowledged potential to deliver low cost administration, or even on their newly assumed capacities for in-house fund management or, more commonly, to harness the fund management capacities of professionals sufficiently competent to provide increased rates of return and expanded benefits for affiliates. After all, the survival to date of most of the extant examples of NPFs can be better explained in terms of administrative inertia than by reference to their achievement of any recognisable effectiveness and efficiency criteria as pension systems. Conversely, among NPFs the 'success stories', Malaysia, Singapore and, most recently, Fiji and the Gambia are the exceptions, not the rule. This indicates that it is important to establish not simply that NPFs can be operated efficiently and effectively as pension systems in rapidly growing economies, but, more positively, to seek to establish that the NPFs themselves contributed identifiably and significantly to the achievement of economic growth sequences. This wider economic impact is most clearly identifiable in the Singapore case where the CPF has been overtly and consistently utilised as a mechanism for macroeconomic stabilisation and for the retention of international competitiveness. Where deemed necessary, the ruling PAP government has prioritised economic over welfare criteria in setting contribution levels to the CPF which are consistent with the perceived needs of the Singapore economy at a particular juncture.

Most recently, but based upon a longstanding policy strategy which has used the contribution rate to the CPF as 'an instrument of macroeconomic stabilisation - increasing the contribution to compress aggregate demand and reducing it to during recessionary times' (Rao, 1998, p.683), employer contribution rates to the CPF were cut by 50 percent from 1 January 1999 in the aftermath of the regional financial crash. Accordingly, for a period, contribution rates stood at 30 percent of covered wages (20 percent and 10 percent for employees and employers respectively). It was envisaged that this reduced contribution rate would be enforced for an initial period of two years to allow macroeconomic stability to return to the Singapore economy. Official announcements stated that the macroeconomic motivation for the cut was to reduce employers' costs, encourage employment and promote export competitiveness (ISSA, 1999a, p.12). An improving macroeconomic environment has now enabled the

Singaporean authorities to increase employers' CPF contributions to 16 percent of covered wages. Regardless of this recent further adjustment in employers' contribution rates, it is axiomatic that this policy decision, overall, has proportionately disadvantaged lower wage earning groups by threatening their retirement savings.

It is in relation to housing that the influence of the CPF has been most obvious in relation to both its economic and its social impacts. Unsurprisingly, there is an extensive literature on these matters, obviating the need for detailed discussion here (see, *inter alia*, Sandilands, 1992; Asher, 1999). John Wong provides a useful summary, specifically noting how 'Singapore's housing system is linked to the saving-investment process of ... Singapore's economy' via the CPF (1992, p.466). At an early stage in Singapore's development, 'public housing, like education, was considered a productive social investment, which can increase the competitiveness of Singapore's labour force in attracting foreign investment', providing an economic justification for the channelling of CPF funds into housing development. Housing investments, in turn, served social purposes. 'The second aspect of public housing is the way that it has been used as an instrument for implementing government social policy' (Wong, 1992, p.466). Overall, therefore, '[t]he CPF fulfils a multiplicity of goals and functions'. Its pool of savings has enabled 'the government to mobilise domestic savings for infrastructural development'. Accordingly, '[i]ts economic function cannot be doubted'. Similarly, '[w]ithout such [a] source of cheap funding, the government would not have succeeded in its massive public housing programme. So it is also a social investment' (Wong, 1992, p.471).

In the Malaysian case, the evidence for the significance of the economic impact of the EPF is perhaps best described as persuasive, rather than conclusive, as some key points readily indicate. First, as the inauguration of the initial NPF, the Malaysian EPF, rapidly underlined, the potentiality of mandatory or contractual savings institutions for generating investment funds extremely quickly is significant, particularly if fund coverage is wide and contribution rates are relatively high. In Malaysia the impact of the EPF was all the more marked since previously it had been considered that the 'scope for raising domestic loan finance was ... negligible' (Edwards, 1970, p.259). Second, contractual savings institutions operating on forced savings principles may, or may not - the evidence is inconclusive - influence aggregate savings upwards, but they do more certainly determine a marked shift in the balance of savings from short to long term uses. Accordingly, the inauguration of an NPF may not have a positive impact on the quantity of savings: it will certainly have a potentially important impact on the quality of savings. Third, the sheer size of potential NPF balances are such as to allow governments to finance development strategies of considerable ambition. EPF balances, for example, have represented approximately 40 percent of GDP since the 1980s and equated to 47 percent by 1996: after a decade of operation the EPF already held 50 percent of domestic debt. In the case of the Singaporean CPF the figure is higher: 56 percent of GDP in 1996 after having fallen from nearly 80 percent of GDP in 1992. Clearly, the autonomy and financial options this concessionary largesse offers to governments can be, and sometimes is, misused.

Overall, therefore, EPF funds can be seen to have significantly underpinned the operations of the Malaysian developmental state, specifically providing the 'monetary magic' that allowed the implementation of the government's long term development strategy (Hicks, 1959, p.179). Similar points can be made even more forcefully in relation to the Singaporean CPF, although as a city state it provides a model less clearly relevant to the concerns of most other countries than its near neighbour. As described above, the savings accrued by the CPF have been, on a consistent basis, invested indirectly in the government's Development Fund, which in its turn has financed extensive infrastructural investments, not least in welfare-related items such as housing and urban development (Sandilands, 1992, pp.128-130). CPF balances, in turn, in a pattern quickly copied by Malaysia, were directly used by affiliates to buy government, and after 1981, private housing. By 1990 more than 90 percent of Singaporeans owned their own homes. Similar extension of CPF services provide health care loans, health care insurance, dependants' insurance, home insurance, preferential access to investments, and loans for higher education. Over recent years, withdrawals from the CPF for housing, medical and education expenditures have been averaging approximately 11 percent of GDP (Rao, 1998, p.683) - a huge sum that would otherwise have been reflected in public expenditure patterns.

This characteristic pattern of on-going benefit expansion and incremental improvement has tended, over time, to blunt at least some of the force of earlier judgements that the main fault of the Asian NPFs was their in-built prioritisation of savings mobilisation over benefit provision. For example, Christine Wallich's comparative analysis of the performance of a number of Asian systems, including Singapore and Malaysia, in relation to the now abandoned Chilean social insurance system, concluded that the former succeeded 'in terms of financial policy' but failed 'on the benefits side' (Wallich, 1983, p.99). Today it is, on the one hand, no longer immediately obvious that simple 'graduation' from NPF to full social insurance is always an appropriate or sustainable pension-enhancement strategy. On the other hand, and more importantly, it is increasingly widely accepted that welfare outcomes cannot simply be inferred from the presence, or absence, of specific welfare instruments or from simply examining direct welfare expenditures in isolation (Gilbert and Moon, 1988, pp.326-340).

Specifically, the high performing Asian economies (HPAEs) in general, and Malaysia and Singapore in particular, come out badly, as serious welfare laggards, if total welfare effort is crudely defined in terms of the instruments used on the basis of levels of direct welfare expenditure. On the one hand NPFs, as with all other mandatory savings schemes both public and private, cannot meet the requirements of ILO Social Security (Minimum Standards) Convention, 1952 (No. 102) on a stand-alone basis because of their inherent benefit limitations (see Appendix, Fig. A2.1). On the other hand, directly budgeted welfare expenditures remain very low in both Malaysia and Singapore, not least because of the respective minimal use in the former and total avoidance in the latter of tax financed social insurance arrangements, facilitated by the expanded opportunities for drawdowns from the respective NPFs for a growing range of covered contingencies. The converse of this situation, of course, is lower taxation requirements, with, for example, Singapore's direct welfare expenditure of around, and in certain years less than, 0.5 percent of its GDP making low taxation demands, at under 20 percent of GDP, possible. Unsurprisingly, therefore, welfare outcomes for both states are far better than crude indicators based on budgeted expenditures would suggest.[1]

Singapore, of course is a special case, with its compactness easing poverty reduction problems. Malaysia, on the other hand, is a much more typically structured DC and its achievements in terms of welfare outcomes provide important and often salutary lessons concerning the importance of defining welfare effort widely, incorporating indirect as well as direct contributions to eventual welfare outcomes. In particular, one significant outcome of the Malaysian government's mandatory savings based investment strategy has been a notable reduction in hard-core poverty. The fact that this effect emerged mainly as an indirect product of strategic efforts to boost economic growth through employment stimulation should not be ignored. However, it should also be duly recognised that, from a comparatively early stage in its post-independence history, Malaysian government investments have had 'a more significant impact on the individual ... than in most other countries of Asia apart from the centrally planned economies and Japan' (Edwards, 1970, p.32).

If welfare outcomes are used to define welfare effort both Malaysia and Singapore can be defined as relatively high achievers with definably 'growth-mediated' social welfare strategies. Within these strategies the respective NPFs have played crucial roles in determining these positive outcomes. The recognition that these crude, low cost, welfare instruments could have such marked indirect effects on welfare outcomes was, no doubt, only gradually attained. Initial government borrowing from the funds simply reflected the absence of alternative domestic and international sources of investable capital. Nevertheless, it is important to stress that these indirect, developmental, uses of the NPF were not a colonial but a properly Asian invention; implemented only after the departure of colonial administrations. Consequently, it was the firm appreciation of both the Malaysian and Singaporean governments that their respective NPFs had rapidly become central to the successful implementation of their respective development strategies that stiffened their resistance to ILO-led efforts to encourage upgrading to social insurance schemes. Retrospectively this resistance can now more clearly be seen to have a basis in both welfare and economic logics.

Singapore and Malaysia: Continuity and Change

Regardless of the consistent criticism levelled at the NPF model, both from outwith but also from within societies operating the NPF model, the respective post-independence development trajectories of Singapore and Malaysia remain of particular relevance to aspirant developing countries currently actively seeking to create a similar degree of development synergy within their respective national pension systems and national economies. Clearly, Singapore and Malaysia provide the best documented cases of the positive outcomes associated with the (generally) successful public sector management and investment of national retirement fund assets. In both these cases significant beneficial social and economic developmental outcomes have been achieved through the state management and investment of the substantial assets of each country's respective NPF.

Although relatively high contribution rates have unquestionably contributed to successful outcomes, a significant factor in the success of the funds has been the overall effectiveness of the public management of the huge volume of assets generated by these contractual savings institutions.

This model of social security provision, nonetheless, remains contentious and consistently attracts criticism from both sides of the ideological spectrum. Thus, criticism comes, on one hand, from market-orientated detractors who challenge the general principle of the public management of pension fund assets and, on the other hand, from those critical of the inherently limited levels of welfare provision given to NPF affiliates. Specifically, the former critics focus on perceived investment performance shortfalls in comparison with, largely hypothetical, commercial alternatives. the latter critics challenge the absence both of the principle of social insurance and the 'explicit' inter- and intra-generational income redistribution which this principle is intended to confer. Objectively, both criticisms are at least partially apt. In response the Singapore government would automatically disregard what it defines as the views of euro-centric or, worse, euro-socialist detractors of this model of retirement income provision, finding some support for its positive views in surveys of the personal attitudes of Singaporeans towards the CPF. These revealed that '(c)lose to half-half (46.5 percent) of the respondents are either satisfied or very satisfied' with the wider welfare outcomes provided by the savings institution (Chen *et al.*, 1997, p.8). Pragmatically, and characteristically, recent reforms inaugurated by the Government of Singapore indicate tacit acceptance of the validity of central elements in both types of criticism.

In recognition of the evolving financial needs of NPF affiliates, the long-term solvency needs of the Funds, and the increasing political risk associated with a continuing state monopoly over the considerable assets of their respective funds, the authorities in Malaysia and Singapore have begun to liberalise their effective control over elements of fund investment. In accordance with continued economic development and a growing level of sophistication within local capital markets, authorities in both Singapore and Malaysia have relaxed investment controls of their respective NPF assets and now permit portions to be managed by licenced private sector fund management companies (McNulty, 1998, p.4; Cooke, 1995, p.8). No less important to these decisions was a growing level of dissatisfaction amongst wealthier NPF affiliates who realised that personal investment opportunities in the developing national capital markets offered the potential of earning higher yields on invested assets than the nominal annual interest rates credited to their personal accounts by their respective NPF institution. Ironically, this 'middle-class' dissatisfaction with the levels of flat-rate state-mandated nominal interest rates credited to personal accounts has disclosed that the NPF model inadvertently permits a small degree of 'implicit' progressive intra-generational wealth redistribution from high earners to very low earners which has not hereto been widely recognised. Notably, a small progressive effect stems from the awarding of nominal interest rates. This, albeit marginally, is a feature absent from overtly regressive private pension funds, such as the Chilean AFPs, where accounts are debited and credited on a more purely 'market' determined basis which in practice favours those with large savings at crucial points, including the purchase of annuities. In theory, the minimum income guarantee provided in Chile to the elderly with insufficient or no retirement income fulfils a similar progressive redistributive function. In practice, as explained more fully in Chapter 7, the availability of a minimum social assistance pension in Chile disguises the fact that the take-up rate is artificially capped by arbitrary numerical ceilings set by the government.

With regards to the liberalisation of NPF investment opportunities, the Singaporean authorities have consistently been more imaginative than their Malaysian counterparts. On one hand, this may reflect the now enormous, indeed unwieldy, size of the Singaporean fund while, on the other hand, it may be more reflective of the Malaysian government's continuing need for cheap long-term investment capital to finance government debt. For instance, as recently as 1995 only 9 percent of EPF funds were invested in stocks (Cooke, 1995, p.8). This relatively low figure of EPF investments placed in shares has, nonetheless, since grown. By 1997, Malaysia had appointed around 30 private fund management companies to invest 'up to 15 percent' (Cooke, 1997, p.8) of the EPF's assets in the local capital market. The motivation for this change appeared to be geared largely towards the twin goals of reducing the political risk associated with monopolistic control over the EPF's not inconsiderable assets and to help promote Kuala Lumpur's position as a contender for a role as one of Southeast Asia's major financial centres.

No less importantly, however, individual EPF affiliates are likely to view these developments in fund management liberalisation positively. To date, EPF fund managers, while producing consistent moderate returns above their own minimum accepted level of 3.0 percent and in some years considerably better, have fallen short of achieving the higher investment yields produced by private fund managers in the UK or the USA. Anecdotal evidence suggests that 'non-Malay' fund managers believe ardently that they could wipe the floor with their Malaysian counterparts, a view, one suspects, officials within the EPF Management Investment Committee are likely to strongly contest. Nonetheless, this point is suitably highlighted by the fact that the City of London has produced average returns of 12 percent a year in real terms on UK equities since 1979 (Riley, 1999a, p.1). Market growth in the USA has been even more pronounced with the American equity market having produced average returns totalling 18.4 percent since 1990 (Hale, 1999, p.20). Nonetheless, and despite the impressive yield figures from the USA and the UK, the Malaysian government is determined that only Malaysian-based foreign fund management companies will be invited to tender for contracts to handle the developing investment programme of the EPF.

In the case of Singapore, where affiliate fund withdrawal rights are more liberal than in Malaysia, the right of fund members to invest portions of personal CPF accounts has proven to be highly popular. By the early 1990s, this had reached such proportions that 'withdrawals for investment exploded to 52 percent of all withdrawals' (Sherraden, 1997a, p.38) taken from CPF accounts. Despite the popularity amongst affiliates for withdrawals made for investment purposes, this option creates further potential risks for the individual and may ultimately prove detrimental to final retirement income. Even prior to the recent Asian financial market instability, it had been suggested that a significant '79.3 percent of CPF members who had used CPF investment schemes suffered losses' (Chen *et al.*, 1998, p.135). As Davis has drily observed, and a view which has wider implications for all countries considering encouraging greater individual responsibility for the provision of retirement income, '(t)his is a sobering illustration of the capabilities of individuals to manage long term investments' (Davis, 1999, Section 6). It must be assumed that, in the aftermath of the Asian financial crisis, this figure is now over 90 percent of CPF affiliates. Regardless of the more liberalised investment policies of the Singaporean NPF, both the CPF and the EPF in Malaysia would have found it very difficult to avoid poor investment returns in 1998. Simply stated, 'public provident funds have been hit hard by collapsing stock markets' (Hemming, 1999, p.22).

In contrast to the reported high levels of satisfaction of Singaporeans, in Malaysia there is apparently a higher degree of public criticism regarding what is now more readily, and openly, perceived to be the state manipulation of NPF assets. The Malaysian academic Jomo has been characteristically forthright in his assertion that the Malaysian middle-classes are 'increasingly outraged about having to pay for the sins and follies of the super-rich with government controlled funds', including EPF assets, 'being diverted to bail out the politically well-connected' (Jomo, 1998, p.1569). In respect of more practical welfare issues and, importantly, in the wake of unprecedented economic turmoil, Jomo portrays ordinary EPF affiliates as becoming increasingly disenchanted by 'another year of yet lower returns' on the invested assets of their personal retirement savings. A large part, if not all, of the blame for this poor investment performance is placed at the feet of government following the decision to allow EPF assets to be used as part of the emergency package designed to help stabilise the national economy in the wake of the recent financial crisis. There is clear evidence that the EPF, 'by far the largest fund in the country' (Cooke, 1995, p.8), played a direct strategic role by intervening to prevent a potential free fall of Malaysian stock market values. Despite substantial losses on the Kuala Lumpur stock exchange, it has been reported that following 'concerted buying by state pension funds' (Kynge, 1997a, p.1), that stock prices responded positively. Considering the pre-eminence of the value of its investible assets, it is likely that this refers predominantly to the activities of the EPF.

Another controversial issue for opponents of NPFs which emanates directly from the state control over investment decisions is the fact that government may decide 'the rate of return on savings to be paid in any given year to contributors of the provident fund, independent of the actual return on the portfolio' (Heller, 1998, p.10). This has apparently always been the case in both Malaysia and Singapore. In Singapore, for instance, 'there is often a difference between the Singapore dollar nominal return on reserves and the nominal interest rate actually paid on the CPF balances of contributors' (Heller, 1998, p.10, fn.9). Accordingly, it is partially misleading to state, as has been suggested, that 'CPF savings are completely tax exempt, both at the time of deposit and withdrawal' (Sherraden, 1997a, p.38). As Chen and Wong outline, the present rate of interest 'credited to members CPF accounts is about 4 percent' (Chen and Wong, 1998, p.135), and is thus above the statutory minimum rate of return of 2.5 percent. Indications suggest that the real rate of interest gained by CPF investments are, at least, closer to 6 percent.

When one considers, on one hand, the level of secrecy which has traditionally surrounded much of the investment policy of the CPF Board and, on the other hand, also consider the more widely known fact that Singapore holds enormous foreign currency reserves, it seems more than likely that the given figure of around 6 percent for the real rate of return on CPF assets investments may prove to be highly conservative. Although the actual level of the real rate of return on CPF investment remains open to conjecture, the official discrepancy between real interest rates earned and the nominal interest rates credited to CPF accounts can best be considered as a significant 'implicit tax' (Heller, 1998, p.10, fn.9). Indeed, using the above cited figures for real investment returns earned and nominal interest credited, the level of the implicit tax on investment returns (capital gains tax) approximates to over 30 percent. It is somewhat perplexing that, on one hand, the lack of disclosure within the CPF prevents independent validation of these figures while, on the other hand, this lack of transparency protects the CPF Board from having to acknowledge that this indeed may be the case. As Asher has stated, although it is 'believed' that the government controlled investment of CPF assets are placed 'predominantly abroad' there is no available information regarding either 'the investment portfolio or the returns obtained' (Asher, 1996, p.92).

One clear indication that personal CPF retirement accounts may be being credited with substantially reduced levels of interest can be drawn from comparing these rates from the levels of interests credited to personal Medishield Fund accounts. The Medishield Scheme is a voluntary 'catastrophic event' health insurance fund which supplements the Medisave scheme, the compulsory health care insurance element of the CPF system. Mukul Asher has shed some light on this issue with the telling observation that, '[i]n 1993 the implicit rate of return on Medishield Fund was 6.7 percent, considerably higher than the rate of return paid on members' funds of 2.5 percent' (Asher, 1996, p.92). Although these insurance funds are managed by institutional fund managers, this alone cannot explain the significant difference in rates of return achieved by these funds and the CPF managed assets. This observation is supported by the fact that the asset value of the 'insurance' funds remain significantly smaller than those held by the CPF fund managers. According to Asher, in 1993 the combined market value of assets within Singapore's three 'insurance schemes', the Home Protection Insurance Scheme, the Dependent's Protection Insurance Scheme and Medishield, was S$142.6 million while CPF personal fund assets in 1994 equated to a staggering S$57 billion (Asher, 1996, p.92). Since 1994 the value of CPF assets has grown considerably, reaching around S$80 billion by 1999 (Luce, 1999a, p.4).

'Future Directions': Ways Forward for NPFs?

Putting to one side the relative success, or otherwise, of specific NPFs, there is a great deal of policy-focused discussion both within and between NPF administrations regarding the 'future direction' (ISSA, 1999c) of NPFs as retirement savings institutions. At its most fundamental, this internal debate is questioning the future relevance of the NPF model itself, a situation which is reminiscent of the confident assumptions of impermanence discussed at an earlier stage in this chapter. Unsurprisingly, the long-standing debate over the future role for NPFs is mirrored by suggestions that the, recently renamed, ISSA Technical Commission for Provident Funds and Allied Schemes may be wound up sometime after its next timetabled meeting at the ISSA 27th General Assembly to be held in Stockholm in 2001. Specifically, the legislative bills approving the transformation of the NPF's of Tanzania and Zambia into social insurance based National Social Security Funds, and some strong indications that Swaziland's NPF is likely to follow a similar reform path can be viewed as indicative of the inexorable decline of the African NPF (this is an issue which we return to in Chapter 6). The reform of the Ugandan NPF is also anticipated, although there are recent indications that the reforms may seek to introduce an element of private sector involvement in parallel with social insurance provision.

Further abandonments amongst African states of existing NPFs would reduce membership of the 'Commission' to less than ten countries. It is increasingly accepted that such a loss of critical mass in membership would render unsustainable a continuing role for the Commission. In the longer term, Kenya has also stated its intent to reform its much maligned NPF, underlining the point that regional trends towards abandonment are likely to be cumulative. Significantly, there is growing speculation that the eventual reforms to be undertaken in Kenya will favour strongly the promotion of non-public provision. As indicated by the ISSA's whole approach to NPFs, the likelihood of the progressive demise of this particular model of social protection has always been held as an expected eventuality. This is a view largely confirmed by the fact that the 'Committee' was never accorded the title of 'Permanent' by the ISSA General Assembly.[2]

Nevertheless, the possible disappearance of the 'Commission' does not auger, at least in the short to medium term, the disappearance of the NPF model in practice. Interestingly, even in Africa where the NPF model is portrayed as being in terminal decline, it is still possible to find evidence of continuing support for this form of state mandated retirement savings institution. As a senior representative of the Ugandan NPF recently argued (ISSA, 1999c, p.105),

> Provident funds have not become obsolete, at least in the eyes of the members themselves. Moreover, not all the problems associated with provident funds are inherent in their structures. Solutions could be sought to improve these systems.

The irony of this strong statement, emanating from the representative of an NPF whose reform has been on the table since 1994, is glaring, specifically underlining the point that African governments may well deviate from, or ignore, consultancy advice from external sources. A further point of importance to be taken from the above statement lies in the fact that it identifies an important populist reason why the NPF model in general has proven to be more enduring than was originally envisaged. Specifically, the lump sum, although negatively viewed by the Geneva institutions, continues to be popular in low income countries where the concept of retirement as a terminal work-free condition is not an option available to many. Lump sums are characteristically invested in income generating projects such as retail outlets and form the basis for work and income generating projects well into old age. Similarly, in states such as Singapore, moving from middle to high income status, the lump sum is now increasingly commonly utilised to purchase an annuity. In 1993, over 5000 annuity policies were in force. By 1996, this figure was approaching 11000 annuity policies and well over 2000 new policies were being purchased annually (Chen and Wong, 1998, p.125 Table 1.4).

In Africa the Social Security and Housing Finance Corporation (SSHFC) of Gambia provides a noteworthy working example of a successful and institutionally stable African NPF, albeit one founded sufficiently recently to have avoided many of the post-independence problems facing its continental counterparts and to be able to learn from examples of good NPF practice in Asia. Designed *ab initio* as a composite institution comprising a traditional NPF retirement saving scheme for private sector employees, a federated pension fund covering mainly employees in the public sector, a housing finance fund, and an Industrial Injuries Compensation Scheme, the Gambian SSHFC is increasingly recognised positively as a '(s)hining light in African social security' (Cooke,

1992, p.10). As the Gambia illustrates, under effective management African NPFs can evolve into effective social welfare institutions, further underlining the point that lack of success across NPFs outside the Asia-Pacific region is not preordained. The effectiveness of the Gambian SSHFC is demonstrated not only by its institutional transparency but also by its successful management of fund assets. As a published profile of the Gambia has highlighted, in the early 1990s, 'the investment return, net of administrative expenses, was 14.5 percent compared with estimated salary increases and inflation of 6 percent' (Cooke, 1992, p.10). Nevertheless, significant problems face most existing NPFs.

One of the most intractable issues for DCs, including the Gambia where NPF membership remains pitifully low, centres upon how to expand the coverage of the formally employed sector characteristically provided for under NPF schemes to incorporate a greater percentage of the national workforce. Specifically, the central problem is the need to expand coverage to those who remain outside the regulated waged economy either in the informal sector or engaged in a self-employed capacity, notably in farming. In principle, the coverage problem for NPFs is greater than that for PAYG schemes which have largely or completely lost any specific connection between insurance contributions and pension benefits. However, as 'pre-Chile' Latin America underlined, in practice, coverage has been a problem for social insurance pension systems in DCs and, as post-Chile Latin America more recently indicates, remains a problem for 'privatised' systems. Accordingly, the coverage issue remains problematic for both NPF and other systems alike across developing regions. As a possible means of addressing this problem, in Fiji and the Solomon Islands schemes exist permitting informal sector workers to join their respective NPF's on a voluntary basis. Clearly, however, this is an offer which informal sector workers often conclude that it is prudent to refuse.

As discussed more fully in Chapter 7, increasing attention is currently being given to assessing the respective potentialities of a number of social protection schemes designed to improve coverage rates for informal sector workers. Major independent initiatives in this regard are currently being co-ordinated separately under the ILO STEP programme and the ISSA 'Initiative'. The issue of poor coverage provided under conventional social security systems is also a major driving factor in the development of World Bank's 'social risk management' approach to social protection. The wider intention of all these ongoing research programmes is to evaluate alternative mechanisms for social protection provision.

Importantly, responses are being sought which go beyond the largely formalistic responses to low coverage rates and irregularity in contributing which characterise conventional approaches to social security provision.

Over and above these wider DC related social protection issues, the most important current development within the NPF model is a widening trend toward the institution of either limited period or full duration pension schemes to complement the lump sum benefit provided by NPFs. A complex series of factors such as increasing longevity, comparatively low retirement ages, a desire to fulfil the welfare needs of NPF members and the increasingly felt irony that the majority of NPF administrators are members of civil servant pension schemes and not of the NPFs which they administer, collectively have contributed to this trend. The recent development of pension schemes operating alongside some NPFs is significant, especially in the Asian cultural context, and as such should be viewed differently from the optional programme in Singapore, and also in Fiji, for NPF members to purchase an annuity at retirement. The first country to introduce such a complementary pension scheme alongside an NPF was India. In 1995, the Indian authorities reformed the Family Pension Scheme (1971), which provided a limited pension for widows and young children in the event of the death prior to retirement of a member of the Indian EPF. The Family Pension Scheme had been financed through the partial diversion of a small percentage of both the employer and the employee's Indian EPF contribution. The defined benefit social insurance scheme (Employees' Pension Scheme 1995), which replaced the 1971 legislation has expanded the benefit entitlements and, as Kaushik (1997, p.3.) outlines, now

> provides for comprehensive pension coverage to the member as an old-age financial benefit as well as in the event of invalidity and survivorship for the family upon death in any eventuality irrespective of whether the death occurred while in service, away from employment or as a pensioner after superannuation.

In April 1996, the Employees' Provident Fund of Nepal established a limited period pension scheme for its members. On 1 July 1999 Fiji enacted legislation for a gradual reform of the existing annuity scheme which, significantly, also introduced a new pension scheme. In Malaysia, where life expectancy has now attained levels approaching those found in OECD countries, there are indications that the Malaysian EPF may also introduce a pension scheme to complement current contingencies for retirement savings. However, despite facing similar shared problems, and not least with regards to concerns over benefit adequacy, not all NPFs are proposing a partial move towards social insurance. Somewhat predictably, the path towards collectivist and redistributive social insurance now being followed in a number of countries with NPFs continues to be eschewed by Singapore.

A recently published independent actuarial study of the Singaporean CPF has noted that the cumulative effects of drawdown entitlements had contributed to rendering current retirement provision increasingly 'inadequate'. Unsurprisingly, the author of the study was led to conclude that 'other sources of income' are necessary if members are to 'maintain a standard of living comparable with that immediately before retirement' (Lee, 2000, p.44). True to form, the policy response from the Singapore authorities to these, and other similar, critical observations appears to have been shaped by a continuing advocacy of the primacy of individual responsibility. Specifically, growing fears over the more widespread inadequacy of CPF retirement accounts has led to the introduction of a 'tax-effective voluntary retirement program' to supplement the old age protection currently afforded under the CPF. It is envisaged that the new voluntary programme, to be known as the Supplementary Retirement Scheme (SRS), will be introduced sometime during 2001 (IBIS, 2000). With the exception of Singapore, the widening trend towards the introduction of social insurance pension schemes operating in conjunction with the traditional savings component of NPFs should be viewed as a positive development as existing NPFs continue to be expanded, modernised and strengthened. These developments, involving NPFs as elements within pillared provision, are indicative of the continuing evolution, and continuing utility, of the NPF model.

The Regional Expansion of the NPF Approach

It was for a time widely assumed that China would be of pivotal importance to any further regional diffusion of the NPF model in the Asian region. Despite reported comments suggesting that the Chinese authorities have rejected both the Singaporean NPF and the Chilean AFP 'pension' models as 'irrelevant' (White, 1998, p.200) to the needs of the PRC, we would argue that Beijing, nonetheless, has carefully distilled from these two special cases the elements deemed appropriate to the scale and uniqueness of the pension situation in China. Clearly, it would be a mistake to underestimate the complexity of the task faced by the Chinese authorities in implementing 'national' pension system reforms. This situation is highlighted, on one hand, by the disparities in levels of economic development existing between the more developed urban coastal regions and the underdeveloped rural heartland and, on the other hand, by the serious problems of financing current and future pensions provision created by the ongoing restructuration of SOEs and an increasingly ageing society. Pension reform options are further limited by the constraining influence of an underdeveloped financial system.

Accordingly, proposals for the introduction of a three pillar unified pension system, including mandatory second pillar defined contribution pension funds, is likely to involve a predominant role for the state, not least in the management of fund assets. As Stuart Leckie has stated, 'there is still a great deal of groundwork to be done before private fund managers can be permitted to provide their value-added services in the PRC' (Leckie, 1999, p.39). As a consequence, all indications suggest that China is set to establish a pension regime developmentally utilising an adapted version or, more likely, versions of the NPF model, but with all chosen models of pension provision both appropriately adjusted to suit that country's size and regionalised administrative pattern and pillared in line with modern practice. Current trial schemes already under active consideration in the PRC suggest possibilities for regional variations in administrative pattern within a pillared system of pension provision that, nevertheless, prioritises the fundamental NPF principles of full benefit funding under an organisational regime that involves state management of contribution collection and state control over investment strategies.[3]

Reported concerns over both the longer-term financing of a growing public sector deficit and perceived weaknesses amongst a number of China's most important financial institutions are likely to reemphasise to the PRC authorities the developmental logic of retaining state control over the management and investment of second pillar pension fund assets. Although it is inappropriate to apply the term NPF within the context of a multipillar pension system, nonetheless, the underlying logic which has inspired the decision to place state control over the assets of the second pillar funds may be assumed to be more sophisticated than the narrow analysis based upon present financial sector capabilities which Leckie's view mentioned above infers. Clearly, the Chinese authorities, being very familiar with the dual roles of NPFs as uncomplex mandatory retirement savings schemes and sources of relatively cheap long term investment capital, will be nothing less than fully aware of the similar developmental potentialities which access to the long-term funds of mandatory second pillar schemes will confer.

In particular, the access to long-term investment capital which the development of pension funds should provide is central to the attainment of what the World Bank has outlined as one of the Chinese government's main development priorities, the 'faster development of its physical infrastructure' (World Bank, 1997d, p.19). The likely importance of these fund assets to the ongoing pump-priming of infrastructural development is highlighted by the fact that central government revenues in 1998 were reported to have accounted for only 12 percent of GDP (Kynge, 1999, p.4). Ultimately, however, the wider success of all reforms, including those of the pension system, may depend upon the Chinese authorities successfully rooting out the potentially seriously destabilising impact of high levels of endemic bureaucratic corruption. The potential for political risk, which is inherent within all state-run schemes, has been further highlighted in China by reports suggesting that in 1999 Rmb100 billion was 'siphoned off from individual pension accounts to pay for state pension obligations' (Kynge, 2000, p.10). While such desperate measures may be deemed, in the short term, politically expedient, this decision will only partially resolve a funding crisis in pensions provision which, in the longer term, and regardless of systemic reform, threatens to become more acute.

At first glance, the pension system reform undertaken in Hong Kong Special Administrative Region (HKSAR) would appear to be even more directly influenced by the NPF model. Ironically, the introduction of the Hong Kong Mandatory Provident Fund (MPF), 'to commence in the year 2000 or later' (Leckie, 1999, p.72), belies the crucial fact, despite its name, that it is more akin to the mandatory private defined contribution pension schemes commonly associated with Latin America. Indeed, the entitlements to be offered under the MPF look likely to mirror closely aspects of the trend-setting Chilean AFP system, including its modified monopillar format. As is the case in the Chilean monopillar AFP system, it is likely that the old age provision of the Hong Kong MPF will be complemented by a means-tested state guaranteed minimum pension for the poorest. Accordingly, while the MPF may be a 'provident fund' by name, it would be totally inappropriate to categorise the MPF as a 'national' provident fund since competitive private providers may be contracted under both employer and employee mandates leading inevitably to the likelihood of a proliferation of funds. Nonetheless, it should be noted as significant that the MPF proposals designed for Hong Kong reflect, albeit largely on the basis of semantic symbolism, the prominent position that the NPF model holds in the psyche of Asian policy makers. In particular, the use by the HKSAR authorities of the term 'Provident Fund' would suggest a subtle and calculated head-nod to regionally acceptable social security terminology while also avoiding the development of expansive, costly and, from an orthodox Asian-values perspective, undesirably 'welfarist' social security practices as well. Importantly for the future evolution of pensions provision throughout the PRC, the proposed developments in Hong Kong will provide a useful *in vitro* experiment from which Beijing can draw, at a later stage, conclusions regarding the appropriate sequencing and extent of possible private sector involvement in Chinese pensions provision.

Conclusion

The evidence outlined above underlines the point that the choice between social insurance based retirement systems and provident funds should no longer continue to be seen as mutually exclusive. This view is supported by policy developments and proposals from India, Nepal, Fiji and also, albeit still tentatively, Malaysia. Arguably, developments in the PRC would indicate that the Chinese authorities are arriving at policy conclusions regarding the structuring of pensions provisions similar to many of their Asia-Pacific neighbours.[4] Simply stated, the virtues of an NPF can most profitably be maximised by operating in tandem with a primary social insurance pillar, thereby jointly satisfying minimum ILO pension provision standards without sacrificing the developmental advantages of an NPF. Multipillar systems inject short, possibly even medium, term flexibility into the search for appropriate pensions options for specific states and regions facing a variety of complex problems and seeking comparably tailor-made institutional provision to match both existing administrative capacities, public and private, and obvious funding limitations.

Within pillared schemes, as the World Bank rightly emphasises, the principles underlying the provident fund model - full funding and no additional budgetary support on the one hand, and defined contributions rather than defined benefits on the other - remain administratively, economically and actuarially realistic ones for many DCs, but particularly so for those of middle income status with relatively larger formal sectors. What we have sought to stress are the advantages of the NPF as a development finance institution capable of influencing welfare outcomes positively within appropriate government strategies. This developmental role, although perhaps achievable in principle under the type of privatised, decentralised and competitive system of fund administration and management currently advocated by the World Bank on the basis of the Chilean AFP model, is not likely, in practice, to be achieved so parsimoniously in the absence of the strategic capacity for investment coordination and targeting afforded by a centralised NPF.

Notes

1. We are aware of the negative aspects of an expanded menu of drawdown opportunities. As the Geneva institutions have consistently argued, excessive expansion inevitably damages retirement savings prospects. Prior to the economic crisis, the government of Singapore estimated that by 2003 withdrawals for housing and other investments would ensure that many Singaporeans would not have retained the CPF's minimum required balance for retirement purposes of S$80,000 accrued by age 55. These estimates may now be seen as conservative given the 25 percent overall cut in contributions to the CPF mandated from 1 January 1999 which will automatically ensure significantly larger shortfalls in the retirement savings of low income earners.
2. There are nine Permanent Committees which meet at the triannual ISSA General Assembly; Permanent Committee on Old-Age, Invalidity and Survivors' Insurance, Permanent Committee on Family Allowance, Permanent Committee on Insurance Against Employment Accidents and Occupational Diseases, Permanent Committee on Prevention of Occupational Risks, Permanent Committee on Statistical, Actuarial and Financial Studies, Permanent Committee on Unemployment and Insurance and Employment Maintenance, Permanent Committee on Medical Care and Sickness Insurance, Permanent Committee on Mutual Benefit Society, Permanent Committee on Administrative Management, Organisation and Methods.
3. Recent reports suggest that the institution of a 'national' social security fund to cater for the retirement needs of former SOE employees in China is in the pipeline. Significantly, the *Financial Times* report that the new national fund will be headed by Liu Zhongli, the director of the State Economic Restructuring Office, indicating that the fund may be envisaged to fulfil a greater strategic investment role than would be the case if it were under the direct control of the Ministry of Labour and Social Security. Mirroring trends

in other Asian state-run pension funds, the Chinese authorities also envisage utilising the 'selected' talent of private-sector know-how to manage and invest an undisclosed portion of the funds' assets on the stock market (McGregor, 2000, p.12).

4. As recently as 1998, the Philippines' Government was planning to introduce legislation to create a mandatory NPF to complement the existing social insurance pension provided by the Social Security System (SSS) for private sector employees. Elsewhere in the Asia-Pacific region, and although not a Provident Fund by name, Iglesias and Palaçios (2000, p.6) refer to the Employee Trust Fund (ETF) of Brunei as a 'Provident Fund'. Although the ETF operates under the Ministry of Finance as a publicly managed defined contribution 'savings' fund it has not been covered by this survey. Also, it has been reported by an official of the ISSA Secretariat that Tonga has developed plans to introduce a NPF scheme in the very near future.

Part III

Pensions *in* Development: Towards Expanded Options

6 Sub-Saharan Africa: Trends and Issues in Social Protection

Introduction

Bibliographic searches, confirmed by archival research, highlight the fact that both the relevant practitioner and the corresponding academic literatures, whether focused specifically on African 'pension' issues, or on formal social security provision more generally, are significantly less voluminous than those relating to other regions of the developing world. For reasons expanded on below, there has been a relative dearth of in-depth empirical studies on the operational impact of those formal elements of old age support statutorily provided for in SSA. Even basic information concerning the organisational and managerial format of pension systems tends to be in short supply, with even the best placed sources typically providing either dated or even inaccurate information. While these informational problems present a stimulating challenge to academics the negative ramifications for SSA social security administrations are clearly significant, undermining prospects for sharing good practice and avoiding bad. Accordingly, as an essential prelude to the required in-depth studies, one important purpose of this chapter is simply, and briefly, to summarise existing information regarding the current statutory and institutional situation in respect of formal 'old age' and 'retirement' pension provision across SSA.

Inevitably, there is also much that we still have to learn concerning the evolution of formal pension provision across the region before it will become possible to be even minimally confident as to how future, hopefully greatly improved and significantly more widely extended, arrangements may best be organised and managed. Following from this point, therefore, a second central purpose of this chapter is to underline areas where further research is badly needed, either to establish more clearly and precisely how Africa's pension systems have come to be as they are today, or to begin to clarify at least some of the policy and institutional directions in which reformed and reconstructed systems should be encouraged to develop. Chapter 7, in turn, takes up these policy and institutional issues and makes specific proposals designed, expeditiously, to secure universality in provisioning.

In developing these reform proposals, we have sought to be as encompassing as possible in our approach, remaining particularly conscious that much of the contemporary pension reform debate is largely perceived as peripheral or tangential to the central concerns of those focussing on *'Ageing and Development'* issues, whose starting point is, quite rightly, defined by the needs of the elderly people of the South. Specifically, for those academics and development practitioners actively involved in researching, highlighting, and seeking constructively to address the burgeoning sets of problems and crises facing the growing numbers of the elderly poor across the region in the face of limited interest from DC governments, and, largely, from donors, the growing fashionability of pension reform in recent years has often been accorded only a limited welcome. This somewhat lukewarm support for pensions reform as a priority policy agenda for DCs rests on entirely understandable reasoning. First, contemporary pension reform agendas and proposals for DCs are often, correctly, perceived as substantially irrelevant to the immediate, and very real, needs of the great majority of the continent's elderly people. 'Paradoxically, while there has been little interest in older people, there has been a great deal of interest in pensions in the developing countries' (Schulz, 1999, p.87). Second, there is a real, and very understandable, concern that reform of formal systems of provisioning for the elderly will be seen as a 'magic bullet' solution, obviating the need for further or additional interventions in support of the elderly. 'Too often development of formal pension and social security programmes is taken as the single reform agenda for older people. This is problematic' (Heslop, 1999, p.27). We largely concur with both these contentions and substantially accept the logic of the reasoning behind them.

Indeed, what this chapter underlines is that, as currently constituted and operated, many of SSA's formal systems of old age provisioning are demonstrably as much, or more, a part of the problem rather than forming a part of the solution to meeting the material needs of the majority of the region's elderly people who remain both chronically poor and acutely vulnerable to economic shocks. Nevertheless, realism suggests that the focus of the pensions reform debate is unlikely to change, and the impact of its currently dominant pensions privatisation agenda is unlikely to dissipate, at least in the conceivable future. What is needed, therefore, is a realistic and positive response from those academics and NGOs advocating the cause of the elderly in DCs, increasingly seeking to influence this debate rather than to distance themselves from it. Bluntly, influence over future international and national policy agendas is only possible through such positive engagement. Although, ironically, the global pensions reform debate has, to date, generated only limited direct interest in the policy needs of the elderly among the major multilateral donors, and even less interest among the bilaterals, this situation appears to have begun to evolve in more positive directions as the donor community comes under increasing pressure from umbrella NGOs such as HelpAge International (HAI) to move ageing issues up donor and aid policy agendas.

Similarly, positive engagement is also essential if DC governments are to be persuaded to give support to the elderly a higher priority within future policy agendas. Just as 'ageing issues have not been a major concern of leaders in developing nations' in general (Schulz, 1999, p.87), concern for the problems of the elderly remains relatively low on the political agendas of the rulers of most of SSA's states. Sadly, but realistically, it must be recognised that DC governments are more likely to respond only gradually to the pressing needs of the elderly, currently pensionless, poor, remaining more likely to respond immediately to the needs of elite public service pensioners. In this respect it is instructive to discover, in relation to Pakistan but with wider DC resonances,

> what the conference called by the federal government on the Senior Citizens' Day discussed by way of problems of the aged. There was talk of poverty, but only in the context of retired public servants and their meagre pensions. These make up about one percent of the total population of people aged 65, the age when you get promoted as a senior citizen. Did the conference also take into account the millions of the really poor and decrepit, including the ageless *baba* ['old' man] who stands at my street corner silently begging for alms?
>
> Rahman, 2000

Needless to say, the question was rhetorical. Accordingly, the positive value of engagingly positively with the contemporary pensions reform debate is that such a strategy, at least, offers the prospect of raising the profile of the needs of the elderly in relation to international policy agendas, with the distinct likelihood that regional and national agendas will progressively be similarly influenced, always provided that there is both sustained donor pressure for such developments and similarly sustained donor support for resultant institutional and policy changes and adjustments.

The Problem in Context

What we do know, and have known for some time, is that a fundamental and far-reaching reform of the continent's formal systems of old age provision is badly needed, ideally as part of a comprehensive strengthening of social security and welfare systems. As the International Labour Organisation (ILO) has consistently recognised, there is a 'long-standing need for the reform and development of social security in Africa' (ILO, 1994d, p.101), including, not least, its old age support elements. Bluntly, as an ILO official has recently suggested, 'Africa is probably the continent which can provide the most striking example of the failure to meet social security objectives'. Clearly, on the one hand, this situation 'is partly attributable to a range of economic and political factors' (Bailey, 1999, p.7), some of which are not only causally exogenous to the systems of social security in place but also are, to some extent, beyond African control. 'If there is hyper-inflation, political unrest, poor human resource development, insufficient resources to meet basic needs and ineffective communications, it is unsurprising that the social security system does not work as it should' (Bailey, 1997, p.7).

On the other hand, it should also be recognised that some of the major shortcomings in social security protection in Africa are substantially endogenous to both region and system, accepting that many of the observed problems are identifiably 'due to weaknesses in almost every aspect from the design of the schemes to their day to day administration' (Bailey, 1999, p.7). In particular, it is possible to highlight a number of long-standing, fundamental, hence chronic, problems which are common to the continent's systems of social protection, irrespective of the institutional variations we outline below. The ILO has succinctly summarised these underlying defects as '(t)he problems of administrative efficiency, inadequate benefits and limited coverage' (ILO, 1994d, p.101). Of these problems the most serious, we would argue, is the very limited coverage so far achieved in most SSA states. Inadequate benefits, crudely, are better than no benefits at all, albeit in themselves remaining as undesirable, if not as avoidable, as the often associated problems of administrative inefficiency, and, in at least some cases, outright and deep-seated corruption.

Regionally a very low percentage of the labour force is currently covered by statutory social protection measures in general (see Appendix Table A6.1). Moreover, the poorer the country, the lower the level of coverage. For example, in the Gambia, Niger and Chad only one percent of the labour force is covered by social security (Bailey and van Ginneken, 1998, p.3). In relation to the formal old age 'pension' schemes operating in SSA, notably social insurance and NPFs, the present position is well summarised by the ILO. Coverage is afforded to 'only a small part of the population, generally less than 10 percent of the labour force plus their dependants' (Gillion *et al.*, 2000, p.520). On the basis of World Bank figures, given in Table 6.1 below, contributory pensions cover just over 6 percent of the total labour force across SSA as a whole, although Southern Africa does significantly better than the rest of the region. Even South Asia, at close to 12 percent, has significantly higher regional levels of coverage.

Table 6.1 Pension Contributors as a Percentage of Labour Force*

Sub-Saharan Africa	6.26
South Asia	11.60
East and Southeast Asia and the Pacific	34.57
Latin America and the Caribbean	35.11
North Africa and the Middle East[1]	35.18
CEE and NIS/FSU	65.73
OECD	90.42

* Unweighted Arithmetic Means
1. Excludes Israel and Turkey
Adapted from: Palaçios and Pallarès-Miralles, 2000

The administrative shortcomings of Africa's state pensions institutions, ranging from excessive administrative costs to rampant kleptocracy, have long underpinned, and provided supporting evidence for, the World Bank's established view that '(t)here is considerable evidence that public management of pension funds should be avoided' (Iglesias and Palaçios, 2000, p.37). What is omitted from the Bank prescription is the role of economic decline and the collapse in both government revenues and civil service morale that accompanied the economic crisis of the 1980s in these developments. As we argue below in this chapter, marked administrative shortcomings became administrative disasters only in the 1980s. Similarly, administrative performance has risen, along with government revenues and morale, quite commonly in the 1990s. Nevertheless, administrative shortcomings still remain commonplace among the continent's social security and pension institutions and examples of gross mis-management and petty, sometimes largescale, corruption are regularly reported particularly outside southern Africa. Quite simply, as, for example, recently reported examples of the mismanagement of social security reserve assets in Tanzania and Cameroon reveal, a great deal remains to be done to improve the governance of many African social security administrations (Iglesias and Palaçios, 2000, p.19).

Moreover, to the underlying inadequacies of existing formal provision have been added mounting pressures on the family and community-based non-formal systems of support on which most of the region's old people have so far mainly depended for survival. For those without immediate families, and therefore unable to rely on kinship ties, the community was expected to provide, for example offering, in South Africa, various 'forms of community reciprocity, including "work parties" and outright charity' (Carter and May, 1999, p.5). Similarly, older people participate across SSA in religious societies, credit associations, savings groups and burial societies as well as, in some countries, traditional councils and many other informal networks. Formerly, such family and community networks were regarded as encompassing and capable of meeting most of the needs of elderly people. For example, a paper published in 1977 referred to the rural areas of, then, Southern Rhodesia, to which Africans were expected to move to as they grew older, as 'indigenous pensions' (Clarke cited in Kaseke, 1999, p.52). Such a depiction is no longer appropriate.

Across Africa, the situation facing the elderly has deteriorated and is continuing to deteriorate (Apt, 1996; Aguilar, ed., 1998; HelpAge International, 1999d). At a high level of generality, the limited research available 'largely supports the view that modernization is detrimental to the social and economic status of the aged' (Lloyd-Sherlock, 1999, p.75). More specifically, sustained economic crises from the early 1980s, as well as changes in government policy in relation to charging for health care and other services, have taken their toll. 'Older people insist that coping strategies have changed over the years - in the past, there was more community support, families were less fragmented, and there was less necessity for money, particularly because health services were free' (HelpAge International, 1999d, p.139). Successive crisis, it seems, have effectively undermined community and family capacity to support the elderly despite an apparent continuing commitment to meeting such 'traditional' obligations. This distinction has important implications for policy. Overall, what interview and research 'findings suggest [is] that it is the *ability* to care and support needy older members that needs to be addressed rather than the *willingness*' to do so (Eldermire-Shearer, 1999, p.99, emphasis in original), as deepening poverty and successive economic crises have reduced both community and familial capacity to assist their elders. In practice, therefore, despite the fact that among DCs generally, 'informal support and continued work remain the most viable options for older people' (Gorman, 1999b, p.6), the balance has shifted progressively towards the latter over recent decades. Across the developing world labour force participation rates among the elderly are rising. By the early 1990s, the ILO found that across SSA the percentage of those over 65 continuing to work was between 74 percent and 91 percent (Heslop, 1999, p.38).

Even within families elderly widows have always been highly vulnerable, often subject to the withdrawal of support. In SSA, as in South Asia, '[w]idows without grown sons tend to face difficulties ... even if their extended families are relatively prosperous' (Expenditure Policy Division, 1998, p.29, fn.30). As an IMF paper has recently reminded us, '[i]n Africa, the term for being poor is often synonymous with the absence of family or friends' (Expenditure Policy Division, 1998, p.27, citing Iliffe, 1987). Both in Africa and more widely across the developing world, elderly people without the support of extended families continue to constitute one of the poorest groups in society. Moreover, there are strong indications that the numbers of such isolated and abandoned old people, sometimes male, but more likely to be female, are rising significantly in the face of a combination of crises. Generally, such solidarity-threatening '[p]roblems arise when there are no male offspring or when there is a breakdown in family relationships - often connected with an inability to provide support' (Expenditure Policy Division, 1998, p.27).

Inevitably, across Africa, albeit still unevenly, such family-threatening problems have mounted over recent decades as established inter-generational support mechanisms, including the remittance economy, which gives rural households shares of migrants' income, have been subjected to a succession of crises as economic, social and political conditions have deteriorated. Since the outcome of this cumulation of crises places similar pressures on the community-based support mechanisms, notably food provision, that had previously ensured the survival even of those among the elderly poor who lacked family support, the situation facing non-formal support systems generally has become increasingly grave, with potentially disastrous consequences for very large numbers of the region's elderly poor. Among the most significant of the sources of these systemic threats have been the cumulative impact of the increasing informalisation of employment over recent decades, the growing economic and social impact of the HIV+/AIDS pandemic across some of the world's poorest countries, and the mounting socio-economic dislocation stemming from the effects of internal wars and insurgencies and other forms of political instability. When these specific crises are added to a socio-economic context in which urbanisation and migration patterns, as well as established demographic trends, had already seriously weakened at least some of the non-formal familial and community support systems 'traditionally' extended to the old, it is unsurprising that the continent's non-formal arrangements are themselves now increasingly perceived as facing the possibility of imminent collapse. This looming possibility essentially adds acute dimensions to the chronic problems facing formal provision; forming a conjuncture that is occurring just as the emerging prospect of demographic ageing looms over the region.

Issues in Research and Policy

Legal provision in Africa for state mandated old age pensions has, with the partial exception of South Africa, only been achieved in the post-World War Two era, most frequently initiated as an easily forgotten adjunct of the post-independence settlement, then characteristically extended on a highly restricted basis ensuring very limited coverage. Implementation of these statutory provisions, therefore, occurred in a post-independence context of limited financial resources, frequently of burgeoning economic crisis, in which newly established, hence still insecure and weakly institutionalised, social security institutions rapidly became mired, resulting in both patchy implementation and characteristically disappointing outcomes. Consequently, the self-serving and myopic assumption of colonial governments that there were 'no old people in Africa' was replaced by the equally self-serving assumption of post-colonial governments that they could not afford 'complex and costly' formal social security systems, at least if such systems were to be extended much beyond the ranks of government employees, who, ironically quickly came to regard generous retirement provision as a right. All too frequently this particular assertion proved to be a self-fulfilling prophecy as pensions institutions increasingly found themselves required primarily to service the cash-flow shortfalls of governments with large expenditure requirements and limited revenues.

This inauspicious background is crucially important in explaining the limited amount of academic research hitherto focused on the old age pensions elements within formal systems of African social security provision. What appears retrospectively to have been a distinct lack of any sustained academic interest in pensions and formal social security, specifically appearing conspicuously to fail to complement the consultancy and basic research activities undertaken by the Geneva institutions in SSA states, in part, at least, simply reflects the sensitivities of African governments on these matters and their associated extreme reluctance to provide research clearance to interested academics. Unsurprisingly, when there have been short bursts of analytical work published on the subject of African social security these have failed to engender either more wide-ranging or more sustained in-depth studies of this field. It is noteworthy that many of the key texts on African social security issues, including Pierre Mouton's path-breaking *Social Security in Africa: Trends, Problems and Prospect* (1975), date from as far back as the 1970s. Similarly, the important and seminal published works of Gerdes and of Tribe also date from this period (Gerdes, 1971, 1975; Tribe, 1976a, 1976b). Even by the mid-1970s many African governments had no wish to allow academic researchers easy access to social security institutions that had, in at least some cases, already been utilised to support patron-client systems of rule both dubiously, for employment purposes, and often corruptly, particularly as direct, and easily tapped, sources of funds. As the largely disappointing performance of social security institutions across SSA in the 1970s turned into downright poor outcomes during the economic and financial disasters of the 1980s, the sensitivity of African governments to adverse publicity increased significantly, locking doors that had been left at least partially open a decade earlier.

Further, the scale and rising importance of non-formal employment in the largely low income countries of SSA, a trend mirrored across the developing regions of the world over the last two decades, has continued to ensure that conventional old age pension provision models are problematic both in relation to maintaining fiscal sustainability and to achieving adequate coverage (see Table 6.2).

Table 6.2 Estimated Trends in Informal Sector Employment in Africa*

Countries (various years)	1980s	1990s
Algeria	21.4	25.4
Egypt	58.7	65.3
Morocco	56.9	n/a
Tunisia	36.0	39.3
Benin	86.0	92.8
Burkina Faso	70.0	77.0
Chad	n/a	74.2
Guinea	64.4	71.9
Kenya	n/a	61.4
Mali	63.1	78.6
Mauritania	69.4	75.3
Mozambique	n/a	73.5
Niger	62.9	n/a
Senegal	n/a	76.0
South Africa	n/a	18.9
Zaire (DRC)	59.6	n/a
Zambia	n/a	58.3

* As a % of Non-Agricultural Employment
Source: Adapted from Charmes, 2000, pp.63-64, Tables 1 and 2

Accordingly, most African countries can be defined as still falling largely outwith the middle-income country focus which has dominated both earlier pension system development agendas and the present debate on systemic pension reform. Just as Africa followed a trajectory of pension system development in the early post-independence era which sat uncomfortably on the margins of the ILO's social insurance-based welfare state model, the region currently remains at, or near, the frontier of the Bank's personal savings-based model of old age security. At least until recent years, the contemporary, largely Bank-driven, 'global' pension reform agenda, increasingly prioritising financial sector considerations above considerations related to social welfare, had been perceived to be substantially inapplicable to the large majority of African states. However, as is graphically underlined by the Bank's pensions web-site map marking the global extent of its consultancy advice (see Appendix Map A2.1), this final regional frontier for systemic pension reformers is currently being actively explored. For example, Elaine Fultz (1997, p.4), then representing the ILO in Harare, noted how, by 1997, there was already

> considerable external pressure here to privatise national pension schemes. The primary source is international financial institutions whose role as creditors in many English-speaking African countries gives them substantial influence on national economic policy. These institutions ... are seeking to catalyse economic growth through strengthening capital markets and perceive pension privatisation as a means to this end.

Significantly, the Côte d'Ivoire has been reported by the ISSA as being favourable to the possibility of introducing pillared pension system reforms based upon World Bank policy prescriptions (ISSA, 1999b, p.4). In turn, the interest voiced by the Côte d'Ivoire in Bank pension proposals is empirically unsurprising: both institutionally and ideologically it constitutes a logical SSA entry-point for the Bank pension reform model. In conjunction with a public social insurance system, the Côte d'Ivoire already operates a number of mandatory occupational private pension funds for specific professions. Additionally, a (francophone) West African regional stock market is now based in Abidjan. This development is institutionally important as both an indicator of financial sector development and indicative of financial sector ambitions. Both these factors are likely to encourage a more immediately favourable reception for World Bank suggestions for a greater degree of financial sector liberalisation than elsewhere in West Africa.

In East Africa, too, there is evidence that the global trend towards pensions privatisation is beginning to influence African pension debates. Kenya, again the logical sub-regional candidate, with 'a well-developed infrastructure of brokers, fund managers, and insurance companies and significant competition in the [private pension fund] sector' (Barbone and Sanchez, 2000, p.29), is in the process of liberalising, or partially privatising, pension provision. The Retirement Benefit Authority Act will permit private pension schemes to compete with the National Social Security Fund to provide mandatory old age provision (ISSA, 1999e, p.7). Recent speculation suggests that the future evolution of institutional old age provision in Kenya may well involve an even more significant movement towards an increasing role for private sector delivery. Similarly, recent World Bank interventions in Uganda have led to speculation that a reform path involving a limited degree of privatisation will be followed by this East African state as well.

Nonetheless, apart from the two, albeit potentially significant, cases of Côte d'Ivoire and Kenya, and the speculative possibility of something similar occurring in Uganda, it is unlikely, even in the medium term, that there will be any stampede towards pension system privatisation in Africa. Within SSA, the southern African sub-region constitutes the most obvious entry point for the privatisation agenda. Here, unsurprisingly, there is an indigenous constituency supporting mandatory pension system privatisation within the well-developed private pension industry of South Africa. In reviewing alternative approaches to reforming social security in southern Africa, Fultz and Pieris cite the proposals to establish Latin American-style 'fully funded, privately managed national savings schemes to replace social insurance ... advocated by the World Bank and some segments of the Southern African pension industry' (1999, p.41). Here, it is important to bear in mind the recency of memories of the apartheid regime, under which South Africa's contractual savings sector played a significant role in cementing Afrikaner control over the economy and in financially underpinning the development of Afrikaner industrial enterprises (Vittas and Michelitsch, 1996, p.277). Accordingly, proposals of this kind emanating from South Africa, designed to promote the private contractual savings sector, do not automatically command an immediately sympathetic audience among neighbouring states despite their largely middle income status.

Across the majority of SSA countries unfavourable underlying economic conditions and low levels of financial sector development highlight the point that institutional infrastructures are not yet even minimally conducive to the introduction of the World Bank's multipillar pension model. Even in Côte d'Ivoire, adoption of a Bank-designed pillared pension model is likely to offer effective multipillar coverage to only a very limited section of the working population well into the conceivable future. As World Bank figures underline, indicating just over 9 percent coverage of the labour force in both 1989 and 1997, little progress has been made so far in this respect under present arrangements in Côte d'Ivoire, leaving policy makers with an uphill task (World Bank, 1994, p.356, Table A.4; Palaçios and Pallares-Miralles, 1999, p.67, Table 4.26). Accordingly, for the majority of African states there is likely to be a breathing space lasting several years at least before the Bank is likely to exert any really significant pressure on governments to prioritise systemic pension reform. This is not unimportant since, potentially, it could allow a reasoned and open debate on both pension system priorities and potential reform options to occur. If such a debate is to take place, however, certain preconditions must be met.

Specifically, it is important to establish exactly when, how and why existing formal pension and retirement provision systems began to fail across SSA. Although the backdrop to this chapter is largely one of disappointment and of failure, or, perhaps more accurately, one of the widespread *perception* of the failure of formal pension provision in Africa, it is, as we argue below, by no means as obvious as it is currently assumed that a combination of inappropriate system design and, more importantly, corrupt and inefficient African states are the principal culprits despite some superficially convincing *prima facie* evidence to the contrary. In particular, (much) past and (some) present evidence of both administrative weaknesses and downright corruption among SSA's pensions administrations are not hard to find, including examples more negative even than that of the former Zambian NPF highlighted by the World Bank as its chosen cautionary tale of the evils of public management in *Averting the Old Age Crisis* (1994, p.224).

Further, the continuing sensitivity of many African states to academic analyses of formal pension provision only serves to reinforce this impression of governmental culpability. Such assumptions, in turn, are consistent with prevailing neoliberal and 'Afro-pessimist' views of widespread state failure leading to the economic collapse of the early 1980s and the deep and sustained economic decline of that 'lost decade' in Africa's development. Crucially, from this irremediably anti-state perspective, it is simply assumed that the failure of formal pension provision predates the 1980s, with such systems perceived to be in terminal decline prior to the rampant inflation that accompanied the stabilisation and structural adjustment programmes imposed by the Washington institutions during that decade. If, however, as we argue below, it was in fact the combination of inflationary pressures and stringent expenditure controls that accompanied SAPs that finally turned the earlier investment inefficiency, savings misallocation and consequently poor, or mediocre, performance of state pension administrations into financial disasters, frequently compounded by gross corruption and massive diversion of funds, the implications are very different. Most importantly, the complete loss of public trust in public pension and provident fund administrations that currently prevails in a large number of SSA states is, at least in part, blaming the victim, if not exactly the innocent. Since the rebuilding of this trust in the capacities of state institutions and state provision is centrally important to any realistic pension reform strategy for the region - which must continue to rely substantially on state provision and management in the absence of credible market-based alternatives - this finding is not a trivial one.

Institutional Dimensions of Old Age Pension Provision in Africa

Institutionally, mandatory old age retirement provision across Africa is somewhat heterogeneous, closely shaped by the predilections of the major colonial powers. Moreover, although, increasingly, most African states at least notionally provide some form of national retirement pension provision, this is not the case for all countries, for reasons related to poverty and instability. As the US Social Security Administration's biennially published survey *Social Security Programs Throughout the World* illustrates, Malawi, Sierra Leone, and Somalia do not provide an old age benefit within their respective national social security provisions. In addition to these three countries, there are a number of African countries which are not covered by this survey which also have no national system for the provision of old age benefits. These countries are Angola, Comoros, Eritrea, Ethiopia, Guinea Bissau, Lesotho, and Western Sahara.[1] For most of the other countries on the continent, it is possible to characterise public pension systems as financed via one of three distinct approaches (see Map 6.1).

Social Insurance

The vast majority of African pension systems, involving some thirty seven countries, are provided predominantly on a social insurance basis. These countries are found predominantly, although not exclusively, in North Africa and among the francophone states of SSA. To a large degree, the diffusion of defined benefit (DB) social insurance systems across much of Africa can be traced to the orchestrated influence of former French and Belgian colonial administrations. Typically, these social insurance schemes were initially designed to be financed using a system of scaled premium financing. As the ILO explain, '(u)nder a scaled premium system, a contribution rate is established so that over a specified period of equilibrium (for example 10, 15 or 20 years), the contribution income and interest on the reserves of the scheme will be adequate to meet expenditures on benefits and administration' (ILO, 1997a, p.56). One important feature of the scaled premium system of financing, and one which distinguishes this method of financing in particular from a pay-as-you-go mechanism, is that reserve funds are accumulated. During each period of equilibrium, reserve funds which have not been used to meet scheme administrative costs and individual benefit entitlements, can provide a ready and cheap source of long term investment capital for public administrations.

For developing country governments in particular, this potential for investment is undoubtedly an attractive feature of these schemes. An important problem for DC governments operating these schemes, and a problem which is shared by privately managed as well as publicly managed funds in general, is that the surplus assets held by scaled premium systems will always remain vulnerable to the deleterious impact of high inflation rates. In practice, therefore, it is largely unsurprising that African social insurance schemes more typically function in practice on a largely PAYG basis. It is worth remembering that the destructive impact of rampant inflation upon pension fund surpluses was one major factor which contributed to the introduction of PAYG in Europe in the post-war era. Colonial regimes failed to internalise this lesson and history may currently be repeating itself. Significantly, Tanzania's newly instituted National Social Security Fund (NSSF) is a scaled premium social insurance scheme, operating initially with a 15 year period of equilibrium.

Minimally, legal changes are needed to provide African social security administrations with some ability to diversify investment portfolios internationally to ensure returns above inflation, for example along the lines pioneered by the Asian-Pacific NPFs discussed above in Chapter 5. In order to avoid future fund destruction due to inflation there is a clear need for donor support for the development of fund management capacities within African social security administrations sufficient to cope with such contingencies. In turn, these requirements clearly indicate a need for the type of international advisory and capacity building regime we outline in Chapter 9.

Map 6.1 Old Age Pensions Provision in Africa

No Public Old Age Provision [1]
General Revenue Financed Pension [2]
Social Insurance Pension [3]
National Provident Fund [4]

Notes

1. No information is currently available regarding national old age pensions provision in Angola, Eritrea, and Guinea Bissau. Comoros intends to expand its current social insurance system to include an old age pension scheme. Ethiopia, Lesotho, Malawi, Sierra Leone, Somalia and Western Sahara provide old age pensions for public servants only;

2. Mauritius, the Seychelles and, albeit to a 'lesser extent', Gabon (Barbone *et al.*, 2000, p.46) operate dual universal and social insurance pension schemes;

3. Côte d'Ivoire operates social insurance and mandatory private pension funds; Mozambique operates a limited social insurance system and a geographically limited means-tested poverty alleviation programme. Due to armed conflict, the social insurance schemes of Liberia, the Republic of Congo and the DRC were totally or substantially destroyed (Gillion *et al.*, 2000);

4. The Gambia operates, in parallel, an NPF and social insurance pension scheme.

National Provident Funds

A second institutional form of old age provision which was previously more common but which is still extant in four 'anglophone' countries is the National Provident Fund (NPF). As of 2000, NPFs were operational in the Gambia, Kenya, Uganda and Swaziland. National Provident Funds, as explained fully in Chapter 5 obviating the need for extended discussion here, are mandatory state-run defined contribution savings schemes which, in their most basic form, provide lump sum payments to affiliates on retirement. The institutional origins and diffusion of NPFs across Africa, as elsewhere in the developing world, is linked closely to these countries' former status as British colonies. However, in contrast with the highly centralised development of social insurance systems in francophone Africa, the development of NPFs was altogether more patchy and ad hoc, particularly in relation to the degree of co-ordination exerted from London. Nevertheless, despite the limited planning involved, London was quick to recognise an opportunity to circumvent the financial and administrative burdens associated with the establishment of 'national' social insurance schemes in the colonies. A further highly influential factor in the diffusion of the NPF model, as underlined in Chapter 5, was the operational experience of the longer established Asian NPFs. Over time, of course, the relevance of Southeast Asian experience to Africa has waned as regional developmental trajectories have increasingly diverged. In the specific case of the NPF model, the positive image derived from Southeast Asian experience contrasts markedly to an almost entirely negative image in Africa. Due, in part, to the continuing characterisation of NPFs, not least by the ILO, as an immature and inadequate form of social security for retirement, and in part also due to performance shortfalls in SSA, a trend towards the transformation of NPFs into social insurance schemes is now well underway in Africa.

Recently, Tanzania and Zambia replaced their NPFs with social insurance pension schemes. Similarly, Kenya and Uganda have received technical assistance and reform advice from the ILO, the ISSA and the World Bank regarding the transformation of their respective NPF's. In the case of Uganda, the nature of reform advice given by the ILO and the World Bank to the Government of Uganda has at times been divergent, with the Bank recently arguing for a degree of partial privatisation inconsistent with the earlier advice of the ILO to strengthen public provision. Swaziland has also stated a future intent to reform its NPF. If such a process of transformation were to be realised, this would leave only one operational African NPF. Significantly, this would be the atypical NPF of the Gambia, only founded in 1981. The Gambian fund, which operates as an element within the Social Security and Housing Finance Corporation (SSHFC), provides a traditional NPF retirement saving scheme for private sector employees. The SSHFC also provides a federated pension fund covering employees in 'quasi-government institutions and in participating private companies' (ISSA, 1999), a housing finance fund, and an Industrial Injuries Compensation Scheme. Of crucial importance to the continuation of the Gambian scheme is the growing international reputation of the SSHFC as an effective, efficient, and transparently managed social security institution, as explained above in Chapter 5. Significantly, and especially so in relation to the experience of other countries that have undergone structural adjustment, these are compliments which are rarely accorded to African social security institutions, and to African NPFs in particular.

General Revenue Financed Assistance Pensions

The third institutional form of public old age provision found in SSA is the non-contributory, tax financed, old age pension. Like social insurance schemes and the NPF model, non-contributory systems of universal provision on a demogrant basis are by no means exclusive to Africa. However, such schemes are rare in DCs. 'Outside the industrialised countries, Eastern Europe and the FSU, cash transfers rarely figure in anti-poverty strategies' (Case and Deaton, 1998, p.1331). Among pension systems, developments in southern Africa are also unusual. As Case and Deaton underline in relation to the South African social pension, 'its non-contributory nature, its large size, and its comprehensive coverage set it apart from other pension arrangement around the world' (1998, p.1331). Internationally, systems of non-contributory old age provision are most readily associated with the means-tested system found in Australia and the New Zealand universal system which bases eligibility on the fulfilment of a residency condition. Similarly, Denmark provides a universal pension wherein eligibility is again based upon the fulfilment of a residency condition. Nevertheless, these examples have not provided models for southern African developments. In contrast to the European colonial heritage of many of the continent's social insurance and NPF systems, the adoption and diffusion of non-contributory old age provision appears to have been largely African-driven. More specifically, evidence suggests a widening trend towards the adoption of this institutional form of old age benefits provision in southern Africa, underlining a developing regional diffusion process as well as largely indigenous origins.

The origins of, and early development within, this emerging sub-regional demogrant system, however, were not, in any respect, regionally coordinated. Specifically, the pre-war establishment of what has now evolved into South Africa's universal 'social pension' system simply reflected the unique socio-economic and political circumstances of that state. 'Most white workers are covered by private occupational pension schemes, and a means-tested state pension was originally introduced as a safety-net to provide for the limited numbers of white workers who reached retirement without adequate provision' (Case and Deaton, 1998, p.1334). True universality in state pension provision, therefore, was first sought by Mauritius, predating South Africa's efforts to extend its state pension to, first, its 'Coloured' and 'Indian' populations, as part of its late-apartheid reforms, then, belatedly, to the black majority of its population in the terminal apartheid era. 'The size of the state pension was gradually equalised across all racial groups during the disintegration of the apartheid regime' (Case and Deaton, 1998, p.1334).

In pioneering universality in pension provisioning within SSA, Mauritius can, retrospectively, be defined as providing a regional welfare model, although its leadership role in this, as in other welfare-related respects, is only now becoming generally acknowledged even by its neighbouring states. Wider sub-regional diffusion of this universal provision model dates from the mid-1990s, initially largely reflecting, albeit for very different reasons, Namibia and Botswana's convergent responses to South African developments. Within the southern African sub-region, wider interest in the Mauritian example has been exhibited from the late 1990s, specifically emerging under the stimulus of exchanges of pensions administration personnel, and other encouragements to expertise and information-sharing, coordinated and supported under the auspices of ILO's Harare-based SAMAT. 'At SAMAT's request, the Mauritian Ministry of Labour and Social Solidarity has provided training in various aspects of social security administration to officials from Zambia, Zimbabwe and Namibia (1996-99). As the oldest pension scheme in the region, Mauritius has provided both technical expertise and inspiration to its neighbours' (Fultz and Pieris, 1999. p.53).

To date, however, in relation to the universal assistance or social pension model, this emerging, and highly encouraging, pattern of inter-state cooperation has probably been mainly important in cementing the regional extension of the principle of universality in old age provision. Currently, even 'old age' remains diversely defined within the southern African sub-region, with eligibility for a state pension set at 60 in Mauritius and Namibia, at 65 in Botswana, and at 65 for men and 60 for women in South Africa. Unsurprisingly, benefit levels also vary significantly between countries, ranging from comparative generosity in Mauritius and South Africa to significantly less generous levels in Botswana and Namibia. Similarly, while entitlements under these schemes are generally provided as flat-rate benefits they are means-tested in the case of South Africa. Universal tax financed schemes also exist in the Seychelles and in Gabon: this last case constituting the first continental example outside the southern cone of SSA. In the case of Mauritius, the universal non-contributory pension scheme, for which all residents are eligible, operates alongside an earnings-related social insurance pension scheme. Seychelles also operates a dual system, combining an universal non-means tested basic pension and a voluntary contributory social insurance old age pension scheme (Justaert, 1995), indicating the possibility of the development of comparably 'tiered' systems as the regional norm.

An interesting variant of tax financed social assistance provision is found in Mozambique where means-tested cash-transfers are available in some areas, centred on the capital Maputo, to urban-domiciled citizens who are aged over 60 and unemployed. For the government of Mozambique such an approach is doubly attractive in that, in the short-term, it permits a strong element of budgetary control while, in the longer-term, the centralised administrative structure and the largely geographically-based criteria for eligibility allows for the future possibility of expanded coverage through incremental growth into other designated geographic areas. Initially, it should be noted, the Mozambique government envisaged a nation-wide scheme but geographical coverage was scaled down in the implementation phase due to the limited financial and other resources available in the face of the multiple requirements for post-war reconstruction.

Clearly, funding problems present a similarly significant constraint to programme development, both in Mozambique and more widely across much of SSA, in the continuing absence of dependable tax revenues and multiple claims on scarce financial and administrative resources. As the Mozambique case highlights, in poor states the road to the achievement of expanded coverage and benefit adequacy under state provision will remain, at all times, problematic, and, in the initial stages of programme development at least, is likely to be significantly dependent on aid disbursements and continuing donor generosity (the potential significance of the role of non-contributory pension provision for poverty alleviation in LDCs is addressed more fully in Chapter 7 below).

Private Sector Provision

The absence, discussed above, of any meaningful continental trend towards the growth of mandatory private pension provision is, we would argue, far from insignificant in its wider implications for pension policy in the region. Currently, with the exception of some elements within the private pension fund industry in South Africa there is no real constituency within SSA pressing for mandatory pensions privatisation as a policy option, let alone as a policy priority. Nevertheless, it must be underlined, a near absence of *mandatory* private provision - with Côte d'Ivoire being the sole, and then only partial, exception to the rule - does not signify a comparable level of private provision in general. Indeed, a focus on issues relating to mandatory provision simply serves to further divert attention away from the roles already widely played by private and occupational pensions providers and financial service operators across Africa. Nor is this private provision an exclusively urban phenomenon. Large agricultural estates and plantations quite commonly provide small cash pensions to their former workers, ensuring that 'private' pension provision is widely, but very unevenly, diffused among both the low and middle income states of the region. Nevertheless, almost no systematic work has been carried out in relation to 'private' provision, leaving us largely ignorant of the current position in most states. Consequently, it is easy to overlook the fact that a number of African countries already have established, if, as discussed below in Chapter 8, often weakly institutionalised, financial service sectors. Within these sectors contractual savings institutions, pension funds and life insurers are already prominent among the region's non-bank financial intermediaries. Among the region's middle income countries generally private pension provision is already well established along occupational lines referred to above in relation to Côte d'Ivoire. Kenya, for example currently has private pension fund assets equating roughly to 10 percent of GDP (Barbone and Sanchez, 2000, p.29).

Nothing in SSA matches the size and the sophistication of the South African financial services sector. South Africa, by global, not just regional, standards has 'a sophisticated financial services industry in terms of products, services and distribution infrastructure'. In 1995, the value of assets held by South African life insurance companies and pension funds was in excess of 80 percent of GDP. In comparative international terms, this ratio is amongst the highest in the world. For instance, the South African ratio is 'higher than in the United States and Canada, though lower than in Switzerland, the Netherlands and the UK' (Munro and Snyman, 1995, p.127). The private contractual savings sector in South Africa has deep roots, originating in the mid 19th century. Over time the sector has developed into the large institutional investors sought after by the World Bank with strategic holdings in key industries. 'In South Africa pension funds and especially the insurance companies that manage most of these funds and other contractual savings are dominant in corporate governance and have controlling stakes in a large number of companies, including other financial institutions, such as commercial banks and even building societies' (Vittas and Michelitsch, 1996, p.273).

Historically, the contractual savings sector in South Africa has been free to invest in domestic equities, and, indeed, was directed to do so by the government during the apartheid era in order to soak up the divested assets of foreign enterprises exiting under sanctions. This equity bias, combined with the investment expertise of South African fund managers developed under the difficult economic circumstances facing the apartheid regime, has contributed greatly to the competent performance of the sector despite episodes of high inflation. During the early to mid-1990s, there was significant restructuring in the South African financial service sector, not least as it responded to the opportunity to diversify its investment portfolios internationally for the first time. Anticipation of the end of apartheid also stimulated demand among private employers for a appropriate savings products for the new era of democracy and equal opportunities. The ILO has reported that between 1992 and 1994 more than 6000 new private provident funds were created (Fultz and Pieris, 1997, p.5). As noted by Case and Deaton, in comparison to other 'racial' groups but particularly to 'whites', black 'African workers in the past have had less attachment to the formal labour force, and even those with long-term employment relationships were generally excluded from their employers' pension programmes' (1998, p.1334). These discriminatory exclusions became increasingly untenable as the apartheid system came under strain. For those black South Africans employed in the formal sector, largely occupying low paid blue collar jobs, the most accessible savings products - usually constituting the only saving undertaken by such workers - have been those provided by the trade unions on a contractual basis for 'retirement' pension provision. By the mid-1990s the trade unions had collectively amassed total pension fund assets approaching 100 billion Rand, giving these organisations significant investment muscle and real influence as financial intermediaries within a steadily expanding private financial sector.

Already regionally significant, the industry is increasingly now gaining importance internationally. In the late 1990s the nature of the South African financial service sector was irrevocably altered by the demutualisation of the two largest life assurers, Old Mutual and Sanlam. Most notably, the dominant South African life assurer Old Mutual, founded in 1845, relocated its operational headquarters to London after demutualising in 1999. Although Old Mutual still retains a sizeable life assurance business in South Africa and other southern African countries, following demutualisation it now markets itself as an 'international financial services group', for example immediately moving into the potentially huge Indian life insurance market as soon as government policy permitted entry. Nevertheless, international expansion within the sector has also been accompanied by continued domestic growth. By the late 1990s, it was estimated that 74 percent of formal sector workers in South Africa were covered by private occupational pensions and provident funds provided voluntarily by employers and trade unions (Fultz and Pieris, 1997, p.5). While the extent of this occupational coverage can be explained partially by the means-tested nature of public old age provision, the growth in private occupational pensions is also indicative of the soundness, responsiveness and adaptability of the South African financial services industry. Moreover, the desire of employers to retain valued workers will be an important contributory factor on the demand side.

In turn, the South African financial service sector rightly prides itself on being innovative and providing new products for its customers. As Munro and Snyman suggest, 'South African insurance companies claim to have invented universal life and annuity policies' (1995, p.127). Of even greater relevance to the concerns of this chapter is the South African industry's continuing responsiveness to its customer base. In particular, it has responded positively to high demand for relatively short-term savings products and to the continuing popularity of lump-sum 'terminal' bonuses taken by workers leaving one employer for another. Nor has the South

African industry entirely ignored the poor and low income workers who constitute the great majority of the working population. One domestic initiative worthy of note, the 'E-Plan', has been designed to offer cost-effective financial services to the urban poor and to redress some of the economic inequalities created by apartheid (Paulson and McAndrews, 1998).

In comparative African terms, the enormity of the South African financial service sector can conveniently be illustrated by contrasting it to the combined value of both the onshore and offshore business conducted in the rapidly modernising and ambitious Mauritian financial service industry. In 1998, the Mauritian financial service sector 'constituted 11.4 percent of GDP' (MOBAA, 1999, p.12). On a continental level, only in Namibia does the importance of the financial service sector to the national economy come close to that of South Africa. Pensions and life insurance assets equate to around 80 percent of Namibian GDP, a ratio only slightly lower than that of South Africa (Kenny and Moss, 1998, p.839). Unsurprisingly, however, given the country's recent 'colonial' history, the role played by South African subsidiaries remains predominant in Namibia. Only after a 1995 reform of the regulatory regime for pension funds were 'the largely South African-owned funds operating in Namibia [required] to invest 25 percent of their assets locally' (World of Information, 1995, p.134). Additionally, the Namibian national civil service pension scheme is 'administered under contract by a private insurance company' (Bailey, 1997, p.19, fn.4), once again underlining the South African connection.

More widely across Africa, although organised financial service sectors, and the insurance industry in particular, often remain 'beset with many administrative and infrastructural problems' (UNECA, 1997, p.153), financial service products, including health insurance and old age pensions, are provided in most countries under employer mandates for salaried employees. Occupational provision therefore tends to provide at least some privileged formal sector workers with a means to compensate for limited state provision. For example, the development of occupational pension provision in Zimbabwe arose, in large part, to compensate for the absence of state provision prior to the introduction of social insurance financed pension provision in the early 1990s (ILO, 1993, p.58). Despite the introduction of a national social insurance system, it is likely that occupational provision will remain important due to the low levels of population coverage so far achieved by the Zimbabwean state system, and given the comparatively wide coverage already achieved by private occupational schemes in a context which, by African standards, has an unusually high level of formal sector employment. Formal sector employment in Zimbabwe involves over 90 percent of the labour force, a figure even higher than in neighbouring South Africa. In the longer-term, however, coverage under the Zimbabwean National Social Security Scheme is, in theory at least, to be gradually expanded in three phases to eventually cover all those who are economically active, including the self employed and informal sector workers, groups currently also falling outside the remit of occupational schemes. Elsewhere in SSA, occupational schemes characteristically have more restrictive coverage, generally remaining heavily biased towards wealthier groups within the formal sector. Unsurprisingly, in relation to access to personal insurance products in general, there is similar evidence of 'bias towards the urban and affluent, as is markedly the case in Kenya, Zambia, Nigeria and Ghana' (UNECA, 1997, p.162).

Even the relatively wealthy, however, are facing significant problems in relation to life and health products. As an actuarially inevitable outcome of increasing mortality rates, HIV+/AIDS is having a significant impact upon the life insurance business. In Zimbabwe, whose population has one of the highest level of HIV+ infection in the world, life insurance premiums have quadrupled over the last two years (Herzberg, 2000, p.3). As this trend is mirrored in other SSA countries, 'life' products will become, at best, very expensive, or, at worst, unaffordable, even for the wealthy. Similarly, the HIV+/AIDS pandemic threatens to weaken occupational pension provision in SSA. In particular, the increased costs associated with the provision of, often AIDS-related, death grants which are provided to members of occupational pension schemes, is causing solvency problems, threatening the financial sustainability of some occupational pension schemes in South Africa. The mounting cost of death grants awarded by occupational pension schemes is forcing some employers to reduce the level of the grants awarded and may even lead some employers to consider suspending this particular form of employees' benefit (Thérin, 2000, p.28).

For SSA countries in general with often very limited coverage under state social security systems and health care provisions, the welfare enhancing potential of private occupational schemes for individual workers and their families should not be under-rated, despite regressive bias. Nevertheless, coverage still remains poor even across the formal sector, except in southern Africa. More significantly, the vast majority of the active labour force in most African countries who work in the informal sector, or in subsistence agriculture, still find themselves doubly excluded from access to social protection measures, both private and public. Moreover, these penalties fall disproportionately on women who occupy ill-paid, often un-pensionable, posts in the formal sector, such as household work, or, even more commonly, are engaged in marginal activities in the informal sector or in rural economies. For all these groupings the most appropriate vehicle to extend coverage quickly is the social assistance demogrant provided on an universal basis, as discussed in detail in Chapter 7.

Structural Adjustment and Pension Provision

Although much further work needs to be done before the full implications of the impact on formal 'retirement' pension provision of what is now almost two decades of debt crisis and IFI-mandated structural adjustment programmes can be delineated, it is clear that this impact has been both marked and significantly negative. Specifically, continuing, SAP-related, tight controls over government expenditure, particularly social expenditure, in a context of low, and in the 1980s often negative, economic growth, ensured that pension and other elements of social security expenditure was pro-cyclically determined and correspondingly, often disproportionately, reduced or curtailed as the recession deepened. Budgetary constraints ensured that the financing of social programmes, always problematic for impoverished states, became a critical problem. As Gruat confirms, IFI-mandated policy responses to a decade and more of continuing weak economic performance across most of SSA has led 'decision-makers and their advisers, more than in the past, to base their decisions on the primary and almost exclusive criterion of economic and financial efficiency...' (Gruat, 1996, p.1).

From the early 1980s a vicious circle of decline set in for social provision across SSA, involving as one of its elements reductions in pensions and in the funding of pensions administrations. The result was levels of societal welfare significantly reduced below the, already low, thresholds previously obtained. The overall outcome of the 1980's crisis and its attendant deleterious impacts, not simply impinging negatively on social spending but also on formal sector income levels and on formal, particularly public sector employment, was to increase overall poverty in the region. Developments in the 1980s specifically added what the World

Bank termed the 'new', structurally-adjusted, poor to the 'old' poor who had always fallen either outside, or at the margins of, both formal sector employment and its attendant formal social security provision. Needless to say, the adjustments of pensions and other elements of social policy on a pro-cyclical basis not only undermines their effectiveness as welfare instruments but also further undermines popular trust in the principle of public responsibility for, and public management of, welfare provision.

As the International Labour Organisation (ILO) and the International Social Security Association (ISSA), have consistently argued, over-emphasising economic and financial cost issues in poor countries obscures the primary concern, and threatens the capacity, of social security to provide adequate social protection or, in ILO parlance, to guarantee 'social justice'. As Gruat highlights for SSA, basing social expenditure criteria exclusively on grounds of economic and financial efficiency can only be 'to the detriment ... of the radically different considerations that underpin the legitimacy of welfare systems' (Gruat, 1996, p.1): the latter essentially requiring counter-cyclical responses in a recession if public trust in state responsibility for welfare provision is not to suffer.

Directly, a major effect of SAPs has been a further worsening of social security coverage (see Appendix Table A6.1). More widely, the implementation of state-shrinking policies under SAPs, particularly the ripple effects from the large-scale retrenchments of state employees, has often further undermined the day-to-day management and the longer term financial health of, already weak, pension systems in many low income countries by significantly reducing the ratio of active contributors both in relation to those actually working and to those entitled to present and future pension benefits. Although poor or very poor coverage levels are a concern for almost all African social security systems, coverage declines have particularly worrying implications for the financial health of the many social insurance schemes which, as outlined above, now operate across much of the continent having been more widely adopted beyond their original base in francophone Africa. The particular problem for such social insurance systems is that the reduction in income from mandatory contributions which result from the retrenchment of state sector employees does not affect on-going state commitments to pay, at a future date, the defined benefit pension entitlements of increasing large numbers of non-contributing scheme members. Moreover, reduced levels of contributions income undermine capacities to pay current benefit entitlements and to meet operating costs, thereby having immediate, as well as medium and long term, negative impacts on pension system performance.

A further, highly significant, corollary of structural adjustment, is that the financial viability and sustainability of many African social security institutions has also been jeopardised by the deleterious impact of high inflation on the value of the accrued assets of national social security systems. In particular, the often sustained bouts of hyper-inflation that accompanied SAPs has been particularly damaging to those African social security systems that have remained partially funded or, albeit less commonly, fully pre-funded. Long periods of double digit inflation plagued African economies throughout the 1980s and, in many cases, persisted well into the 1990s. These inflationary episodes, at least partly attributable to the policy choices mandated by the IFIs as essential to the process of economic restructuring, coincided with an identifiable turning-point for the worse in the financial health of a number of social security administrations, not least those in the anglophone states which, following the processes outlined above in Chapter 5, had adopted NPFs as their preferred mechanism for providing mandatory retirement savings to formal sector workers. Prior to structural adjustment, it must be emphasised, Africa's now much maligned NPFs were, overall, in a financially sound condition, albeit hardly star performers in comparison to their Southeast Asian counterparts. By the early 1990s the same NPFs were effectively insolvent. This point is particularly significant given the negative image that the World Bank has given to the region's NPFs, thereby contributing significantly to the NPF model's apparently inexorable decline, and possibly eventual disappearance from SSA. Specifically, whilst SAPs have had a negative impact on African social security administrations in general, the effects, both directly felt and indirectly mediated, of structural adjustment programmes have clearly been most profoundly deleterious in relation to the region's fully funded national provident funds, thereby contributing significantly to the ongoing demise of the NPF model in Africa.

By the end of the 1980s, a decade characterised by SAPs and high inflation rates, the condition of Africa's NPFs had changed dramatically for the worse. In the case of Tanzania, the average inflation rate for the period 1981 to 1987 was 30.5 percent. Inevitably, double-digit hyper-inflation over this period led to a severe depreciation of the Tanzanian currency. As the, then, Director General of the now defunct Tanzanian NPF reported in 1994, referring to the seven year period between 1986 and 1993, 'through the depreciation of the Tanzanian currency alone, the Fund's investment in government stocks on 1 July 1986 had diminished by 28 times in US dollar terms' (Mkulo, 1994, pp.9-10). The impact on the financial position of NPF administrations was clear-cut and profound, turning previously average or poor investment returns into financial disasters. At the end of 1979, the Zambian NPF, which later would come to be characterised as *the* prodigal 'enfant terrible' of National Provident Funds, held fund assets valued at a respectable 11 percent of GDP after fifteen years in operation (ILO, 1987, p.13, Table 3). As the less well known accompanying 'diskette' database to the World Bank's *Averting* (1994) demonstrates for the period 1980 to 1988, the already negative investment returns of the ZNPF nose-dived catastrophically from 1983 onwards, as the Zambian economy declined disastrously during the decade of debt crisis and structural adjustment (see Table 6.3).

Table 6.3 Zambian NPF Investment Returns 1980-1988

1980	1981	1982	1983	1984	1985	1986	1987	1988
-7.2	-1.4	-8.1	-14.0	-14.5	-32.0	-46.3	-37.5	-50.0

Source: World Bank, (1994), Averting the Old Age Crisis, Data on Diskette

The severity of Zambia's economic decline during the 1980s is reflected in its movement during the decade out of the Bank's middle income category and into its present position as a LIC, with triple digit hyper-inflation persisting into the 1990s. It is worthy of mention that the World Bank, in *Averting*, chose to highlight a limited time period of only two financial years, 1988-89, rather than fully presenting their longer time series of available data. By focusing on this period, the operational nadir of the ZNPF, the Bank drew attention away from longer-term trends, in particular obscuring clear analytical linkages between the declining health of the NPF and the impact of economic decline in an era of structural adjustment. The outcome was that the value of assets held by the Zambian NPF fell in the period 1980 to 1987 from 9.1 percent to 5.8 percent of GDP (World Bank, 1994, data on diskette). Furthermore, the fact that this period also witnessed negative growth in Zambian GDP underlines the speed and degree to which the fortunes of the ZNPF had deteriorated over the decade.

Inevitably, as the authors of the Zambian case study in a recent ILO reassessment of structural adjustment programmes in central and eastern

Africa conclude, all the country's various social security schemes, including the ZNPF were rendered 'ineffective in providing adequate protection', and this ineffectiveness 'can be attributed *to a great extent* to the various aspects of the economic crisis and the SAP reforms adopted' in response (Seshamani and Kaunga, 1999, p.185, emphasis added). In turn, this finding puts the criticisms, not least those highlighting the specific financial failings of the ZNPF, but also those more widely levelled at the NPF model by the World Bank in *Averting the Old Age Crisis*, in a very different light. Clearly, African governments, not least those politicians and bureaucrats directly charged with responsibility for pension and NPF administration, were far from blameless in these developments. At the very least, the failures of Africa's politicians and bureaucrats, combined with poor system design, contributed significantly to some of the problems of financial collapse and insolvency that emerged during the 1980s. As Seshamani and Kaunga carefully conclude in relation to the Zambian evidence, inadequacies in social protection in that country were not simply the result of the combination of economic crisis and SAPs. Specifically, 'other factors have also played a significant part. There are deficiencies in the benefit structure of the schemes, in their management and in their financial systems' which were far from unimportant in explaining the performance shortfalls highlighted by the World Bank (1999, p.185).

Nevertheless, recognition of these shortcomings does not make African politicians and bureaucrats entirely responsible for all the subsequent performance failures duly recorded by the Bank and mobilised as evidence against state management of retirement savings provision in general and the NPF model in particular. Specifically, it is not exactly fair for the World Bank to use the institutional failings of an NPF, whose operational capacities had been severely undermined by the impact of its own policies of structural adjustment, as one important justification for the promotion of privately managed defined contribution pension funds. The particularly ironic element in this situation is that the combination of economic recession and SAP-induced inflation would equally comprehensively have undermined, indeed bankrupted, any conceivable alternative, domestically managed, system of mandatory private pension provision in most SSA states, had such systems been inaugurated during the 1980s. Specifically, the government paper-dominated investment profile of Chile's private AFPs in the 1980s, discussed in detail in Chapter 8, paralleled the similarly government bond-dominated investment portfolios of SSA's NFPs. As Vittas and Michelitsch of the World Bank confirm,

> [t]he extremely high performance of the Chilean pension funds stemmed ... from two unusual factors that prevailed during the 1980s in the Chilean economy. These were the high level of real interest rates following the severe financial crisis of the early 1980s and the subsequent large capital gains earned on bonds and other debt instruments that resulted from the large fall of real interest rates when the economy recovered and financial confidence was restored.

> 1996, p.271

Needless to say, the AFPs would not have prospered in the quite different economic context of SSA in the 1980s. Bluntly, it is fortunate for the advocates of pension system privatisation in DCs that comprehensive pension system reform was not perceived initially to be important by the World Bank to macroeconomic adjustment strategies, and, consequently, that its staff largely ignored the Chilean model in the 1980s and omitted pension reform from the content of SAPs implemented across the developing world during that decade. By the time, into the 1990s, that the Bank's financial sector liberalisation policies came to include the strategic reform of state managed retirement pension systems as one of its key institutionally-focused elements, inflationary pressures had declined significantly across the developing world. Similarly, where the financial instability that is an inherent accompaniment of the policies of financial system openness advocated by the Bank has more recently led to serious bouts of hyper-inflation, as in Southeast and East Asia, the investment performance of funded retirement savings systems has inevitably suffered, to the equally inevitable detriment of their capacity to continue to deliver satisfactory retirement savings to their affiliates. Although, therefore, it has been the turn of the previously highly successful Southeast Asian NPFs to face this particular problem the implications would be identical for any privately managed alternatives operating under comparable legal and regulatory regimes.

Trends and Implications: The Limits of the SIPS Model

With only four NPFs remaining in Africa, the incipient demise of the original NPF model in Africa can be anticipated. A clear-cut regional trend away from the provident fund model in anglophone states towards social insurance is on-going. Nevertheless, it is important to stress that the recent expansion of social insurance in Africa, as typified by the reforms in Tanzania and Zambia outlined above, is more indicative of the continuing policy influence of the ILO across the continent than of the inherent or practical merits of the principles of social insurance *per se*.[2] As will become clear in the course of the next chapter, we not only have significant reservations concerning the appropriateness of social insurance based systems as the primary mechanism for providing protection to the elderly in DCs but also, positively, advocate the wider relevance of the general revenue financed social assistance pension model, discussed above, and currently well established in the MICs of southern Africa, but, until recently, little known outside this sub-region. In this regard, the Gabonese Social Guarantee Programme represents an important geographical breakthrough.

However, we are also keen to stress the almost equal importance of reforming existing systems of formal provision alongside the establishment of universal social assistance pensions. In particular, it is important to stress that our proposals neither involve the abandonment of existing state-run formal provision, whether NPF or SI-based, nor do they involve the discouragement of the continued expansion of existing forms of private pension and provident fund provision, provided that these continue to be offered on a voluntary rather than a mandatory basis. However, for reasons outlined below, we also regard it as imperative that the focus of formal protection systems increasingly shifts beyond the needs of the formal sector worker. Specifically, we recognise the looming possibility that, if meaningful reform of social security provision is further delayed, the damage already done to the credibility of existing social protection systems may ultimately, and potentially irrevocably, undermine any residual regional belief in social security as a 'concept' - an issue of relevance to the likely pro-privatisation reform path to be followed, in particular, in Kenya and, albeit to a lesser degree, in Uganda. To date the ILO have continued to argue, and have continued to have the support of most African governments in their view, that the serious failings which affect formal social security in Africa 'lie in their operation rather than in the concept' (ISSA, 1994b, p.96).

Maintaining this position, however, is likely to become increasingly difficult, possibly untenable, if social insurance principles continue to form the main basis of regional systems of social protection. The problems facing existing social insurance systems in SSA are profound. Currently, limited levels of population coverage leave the vast majority of people on the continent without any form of income protection for old age. Although, as the ILO are correct to emphasise, it is important to remember that, despite their problems, '(s)uch schemes do... provide for many millions of people the only form of income or social protection...' (ILO, 1994d, p.96) that is currently available, this is no comfort to the much larger numbers currently excluded from participation and benefits. Coverage of the poor is the crucial problem for all social insurance-based social security systems in developing countries and, therefore, SSA provides a challenge in this respect that social insurance alone has not, and now cannot, meet. As Guy Standing, from within the ILO, has underlined, 'social insurance *in practice* has not been providing protection to the poor and the vulnerable' (Standing, 1999a, p.363, emphasis in original). Fully facing up to the implications of this point clearly requires the ILO to reconsider many of its established perspectives and approaches: a process that is currently underway and ongoing.

Accordingly, the most pressing, and potentially the most damaging, issue among the numerous institutional problems associated with the administration of African social security systems, pre-dating SAPs and still awaiting attention, are low levels of system coverage (ISSA, 1994b). As a result of this long-standing coverage problem, there is a growing acknowledgement of the institutional impossibility of attempting to provide, in the African context, universal social security exclusively through social insurance financed provision. More widely, the persistent growth of informal sector employment in middle and low income economies has played a significant role in undermining the contributions base, and in highlighting the design limitations, of social insurance financed social security among developing countries generally. Undermined by operating in a context of low and declining national levels of formal sector employment, it is clear that the 'universal' expectations placed upon contributory social security in many African countries have become unrealistic.

In particular, a continuing emphasis placed upon the *conventional* approach to social security funding, whereby entitlement to social security benefits is, most commonly, achieved through paying contributions deducted from the wages of formal sector employees, renders the majority of individuals within national labour forces across much of Africa ineligible for any form of formal social security protection, and will continue to do so into the foreseeable future. The fact that the vast majority of African countries operate social insurance financed social security systems within economic environments in which non-formal sector activities underpin a significant proportion of national productivity, highlights this point well. It is important also to recognise that, typically, there is a heavy, institutionalised, male-bias built into established formal social security provision. This arises, in part, from the historical male-bias already inherent in the European social security systems upon which most African schemes are modelled. From an African perspective, however, the primary problems of male-bias arise from the fact that a disproportionately large proportion of women work within non-formal sectors, leaving formal sector, 'pensionable' employment heavily male-dominated.

Despite the merits of the risk sharing principles of social insurance in particular, it is clear that contributions financed social security provision cannot be expected satisfactorily to alleviate old age poverty in Africa. The acknowledged failure of social insurance systems to provide any reasonable degree of protection to those in irregular, unregulated or any other form of non-formal employment, including those working in subsistence agriculture, underlines one reason why the social security approaches that were central to the development of European-style welfare states have become increasingly irrelevant to many, especially the poorer, developing countries, not least those in Africa. Nevertheless, established systems of formal protection should not simply be abandoned; rather, existing systems should be reformed and strengthened (Fultz and Pieris, 1999). Accordingly, the challenges facing African policy makers remain clear cut. First, they are faced with the problem of consolidating and improving the governance and administration of social security institutions. Second, they face the task of extending the population coverage provided by current social security arrangements. Third, policy makers should be encouraged to seek and to harness alternative and additional mechanisms, including 'traditional', non-formal, social security arrangements, to address the welfare needs of the growing numbers of destitute elderly in the region. These last issues are the focus of Chapter 7 below.

Exploring the Policy and Institutional Implications for SSA

Typically, perceptions of the achievements and impact of formal social security provision in Africa remain largely negative. Such unflattering perspectives are confirmed by very poor levels of population coverage, generally inadequate benefit provision and evidence of institutionalised administrative corruption. In short, in regard to the efficient and effective delivery of systems of social protection to the great majority of its citizens, Africa has everything to learn and nothing to offer. Although overdrawn, such predominantly negative perspectives are not significantly misplaced in focusing on the poor and sometimes dismal performance of the majority of SSA's formal social security systems. In contrast, African 'success stories' of effective and efficient social security provision remain rare: those that fall into that category, notably the largely unconcerted regional movement towards universality in old age pension provision across southern Africa, have remained little publicised even within the region until comparatively recently. Nevertheless, there are some hopeful signs, not least the increasing possibility that any future pension debate in Africa may follow a trajectory which will sit uncomfortably both with the ILO's social insurance-based approach and with the World Bank's personal savings-based model of old age security.

Any realistic debate on the future nature of and optimal trajectory for pensions provision across Africa requires a reconsideration of the fundamental purposes of support to the elderly, and an equally far-reaching reconsideration of the policy and institutional bases on which that support can be extended, if such provision is to form a more effective element within wider strategies of poverty alleviation, or, as it is currently more fashionably presented, poverty eradication. For the poor in developing countries, not least those of SSA, the importance of guaranteeing 'social justice' for all cannot be overstated, irrespective of which approaches and mechanisms are ultimately selected and employed to achieve this end. In the African case it is clear that a continuing primary emphasis upon contributory social security will leave very significant portions of national labour forces excluded from formal social security arrangements whether these are based on social insurance principles or on the NPF model of retirement savings provision. Similarly, the current fashion for basing provision on private defined contribution retirement savings schemes remains largely inappropriate to the needs of most people in most African countries.

Arguably, the complex specificity of the problems facing African social security administrations, combined with the equally complex specificities of Africa's economic, political and social experiences, would suggest that all conventional western-style, and, indeed, Southeast Asian-style, approaches to social security provision are likely to be substantially inappropriate as mainstream social protection mechanisms. Both these approaches will remain largely irrelevant to the needs of the majority of Africa's populations, well into the conceivable future. Nevertheless, existing approaches to formal provision of social protection should not, indeed cannot, be left unreformed and unreconstructed. Accordingly, as well as actively seeking additional and alternative mechanisms designed expeditiously to secure the widening, and maximal extension, of social protection coverage, there also remains an urgent need to continue to press for the reform of the administration and governance of existing formal social security systems and institutions, however limited their achievements to date. Such programmes of reform are required if formal social protection mechanisms are realistically to begin to perform their functions as effective instruments within poverty alleviation strategies and to contribute significantly, at least in the longer term, to the rapid expansion of benefit coverage that is required. To repeat a point made earlier, if meaningful reform of existing formal social security provision is further delayed, the resultant damage to the credibility of social protection systems may also destroy any lingering belief in the value of social security as a 'concept'.

Positively, it may be suggested that the most practical way to make African social protection both more inclusive and more effective in reducing poverty amongst the elderly is to follow an institutionally heterogeneous and a policy eclectic pathway, specifically taking note of successful attempts to address coverage, and related poverty alleviation problems, creatively. In these respects, innovative developments in India aimed at improving coverage for the elderly poor under contributory and non-contributory schemes provide potentially useful models for African administrators to consider. Specifically, the mechanisms developed to secure incremental expansion of coverage in India may provide useful policy lessons to SSA, both for the widening of contributory social security and for the non-contributory inclusion of the unprotected destitute elderly. As the available evidence, outlined in Chapter 7 below, suggests, both these approaches can be administratively feasible and financially affordable, even for the poorest countries. The extension of general revenue financed, even, in the case of South Africa, means-tested, provision on an universal basis across southern Africa, in turn, demonstrates that a more comprehensive level of coverage of the elderly is both an appropriate and a viable policy option for African countries.

Crucially, what is now required across SSA, particularly if poverty alleviation aims are to served by 'formal' social security mechanisms, is that serious consideration should be given to the design and implementation of consolidated administrative arrangements that will manage and deliver existing and reformed programmes of 'pensions', and related transfers, to eligible beneficiaries increasingly economically, efficiently and effectively. In practice, achieving these aims involves a set of complex, therefore initially costly, tasks that can only be implemented gradually over a number of years in most of the region's states. Currently, typically, contributory state pension provision is organisationally separated and insulated both from social assistance programmes and from any formal, as well as informal, private provision to such a degree that no information flows between them and cooperation, let alone coordination, is neither envisaged nor attempted either in programme design or in implementation. Accordingly, even to take some initial steps towards a more rational set of arrangements requires the commitment of significant additional administrative, financial and human resources, not to mention a degree of political will and commitment that has hitherto been conspicuous by its absence. Potentially, however, the payoffs are large even in relation to the investments of money, resources and time that are needed to move towards integrated administrative arrangements coordinating, within consolidated programmes, existing disintegrated *melanges* of disaggregated and disjointed elements of social support to the elderly.

Interestingly, although atypical of SSA states in facing few significant financial constraints, Botswana has recently begun to implement the type of policy coordination and institutional consolidation programme suggested here. On the basis of recent studies undertaken sub-regionally, covering Mauritius and the Seychelles as well as neighbouring Namibia and South Africa, and building on a series of consultancy reports provided by both the ILO and by local organisations, the Government of Botswana is planning to move, albeit gradually in a carefully phased process, towards the organisational consolidation of the administration and management of existing social security and related social assistance programmes within a single Ministry (ILO, 1980, 1997c; Ernst and Young *et al.*, 1998).

The basis of this proposed organisation would be to ensure that all administrative procedures and organisational structures are streamlined, and only one single entity is involved in the development of social security policy and delivery of services. *In imparting this responsibility to a single Ministry, delivery efficiency should increase as well and the current confusion among the various social security benefit stakeholders could be alleviated.*

Ernst and Young *et al.*, 1998, p.26, emphasis added

Within this consolidated organisational format for the coordinated provision of social protection to the vulnerable, 'the proposed Department of Social Security would focus on the development of legislation and delivery of benefits to all areas of society including the elderly and destitute irrespective of an individual's employment history or status' (Ernst and Young *et al.*, 1998, p.25). In turn, this consolidated organisational format is to be implemented to deliver the Government of Botswana's planned 'consolidated welfare policy'. This is specifically to be formulated as a 'comprehensive' programme in order 'to develop cohesion among social welfare operatives' and, as such, will explicitly be 'aimed at facilitating coordination of central and local government organs with social welfare functions' (Phirinyane, 1999, p.1). As the Minister of Finance and Development Planning underlined in announcing this policy initiative, such 'coordination was critical to avoid duplication and [in] ensuring economic and efficient utilisation of scarce resources' (Phirinyane, 1999, p.1). Arguably, the need for such coordination is even more pressing in the great majority of African states which lack Botswana's financial resources, but, ironically, thereby also lack that state's capacity either to continue to support existing, inefficient, programmes or to develop the requisite operational alternatives. In these cases domestic reform efforts must be underpinned by sustained external support from donors, initially in the form of policy advice and institutional capacity building, for comparable programmes of policy, institutional and organisational development and associated administrative and procedural reforms.

Conclusion

The implications of the trends and findings outlined above both pose particular problems and offer significant opportunities for the International Labour Organisation, given that its long-standing commitment to the principles of social insurance is matched by equal commitment to the maximal extension of social security provision. Specifically, the ILO's long-standing belief in the virtues of social insurance has been paralleled by its tireless work in championing the growth of social security protection and advocating its maximal extension. This promotion of the importance of providing expansive and wide-ranging social security coverage crystallised in the ILO Social Security (Minimum Standards) Convention No. 102 (1952) (see Appendix, Fig. A2.1). Although it is increasingly acknowledged that this Convention was drafted in an era characterised, at least for a time in HICs, by a pattern of male-dominated full-time employment and stable family structures, it continues to provide a widely accepted benchmark against which all national social security provisions are evaluated. Nonetheless, it remains significant that, to date, no country in southern Africa, the sub-region within SSA with the most developed set of social security arrangements reflecting above average national incomes, has ratified Convention 102 (Fultz and Pieris, 1999, p.2). In relation to SSA, specifically, the current challenge is both to design new and to adapt old policy instruments and institutions to deliver these benefits to all those who need them. It is to these policy challenges that we now turn.

Notes

1. Western Sahara is here presented as a sovereign independent territory. The UN has stated openly its support for a referendum on the self-determination of the people of Western Sahara.
2. It has been reported that Namibia is considering adding a social insurance element to its existing universal tax financed 'first tier', in line with standard ILO advice. It is also reported that conflicting advice is emanating from the private sector and that civil servants are opposed to the proposals.

7 Alternative Agendas for Least Developed Countries

Introduction

As will have become clear from reading Chapter 6, the policy challenges facing those charged with designing and providing more effective, as well as more comprehensive and inclusive, African systems of social security are immense. These policy challenges frame the concerns of this chapter: namely to sketch out, albeit tentatively and provisionally, some suggestive directions and possibilities for reform strategies, particularly focused at sub-Saharan Africa (SSA), but utilising examples of good practice from other regions where appropriate. Specifically, as the ILO has long understood, the extent and scope of the problems to be solved, and the scale of the needs to be met across SSA, suggest that the appropriate policy strategy remains that of reforming social security systems *in toto*. For reasons explained above in Chapter 6, SSA, especially low income SSA, is unlikely, at least in the short term, to be pressed by the Bank as hard as other Third World regions to adopt its private sector-based version of pillared pension provision, leading to the prospect of serious regional consideration for more state-friendly versions such as the ILO's 'tiered' variant, discussed above in Chapter 3. What we would wish to emphasise is that it is as important that this reform debate should break out of the confines of the social insurance model of 'welfare state' provision as it is vital for it to transcend the Bank's private sector bias and capital market development focus. What we would wish to add to the debate is the need for a reform agenda to actively incorporate social assistance approaches in order to achieve universality in coverage and comprehensiveness in contingency provision - and to do so quickly.

Significantly increased acceptance of the importance of well institutionalised social assistance programmes offered on a long term basis is essential if low income, often aid dependent, states realistically seek to aspire to the goal of universality in coverage of eligibles. In this emphasis on the fundamental importance of social assistance within our suggested pension reform strategy we depart from both the ILO's, traditional, and the World Bank's, more recent, acceptance of social assistance as necessary, but, equally, largely temporary, palliatives. The ILO has long accepted that 'social assistance has a role to play, at least as an interim measure under economic and social conditions which preclude the extension of social insurance protection to the majority of the population' (Midgley, 1984b, p.26). For the Bank in recent years, support in a social assistance format has involved a series of *ad hoc*, aid financed, hence always provisional and uncertain of continuing funding, 'safety nets', specifically characterised by administrative structures deliberately located outside regular government bureaucracies. This approach was exemplified, first, by a series of 'emergency' social funds initially implemented across Latin America as temporary measures within structural adjustment programmes and then institutionalised on a more established basis in the form of social 'investment' funds inaugurated across Latin America and in SSA.

Our contention is that neither of these perspectives on and approaches to social assistance is satisfactory, underlining the clear need to reconsider available modalities and mechanisms for delivering social benefits on a social assistance basis in low income countries as an important research priority. For example, even the Bank's core social protection researchers readily acknowledge that the role so far played by its social funds in 'social risk management' has been 'mainly in [the] area of risk coping', recognising the largely retrospective focus of such programmes on those already poor (Jørgensen and Van Domelen, 1999, p.21). As Jørgensen and Van Domelen acknowledge, social funds remain only 'potentially important vehicles for risk reduction and mitigation', requiring substantial adjustments in focus to '[m]ove from poverty to vulnerability targeting' (1999, p.21).

As we expand on below, utilising southern African evidence supplemented by examples of innovative approaches from India and Latin America, there are numerous relevant examples of good policy and institutional practice in providing effective social assistance on a regular basis to very large numbers of the elderly poor among schemes already operational in a number of DCs. Nevertheless, in this field in particular, much further comparative work is needed to provide appropriate policy models and relevant institutional examples for LICs. There are, however, some positive signs, not least the evolution of ILO thinking on such matters, largely paralleling Bank initiatives outlined above and in the Introduction. Recent ILO thinking has also moved to consider an increasingly encompassing 'social risk management' approach to social protection, updating and incorporating its earlier view of social security, 'as an umbrella term, incorporating social insurance and social assistance' (Lund and Srinivas, 2000, p.17) within its parameters.[1] This evolution has allowed for an increasingly positive attitude to social assistance and to its potential for supporting increased social protection in economies with large informal sectors. These developments are already having an impact on core ILO activities, for example within its increasingly influential global STEP programme (Strategies and Tools against Social Exclusion and Poverty) and its InFocus Programme on Socio-Economic Security (IFPSES). 'In many countries the conventional forms of social security perform poorly and are often inefficient ... The InFocus programme will assist in formulating cost-effective and equitable ways by which social protection can be extended to all groups in society and will advise on the relative efficacy of alternative policy options to promote social and economic security' (ILO, 1999c, p.24). This social assistance-friendly strategy complents the ILO's current 'first tier' proposals outlined in Chapter 3.

Universality: Establishing Feasibility

For least developed countries (LDCs) whose poverty and macroeconomic weakness renders them largely *outwith* the parameters of the current 'global' pension reform agenda, important lessons can be taken from the largely overlooked trend, outlined in Chapter 6 above, towards the provision of universal and, in the South African case, means-tested state pension provision in Africa's (middle-income) southern cone region. Conventional wisdom has always been that LDCs cannot afford to implement, and expect to sustain, complex and costly Western-style welfare systems. Our contention is a simple one. Conventional wisdom is wrong, perhaps not comprehensively so, but at least in large part. Specifically, if welfare systems are broken down into their component contingencies it is feasible for even the poorest of the world's states to consider providing 'universal' coverage for at least some of the central pillars of support associated with conventional welfare states, either by supplementing existing social insurance or NPF provision with non-contributory incorporation of the poorest, or through stand-alone social assistance programmes. The appropriate starting point for expanded state welfare provision, we would suggest, would be the most vulnerable, and currently the least considered, segment of the population of LDCs, the old. Specifically, contrary to the assumptions of the 'complex and costly' argument over the extension of social insurance principles and programmes to DCs, the available evidence from those few DCs that have in recent years swum against the global tide and instituted universal general revenue financed systems is that this is an immediately fiscally affordable option for those states with significant formal sector employment profiles and, therefore, with relatively accessible tax bases. No less important, the provision of state minimum retirement provision is also an administratively feasible goal for all states. In principle, universal coverage for all old people, via a small cash income support programme, is achievable for the poorest LDC given the continuance of existing levels of foreign assistance.

The supporting evidence for this argument, we would suggest, is as straightforward as it is compelling. In 1995, for example, Egypt, admittedly with per capita income at the top end of the scale of LICs, was able to achieve 83 percent workforce coverage for its SI retirement pension at a cost equivalent to 2.5 percent of GDP. Outreach, incorporating substantial segments of the informal sector and the rural workforce, is maximised by the simplest of fiscal incentives. Farmers, for example, in return for a nominal contribution of 1 Egyptian pound receive a minimum pension of 45 pounds (Vittas, 1998b, p.17). South Africa, admittedly at the bottom end of the upper middle income category, has successfully extended its (means tested and individually-based) retirement pension provision to a point where it is reasonable to claim 'universality' as well as 'generosity'. Specifically, with in excess of 90 percent coverage of eligibles (males over 65 and females over 60) in the black community, and with the majority of those 'excluded through eligibility criteria (the means test) rather than administrative obstructions' (Ferreira, 1999, p.55), '[p]ensioners are ... a principal source of cash income for a large number of households'. Nor is the South African experience an isolated one regionally since Mauritius, Namibia and Botswana have also established similarly 'universal' schemes. Moreover, Mozambique, one of the world's poorest countries, has a means-tested scheme, albeit not officially described as a pension but as a cash-transfer programme, for unemployed urban citizens aged 60 or over, although it is currently operating with restricted geographical coverage.

LDC Social Assistance Pension Programmes: Indian Examples

Outwith Africa, means-tested old age pension schemes designed to provide protection for the destitute elderly are found across India. Initially, the introduction of means-tested old age pensions was legislated for at State level. In 1957, 'Uttar Pradesh was the first to introduce such a general 'old-age' pensions scheme'. As Guhan outlines, following this initial development in Uttar Pradesh, during the 1960s old-age pension schemes were introduced at State level in Kerala (1961), and Andhra Pradesh (1961), to be joined by Tamil Nadu (1962), West Bengal (1962), Punjab (1964) and then by Karnataka (1965), as simple mechanisms designed to provide social security to the destitute elderly. During the 1970s similar initiatives were introduced in Orissa (1975), Gujarat (1978), Madhya Pradesh (1979) and Maharashtra (1979) (Guhan, 1992, p.287, fn.14). During the 1980s, various Indian states independently introduced old age pension schemes for agricultural workers, thus, in principle, further widening the percentage of the population with access to some form of old age protection. Accordingly, it is now the case that 'each and every state in India has implemented old age pension schemes for elderly destitutes' (Kumar, 1998, pp.14-15).

Despite the widening availability of social assistance for the destitute elderly and other disadvantaged groups, these State schemes, nonetheless, 'have been berated for their poor coverage and inadequate financial assistance' (Arun and Arun, 2000). One significant response to the recognised shortcomings in provision under State-level social assistance has been the introduction in 1995 of the National Social Assistance Programme (NSAP). The NSAP aims to provide a unified rate of Rs. 75/- per month for the destitute elderly across all the States and Union Territories (UT) of India. Under the State schemes, the level of monthly benefits varied considerably between States, ranging from Rs 30/- to Rs 60/- per month, were set at a lower rate than that provided by the NSAP. However, in practice, the introduction of the NSAP has not been without its own problems. Simply stated, the NSAP has encountered many 'institutional and procedural complications' which have hindered the implementation of a uniform programme of social assistance at the national level (Kumar, 1998, p.16). Importantly, it was intended that the introduction of the NSAP would complement existing State and UT social assistance provisions. In practice, the introduction of the centralised NSAP has tended to displace independent local social assistance provision for the elderly as the Indian States and UTs have 'diverted their own resources to other programmes' (Kumar, 1998, p.16).

Such severe, albeit merited, criticisms of social assistance programmes in India should, however, be seen from a wider perspective of weaknesses in formal pension provision, specifically taking cognisance of the fact that around 28 percent of salaried employees and nearly 90 percent of workers, including the self-employed and farmers, 'are not covered by any pension scheme that enables them to save for economic security during old age'. In total, this equates to nearly 300 million people. As a government sponsored report states, 'the present formal provisions for old age income security in India cover less than 11 percent of the estimated working population' (OASIS, 2000). This sobering fact would suggest that, despite the acknowledged problems associated with the NSAP, the policy prioritisation of a national social assistance programme is, in principle, justified. In practice, however, the criticisms validly levelled at the NSAP demonstrates that there is an immediate need to improve the administration and coordination of both national and state social assistance programmes, not least in order to secure expanded coverage. The problematic issues specifically identified, namely the difficulties of guaranteeing adequate funding and of improving accessibility to entitlements on a nation-wide basis, which currently preclude the development of more effective and efficient benefit provision in India, in turn, are indicative of comparable financial and administrative problems common to many, probably most, large-scale social assistance programmes in low income developing countries. Our simple contention is that the sources of such problems are to be located in the inauspicious economic, social and political contexts in which ambitious benefit schemes have been implemented, and are not to be found in either the specific policies and instruments utilised, or in the wider, social assistance approaches on which these policies are based.

Achieving Universality: Key Issues

Specifically, we would argue that the problems currently facing the elderly poor in low income countries are of such magnitude that early implementation of provisions for universal and regular, even if only small, cash incomes on a social assistance basis is now a necessity rather than an option. Acceptance of the inevitable administrative shortcomings and implementational shortfalls should be built into country policy strategies. Latin American experience with comparable large-scale social assistance programmes underlines the point that the capacity both to design and to manage such programmes accumulates over time, whilst also confirming that such capacities are more effectively and efficiently mobilised by middle income countries than by their low income counterparts (Aedo and Larrañaga eds., 1994). Even among LICs administrative, managerial and implementational capacities vary quite widely, with India among the most capable. Accordingly, the example of Mozambique is arguably of even greater relevance to most LDCs than the well-established case of India's NSAP, albeit remaining one of ambition rather than of firm achievement. If Mozambique, with an UN estimated level of per capita-GDP in 1997 of $199, can aspire to old age provision universality any country can, and, arguably should, as an anti-poverty priority.

Due to the comparatively low numbers involved - currently, over 60s approximate roughly to only 10 percent or even less of total populations in SSA [see Appendix Table A1.1] - the budgetary costs of universal provision are not high, even if LDCs are not able to fund individual pensioners at the $85 per month level achieved in South Africa. Universality is fiscally feasible for LDCs if it is pitched at below the 1 percent of GDP, equating to 8 percent of government expenditure, that the current South African scheme requires (Ferreira, 1999, p.55). Indeed, in the context of most LDCs, even tiny injections of cash income delivered on a regular basis would have significant poverty reducing impacts for the poorest of the old. For example, in the mid-1980s, Guhan argued that the social assistance pension systems of Kerala and Tamil Nadu in India, though very small in cash income terms, provided significant additional support for the poorest households in these states (Guhan, 1994, pp.47-48; Nair and Tracy, 1989). Specifically, in Kerala and Tamil Nadu pensions were calculated to meet 50 percent or more of subsistence needs. Significantly, the extrapolated cost of the latter's full social assistance programme to the whole of India, and thus a figure likely to equate to the hypothetical total cost of the NSAP if it were adequately implemented, would provide a comprehensive social security package for poor households equating to no more than 0.3 percent of India's GDP and involving the commitment of about 1 percent of total revenue (Guhan,

1994, pp.48-49). As Guhan rightly concludes such a 'minimum package can thus be both affordable and sustainable' (Guhan, 1994, p.49).

At a more basic level, Russian experience reminds us that cash incomes through pensions remain important to poor households in all countries however small these incomes are. Despite the fact that Russian pensions have steadily lost value, equating to only 33 percent of the average wage in 1999, a Siberian respondent was recently quoted as claiming that 'it is better to have two live grandparents than to have two cows' (as cited in Kandiyoti, 1999, p.506). Confirmatory evidence of the wider applicability of this point is provided by a sample from interview data collected by UN researchers in the town of Shkrodra, Albania. Quite simply, in many of the transition economies pensions are the sole source of cash income in the poorest households.

> In this house four families live: my parents, myself with my wife and children, my two brothers with their wives and children. We live on our parents, 3,600 Lek a month each, since one of my brothers is unemployed and we just do temporary jobs from time to time.
>
> Kudat and Youssef, 1999, p.31

Across much of the developing world the poorest households similarly have to survive on cash incomes that are a fraction of minimum or average wages. In Zimbabwe, for example, the elderly were, by 1995, on average subsisting on a mere 20 percent of the formal sector minimum wage. The poorest category of all, widowed females, were surviving on a derisory 6 percent of the formal sector minimum wage, down from 16 percent in 1988 (Adamchak, 1999, p.54). Supplementary support in the form of a social assistance 'pension', even if set at very low levels, would have significantly positive impacts on the increasingly large numbers of such households, not least in boosting their prospects for retaining some degree of inter-generational solidarity. Specifically, recent research in South Africa has confirmed that pensions are vital to underpin the status of the old in multi-generational households (Sagner and Mtati, 1999). Moreover, South African evidence also indicates that household size rises when even one member is in receipt of an old age pension, underlining the point that assistance pensions constitute a cost-effective mechanism for underpinning family solidarity at the household level (Carter and May, 1999, p.20).

Across SSA and in the rest of the developing world such multi-generational households are under multiple threat, from economic decline, from socio-political instability and rising crime, resulting in the increasing breakdown of traditional informal support systems. In SSA in particular, the debilitating impacts of the HIV+ virus and the deadly consequences of full blown AIDS upon the middle cohort of multi-generational 'family' groups is increasingly obvious. Reversing this wider decline requires the injection of cash incomes directly into the hands of the elderly, preferably delivered as individual entitlements rather than on a household basis, to achieve equity and to avoid male-bias problems. The state, in turn, is the only feasible source of such incomes for the elderly poor.

Social Assistance Pensions: Achievements and Potential

Accordingly, although there is still an urgent need to continue to press for the reform of the administration and governance of the existing formal social security institutions across SSA, as discussed above in Chapter 6, the even more urgent requirement is to seek additional and alternative social protection mechanisms designed specifically to widen social protection coverage both expeditiously and comprehensively. Among the various obvious cohorts requiring enhanced support as a priority, notably women and young people, there is sound evidence emerging from within SSA that would confirm the potential importance of provision to the old as a central element in any comprehensive anti-poverty strategy for the region. Crucially, as recent research in South Africa has underlined, it is clear that the provision of universal old age pensions has welfare enhancing outcomes which go far beyond their immediate goal of providing a source of income for the elderly recipient, specifically also providing enhanced income security, hence also forming a source of collective security and solidarity, for larger family groups (Ardington and Lund, 1995, pp.557-577). Collective consumption means that '[i]n rural communities, pension income circulates widely and is crucial in combating poverty and reducing material insecurity' (Ferreira, 1999, pp.55-56). As a government report on the early impact of the social pension found, effects on local economies in rural areas were profound; '[p]eople are fed and sent to school out of this pension money, it enables investments in farming activities, and in general it is crucial for the very survival of these communities' (Le Roux, 1995, as quoted in Heslop, 1999, p.27). Household surveys have confirmed similar poverty-reducing impacts in urban areas (Sagner and Mtiti, 1999). As the government review concluded, the social pension constituted 'an imperative for the very survival of many urban poor' (Le Roux, 1995, as quoted in Heslop, 1999, p.27).

As Ardington and Lund summarised on the basis of fieldwork undertaken shortly after the post-apartheid implementation of South Africa's universal 'social pension' programme, such transfers to the elderly constitute, variously, 'a significant source of income, with marked redistributive effects; they are a reliable source of income, which leads to household security; they are the basis of credit facilities in local markets, further contributing to food security; they deliver cash into remote areas where no other institutions do; they are gender sensitive towards women; and they reach rural areas as few other services do' (1995, p.571). Subsequent experience has only served to confirm the widespread positive economic and social impacts of this now well established transfer programme. Lund and Srinivas (2000, p.107) provide a convenient, updated, summary of impact;

> The South African state assistance to pensioners has been vital in ensuring household security, has acted as proxy unemployment coverage for younger household members with no access to the formal scheme, has helped smooth income and consumption, and contributed to agricultural inputs - apart from assisting with the care of children.

Although much further research is required to fully explore the potential ramifications of these findings and to develop their implications into firm policy proposals, it is appropriate to make some initial, albeit tentative, suggestions. The first of these relates to the urgent need for enhanced support to the old, as a necessary response to evidence of widespread and severe income insecurity and vulnerability. Although the set of focused household-level studies called for by Tribe (1976a; 1976b) in the 1970s, specifically to cover sources of income and other forms of support in order to fully establish the position of the elderly across SSA, have, for the most part, still to be undertaken, the cumulative evidence from the more general household and village-level studies undertaken increasingly widely in recent years is clear-cut. The already precarious position of the elderly in Africa is deteriorating and will continue to deteriorate further as the proportion of the old within the region's populations begins to rise, requiring increasingly urgent policy responses.

For example, recent research in Tanzania, replicating similar findings from across SSA, confirms that '[m]ore than half the most vulnerable older people have no identified source of support in a crisis', with old women, largely lacking 'social capital' in the form of a network of group affiliations and social networks, significantly more vulnerable than old men (HelpAge International, 2000, p.12).

The second suggestion follows the paradoxical finding, established by numerous studies, 'that the family is the main source of day-to-day support for older people, but family relationships can also be exploitative and contribute to older people's vulnerability' (HelpAge International, 2000, p.12). Importantly, in an era of increasing urbanisation and population mobility there is mounting evidence that the breakdown of 'traditional' family structures and 'traditional' family and community-based 'social security' mechanisms have had the most serious negative impact upon the elderly, and particularly so on the elderly poor. Specifically, the remittance economy, always regressive in that the incentive to remit was always stronger for those with the prospect of eventually securing assets held by the elderly, has not only declined significantly overall in the face of continuing economic crises but has all-but disappeared for the very large number of old people who are now effectively assetless. In this context the provision of old age pensions can act both to protect the old and to encourage the retention of threatened non-formal family and community support structures.

Moreover, for many old people in Africa a narrowing of sources of support and reductions in resources of cash and other assets has, if anything, been accompanied by enhanced responsibilities as a, relatively, stable element within increasingly insecure inter-generational family and community structures. In this respect, the importance of providing cash incomes directly to the elderly poor has been recently highlighted, in central and southern African states in particular, by the growth of the tragic phenomenon of 'AIDS-grannies' who find themselves exclusively responsible for the upbringing and financial support often of several 'AIDS-orphans'. For example, it is reported that Botswana's Minister of Local Government and Lands, and as such responsible for the country's old age pension system, 'visited an elderly woman who was attempting to support nine orphaned grandchildren with her pension' (Fultz and Pieris, 1999, p.23, fn.52). The positive outcome of this visit is that 'Botswana is providing in-kind support to pensioners who provide care for AIDS orphans' (Fultz and Pieris, 1999, p.23). Overall, therefore, it is important to recognise the important role that old age pensions could play in SSA in achieving wider welfare enhancing and poverty reducing outcomes. By providing regular cash incomes to the elderly, 'pensions' have the potential to form highly flexible instruments of social support, not simply providing much needed crisis-proofing for the assetless old but also with significant spread effects, thereby reducing vulnerability significantly across wider family groupings.

In relation to potential benefits, therefore, likely costs are not high, provided administrative overheads are minimised and corruption is controlled by careful monitoring. Donor funding, and administrative support, would, of course be crucial for the many LDCs that have never previously attempted universality in social assistance coverage, not least in providing capacity building administrative support and in monitoring both programme overheads and transparency. However, rationalisation of existing provision rather than new money would be the appropriate mechanism. Excluding Nigeria and South Africa the average SSA country was receiving aid equivalent to 13.2 percent of GDP annually by 1995. According to van de Walle, in a typical SSA country '30-40 donors in addition to 75-125 foreign NGOs fund a thousand or so distinct projects, involving 800-1000 foreign experts' (1999, p.339) making foreign aid the region's second largest employer after government. Currently, there is much concern about the dissipation of impact inherent in existing aid management and delivery strategies. Support for a universal retirement pension would offer a cost effective mechanism for delivering pooled funds to the neediest of the poor. Donor support, on a more decentralised basis, would also be crucial to achieving universality of coverage and regularity of payments. However, it is important not to understate the existing administrative capacities of LDCs in this respect. Many already have experience with the management of community programmes which often achieve surprisingly wide coverage with very limited resources.

Social Assistance Approaches: Learning from Bad and Good Practice

Similarly high administrative costs, often associated with similar diversity and multiplicity in provisioning arrangements, are also characteristic of social assistance programmes in most DCs, both low and middle income. Accordingly, it is clear that social assistance is far from immune from many of the same administrative problems that have been characteristic of the contributory social security programmes with which this volume has primarily been concerned. Although space considerations preclude a full discussion either of evidence or of the relevant issues and implications, it is amply clear that many existing social assistance programmes in DCs, including, not least, those focused on the elderly, are both poorly designed and poorly run (see Lloyd-Sherlock, 1997, for rich empirical detail based on research in the *Shanty Towns of Buenos Aires*). Widely identified design problems relate to opaque eligibility criteria, cumbersome registration arrangements, and complex delivery mechanisms, collectively leading to low take-up among intended beneficiaries and, often, the effective exclusion of the most needy who, as commonly occurs in the case of the old, the illiterate, the infirm and the disabled, either simply give up pursuit of their entitlements in the face of the bureaucratic barriers and other impediments they face or, commonly, simply remain unaware of benefits to which they are theoretically entitled.

Characteristically, the inaccessibility of social assistance programmes in DCs reflects underfunding, and associated problems such as an absence of necessary administrative infrastructures and a scarcity of trained and motivated professionals; all problems that are particularly acute at local and community levels. Equally characteristically, programme inaccessibility, in the form of bureaucratic, sometimes physical, barriers to access, may also be indicative of corruption, favouritism and the deliberate diversion of funds to other purposes. Other commonly noted problems relate to the sharing of administration and management of social assistance programmes, and sometimes even the different elements within a single programme, either between different central government ministries and agencies or among different levels of government, frequently leading to duplication and invariably decreasing efficiency by wasting both time and money as well as dissipating impact.

Among the numerous examples of bad practice in large-scale, national or nation-wide, social assistance provisioning from DCs and transition states, it is notable that examples of good practice tend to come mainly from MICs, thereby underlining the importance of both adequate and secure sources of finance and of significant administrative, including human, resources in underpinning programme effectiveness on a sustained basis. Costa Rica's FODESAF (Fund for Social Development and Family Allowance) is indicative of what can be achieved if guaranteed funding and continuity in other resources permit. FODESAF was established in 1975 as a permanent element in the central government bureaucracy and was designed 'to provide assistance to low income Costa Ricans' (Trejos *et al.*, 1994, p.75). 'The FODESAF is funded through earmarked taxes. The funding level is, therefore, relatively stable over time and does not compete with resources allocated to comprehensive programmes'. Consistently accounting for around 1.5 percent of GDP, FODESAF operates on a very large scale, with regular coverage of well over half a million individuals and with close to $1 billion spent in its first 15 years, but also operates with a good degree of flexibility. This has ensured that the distribution of funding between its more than 50 separate programme elements, mainly administered on a decentralised basis, can be adapted and varied in response to changing economic circumstances and trends. This meant, for example, that support to the elderly poor in the form of social assistance pensions to those 'indigents', almost 75,000 in the mid-1990s, not covered by the contributory pension system, could be expanded during the economic crisis of the early 1980s to meet increased needs (Trejos *et al.*, 1994, pp.75-77).

Nevertheless, FODESAF is not without its problems and the assistance pension programme, in particular, has been criticised for poor targeting, 'with the result that less than 60 percent of the users are among the poorest 40 percent of the population' (Trejos *et al.*, 1994, p.79). As Trejos *et al.* underline in respect of the Costa Rican experience with assistance pensions, an otherwise largely positive experience is somewhat undermined by targeting deficiencies. Moreover, their explanation for this poor targeting achievement is a familiar one, largely reflecting exogenous pressures to misallocate that are endemic to subsidy and assistance programmes in poor countries. 'Even though the process is carried out entirely by professionals, the lack of concrete criteria and of a standard methodology for identifying beneficiaries, as well as the presence of political pressures affecting the grant of benefits, explain the poor targeting results' (Trejos *et al.*, 1994, p.79).

Extending Coverage to the Informal Sector

A further noteworthy and relevant development from India is the development of geographically-limited and occupationally-specific welfare funds for informal sector workers; arrangements which both begin to address some significant coverage gaps and offer the prospect of more effective integration between social assistance programmes and formal social security provision. At present, formally mandated welfare provision in India only provides coverage for about two million 'unorganised workers', a figure which constitutes 'only one percent of the workers in this sector' (Jain, 1997, p.32). Significantly, the establishment by the Indian Government of five welfare funds has sought to provide a degree of coverage to some of the many previously uncovered workers. These five funds now provide coverage for around 4.5 million people employed as *beedi* (cigarette) rollers, cinema workers and certain groups of mine workers. The financing of the social welfare benefits provided by these five welfare funds is 'derived from a tax or levy on the produce of that occupation' (Bailey, 1997, p.9).

In addition to these non-contributory centralised welfare funds for formerly excluded occupational groups, contributory, occupationally specific, welfare funds also exist, in some places, at State level. In Kerala, reinforcing an established reputation for innovative pro-poor policy initiatives, the State has created over 30 contributory welfare funds for marginal occupational groups. In some industries, such as the cashew sector, it is possible to talk of 'maximum coverage' with up to 90 percent of employees covered. Within other informal sector group insurance schemes, however, the percentage of the labour force covered has been much less extensive. For instance, less than 17 percent of coir workers are members of their respective scheme. From a welfare perspective, although covering a similar number of benefit contingencies, there are some important variations between the various occupational schemes in terms of the level of social protection offered and the length of eligibility periods which must be satisfied before entitlement is permitted (Arun and Arun, 2000, pp.10-12). Interestingly also, as Jain has highlighted for Kerala, '[t]he multiplicity of funds has led to high administrative costs and the State Government is considering their integration which is a difficult and complex venture' (Jain, 1997, p.33).

Despite the many, and often innovative, mechanisms adopted in India to improve levels of population coverage under social protection measures, it is unsurprising, therefore, that, in a country where the sheer numbers of those in poverty presents an insuperable set of challenges to the limited administrative and financial resources available to both central and state governments, much still remains to be done, not least in relation to the development of efficient and effective, as well as economic, mechanisms for delivering benefits expeditiously and securely to all the appropriate recipients. Nevertheless, equally, and despite many problems, what Indian experience underlines above all is that improving population coverage, even in a low income country with teeming millions of very poor people, may be a difficult task, but it is not an impossible one. Moreover, what recent Indian experience also indicates is that coverage of informal sector workers, even if initially sought through *ad hoc* and stand alone assistance programmes, can provide a useful basis for later incorporation into established programmes originally designed exclusively for formal sector workers. As evidence from the Indian State of Andhra Pradesh shows, it is possible to use membership of informal sector welfare funds as an initial stepping stone towards inclusion under formal national social security provision (Jain, 1997, p.41). Specifically, the State of Andhra Pradesh has issued identity cards to a large majority of the State's *beedi* workers who are members of the *Beedi* Workers' Welfare Fund, one of the five national welfare funds. By so doing, the *beedi* workers will now be able to gain lump sum and periodic old age benefits under formal social security provision from the recently reformed hybrid Indian Employees' Provident Fund, which now also incorporates the Employees' Pension Scheme within a newly consolidated organisational format.

By repeating this process of inclusion in an incremental fashion, social protection under semi-formal and then under formal national provision is a feasible and practical policy option. In Africa, proposals of a similar nature involving the extension of formal social security protection to non-covered workers who are members of cooperative societies have been proposed by the ILO and considered in a number of countries (Bailey, 1994, p.49; Mulozi, 1994, p.31). Nonetheless, and despite these various proposals for enlarging coverage, one very large group of workers are likely to remain substantially excluded from most social protection measures: the self employed. In the Indian case the self employed comprise 54 percent of the total workforce. Typically, in the development of western welfare states, the self employed were the last occupational group to be afforded social protection under most national social security schemes. Therefore the current exclusion of the self employed in developing countries largely mirrors international experience. Problematically, however, the large numbers of the self employed within developing country labour forces will make it difficult to improve quickly upon the low national social security coverage rates currently pertaining. Accordingly, in countries where social assistance programmes for the destitute elderly operate, a significant proportion of the population are likely to remain dependent upon the small, often very small, cash sums provided by such schemes for some time to come. As is the case in India, and regardless of the higher level of monthly entitlement now available under the NSAP, the value of the pension provided to this numerically significant portion of the population will remain, at best, 'meagre' (Jain, 1997, p.41) into the conceivable future. Nonetheless, as the limited prospect for extending coverage to the self-employed highlights, extending coverage under the aegis of formal social security both widely and quickly is currently infeasible for developing country social security administrations. Consequently, social assistance, even set at niggardly levels to ensure sustainable affordability, constitutes a necessary initial, but neither an 'interim' nor an 'emergency' stop-gap, response.

At the same time it is imperative to underline the point that such 'social assistance pensions', despite their potential value both directly to their elderly recipients and indirectly, as strategic interventions within wider poverty alleviation/eradication strategies, are, in themselves, likely to constitute merely a necessary part in providing solutions to the wider problems of providing the old in DCs with sustainable livelihoods. Heslop's stricture that '[t]oo often development of formal pension and social security programmes is taken as the single reform agenda for older people' (1999, p.27), provides a convenient reminder that sufficient solutions require many additional elements to be in place.

Issues for Further Investigation

I) Integrating Formal and Non-Formal Approaches to Social Protection

Accordingly, it is appropriate to highlight two, among many, salient issues that demand further investigation as an essential prelude to, and basis for, improved policy and institutional strategies for securing more appropriate, more adequate, more comprehensive, and better integrated mechanisms and instruments of old age protection across LDCs and SSA in particular. The first issue stems from the necessity both to acknowledge the continuing importance of, and to respond positively to, the on-going need for, 'traditional', non-formal, family and community based social protection mechanisms. The contemporary relevance of such 'traditional' social protection mechanisms across Africa is not simply a corollary of the ineffectiveness of existing formal social protection systems in the face of predominantly non-formal systems of employment but also, and increasingly, reflects the insecure nature of 'modern' formal sector labour-markets. Unsurprisingly, therefore, and not simply across Africa but more widely among adjusting developing countries generally and including many of the transition states, the observed trend in the 'contra-cyclical' (Charmes, 2000, p.63) rise of non-formal and informal sectors has been accompanied by increased reliance on such, largely family-based, non-formal network mechanisms of social protection, resurrected, renewed and even reinvented in the face of failing and increasingly inadequate formal provision. To the extent that the neoliberal assumptions underpinning the Washington and post-Washington consensuses (see Appendix Figs. A1.1, A1.2) have become embedded in regional and national economic strategies, as has happened most obviously in Latin America, increased resort to, and reliance on, non-formally based social protection mechanisms represent logical, properly 'modern', responses to the insecurities inherent in the liberalised, increasingly 'flexible' labour markets that such strategies demand. In this fashionably liberalised employment policy context, expansion of non-formal coping and survival mechanisms, therefore, represents both an inevitable and a valid response.

Consequently, realistic social and welfare policy strategies for DCs must recognise that such non-formal mechanisms have continuing roles to play both in their own right and as important adjuncts to more formal protection mechanisms in reconstructed support systems. Although a very significant body of research has focused on non-formal social security provisioning in DCs, including SSA, and some important work has been done on the complexities of the interactions between formal and informal elements within established systems of social support (e.g. see various of the essays in von Benda-Beckmann *et al.* eds., 1988, and in Ahmad *et al.* eds., 1991), much further work is still required if the non-formal and the formal are to relate to each other sympathetically and effectively within the articulated systems of social protection required to more effectively attack poverty in both developing and transition states. Specifically, there is an obvious concern that, at least as they are currently constituted, the relationship between public support and private transfers may be, to some degree, mutually exclusive. For example, referring to recent studies of the currently highly significant role of intra-family support networks as social safety nets in Poland and Russia, Chu and Gupta of the IMF restate the standard concern, and one regularly expressed by Bank-funded researchers, that an expanded system of 'public social protection payments could crowd out these private transfers, which are voluntary, efficient and well targeted, making an important contribution to social protection in many transition countries' (1998b, p.106, fn.9).

For Africa, unsurprisingly, little firm empirical evidence is available concerning the impact of public pensions on private transfers. Nevertheless, replicating similar research findings from both Latin America and Southeast Asia, one study of South Africa's social pension programme found a significantly negative impact on the remittances previously sent to the elderly, recording average falls of between twenty and thirty percent (Jensen 1997, as cited in Case and Deaton, 1998, p.1334). More precisely establishing the reasons for this dramatic fall in remittance levels is clearly of some importance to future policy strategies, particularly since it is not unreasonable to suggest that 'in the World Bank's view, pensions and other public social welfare programmes *cause* reduced support by children for their elderly parents' (Gorman, 1999b, p.6 (emphasis in original), citing Lloyd-Sherlock and Johnson, 1996, pp.24-27). Accordingly, evidence of drastically reduced remittances to South African households in receipt of social pensions may seem to offer *prima facie* evidence in support of the Bank's view 'that the extension of formal pension programmes in regions such as sub-Saharan Africa runs the risk of undermining ... informal sources of support' (Lloyd-Sherlock, 1999, p.76).

In practice, however, this interpretation of the South African evidence is likely to be, at best, a partial one, and, at worst, seriously misleading, specifically in danger of confusing evidence of declining ability to remit with reduced willingness to do so. Anecdotal evidence from across SSA consistently refers both to the declining importance of remittances and to the determining role of chronic poverty in this widespread trend, thereby largely obviating the need for concern that public income transfers to the old might crowd out private transfers. For example, a recently undertaken survey of the Tanzanian situation revealed 'a general opinion that support from the family has declined drastically. The chief reason given is poverty' (HelpAge International, 1999d, p.137). Even where, as in southern Africa generally, remittances remain important, cash amounts tend to be very small and remittances in kind outweigh cash transfers.

More significantly, the evidence from the 1993 South Africa national living standards indicates that receipt of the state pension actually serves to cement and underpin household claims on remittances. 'Some households which are remittance dependent also combine this income with incomes derived from pensions and other welfare payments. These would appear to be elderly households who are able to press intermittent claims on their children. These pensions form a vital component of their income and serve to boost the average income earned by this group' (Carter and May, 1999, p.8). Nevertheless, of the 32 percent of rural South African households found by the survey to be in receipt of a pension, 11.5 percent are defined by Carter and May as 'welfare dependent' in that these transfers provide 95 percent of household incomes (1999, p.7, Table 3). In urban areas, the crucial issues in relation to the impact of the receipt of the social pension are rather different. For example, '[o]ne study with older people in a Durban township, found that older people were highly vulnerable to physical and psychological abuse because of the pressure on this income' (Heslop, 1999, p.27, citing the findings of Heslop, 1996). Clearly, further study of this and related behavioural impacts of formal pension provision are urgently needed, not least if observed trends are to be fully and comprehensively explained as a prelude to the development of informed policy strategies.

In relation to the policy strategies needed, fuller understanding will allow for the achievement of enhanced complementarity between formal pension provision and existing non-formal arrangements, with the aim of developing 'programmes designed to protect the informal systems, which are the mainstay of old age security in most developing countries' (Heslop, 1999, p.27). As Amanda Heslop rightly underlines, '[i]t cannot be assumed that guaranteed income is enough to provide social security in old age', particularly given the current, highly precarious, state of all LDC, and most DC economies, and the consequently fierce competition among poor people for access to cash incomes that this precariousness ensures. Accordingly, as a research, and policy, priority, investigation is required into possibilities for ensuring, minimally, that formal social security provision does not undermine existing non-formal provisioning, preferably seeking approaches and instruments that are mutually supportive.

Here, an obvious starting point would be detailed analysis of the reasons for the continuing popularity in SSA of lump sum payments on termination of formal employment; analysis badly needed to confirm the ample anecdotal evidence of the utility of such payments in underpinning the transition from waged work to the self-employment, typically as trader or farmer, that constitutes a more realistic goal for most elderly Africans than abstract notions of 'retirement'. Indeed, for most Africans, male and female alike, what changes most as they grow older is simply the locus of the work that they continue to undertake, which is progressively undertaken closer to, from, and finally within, homes as mobility and strength declines with age. Unsurprisingly, what we do know in relation to the informal social security arrangements of most salience to the elderly in DCs and transition economies, continues to underline the central importance of the family as a key, often still the key, social protection mechanism for the old in both developing and transition economies. As a recent IMF paper summarises: 'The extended family remains the principal source of support for the elderly in societies as diverse as rural China, Indonesia, India, sub-Saharan Africa, and some BRO countries' (Expenditure Policy Division, 1998, p.27).

Policies supporting the family, therefore, form an essential complement to the social pension strategy outlined above; the latter raising the economic and social status of the old within families and the former supporting family structures more widely, thereby collectively underpinning the survival of the family as an inter-generational unit providing solidarity and security. Since, as we have underlined at an earlier stage in this chapter and in Chapter 6 above, both the extended family and community-level support mechanisms are under serious threat across large parts of SSA, there is considerable urgency for governments, and donors, to respond positively and to act quickly. In order to do so, however, considerably more information is required on family survival strategies. For example, utilising South African data, Bertrand *et al.* find a significant reduction in the labour force participation of younger males in households containing a male and, especially, a female pensioner (2000). The reasons behind this behaviour are likely to be both complex and multifaceted, reflecting falling formal sector opportunities in a context of continuing economic recession and indicating that informal or self-employment may have become feasible. Clearly, much further investigation is required, for example in relation to the predilection of South African workers for withdrawing pension savings whenever employment is terminated. The fact that the early withdrawal of pension savings remains 'a popular option among workers in Southern Africa' (Fultz and Pieris, 1999, p.51) is consistent with the possibility that such savings, if available, may be deliberately accessed by younger workers once a male or female household member becomes eligible for a pension. Under such circumstances, it may be that rather than dwelling on the negative labour-market implications of such behaviour, the approach of Bertrand *et al.*, we should more positively anticipate that lump-sum savings, and the pensions themselves, will be utilised for constructive purposes. For example, these funds could possibly underpin investments in income generating activities with household-wide implications or support movements of household members from marginal formal sector employment into informal activities or self-employment.

Interestingly, in this regard, the region's private pension providers have so far shown considerably more initiative than state institutions in responding positively and creatively to the demands of their customers for regular access to their saved funds in a pattern that is replicating the demand-driven 'drawdown' developments previously described for the Southeast Asian NPFs. Governments across SSA, sadly, have either ignored these developments and the popular demands on which they are based, or, have even been actively critical of them. For example, the Government of Botswana recently complained about the negative impact on the country's private pension industry that resulted from the continuing popularity of early access to accrued funds among Batswana. 'The growth of the industry is inhibited by the availability of short term employment benefit schemes, *which appear to be the preference of the working population*' (Ministry of Finance and Development Planning, 2000, p.33).

II) Achieving Administrative Flexibility and Improved Service Delivery

The second issue relates to the need for a significantly enhanced degree of administrative flexibility in the future organisation and management of formal state-provided social security. Hitherto, in particular, too little creative imagination has been applied to the design of benefit delivery arrangements that are both cost effective and user-friendly.[2] Commonly, among developing countries generally, but in low income countries in particular, control over formal social security and other forms of social protection has remained highly centralised, even in an era in which decentralisation of service delivery has become both fashionable and increasingly prevalent. Currently, what is required in rethinking administrative arrangements for providing formal social security provision is a more flexible attitude to institutional design, with appropriate arrangements to be determined pragmatically, relating organisational formats closely to meeting needs effectively. Such flexibility should allow, where appropriate, for a substantial degree of decentralisation in the administration and delivery of poverty alleviating cash, and other, benefits, responding to the finding that the costs of identifying and providing for those in greatest need are minimised if undertaken directly at the local level where the varying circumstances of individuals are well known and where direct responses can most easily be tailored to circumstances. The rationale for decentralisation, therefore, is to ensure that full coverage of those eligible to receive benefits is achieved as expeditiously and as inexpensively as possible; a goal that would remain infeasible under the more centralised, and commonly highly inflexible as well as inaccessible, administrative arrangements that currently prevail in most DCs.

Among low income countries there are numerous examples of the effectiveness of the local, community-level, management of both the revenue and the expenditure elements of social assistance programmes. Many of the most successful of these, providing the most widespread model of good practice in this regard, are associated with the Islamic principle of *zakat*, a religious tax traditionally raised and allocated to the needy on a purely local basis. 'The *zakat* is formalised in some Muslim countries and based entirely on personal responsibility for others'; a straightforward precept that has facilitated its wider utilisation beyond the Middle East and western Asia, albeit often on a more informal basis, for example in a number of those SSA countries with significant Muslim populations. For instance, 'in the Gambia, deliveries of staple food for the needy are based on the precept of *zakat* ...' (Expenditure Policy Division, 1998, p.27). What are less commonly found among DCs, including most MICs, are successful examples of the decentralised management of national programmes. Here the positive evaluation of one development of *zakat* principles in a transition economy, the *Mahallas* in Uzbekistan, is noteworthy, since this programme combines centralised funding with decentralised administration in a creative fashion with obvious potential relevance to many other DCs (Coudouel *et al.*, 1998).

Equally interesting in these respects is Chile's PASIS programme (*Pensiones Asistenciales*), social assistance pensions theoretically provided to all 'those whose monthly per capita incomes do not exceed 50 percent of the minimum pension payment', and in practice effectively targeted at the poorest households who receive about 80 percent of the budgeted cash benefits, would provide an appropriate model for other DCs, if only it did not exclude almost half of those elderly persons technically eligible for benefit because of the arbitrary numerical ceilings placed on take-up by the government (Aedo and Larrañaga, 1994, p.28). With enrolment and selection of beneficiaries decentralised to the country's local governments, the *municipios*, on the basis of detailed socio-economic data collected on a nation-wide basis, PASIS effectively demonstrates how to combine the advantages of centralised control over accreditation criteria and data collection with the advantages of decentralised administration and management of programme implementation. Moreover, an additional advantage of instituting more administratively flexible arrangements, also providing a further rationale for decentralisation, would be to maximise possibilities for institutional and operational interactions with non-formal, hence possibly locally-specific, welfare initiatives.

Conversely, centralised approaches and institutional arrangements remain more appropriate for the effective financial monitoring and control of contributory social security mechanisms, such as the administration and management of social insurance systems and NPFs where huge sums of money need to be collected on a regular basis. China provides an instructive case study in this regard, moving decisively in recent years 'to relieve individual enterprises of full, direct responsibility for their workers' retirement pensions by establishing funds that pool resources and risks among enterprises and across regions' (Hu, 1998, p.143). Since 1986 such consolidated mandatory retirement funds have been widely established at both city and provincial levels, utilising a format that an IMF commentator describes as 'generally modelled on the Central Provident Fund of Singapore' and deliberately designed to capture economies of scale and scope through centralisation. 'Retirement pension pooling has eased the financial burden on many enterprises of supporting the growing number of retirees. Pension pooling has also helped maintain workers' retirement benefits when changing jobs and, hence, improved the conditions conducive to greater labour mobility' (Hu, 1998, p.143; for ongoing developments in this regard, see Chapter 5, footnote 3 above). However, even in the case of contributory programmes where the advantages of a high degree of centralisation are clear-cut, there are still rationales for the decentralised management of some programme elements, notably to ensure effective and efficient benefit delivery but also, for example, as the administrators of Malaysia's EPF discovered (McKinnon, 1996, p.49), to ensure more effective compliance monitoring where detailed local knowledge of enterprises and employment patterns is vital.

Conclusion

Ultimately, therefore, the goals of achieving comprehensiveness and inclusiveness in social protection for the elderly in LDCs, and across SSA in particular, should be pursued via two distinct modalities informed by convergent purposes, and increasingly, we would suggest, organised and managed under coordinated and consolidated arrangements. On the one hand, enhanced inclusiveness should stem from ensuring the widest feasible expansion of 'formal' social security coverage utilising a combination of contributory and non-contributory social protection measures; the former to be extended first to formal sector workers and then offered more widely with appropriate incentives to encourage participation, utilising the latter, in the form of social assistance pensions, to provide cash incomes more immediately to the elderly on an universal basis. On the other hand, in line with the continuing prevalence of non-formal sectors and the important roles of family and community in poor countries, expanded coverage should also be sought by encouraging the development of as wide a variety of non-formal social protection and assistance mechanisms, including non-formal financial intermediaries, as is appropriate and necessary both to reach the elderly poor and to provide more effectively for their survival needs. Here again, the aim is to provide sustainable support on an universal basis and, overall, to begin to mitigate the risks and uncertainties currently faced by the region's millions of elderly poor.

Notes

1. The driving impetus behind the development of social risk management approaches to social protection has been provided by the World Bank, see also Preface and Chapter 1.

2. South Africa provides an increasingly well known user-friendly example of organisational flexibility in benefits provision whereby 'public' old age pension benefits entitlements are delivered on a decentralised 'private' basis by a number of companies. As Lund and Srinivas report, 'private firms have developed sophisticated and robust systems for mobile delivery. Each month, hundreds of vehicles, holding automatic teller machines, millions of rands, and many armed guards, take to the rural roads, stopping at pre-determined pension points along the way' (2000, p.83). In what has been characterised as a system of 'First World Smartcards and Third World Pensioners' (Ashurst, 1996), entitlements are accessed by eligibles, first, by entering a PIN number and, second, through the innovative use of state-of-the-art biometric technology used to scan and recognise the individual's thumb print. Although this decentralised and private solution to the problem of delivering benefits to individuals living in areas with 'undeveloped telecommunications and financial service infrastructure' remains costly, and potentially problematic for the longer-term development of 'more fixed and permanent' local financial services providers, the service provided to the elderly has improved, not least through making entitlements more readily, and thus more regularly, accessible. Nonetheless, the South African authorities have missed important opportunities to improve and widen services to pensioners and South African citizens more generally. As Lund and Srinivas argue, the South African authorities could have 'promoted the expansion and delivery of more general financial services, such as paying salaries of civil servants; insisted on state ownership of the database which has been developed; [and] used the delivery event for dissemination of information ... [to] ... improve overall knowledge about state services' (Lund and Srinivas, 2000, p.83).

8 The Pension Fund-Capital Market Nexus

Introduction

Many of the central long-term economic problems facing the low and middle income economies of the South relate to worryingly low savings and investment rates, and these problems are particularly marked in SSA. For that region in particular underlying problems have been significantly exacerbated by the effects of on-going structural adjustment programmes (SAPs), as domestic investment levels, already at a disturbingly low level in the early 1980s, fell even further as conditionalities imposed under SAPs, notably debt service obligations, further reduced domestic savings and constrained investment possibilities further still (World Bank, 1994b, pp.37-38, pp.153-158, pp.250-253; World Bank, 1996, pp.41-43; Killick, 1998, pp.22-27). In this continuing, indeed deepening, vicious cycle of low national savings and inadequate domestic investment programmes, the weaknesses of financial systems and financial sectors have been constant factors, forming important independent and intervening variables. 'Throughout the continent, inefficient financial intermediation both exacerbates and contributes to the problem of low savings and investment rates, figures which have not been improved by structural adjustment policies' (Kenny and Moss, 1998, p.832). In turn, the macroeconomic policy priorities mandated under initial stabilisation programmes and on-going SAPs have ensured that little attention has been paid, either by governments or by their IFI 'advisers', until comparatively recently, to the constraints on developmental possibilities imposed by the continuing structural weaknesses of the institutions of financial intermediation. Currently, however, there is significant interest being shown by the World Bank in African financial sectors in general, and in the development of non-bank financial intermediaries (NBFIs) in particular. Not only is the focus of this interest understandable, given the high fashionability of the view 'that a more advanced financial infrastructure ... might play an important causal role in explaining economic development', it is also appropriate. In the light of the considerable body of evidence from Africa linking poor savings and inefficient distribution of capital to the 'lack of efficient or reliable financial institutions', it is clearly logical to suggest in response that appropriately '[d]eveloped financial intermediaries, once established as reliable and offering real returns, can facilitate the unleashing of dormant domestic capital' (Kenny and Moss, 1998, p.836).

Among the wide array of NBFIs, it is contractual savings institutions, and particularly pension funds, that are seen as key financial intermediaries, improving savings quality by tying funds into long-term investments, as well as swelling savings quantity. For example, the establishment of a mandatory fully funded pension system, whether publicly or privately managed, generates huge quantities of savings very quickly. Such schemes amass funds at the rate of 2 percent of GDP per annum from their inception (Reisen, 1997, p.1181; following Vittas, 1995), thereby supplying, on a predictable and continuing basis, vast amounts of investment capital actively seeking long-term outlets. Either or both privately and publicly managed contractual savings institutions may invest the huge sums generated under mandatory systems efficiently and effectively, just as both public and private fund managers will be constrained by their requirements for efficient financial sectors and developed financial market institutional infrastructures to ensure productive channelling, and subsequent oversight, of invested funds (Heinrich, 1997, pp.41-42). Clearly, these funds will achieve variable consequential growth impacts dependent on investment appropriateness and efficiency.

Nevertheless, there is significant potential for meeting wider economic needs in relation to existing domestic investment shortfalls, with the establishment of pension funds promising the possibility of matching savings to long-term investment requirements across the South both more comprehensively than any foreseeable combinations of foreign direct investment (FDI) and overseas development aid (ODA) could achieve, and certainly more sustainably than any conceivable enhancement of portfolio investment activity might indicate. However, it is the key contention of this chapter that the choice between public and private pension and retirement savings provision is not an equal one, and this inequality in performance is demonstrable in relation to both welfare and economic development potentialities alike. Specifically, funded systems, both private and public, will, if properly managed, serve both the purposes required of pension systems, securing income security for individual pensioners and driving, or helping to drive, national economic growth sequences, adequately: only public management, however, offers the potential for achieving truly creative synergy between them.

Pension Funds in Capital Market Development

Although the synergies between pension funds and capital markets in achieving positive financial sector outcomes are obvious, at least in principle, both the direction of causation within, and the developmental impact of, this pension fund-capital market nexus can easily be misleadingly interpreted or over-stated. Thus, current thinking identifies 'an important virtuous cycle [that] links stock market development with the maturation of banking and other financial intermediaries' (Kenny and Moss, 1998, p.837). How this virtuous circle is formed and how it operates, however, is far from clear. Demirgüç-Kunt and Levine, summarising the available evidence, 'find that market capitalisation and the value traded ratio are positively correlated with all of the indicators of financial intermediary development, showing that stock markets and financial intermediaries are generally complements'. However, both tend to emerge at later rather than at earlier stages in financial system development. Specifically, 'a rough evolutionary path of a financial system can be observed from crosscountry differences ... [The] evidence suggests that as economies develop, self-finance first gives way to intermediated debt finance and later to the emergence of equity markets ... [with] non-bank financial intermediaries and equity markets develop[ing] together at later stages of economic development' (Choe and Moosa, 1999, p.1072, citing Demirgüç-Kunt and Levine, 1996). In relation, therefore, to the still open issue of the direction of causation, one area in need of much further clarification relates to the optimal temporal sequencing of the two institutional component elements in the nexus. As Ajit Singh has highlighted, the highly significant recent growth in the numbers of, and, more significantly, the capitalisation values held by, stock markets in both the developed and developing world 'has occurred in most countries without private pension schemes of the kind advocated by the Bank' (Singh, 1995, p.8). This simple fact highlights the comparative rarity of examples of the UK, US and Chilean type, where pension fund growth and stock market development may most appropriately be seen as mutually supportive within a virtuous circle of financial sector expansion and deepening.

Clearly, on the available evidence, pension funds do not even form a necessary, let alone a sufficient condition for the achievement of a significant degree of stock market expansion and development. Moreover, having made precisely this point in a recently published, significantly revisionist, paper, Dimitri Vittas, of the World Bank, suggests, on the basis of evidence from countries such as Greece within the EU, that the direction of causality in such cases may be the reverse of what is generally anticipated.[1] Specifically, 'the link may be from capital market development to pension reform rather than the other way round' (Vittas, 2000, p.16). Overall, Vittas provides a convenient, and balanced, summary of the implications that can legitimately be drawn from existing evidence regarding the impacts of pension funds and other institutional investors on financial systems, specifically suggesting

> their large potential impact on capital market development and the dynamic interaction that is likely to evolve between pension funds and capital markets. But other forces, such as advances in technology, deregulation, privatization, foreign direct investment, and, especially, regional and global integration, may have the same impact.
>
> Vittas, 2000, p.16

For example, as underlined below the 'southern cone' of SSA contains four examples, South Africa, Zimbabwe, Botswana and Namibia, in which the expansion of private contractual savings sectors, comprising pensions and life insurance, has clearly been developmentally significant in underpinning the growth of stock markets, underlining in practice the 'dynamic interactions' described by Vittas.

More widely, of course, just as the increasingly bewildering array of commercially available financial products on the UK retail market must legally now carry an official UK government health warning - 'Past performance is not necessarily a guide to future performance. Both capital and income values may go down as well as up and you may not get back the amount you invested' - so too must financial markets face continuing doubt as an appropriately stable basis on which to build saver and investor-friendly financial systems. The issue of the optimal financial system type in relation to achieving the appropriate balance between risk and return is clearly both complex and open. If, however, financial system stability is prioritised then there is considerable force in the argument 'that bank-dominated economies in which banks do not face considerable competition from financial markets have a greater ability to smooth asset returns over time than [capital] market-dominated economies' (Thakor, 1996, p.943). Nevertheless, beyond this rather imprecise point, it is clearly unsafe to draw firm conclusions to the effect that bank-dominated financial systems are inherently more stable than their capital market-based rivals. Specifically, existing work 'does not deal with a multibank financial system with the possibility of bank runs and contagion-induced panics. The question of which system is more stable remains open at this point' (Thakor, 1996, p.943). Recent banking crises across the developing world, including the transition economies amply underline the importance of this caveat.

In relation to potential impacts of pension funds on financial sector development there is a similar problem of causal circularity. On the one hand, any proposal for the fundamental reform of national pension systems intrinsically implies a commensurate potential opportunity for a parallel restructuring of the format of a country's entire financial system. On the other hand, the converse also applies: the structure and limitations of existing financial systems and related market and state-based governance institutions provide important constraints on the prospects for successfully implementing pension reform, particularly if reform proposals are of a radical nature involving significant expansion of private provision. 'As a prerequisite to introduce funded pensions, some kind of financial market must already exist to which the introduction of funded pensions should contribute' (Holzmann, 1994, p.202). Otherwise, as in the weaker and poorer economies among the transition states as well as, more widely, among the low income economies of the South, the effective absence of soundly based and operationally entrenched financial markets offering a menu of long-term instruments removes a necessary precondition for the development of a secure and sustainable system of long-term savings.

Conversely, it has been argued that the creation of fully funded systems of pension provision, with individual savings accounts tying benefits directly and strictly to contributions made, will, in itself, particularly if these schemes are privately delivered, stimulate financial system development, thereby expanding capital market activities and capabilities and providing for the deepening and strengthening of financial sectors deemed necessary for sustained economic development in a market economy. Nevertheless, if internal, market-based, and external, state-based, monitoring, control and governance mechanisms remain weak, such regulatory limitations render savings at considerable risk from both inefficient institutions and unscrupulous individuals as well as from the vagaries of market forces. As Robert Holzmann rightly underlines, '[t]he introduction of funded pensions in economies with no or only rudimentary financial markets resembles the hen-egg problem ...' in its circularity (Holzmann, 1994, p.202).

Recent World Bank thinking centres on breaking through this circularity dilemma faced by low or middle income countries with rudimentary financial markets through creative policy interventions, notably imaginative proposals to encourage the increasingly trans-national development of existing capital market institutions initially on a regional or sub-regional basis. One such creative but feasible market expansion mechanism is the establishment of regional equity markets of the type currently in the final stage of implementation for the common currency area of the CFA Zone in West Africa and centred on the expanded operational remit of the established Abidjan *Bourse* in Côte d'Ivoire. Accordingly, whilst accepting the argument that 'private provision of social insurance is only workable if financial markets are well enough developed so that financial intermediaries can readily match these long-term liabilities with long-term assets', the Bank contends that, given the activation of appropriate policy instruments and legal underpinnings, 'even in poor regions such as sub-Saharan Africa, thin capital markets need not be a bar to the development of private pension funds' (World Bank, 1997c, p.58).

In turn, the recent survey of the development of stock markets across sub-Saharan Africa, undertaken by Charles Kenny and Todd Moss, rightly underlines the fact that capital market growth in the region remains constrained by the underlying, and continuing, weaknesses of host economies, not least in relation to other, necessary, dimensions of healthy financial systems. 'Financial infrastructure is particularly restrictive' across the continent (1998, p.832). Not only are banking sectors themselves poorly, and often inappropriately, developed but the non-bank financial intermediaries that, alongside the banking system, collectively define the institutional architecture of financial sectors, 'such as pensions and insurance, are also very small' (1998, p.832) and insecurely institutionalised as investment agencies in most of the countries of the region. There are, however, growing numbers of exceptions, providing important policy indicators to the rest of the continent. As the Bank underlines, '[a]lready some equity markets in sub-Saharan Africa compare favourably in terms of market capitalization with those in Latin American countries that have recently privatized their pension systems (such as Peru)' (World Bank, 1997c, p.58). Significantly, standing out among these examples of capital market success both South Africa and Zimbabwe have long had large contractual savings sectors with a significant presence of funded pensions schemes largely based on company plans and, as a consequence, possess relatively big stock markets. Both Botswana and Namibia have seen more recent, but also very rapid, growth of contractual savings sectors. Namibia, for example, had, by 1996, pension and life insurance assets totalling 80 percent of GDP (Kenny and Moss, 1998, p.839). In both cases it is clear that stock market expansion has paralleled the rise of contractual savings.

If, as the World Bank has consistently argued over recent years, the long-term aim of policy should be to strengthen the continent's capital markets sufficiently to ensure that they can become effective and efficient providers of finance for the necessary infrastructural and other developmentally essential long term investment funding needs of the real economy (World Bank, 1994b, p.104), then '[g]etting there will require broad investor participation, a variety of market-making players (brokers, dealers and underwriters), and a wide range of financial instruments' (1994b, p.104); all items currently in comparably short supply. On the one hand, what is required for the sustainable growth of financial sectors is the considerable augmentation of the supply of long term securities on offer through capital markets. On the other hand, 'for the market to function well, there must be a matching demand for such securities' (1994b, p.104); a demand only sustainable through expansion in the size and activities of contractual savings institutions, pension funds and life insurers, collectively mediating financial systems which can guarantee the more effective mobilisation of savings into long term markets for investment funds across the region.

Currently fashionable financial sector development scenarios for Africa, rather than looking to regional models, such as South Africa, are, as in the earlier case of the transition economies described above in Chapter 4, largely based upon an optimistic reading of the Chilean experience, and suggest that the demand-driven supply of long-term securities can be most effectively generated and most appropriately managed by expanding the activities of mandatory private contractual savings institutions, particularly private pension funds. Kenny and Moss, for example, suggest that African '[g]overnments can ... encourage the establishment of private savings and pension plans which could invest in the local stock market - Chile has done so very successfully, increasing the funds under management by private pension funds from next to nothing in 1981 to US$12 billion by 1992' (1998, pp.838-839). In turn, private pension provision is positively viewed as avoiding what are perceived as the inherent defects of state-run institutions. The latter are characteristically presented as both unprofessionally operated and as inherently lacking sufficient autonomy to invest their assets either prudently in the long term interests of their savers or developmentally in the interests of the wider economy. Specifically, in the first place, 'government-sponsored pension funds have often suffered from mismanagement and misuse'. In the second place, 'even when they are technically autonomous, pension funds within the public sector often come under pressure to finance government consumption spending and low-yielding investments' (World Bank, 1994b, p.107).

To a certain extent, but only to a certain extent, the currently fashionable assumptions outlined above are well-founded. In particular, rapid expansion, on a mandatory basis, of contractual savings sectors in the form of pension funds generates very effective pressure for both an expanded supply of securities and for the diversification of investment instruments on offer, thereby contributing highly effectively, as well as expeditiously, to financial sector deepening. In the Chilean case, for example, the pension fund system was successfully utilised to promote the privatisation of a number of large public utilities with the AFPs purchasing up to 35 percent of the equity capital of organisations as diverse as the Santiago subway system and Chilean telecommunications utility. Similarly, the active involvement of the AFPs in the capital market encouraged suppliers to diversify and expand the variety of investment products available for purchase, for example directly leading to the marketing of 'more complex products' such as 'swaps, derivative securities and asset-backed securities' (Rowat, 1999, p.277). Conversely, considerable evidence can be marshalled in support of the often developmentally negative impact of government-managed pension and retirement savings funds. As was addressed in detail in Chapter 6 above, a particular, and carefully chosen, World Bank favourite as a cautionary tale of governmental improvidence is the now defunct Zambian NPF, but a number of other, significantly also African, NPFs could be similarly negatively cited.

Nevertheless it is important here both to reiterate the point, originally made above in Chapter 4 that it is still largely unclear as to whether it was capital market expansion that drove AFP expansion and 'success' in Chile or whether, as the Bank would wish it to be, the reverse is the case, and also to add some further caveats concerning the specifics of the capital market impact of the Chilean reforms. In particular, given the magnitude of the advance publicity that preceded the creation of the AFPs, essentially tax-financed, and state-provided, free-market propaganda that largely involved the denigration of state capacities to administer pension funds and manage complex financial transactions, it is important to underline the significant extent to which early AFP performance fell short of the pre-reform promises. In this public relations *blitzkrieg*, orchestrated by the author of the pension system reforms, Minister of Labour José Piñera, it was argued, well in advance of the reforms, that 'the new private funds were expected to have a positive impact on the private sector of the economy at large by contributing to the formation of a local capital market which, in turn, would foster economic development' (Borzutzky, 1991, p.94, citing Costabal 1981). In this regard, one key test of AFP performance clearly relates to the extent to which establishment of the AFPs encouraged the move towards the long term savings and investment bias expected of such pension funds. In this regard, Mesa-Lago, observing the portfolio performance of the private pension funds over a decade of operation, found that among Chile's AFPs in the 1980s '[t]he average term of all invested assets is two years' (1991b, p.18). Moreover, to the extent that there was a shift towards the longer term in Chile's financial markets in the aftermath of pensions privatisation it was in the country's bond, not its equity markets (EBRD, 1996a, pp.97-98). Overall, what the Chilean evidence reveals is that institutional investors

> gave a boost to the development of bond markets, including corporate ... bond markets, and the creation of rating agencies. But their impact on the equity market was more subdued.
>
> Vittas, 2000, p.9

Bond Markets, Government Debt and Pension Funds

The empirical evidence from Chile is clear-cut. As Kuczynski forcefully suggests, '(t)he most tangible contribution of the much-studied privatisation of the Chilean social security system, and its conversion into private pension funds after 1980, has been that it has made possible the creation of a significant long-term domestic bond market' (1999, p.223). Moreover, as indicated by the common experience of the other countries following Chile in implementing 'radical' pension reform, and discussed in Chapter 3, this point can be generalised. In terms of financial market outcomes recorded to date, the most likely future scenario to occur from the introduction of prefunded pension sectors, in developing and transition economies alike, is the development of a national bond market. In itself this impact should be viewed as both positive and significant. The development of domestic bond (securities) markets is widely accepted as an important element in financial market widening and deepening. As Claessens and Glaessner suggest, '(b)etter securities markets are needed because they can be a competitive force for improving banking systems and because bank and securities markets are complementary sources of finance' (1997, p.18).[2]

Ironically, and especially so from the perspective of neoliberal proponents of market-driven economic growth, it is important to recognise that when bond market development occurs, as in Chile, it is likely to be reliant, to a not insignificant extent, on state bond offerings. In Chile in 1994, for instance, when total combined investment in government and corporate bonds was at an all time low of 67.0 percent of total portfolio investments, the public sector still accounted for 39.0 percent of total invested AFP assets. During the remainder of the 1990s the value of total assets invested in public bonds remained largely unchanged at around 40.0 percent. In 1998, the exact figure was 40.96 percent of total assets (Rodriguez, 1999). Clearly, state bond offerings can help promote securities market developments in two ways. First, as was the case in the development of the Chilean bond market, the securities market may benefit initially from being pump primed by the securitisation of government implict pension debt which is made explicit by the transition towards the full implementation of a new pension system. In the case of Chile, state bonds, or 'recognition bonds', were sold in order to finance the transition costs of the pension system reforms (for an overview of the fiscal cost of the Chilean pension reforms between 1981 and 1996, see Appendix Table A8.1). Second, in the likely absence of sufficient suitable investment opportunities in domestic corporate securities and stocks and the enforcement of strict government control over international investments, investors may be severely restricted in their choice of investment portfolio. Accordingly, in the overall context of the development of emerging financial markets, such financial system developments are likely to be most beneficial, in the short to medium term at least, to the restructuring of government debt. Simply stated, it is likely to be government, and not the private sector, that will be the major beneficiary of a developing private pension fund-financial market nexus in emerging economies.

Further evidence to support the view that it is government and not the private sector which is commonly the major beneficiary of a developing private pension fund-financial market nexus is provided by portfolio investment figures from Chile for the period 1981-1998. Up until 1998, the annual average value of the AFP portfolio invested in government bonds was 37.24 percent of total investments. Although corporate bond holding were very significant throughout the 1980s, throughout the 1990s their value as a percentage of total assets has been consistently lower than government bond holdings (see Appendix Table A8.2). It is also important here to mention the investments placed in stocks by the AFPs. After rising to a peak of 32.10 percent of total assets in 1994, AFP investments in stocks declined every year up until 1998 when they represented only 14.90 percent of total invested assets (Rodriguez, 1999). A characteristic feature of equity investments made by the AFPs has been a consistent and heavy concentration in a very limited number of privatised utilities companies. Such herded concentration of investment clearly has limited the scope for earning above average yields while leaving the AFPs vulnerable to losses in periods of sectoral downturn as well as wider economic recession. This analysis suggests, at least in financial markets which remain largely underdeveloped, that it is misleading to talk too generally about a pension fund-capital market nexus. In the context of emerging financial markets it may be more appropriate to talk more specifically of a *ménage à trois* between pension funds, government debt and national bond markets.

A further important issue, illustrated by the similarity between developments in Chile, Singapore and Malaysia, is that securities market development is not necessarily better aided by the existence of privatised defined contribution pension funds. The evidence from the expansion of bond market activity in Singapore and Malaysia underlines the point that the accelerated development of a national bond market is not dependent upon the creation of private sector pension funds nor upon the prior existence of other private sector contractual savings institutions. State run retirement saving schemes, such as the NPFs utilised by both these Southeast Asian examples, are also capable of producing similarly positive outcomes in the form of national bond market development. In addition to the well understood fact that NPFs have commonly held a vast proportion of their respective governments' debt, reports from Singapore indicate that the CPF is now becoming more actively mobilised to play a strategic role in the island state's drive to develop itself as the region's leading financial centre. These strategic ambitions intend to place Singapore in direct competition with the current leading regional financial centre, Hong Kong. A key element to fulfilling these ambitions is the leveraged development of the domestic bond market. One important element within this strategy has involved the CPF purchasing bonds at the request of the Singapore authorities. More specifically, the Singaporean authorities have, somewhat controversially, induced 'artificial' demand within the domestic bond market by using CPF assets to purchase bonds to finance debt for which the government has no obvious practical need (Luce, 1999b, p.36).

Similarly, in Malaysia, the EPF has played a central role in guaranteeing the success of government bond issuance. In 1997, for instance, the government investment arm, Khazanah, issued a 'zero-coupon, three-year M$1 billion government guaranteed bond' in an attempt to bolster the flow of finance in the domestic market which had suffered as a consequence of the currency depreciation of the Malaysian Ringgit. Mirroring previous trends in the ownership of government debt, these bonds were purchased 'mainly by financial institutions such as pension funds that are either state-owned or have links to the government' (Kynge, 1997, p.40). More precisely, it can be assumed that this particular response in Kuala Lumpur to the financial crisis of 1997 was, once more, largely dependent upon the strategic mobilisation of the financial might of the EPF. In addition to the issue of these relatively short-term bonds, the Malaysian government also scheduled the sale of medium to long term Khazanah bonds with five, seven and ten year maturities. Likewise, it is widely assumed that the EPF will continue to play an important purchasing and pump-priming role in these bond market developments.

Clearly, as is evidenced by developments in Chile, Singapore and Malaysia, the trajectories of funded national pensions systems and national financial systems are closely entwined. More specifically, however, it would appear that, in practice, bond markets have profited more, and more immediately, from this relationship than have equity markets. Nor should this association, which is currently being replicated in CEE states, be seen as limited only to DCs and transition economies, or, indeed only to countries with funded pension systems.[3] Pension system interaction with bond markets is likely to increase dramatically for many developed country governments currently aspiring to parametrically restructure their existing PAYG schemes in the first two decades of this century, as significant fiscal debt obligations are now more specifically identified as emanating from future national pension system liabilities. In addition to the use of bond markets as one risk hedging mechanism to protect the value of financial assets, it is also of interest to note that, in a similar manner to the way that governments use domestic bond markets to restructure, forestall and potentially reduce existing levels of fiscal debt, it now appears increasingly appropriate for governments to do likewise when dealing with the specific issue of future state pension system debt liabilities. The Italian government, for instance, have recently announced proposed plans to restructure and forestall social security debt, including pension liabilities, though the securitisation of the social security budget deficit. Innovatively, the proposed sale of government bonds will be 'backed by unpaid social security contributions' (Luce and Blitz, 1999, p.1). Although this planned 'securitisation' of fiscal debt will ultimately require budget transfers in order to meet the final costs of the deficit repayment, the bond issue will both delay and significantly reduce the required transfers.

A Balancing Act: The State in the Market

In the absence of the important financial sector preconditions which are rightly perceived as necessary to ensure the healthy development of private defined contribution pension funds, developing country governments may, alternatively, seek to harness the developmental potential of public sector pension funds. For countries with underdeveloped financial sectors, the state mandated mobilisation and state directed investment of national savings channelled through state pension funds provides an altogether more logical alternative modality through which to stimulate economic development. Despite the continuing anti-state sentiments emanating from the Washington institutions in relation to the effective management of 'retirement' savings, the principle of state-led mobilisation of pension fund savings should not be discounted out of hand, or viewed, in practice, as an inherently 'second-best' option for DCs.

To the contrary, the state-led mobilisation of savings can provide important inherent advantages of its own. Most notably, state intervention has the potential to produce significant direct, as well as indirect, welfare enhancing developmental outcomes through the strategic targeting of a concentrated pool of investments. Especially in the least developed of the South's economies, there are many specific development objectives which may be better accomplished, conceivably will only be accomplished, through active state intervention rather than through the market allocation of an inevitably limited pool of national savings to competing private funds. Specifically, state control of national pension fund assets remains essential for those countries without the allocative financial capacities of developed national capital markets, and therefore lacking experienced institutions of financial intermediation. State control over such important assets remains advisable more widely across DCs, including most MICs, where an active policy of state allocation of finance for development is altogether a more logical, coherent and feasible strategic policy choice than the total surrender of scarce investable funds to a number of insecure and untried private entities.

Evidence in support of these propositions is provided by the performance record of the more strategically managed of the NPFs discussed above in Chapter 5. Singapore provides the clearest examples of the direct and indirect economic and welfare benefits accruing from appropriately targeted usage of savings amassed by the CPF for creative investment purposes. Although neoliberal critics describe the CPF as a form of 'pension fund socialism' and characterise its essential feature as 'forced savings', the early key to its wider developmental impact lies in the imaginative government policies that turned high savings into highly productive and successful investments, using tax concessions and other fiscal incentives, effectively large subsidies, alongside infrastructure provision to attract FDI (Ermisch and Huff, 1999, pp.31-32). There is, however, much, much more to the case in favour of the CPF than the simple point of the effective investment of mandatory savings. The public-private provision of housing in the post-independence era, with its important growth impacts on the Singapore economy and its equally significant welfare impacts on Singaporeans (see Chapter 5), provides the clearest, and most commonly described, example of both the impact duality and the impact effectiveness of the CPF.

The wider, indirect, but significantly positive, effects of these long-standing policy strategies have also become increasingly recognised. For example, as Jeffrey Henderson has recently underlined, the CPF forms an important link in explaining the East and Southeast Asian crisis' uneven impacts, specifically indicating why Singapore 'escaped relatively unscathed', conspicuously avoiding the 'property-market speculation [that] has been a central component of the construction of economic turmoil in the [other] Southeast Asian economies and Hong Kong' (Henderson, 1999, p.353 and pp.359-360). This important counter-cyclical effect emerged essentially as an offshoot of the long-standing use of the CPF as the key financing instrument in the Singapore state's utilisation of housing policies as an instrument of economic stabilisation. Collectively and cumulatively these policies, in turn, 'have had the effect of substantially removing housing as an object of speculative investment' in the island city state (Henderson, 1999, p.360). More widely, these policies have also been material in securing the effective containment of real-estate speculation. In securing these outcomes 'the state's decisive role in housing provision and finance has been a major contributing factor ... State-enforced savings through the Central Provident Fund have ... circumscribed funds that might otherwise have been available for speculative purposes' (Henderson, 1999, p.359).

Counter-cyclical effects, in turn, have been matched by some very specific and very deliberate microeconomic interventions frequently undertaken largely by means of the strategic manipulation of the CPF. For example, '[t]he Singapore Government ... has successfully levered foreign and domestic firms alike to invest in technological upgrading and higher value-added activities. This has been done partly through forcing up labour costs (via increased Central Provident Fund levies) and thus squeezing some of the labour-intensive assembly industries out of the economy' (Henderson, 1999, p.360). Among other important examples of the policy utility of the CPF, is the reinforcement effect on Singapore's strategy of constant technological upgrading that is provided by the enhancement of the educational assets of the workforce that are substantially financed via CPF drawdowns. CPF drawdowns have become similarly supportive of health sector expansion and for ensuring the sustainability of costly medical infrastructure provision (see also Chapter 5, footnote 1).

Among other important growth and welfare enhancing effects of the CPF, the lessons of greatest relevance to the specific, financial market, concerns of this chapter relate to the vital, indirect, role played by CPF funding in underpinning Singapore's outstanding record of success in the moderation and containment of stock market speculation. Secure in its vast stockpile of savings, courtesy of the CPF, 'the Singapore government has been more concerned to control the potentially disruptive effects of stock-market speculation than it has to encourage stock-market expansion for its own sake' (Henderson, 1999, p.359). Relative to its regional near-neighbour, Kuala Lumpur, the volume of trade on the Singapore exchange is low, despite the fact that Singapore is a much more important international financial centre. Specifically, one obvious spin-off from the CPF effect, vast savings in an economy without an agricultural sector and effectively without an urban informal sector, is that there is less need than in Malaysia for portfolio investment. Due to both the direct impact of CPF savings, providing more than adequate domestic sources of coverage for all infrastructural needs, and its related, but indirect, impact in underpinning Singapore's outstanding success in attracting large quantities of high quality FDI, there is simply no need actively to seek other, inherently less stable and more volatile, forms of international investment finance. Quite simply, as Henderson argues, the extraordinarily high level of FDI apparently permanently attracted to Singapore 'has probably meant that there has been no need for the extraordinary levels of short-term portfolio investment - and its destabilising potential - evident elsewhere in the region' (1999, p.360).

Equity Markets: Development and Control Issues

Other DCs, clearly, cannot hope to emulate Singapore's, essentially unique, good fortune in being able largely to avoid, or solve, most of the savings and investment problems that characteristically face them. For a few MICs the central problem has become one of controlling foreign investment capital, particularly the destabilising short-term inward and outward movements commonly viewed as characteristic of the more volatile, 'footloose', elements within portfolio flows. For all LICs, and many MICs, the central problem remains one of attracting and stimulating investment, for some by any means possible. For the fortunate few, the most obvious immediate response to the potentially serious problems posed by volatile and unpredictable short-term capital movements is to replicate the Chilean model of outflow taxation; a simple but effective strategy now rather widely advocated, and well described, in the literature, obviating the need for further consideration here. However, what it is important to underline at this point is the sheer complexity of the subject of financial flows and the substantial inadequacy of current breakdowns of its composition, however confidently this information is presented. In particular, serious doubt has been cast on the explanatory validity of the conventional classification of capital flows into tightly defined categories such as portfolio investment and FDI. The latter, in practice, may be far more liquid than is assumed whereas 'some types of portfolio investment are largely illiquid. Moreover, flows are often misclassified, especially as derivatives markets grow in importance' (Lukaukus, 1999, p.277, citing Garber). On an increasingly global basis over the last decade, a significantly diversified set of 'financial instruments have entered the scene ... Theory needs to account for a variety of international financial instruments, some of which are highly illiquid and not easily incorporated into a capital strike' (Lavelle, 1999, p.221).

The implications for DCs seeking investment funding are large and important. 'Increasingly, multiple financial instruments are available to finance any project, and so if a tight link ever existed between the financing method and the underlying nature of the project, it is probably becoming increasingly loose. A Treasury Bond with a thirty-year maturity can be sold on the secondary market, and short-term assets can be continuously rolled over ... In addition, the explicit label given to a flow may not cover its implicit nature' (Claessens, Dooley and Warner, 1995, p.155). Clearly, appropriate DC responses to this funding complexity and confusion are themselves likely to be far from straightforward and clear-cut. By definition, their characteristically weak financial systems, based on shallow capital markets and tiny savings bases and lacking the depth liquidity and breadth instruments found in the financial systems of more developed states, require strengthening (Howell, 1999, p.66 and pp.68-69). The key problem, exactly how best to achieve this strengthening, remains as contentious as it has always been, with the issue of the appropriate sequencing of financial sector and financial policy reforms continuing to generate significant controversy. Insofar as there is any emergent consensus in the literature, it is to the effect that institutional reform should precede policy reform, at least if financial instability is to be avoided.

Specifically, financial liberalisation, the policy fashion of the 1980s, is now increasingly seen as quick and easy, but dangerous unless appropriately underpinned by risk averting institutions. The key principle, learned the hard way by numerous DC and transition economies during the 1990s, is that financial opening in DCs must not be allowed to run ahead of the financial infrastructure required to constrain financial risks (Reisen, 1999, p.127). Although the liberalisation and international opening of the financial systems of DCs clearly creates effective demand for better financial infrastructure, it also tends, in practice, to undermine financial stability, and to do so, often disastrously for the citizens of the states involved, before risk averting institutions have had time to emerge in response to this demand. Clearly, as is now increasingly argued, the appropriate lesson to be drawn from recent DC financial crises is that the supply of stabilising financial institutions should precede rather than follow the demand for their services. Nevertheless, however sensible and prudent such a strategy may seem, it is significantly at odds with continuing calls for rapid global financial liberalisation. The task of building institutional capacity within financial markets is inherently slow and complex, particularly so if, as in the case of most DCs, institutional capacity building is being undertaken from a low, or no, base (Reisen, 1999, pp.127-128, quoting Claessens and Glaessner, 1997). Given the rapidity with which global financial integration is perceived to be progressing, the understandable fear of being left behind in a globalising world places significant pressures on DCs to conform and liberalise expeditiously, essentially pressed into financial opening, perhaps prematurely, by their understandable fear of marginalisation in the intensifying competition for foreign capital.

Helmut Reisen, in particular, has emphasised the potential 'benefits of global capital mobility' to DCs. Specifically, Reisen is optimistic about the mutually beneficial, developmentally positive and wealth enhancing, outcomes to be derived from what he envisages as 'the interaction between the capital-rich, moderately-growing and fast ageing OECD economies and the capital poor, fast-growing and slowly-ageing emerging economies' (Reisen, 1999, p.6). Significant movement of finance capital in this regard has already occurred as the search for asset diversification has increasingly led fund managers into 'exposure' to an increasing number of emerging markets. Recent estimates suggest that the value of pension assets worldwide had reached US$11,000 billion in 1998. Significantly, in the same year the value of assets held by tax-exempt US financial institutions, comprising of mutual funds as well as pension funds, equated to over 50 percent of this figure at US$6,000 billion. Riley has, arguably, understated the significance of US financial institutions to the global economy when he explains that, in response to meeting the financial needs of an ageing American society, 'Americans have become important operators in the world stock markets' (Riley, 1999b, p.1). To date, however, it is less easy to identify the benefits that DCs have gained from these large capital flows than it is to identify their less welcome contribution to global financial market volatility, with a now well proven propensity of fund managers to exhibit their tendency towards herd-induced panics and to exercise *en masse* their legal right to practice capital 'flight' towards the greater liquidity and safety of more developed markets at the first sign of danger.

The deleterious financial and economic impacts of this type of market withdrawal contagion on the most dynamic of DCs is underlined by recent experience of the 'tequila effect', culminating in the peso crisis of late 1994, which followed the Mexican crisis of the 1980s and, even more devastatingly in relation to welfare impacts, the 'Asian contagion' which spread out widely across Southeast and East Asia from its origins in Thailand in 1997.

Once out, fund managers may well remain reluctant to return to emerging market for long, often irrationally long, periods, once again underlining the importance of the herd behaviour and pressures to conformity that, paradoxically, is largely induced by the highly competitive nature of the business in which they are engaged. The Institute of International Finance (IIF), in a recent evaluation of short-term capital flows to developing countries, underlines the point that, in the present economic climate, 'financial institutions remain cautious about lending to emerging markets following the series of financial crises which these economies have experienced' (IIF, 1999, p.1). Accordingly, from a DC perspective there is limited certainty and significantly less predictability about such portfolio capital flows than their enthusiasts originally suggested. Nor should this seem surprising. Despite the common assumption that the investment proclivities of institutional investors (IIs) and, in particular, contractual savings institutions, pension funds and life insurance, are inherently market smoothing and stabilising because of their long investment horizons, the reality of investment practice is much more complex. In direct contradiction to this 'patient investors' view the evidence suggests that, above all, what institutional investors demand is market liquidity, essentially institutionalising short termism (Bloomestein, 1998, p.67). Bloomestein, in a succinct summary of available information on the investment habits of IIs, refers to the UK Pension Law Reform committee's finding that the average period that a pension fund held a share over 1983-1987 declined from 7 to 2.5 years (Bloomestein, 1998, p.106, fn.70). Many shares will, however, be held much longer than the average period by pension fund managers but, crucially, these are not very likely to be those floated on emerging markets. 'In analysing the average holding period of institutional assets it is important to distinguish the core portfolio - representing the bulk of a fund's assets - from the satellite portfolio (*i.e.* the remainder of the fund's assets) ... The holding period of the core portfolio is much longer than of the satellite portfolio' (Bloomestein, 1998, p.67).

Accordingly, the fact that 'not all institutions are alike: mutual fund portfolios are often traded much more active[ly] than pension funds or insurance companies' (Bloomestein, 1998, p.68), offers cold comfort to emerging markets in DCs, particularly the more marginal ones, as in SSA, where, ironically, the need for stable sources of investment capital is most marked. What DCs need primarily is good quality capital and not just quantity of capital. Low quality capital essentially guarantees financial market volatility (Howell, 1999, p.73). However, sadly, it is such low quality capital that DCs, particularly those aspirant LICs with ambitious and optimistic expectations of rapid capital market expansion, are largely condemned to receive. As Kenny and Moss summarise: 'Because Africa represents the most risky cutting-edge market for investors, capital there may be cautiously invested but quickly divested ... it is clear that these stock markets will remain extremely unstable for the short to medium term ... ' (1998, p.834).

Bluntly, stock markets remain, as they have always been, important elements within financial systems continuing to be especially useful for 'financing riskier ventures' that banks in DCs would never fund and, thereby, for attracting foreign capital. Nonetheless, '[t]he small size of African stock markets will also be a particular problem when transacting with global institutional investors ...', underlining the political risks involved in economic opening with its potential for displacement of nationals from key economic sectors (Kenny and Moss, 1998, pp.834-835). As the Chilean case nicely underlines, these key sectors may well include newly created private financial institutions such as pension funds. Specifically, the banking crisis which followed hard on the heels of pensions privatisation in 1981 and led to the 1982 recession, had a major impact on the ownership of the AFPs due to the bankruptcy of the *Grupos*, their original Chilean owners. Subsequent state administration of AFP assets, events conveniently forgotten by the exponents of pensions privatisation, was followed by a process of re-privatisation this time, however, involving offerings to Chile's international creditors on a 'debt for equity' basis. The outcome was that a significant portion of the AFP sector became 'totally or partially owned by US companies'. Crucially, re-privatisation of the AFPs left 'the four largest funds ... controlled by foreign corporations'. As Borzutzky comments, this change of ownership 'certainly change[d] the impact that the funds have on the local economy', and, it might be added, served also to undermine previously positive Chilean perceptions of pensions privatisations (Borzutzky, 1991, p.97). In the light of all the available evidence, therefore, it is sensible to heed the warning that stock markets offer 'no panacea for Africa's financial problems ...' (Kenny and Moss, 1998, p.838).[4]

The Mobilisation of Domestic Savings for Development

It is currently fashionable to emphasise the desirability of 'stable' FDI as the optimal investment source for DCs, and there is much sense in this view, given the obvious medium and long term commitments inherent in most direct investments in DCs (for example, Reisen, 1999, pp.130-131). However, we would suggest that there are sound reasons for DCs to focus, at least initially, primarily on improving the quality of their domestic sources of finance. In the first place, for most DCs the problem remains one of attracting FDI, with multinationals for the most part apparently stubbornly unprepared to diversify beyond the narrow range of MICs on which they currently concentrate their activities. As discussed above in this chapter, even uniquely privileged Singapore initially had to work extremely strategically, actively mobilising CPF savings into investment programmes designed to provide the infrastructural and human resource bases on which its attractiveness to foreign investors has been built. The clear implication is that it is as important for DC policy-makers to foster and to stimulate financial system development as it is for them to encourage industrial development. As underlined in the Singapore case, the two have been complementary elements in economic success, the CPF providing the government with a bottomless pool of domestic savings and FDI providing long term access to updated technologies.

In the second place, as pointed out recently by Robert Wade, and as confirmed for DCs in the IFC's annually updated statistical compilation of private capital flows, 90 percent of domestic investment globally continues to be financed by domestic capital (Wade 1996, cited in Lukauskas, 1999, p.286, fn.22). Accordingly, it is difficult to disagree with the logic of the International Finance Corporation's assessment that national economic development is 'simply impossible... without domestic capital accumulation based upon domestic savings mobilization' (Barger, 1999, p.v). In developing economies, therefore, as the IFC stresses, there is a clear need for 'efficient domestic financial institutions that can manage risk and allocate capital to productive investments' (Barger, 1999, p.v), if DC governments are successfully to achieve economic development policy objectives, including, crucially, the effective mobilisation of domestic savings and their efficient channelling into profitable investments. However, as this chapter has sought to emphasise, recently gained appreciation of the fundamental importance of building institutions within financial markets has not really significantly clarified the issue as to which types of financial institutions to focus on for greatest effect.

The IFC, with its explicit mandate to build private sectors and market economies among DCs and the transition states, understandably advocates the prioritisation of a capital market focus, essentially seeing the process of financial market expansion as inherently self sustaining in an increasingly financially liberalised and hence financially integrated world. Nevertheless, despite the obvious impacts of the increase in global financial liberalisation advocated by the IFC, developments which have ensured that 'the importance of private flows ... increased markedly in the economies of developing countries' (World Bank, 1997a, p.9) during the 1990s, it is important, if ironic, to stress the fact that one key side-effect of these developments has simply been to reemphasise the crucial importance of domestically-sourced finance as the only fully stable and predictable source of investment funding. First, private capital flows to developing countries remain targeted on an unsatisfactorily small number of preferenced middle income DCs, leaving the majority of developing countries without significant access to foreign commercial capital, and leaving the poorest countries, precisely the states both in greatest need of heavy infusions of investment funding and with the lowest domestic savings potential, largely, in some cases wholly, dependent on ODA. Second, the sheer volatility of recent global capital movements, particularly portfolio flows into and out of DCs, has highlighted the fickle nature of global finance while simultaneously reinforcing the strategic importance to developing country governments of mobilising domestic savings.

The International Finance Corporation (IFC) currently defines emerging capital markets in different ways. According to the IFC, the term emerging market 'can imply that a process of change is underway, with capital markets growing in size and sophistication, in contrast to markets that are small and stagnant'. Alternatively, the IFC state that this term 'can also refer to any market in a developing economy', with the implication that all have the potential for development. Consequently, the IFC suggest that an 'emerging' capital market must meet 'at least one of two general criteria; (i) an Emerging Economy Criterion, and (ii) a Developing Capital Market Criterion' (1998, p.2). A more simple, if more cynical, definition of emerging markets refers to them as 'places where financial institutions and multinational companies see profitable opportunities for investment or speculation in what used to be called the Third World' (Fidler, 1997, p.15). However, as underlined already in this chapter, in the lingering aftermath of the financial contagion which swept developing country, and transition economy, financial markets in 1997-98, private capital flows to the developing world are likely to remain much more subdued than they were in the mid-1990s for some time to come. This is essentially good news for MICs, potentially promising more cautious, but hopefully also more stable, patterns of reinvestment in emerging markets as investor confidence gradually returns.

For LICs, especially the poorest countries, the ebbs and flows of private capital are essentially irrelevant; absence of a stock market is the surest way to guarantee insulation from the effects of panic-induced capital outflows. For such countries the most serious problem remains the, now highly significant, relative, in some years absolute, fall in the levels of overseas development aid provided bilaterally and multilaterally by the developed world. As the OECD have reported, financial flows in the form of bilateral and multilateral overseas development aid to developing countries were, by 1997, already at their lowest absolute levels for nearly a decade (OECD 1999a). More importantly, as the World Bank states in the 1999 Global Development Finance Report, 'net ODA fell, in real terms, ... to their lowest levels since 1981' (World Bank, 1999a). From a DC perspective, the steady fall in ODA budgets over the 1990s may be cited as one post-Cold War 'dividend' which developing countries could have well done without. However, of even greater medium term significance to LICs is the fact that the on-going debate over the very fundamentals of the existing aid system, substantially questioning its past impacts and, therefore, its continuing relevance into the 21st century, is currently intensifying, leading to a potentially even more uncertain funding future for the poorest countries.

Arguably, therefore, for MICs and LICs alike, albeit for very different reasons, the strategic importance to development policy of answers to the perennial question as to how best to meet long-term financing and investment needs, has never been more significant or more pressing. As the World Bank noticed about a decade ago, an obvious mechanism for mobilising significant amounts of domestic savings for investment purposes is, in most countries, already lying or potentially lying to hand, in the form of national old age pension scheme assets. Importantly, however, as a consequence of the varying mechanisms which may be used to finance pension provision, not all forms of pension scheme are considered to offer the same potential for national savings mobilisation. Whereas it is possible to identify various partially funded and fully prefunded 'pension' systems which produce an investable fund surplus, the mechanism most favoured by policy makers as being likely to provide the optimum development financing opportunities are defined contribution financed pension schemes.

Clearly, it is the large potential volume of investable financial assets produced by defined contribution retirement schemes which currently attracts policy-maker attention to this mechanism for retirement provision. Arguments preferencing a dominant role for private sector agents and institutions in managing and directing this savings and investment process have been forcefully put by free-market proponents, not least, by the World Bank group of institutions. The World Bank's considered perspective on retirement provision and savings allocation can be suitably summarised as assuming that the mobilisation and allocation of domestic savings is most effectively achieved when channelled through defined contribution mechanisms operated by the private sector. Specifically, pension fund asset investments are expected to be more productive when allocated by the private sector, under competitive conditions and according to market determinations, rather than by states and, hence, potentially open to political misuse and misappropriation. These privately managed funds would be expected, in due course, to fulfil wider roles within the market as institutional investors (IIs). Institutional investors are perceived as having two vital economic roles to play. First, as large and influential investors, IIs play a vital role in the development and expansion of domestic capital markets as a direct consequence of their dominant market position. Second, although of more significance in the longer term, it is expected that IIs will progressively fulfil an increasingly overt corporate governance role, acting both to engender greater overall economic competitiveness and to moderate its more deleterious off-shoots such as insider trading, overall, acting responsibly to increase the shareholder-value of national blue-chip companies. More widely, such developments are expected to enhance the everyday functioning, and encourage the continuing modernisation of, the world's capital markets as IIs, initially mainly in the form of pension funds, perform the role of 'active managers' on company boards whilst remaining stabilising 'passive investors' on stock markets.

Current reality, however, offers little evidence for this virtuous scenario, lending limited credibility to the expectation that IIs will play their expected parts in envisaged scenarios, at least into the conceivable future. If, as underlined at an earlier point in this chapter, IIs in HICs continue mainly to play the roles of 'active investors but passive managers' it is hardly surprising that their counterparts, frequently their wholly or partially owned counterparts, in DCs should follow suit; expectations amply confirmed by AFP investment strategies in Chile. Similarly, as the evidence presented by Vittas and Mitchelitsch in their mid-1990s survey of private pension fund activity across Russia and the CEE states underlined, what we have termed in Chapter 4 the 'outgrowing' strategy of non-mandatory pension fund development neither generated any noticeable corporate governance impacts, nor, to reiterate, much positive investment impact on emergent capital markets.

Accordingly, for the reasons, both positive and negative, expanded on in the course of this chapter, we remain convinced that continuing public, rather than increasingly private, management of pension fund assets remains the most sensible, certainly potentially the safest, option for almost all DCs. At the same time we are aware that our preference for utilising state institutions rather than (prematurely) developing market mechanisms as the conduit for the significant volumes of saving involved is far from uncontroversial in a number of highly significant respects, not least those raised by the perennially difficult question as to the most efficient manner in which to allocate pension fund investments productively and effectively in the interests of all relevant stakeholders, not least the pensioners themselves. It is to these crucial issues that we turn in the next, and final, Chapter.

Notes

1. What Vittas wrote is worth quoting in full, particularly given its potential implications for the Bank's pension reform agenda. 'As the experience of many countries in Europe and Asia shows, *pension funds (and domestic institutional investors more generally) are neither necessary nor sufficient for the development of securities markets*' (2000, p.16, emphasis in original). It is to be hoped that this paper stimulates the positive internal debate within the Bank that its content deserves, rather than engendering the negative, and unnecessarily defensive, response accorded to the comparably stimulating and

provocative Orszag and Stiglitz (1999) paper criticising the Bank's inflexible approach to pension reform, as discussed in detail above in Chapter 2.

2. A factor of importance to the development of a national bond or securities market is the existence of a healthy banking sector; itself a rarity among DCs, including, it must be emphasised, a number of the most economically dynamic among them. Among a number of other obvious and important recent cases across Southeast and East Asia, this issue has come to the fore recently in China. A growing recognition of severe problems within the Chinese banking system, especially in relation to non-performing loans, threatens to impede the smooth expansion of ongoing pension system reforms and the development of a national securities market. Reform of the Chinese banking system remains crucial to Chinese development, arguably more crucial even than pension reform at least from a macro-policy perspective. Similar cases for the prioritisation of banking reform could be made very widely across DCs, not least in SSA.

3. Bond markets are important sources of income for the World Bank Group but in particular the International Bank for Reconstruction and Development (IBRD) which provides market-rate loans to the governments of MICs and credit-worthy poorer countries. IBRD lending accounts for the provision of around 70 percent of the loans disbursed by the World Bank. In 1998, for example, the Bank raised $32 billion on the international bond market (Fidler, 1999, p.5), a figure equating to over 125 percent of the total value of the Bank's lending of $25.5 billion in fiscal year 1998 (World Bank, 1998b). The remaining 30 percent of 'Bank' loans are disbursed by the International Development Association (IDA) which provides interest-free concessional loans to the world's poorest countries. The finance for IDA loans comes from the subscriptions made by wealthier governments. George and Sabelli provide a useful explanation of the important role played by international bond markets in the financing of World Bank lending operations. 'The funds lent by the Bank do not come, predominantly, from capital subscriptions from member countries. In effect, the Bank procures billions by selling its own bonds on the global financial markets. The Bank charges a level of interest to borrowers which is slightly higher than that which it provides to the holders of its bonds. Bank bonds are guaranteed by member-country governments and are thus considered very safe investments to the degree that they are AAA quoted by credit measuring institutions such as Moody's or Standard & Poor. The buyers are as likely to be institutional investors (like pension funds) as they are private individuals' (1994, pp.21-22; authors' translation from French edition). Clearly, this insight into the institutional financial operations of the World Bank which may have appeared largely mundane when presented by George and Sabelli in the early 1990s may be now interpreted somewhat differently when considered in the combined context of the Bank's traditional heavy use of finance sourced from the sales of bonds and its recent active

(arguably, vested) interest in the promotion of mandatory private pension funds; *de facto* institutional investors. It is worthy of note that, in contrast, the World Bank's sister BWI, the IMF, has steadfastly avoided using private capital markets to raise finance. As Fidler reports, periodic attempts to encourage the IMF to adopt similar methods to the Bank for raising finance have always been opposed by Fund staff on the grounds that such proposals were 'inimical to the co-operative nature of the institution' (1999, p.5). Moreover, and not insignificantly, as was noted in Chapters 1 and 2 of this volume, the IMF has consistently also been more balanced than the Bank in its appraisal of the respective pros and cons of pension system reform involving the introduction of mandatory private pension funds in both developed and developing economies alike.

4. Interesting developments in Oman and Canada have shown that not only can publicly managed pension systems contribute to equity market development but also that pension systems do not necessarily have to be fully prefunded on a defined contribution basis to do so. The Sultanate of Oman provides an interesting and infrequently documented example of social security asset investment practice which is geared towards encouraging economic and, in particular, capital market growth. Oman operates a partially funded state run social insurance social security system. A recently legislated directive from the authorities in Oman requires 'social security and pension funds to invest 30 to 80 percent of their assets in companies listed on the local capital exchange' (ISSA, 1998, p.12). The rationale for this investment policy appears to be closely linked to the current rapid development of the Oman capital market. According to IFC figures, the Oman capital market obtained the world's second highest percentage increase in its market price index in 1997 (IFC, 1998, p.14). The Oman authorities, anticipating continuing development in the capital markets, aim both to bolster and to stabilise this growth through the medium of a steady flow of funds from social security and pension fund assets. Crucially, it will be expected that the social security and pension fund assets will, in turn, benefit from rising yield returns from the currently booming domestic capital market. Ironically, the investment strategy of the state run, partially prefunded, social insurance system is likely to have a greater impact on equity markets than the private defined contribution pension funds established elsewhere. The 1998 reform of the Canada Pension Plan (CPP) is noteworthy for several reasons. This reform has led to a move away from PAYG funding towards a different system of social insurance funding called Steady-State Funding, or a General Average Premium System of financing. Within a 'Steady-State' system contribution rates are set at a level higher than is currently necessary to meet expected costs and thus creates an investable surplus. Significantly, this newly created surplus will be invested by commercial fund managers only in indexed equity funds. A total of eighty percent of the fund assets will be placed with domestic Canadian funds. In the

longer term, the portfolio balance will be re-assessed by the statutory Investment Board and may, at a future date, be altered to also include investment in bonds.

9 Pensions *in* Development: From Monologue to Dialogue

In this final chapter we present a summary of the key institutional and policy implications of our modified version of the PID approach, framed in the form of ten contentions. Underlying our approach is an emphasis on the continuing appropriateness of active state involvement in the management of 'pension' provision in developing countries; pension provision to be widely defined to include all existing modalities for providing cash to the old either on a regular, income, basis or in the form of a lump sum. The bulk of this book, reflecting the bulk of existing, particularly of recent, work has focused on the management of 'retirement' savings provision in DCs. Here the case for retention, and, in almost all cases, substantial expansion, of existing state 'retirement' and pension provision, albeit increasingly to be offered, wherever a sufficient level of formal sector employment makes this feasible, on a partly or fully funded basis, is made with particular reference to the appropriateness of public savings institutions, sustainably financed and suitably managed, for meeting some of the crucial long term developmental funding needs of the South's generally weak economies. By rapidly expanding the pool of long-term savings available and offering the potential for matching savings to key national investment needs, such as major infrastructural projects with economy-wide impacts, the 'investment' case for funding is strong. Moreover, this 'investment' case is proportionately strengthened as the size of the formal sector labour force increases. Where, as in 'India, for example, formal sector employment, although a small part of the total labour force, accounts for 27 million persons', the investment case is very strong indeed (Expenditure Policy Division, 1998, p.28).

259

It needs to be underlined that this 'investment' case for public pensions funding is made in full awareness of the convincing arguments against the crude, 'picking winners', versions of industrial policy, and with a similar awareness of the care needed in appropriately defining the focus and emphasis of public investment programmes. As Alice Amsden has recently argued, forming her case on a deep understanding of the bases of Asian developmental success, there is convincing *prima facie* evidence of the importance of the state in late industrialisation, specifically of the need for active governmental roles in channelling investments into projects that develop productive capacity (1997, p.477). In these processes public finance obviously forms a key element, with 'off budget' sources of finance, notably in the form of postal savings systems and pension funds, forming identifiable and important features in Japanese and later East and Southeast Asian success stories alike. As Amsden underlines, it is precisely this 'fiscalisation of finance', the characteristic and creative combination of publicly or quasi-publicly owned financial institutions orchestrating the public disposal of private savings, that has so effectively underwritten both the consistently high rates of investment in the region and the consistently successful channelling of these investments into productive activities (1997, pp.473-474).

Our first contention, therefore, is the particular salience of the retention of state control over the management and disposal of pension funds to enhanced prospects for the effective mobilisation and strategic utilisation of long term savings for the achievement of economically and socially coherent developmental impacts with welfare enhancing outcomes, even, or perhaps especially, in low income economies. However, as this volume has underlined at a number of different points, the effective impossibility of extending 'coverage' to the great bulk of the informal sector workforce and the self-employed - long acknowledged both as the Achilles' heel of contributory 'Bismarckian' social insurance systems and as an inherent limitation of the NPF 'mandatory savings' model - renders all the existing formal, state-provided, mechanisms for 'retirement' and 'pension' provision largely irrelevant to the bulk of the South's populations for the foreseeable future. The fact that private providers, by definition only seeking profit, have even less incentive than the state to cater for the needs of those on low incomes and no incentive to involve themselves either with those without identifiable incomes or with irregular earnings, does not alter the impact of this uncomfortable fact.

Accordingly, our second contention is that the central focus - funded systems - of recent work on pension provision, including our own, must, in current circumstances of burgeoning non-formal sectors among DCs and transition states, be defined as of tangential rather than of direct importance precisely to those, many many million, citizens of the Third World most clearly in urgent need of enhanced income support, the elderly poor. As we have argued above, those in greatest need of support in old age are, by definition, poorly served in practice by all formal systems of 'social security' currently available. These effectively exclude the elderly poor from forms of formal 'pension' provision other than those provided, apparently quite widely, but often erratically, and always marginally across the South on a social assistance basis. It is for the elderly, often female, poor in LICs that pension, not of course retirement, options are most urgently needed to provide regular cash incomes universally. Fully developed options in this regard, however, require much more information and much additional research to establish their administrative feasibility and their financial sustainability, bearing in mind that their intended beneficiaries, the absolute poor, are notoriously difficult to reach on a consistent basis.

There is, bluntly, too much concerning the contemporary realities of old age in DCs that we either do not know or that remains scattered between diverse and, as yet, unintegrated literatures. First, as indicated in relation to SSA in Chapter 6, very limited detailed work has been undertaken on the realities 'on the ground' of formal pension provision in the poorest countries: we simply do not know for most LICs who receives pensions or lump sums and what impact they have. Second, whilst a very great deal of useful and informative work has been undertaken on the nature and impacts of poverty at the household level, including the risk coping strategies utilised by the poor, most of this research deals with the old only incidentally rather than specifically, albeit still remaining highly, if tantalisingly, illuminating in its findings. Third, the subject of social assistance to the elderly poor, arguably the formal support mechanism offering the clearest potential for achieving or approaching universality in coverage of the needy old, is particularly badly served in the existing research literature. Compared to the massive literature on the merits and demerits of alternative pension delivery systems there is only a very limited, and then not particularly illuminating, literature on alternative social assistance mechanisms and modalities. Fourth, work on the subject of 'traditional', 'informal' or 'non-formal' social security, arguably the focus of the most comprehensive corpus of research on the elderly poor in DCs, remains largely detached from the other literatures.

Accordingly, we are painfully aware of how much more work is required before we can finally propose a more fully developed strategy, one that is manifestly both administratively feasible and fiscally sustainable, for achieving universal provision of cash incomes to *all* the elderly in DCs with any degree of confidence. That said, we find the available evidence, outlined in Chapters 6 and 7, sufficiently persuasive to propose, as our third contention, that, a policy priority for DCs, should be to provide (small but regular) cash incomes, preferably on an individual, not simply a household, basis, universally to all the elderly, including, especially, the 'hard to reach' elderly poor. These universal benefits, although provided as social assistance provision, should be presented and provided as permanent entitlements, and therefore inflation linked and adjusted in a guaranteed manner. They should not be presented or provided in the currently fashionable, *ad hoc* and temporary, demand driven and uneven, 'safety net' format. Specifically, for this key element in provision at least, we are suggesting that establishing universality of provision and achieving predictability, regularity and consistency in payment are more important initial policy priorities than demanding, adequacy of provision, at least *ab initio*. Even providing tiny, seemingly inadequate, cash incomes universally, and on a regular basis, to all the elderly poor in individual LICs, would constitute an important step forward, not simply in helping to soften the impacts of absolute poverty, but also in establishing the relevance, validity and operational viability of the workable administrative mechanisms for effective outreach to the poorest households that DC governments currently lack but desperately need.

Consequently, our fourth contention is that the currently fashionable, and currently dominant, rather hard-nosed economic growth-oriented version of the PID approach to pension system design and reform espoused by the World Bank should be softened and appropriately adjusted to more clearly and comprehensively incorporate those aspects of the earlier PAD approach that have continuing validity and relevance. Specifically, in its view of pension systems as passive welfare instruments, essentially forming dependent elements in developmental sequences, the PAD approach exhibited the limits of the 'complex and costly', welfare state, approaches to welfare provision, particularly in its limited interest in, and substantial irrelevance to, the specific problems of pension provision in poor countries. For all its faults, however, it is also clear that PAD perspectives have been too comprehensively displaced by the growth oriented PID approaches, with the latter particularly prone to lose sight of the enduring importance of pensions as welfare instruments intended primarily to protect a vulnerable, and increasingly large, segment of total populations. PID perspectives rightly emphasise the growth functions of pensions, but should not need to do so to the detriment of their equally important welfare functions. As the World Bank argues, '[o]ver the long haul the only way to reduce poverty is to foster economic growth ...' (World Bank, 1996, p.84).

Happily, as the Bank also stresses, appropriately structured and managed pension systems are potentially significant independent variables in generating such positive growth outcomes, offering tantalising possibilities for virtuous growth sequences to emerge on the basis of pension reforms. In searching for innovative policies and instruments for stimulating economic growth in DCs, the World Bank has prioritised private pension funds and focused increasingly on the virtues of what we term the 'pension fund-capital market nexus' (see Chapter 8), thereby also prioritising the importance of growth over welfare in pension system design. In the variant of the PID perspective espoused in this volume the growth and welfare elements in, and purposes for, pension system design are regarded as both of equal importance and as mutually consistent, indeed becoming significantly synergistic in appropriately structured and operated public systems. The Singapore example, discussed in detail above in Chapters 5 and 8, provides the classic case of such synergy.

Our fifth contention is that the neoliberal assault on existing social and welfare policy has been too easily accepted. As Bob Deacon has underlined, social policy responses to recent global developments have been limited, to say the least. 'The implications for national, supranational and transnational social policy of this present phase of globalisation is an under-theorised and under-researched topic within the subject of social policy' (Deacon, 1997, p.1). As a result social policy objectives have become subjected to the will of the market (Ramonet, 1999). Put bluntly, social policy becomes yet another mechanism to 'promote capital accumulation though financial manœuvres' (Vilas, 1996, p.18). In the face of this assault, traditional social policy standards and objectives, not least the provision of reasonable living standards for all old people, have been too easily surrendered and abandoned. Yet social policy, as Margaret Sherraden has rightly noted, 'does not have to be a drain on economic production and can even contribute to it' (1995, p.188). Sadly, this is an insight rapidly grasped, and readily utilised, by neoliberals but not so often or so effectively, at least so far, by their critics.

The Bank's approach to pensions policy, in turn, equates neatly to one possible type of 'growth-oriented social policy', which, appropriately, is similarly epitomised by Chile (1995, p.189). The advantages and disadvantages of this approach are succinctly and fairly outlined by Margaret Sherraden: Chile at once provides a 'striking example of growth-oriented social policy' and at the same time must be deemed 'a failure' in respect of its neglect of 'mechanisms that adequately address the needs of the poor'. As Sherraden rightly notes, what is required in response is a more coherent alternative perspective. Approaches to social policy which either 'emphasise the free market simplistically ...' or, alternatively, 'those that emphasise redistribution only ...' are both too narrow when viewed 'from a development standpoint' (1995, p.188). Specifically, Sherraden 'suggests an overall rejection of the debate over growth versus equality. A better focus might be growth and equality, with a major role to be played by social policy. If we can learn anything from examples of East Asian development, this dual goal would surely be at the top of the list ...' (Sherraden, 1995, p.188, citing Birdsall, Ross and Sabot). It is our contention that pensions policy and pension system design for DCs should, and can, actively contribute to the pursuit of this dual goal.

Our sixth contention is that neoliberal impacts on DCs over the last two decades have both deliberately and accidentally, or incidentally, made this task more difficult. Ramonet's depiction of a dominant reductionist HIC policy perspective in which 'politics is economy; the economy is finance; and finance is the market' (1999, p.1), provides a neat depiction of the approaches adopted by the Bretton Woods Institutions (BWIs), particularly the Bank, in implementing the requisite 'market-friendly' structural adjustments in DCs. A vast literature has recorded the comparatively limited successes of structural adjustment programmes across the South, their numerous shortcomings, not least in relation to their negative welfare impacts, and the inherent limitations of the imposed conditionalities utilised to enforce the terms of policy-based lending. What we would wish to add to this large catalogue of failings is the simple point, at once both paradoxical and ironic, that the impact of SAPs, despite their slow and patchy implementation, has been very effectively to undermine the existing bases of, and the short and medium term prospects for achieving, precisely the dynamic formal private sectors that the IFIs are so committed to encouraging.

Alice Amsden's view, based on deep understanding of the mainsprings of East Asian success, is that the neoliberal medicine packaged as SAPs especially in Latin America and across SSA, required the sudden and abrupt dismantling of the original, well established, social constructions of competitive assets that had slowly evolved over many decades, resulting in sustained falls in investment in productive capacity across the South from the early 1980s (Amsden, 1997, p.478). What is now required, therefore, is precisely what World Bank policies have so effectively undermined; the development of a completely new social construction of competitive assets, to be based on renewed public-private partnerships not on neoliberal zero sum state-market dichotomies. Moving closer to the world technological frontier and becoming internationally competitive requires that governments join with the private sector to socially construct 'competitive assets', comprising resources, capabilities and organisations, rather than create perfect markets, Amsden argues convincingly (1997, p.478).

The rhetorical question that Marc Wuyts asks in the context of structurally adjusted Mozambique has a DC-wide relevance: can 'a state which operates on a short time horizon ... in fact support a shift to a private sector culture of longer term investment?' (Wuyts, 1996, p.747, fn.10) What the Bank's 'market friendly' policies actually produced, albeit as an unintended by-product of their assault on the state, were burgeoning informal, and non-formal, sectors, instead of the dynamic formal sectors they intended. As the World Bank has slowly, grudgingly, and still only to a strictly limited extent, acknowledged during the course of the 1990s, tentatively in the *East Asian Miracle* (1993) and then more explicitly in the 1997 World Development Report, *The State in A Changing World*, developing a dynamic private sector in DCs demands, as a necessary precondition, an equally dynamic state. This was the essential lesson from both Gerschenkron's 'late' industrialisation (1962) and Amsden's East Asian 'late, late' industrialisers (1989), and should have been well internalised by those charged with the responsibility for the success of currently aspirant 'late, late, late' industrialisers. It is particularly strange that the Bank's pensions experts have not exhibited enthusiasm for the positive virtues of a dynamic and innovative state. After all, the so-called 'Chicago boys' responsible for the seminal set of neoliberal social policies in Allende's Chile - Piñera was in fact a Harvard graduate - were themselves state technocrats, not products of the market.

Our seventh contention, therefore, is that the Bank model of pillared pension provision - never likely to be particularly appropriate for the great bulk of DCs, including the MICs for which the model was designed - has become even less appropriate as a model for developing and transition economies as a direct consequence of the outcome of the cumulative impacts of the World Bank's own policies. Specifically, in orchestrating donor activities, via cross-conditionality, in so successfully undermining state effectiveness across the South, as well as, albeit inadvertently, stimulating the expansion of informal economies, the Bank has also, and with equal effectiveness, undermined the prospects for the successful implementation of its pensions policy preference, private funded schemes extended on a mandatory rather than a voluntary basis. For success to be ensured, this agenda requires, on the one hand, a ruthlessly efficient state to initiate, to enforce, and to continue to guarantee, successful reform implementation, and, on the other hand, an expanding and dynamic private sector to provide both healthy savings inflows to the funds and profitable outlets for their investments. Yet, courtesy of the Bank, both sound states and healthy private formal sectors are now in very short supply in DCs and the transition states alike. It is also worth remembering at this point that the disasters that struck African pension systems, and NPFs in particular, in the 1980s, and which contributed to the evidence that the World Bank has mobilised so effectively against the public management of pension funds, were the immediate result of rampant inflation, one underlying cause of which were SAPs. Had Africa followed Chile in the early 1980s the performance of private pension funds would have been equally disastrous.

The Bank's pensions reform agenda is based on the assumption that savings grow best when they are placed in the hands of private sector fund management 'professionals'. Our eighth contention is that this assumption is at least ill-judged and at worst highly risky with the life-savings of the citizens of DCs who can ill afford the potential consequences even of poor returns on their investments, let alone the consequences of total loss. Such a gamble, is, as Paul Johnson pointed out at an early stage in the transition from communism, particularly inappropriate for small and poor DCs (1996, p.15). These are, by definition, ill equipped to support private pension funds, and the latter, if domestically owned and managed, are liable to fall rapidly into a vicious cycle of unproductive competition, as too many potential providers compete increasingly desperately for a limited pool of savings, leading in Latin America to what has been termed 'transfer wars' as funds compete ruthlessly for customers (*Economist*, 1999a, p.119). Limited profitable, other than risky and speculative, domestic investment opportunities, hence limited portfolio diversity, completes the negative circularity. The likelihood is that most private funds would rapidly become bankrupt in such contexts, and that a degenerative cycle of competition would lead to institutional consolidation, probably on the basis of mainly foreign ownership of a few larger funds. These larger funds would clearly be more viable, particularly if permitted to diversify their portfolios globally, but would almost certainly survive only at the margins unless they tacitly reduced competition, thereby totally negating the original reform objectives. Accordingly, we find the investment case for private provision in DCs largely unconvincing, throwing back at the Bank a mirror image of its own verdict on the poor investment performance of public pension funds.

Nor are these points simply hypothetical. As *The Economist*, admitted in an otherwise enthusiastic overview of 'Latin lessons on pensions', '[c]ompetition among funds has failed to curb their operating costs, which amount to a steep 3 percent of wages in some countries: instead of competing on price, the firms have spent heavily on advertising and sales agents' (Economist, 1999a, p.119). Moreover, the empirical evidence of poor domestic investment performance and limited positive investment impact of private pension funds in DCs is also mounting steadily, as the actual investment impacts and outcomes of recently implemented reforms become increasingly clear. We have dealt in detail with the weaknesses and extremely limited impact of the voluntary 'outgrowing' pensions privatisation strategy originally pursued in CEE and the NIS/FSU in Chapter 4. Similar points could be made about the disappointing outcomes of the more radical pension reforms undertaken, under Chilean influence and with Bank support, in other Latin American states and beyond in the course of the 1990s. Argentina - itself an influential reform model, arguably, in practical system design terms, providing an even more influential model for pension reformers than Chile - provides confirmation of the limited positive outcomes of recently 'reformed' pension systems.

As a recent *Economist Survey* underlined, finance remains the Achilles' heel of the Argentinean economy. 'Bank loans, if available at all, cost a bomb ... Nor is longer-term capital easily found. One obvious source turns out to be useless: the stockmarket ... The much-touted private pension schemes, born in 1994, are little help. A fine idea for their purpose, they have now won 8 million subscribers, but over half of these are not actually paying up. In all, the funds manage $17 billion. But tight rules limit their equity investment, overall or in any one company, even were more equities available' (Economist, 2000c, p.7). Add disappointing investment impact to unacceptably large running costs, the one negative feature of the private funds that is actually accepted even by pension reform enthusiasts (see Queisser, 1999), and the impending threats posed by the cumulative impact of these factors to the long-term integrity of invested funds, hence also to the pension prospects of savers, becomes obvious. Nor should we be surprised by these developments. South Africa provides the clearest case of both the achievements, and the inherent limitations, of the 'outgrowing' strategy of private pension sector development. As underlined above particularly in Chapter 6, the South African industry is innovative and even, to some extent, pro-poor. Nevertheless, returns from South African funds are merely respectable, largely conforming to international standards in this respect. More widely, in the rest of 'Southern Africa there are fewer productive options for investment, capital markets are less well developed and regulated, and returns are often offset by currency deterioration', further undermining returns to the affiliates of South African financial services subsidiaries (Fultz and Pieris, 1999, p.45).

The standard riposte of radical pension reform enthusiasts, justifying their continued enthusiasm for private provision, is that the investment performance of public pension funds both has been, and will always be, worse than that of their private counterparts. We largely accept the Bank's strictures on the past performance of public pension funds, but reject the implication of the inherent investment inefficiency of public provision, leading to our ninth contention. This is to suggest that, for DCs in general but for small and poor DCs in particular, there is significant, as yet largely unconsidered and untapped, potentiality in the public management of the investment function of pension funds. Bluntly, big public savings institutions dealing with consolidated pools of national savings can much better afford to buy in the best fund management advice available internationally than small private providers.

All the evidence that is publicly available - these are highly secretive institutions - suggests that the large international investment funds operated by some astute DCs, classically the Kuwait Investment Authority (KIA) and Singapore's Monetary Authority (MAS) but also, albeit more quietly, the Bank of Botswana, achieve high, perhaps extremely high, returns on their globally diversified investment portfolios. The main problem facing most DCs in seeking to replicate this type of international investment fund operation is that few can afford to do exactly what Botswana, Kuwait and Singapore have done, namely utilising the luxury of the surpluses accruing from their huge revenue bases, relative to populations, to undertake their major domestic investment programmes mainly or even entirely on the back of the profits made by their internationally diversified portfolios. However, even if consolidated public pension funds were obliged to exhibit the same domestic market investment bias characteristically required of their private counterparts, the central points stand: the potential returns on investment portfolios would still be better, overhead and administrative costs could and should be significantly lower, and the security of savings can be most directly and comprehensively guaranteed by governments.

The fact that the MAS, in acting as an investment conduit for CPF savings, is known to achieve investment returns far higher than those subsequently passed on to the retirement savings accounts of individual Singaporeans, simply reflects the priorities of the Government of Singapore. For our current purposes the salient point is to underline the clear potential for returns to be credited to the accounts of CPF savers at higher rates of interest than are currently sanctioned, if the Government of Singapore chose to do so. Ideally, under good governance requirements for public management to be transparent and accountable as well as effective, this form of, hidden, implicit taxation of CPF savings would be made public and explicit, even if the operations of the MAS itself remained less than fully transparent to protect its competitive edge on international markets. In the medium to long term, at least, this is the likely scenario for Singapore, as an increasingly aware public exerts pressure for improved returns on their savings on the Government of Singapore, and as the latter has less and less reason to hoard huge sums of money for public investment purposes.

For most DCs the key need, either in contemplating the establishment of a public pension fund *ab initio* or, in a few cases in reconstructing an existing hitherto poorly performing NPF and turning it into a high performing National Pension Fund, is for a combination of sound advice and practical assistance. These requirements could and should be readily met simply by utilising the combined expertise of the existing community of international advisory institutions. For example, at an early stage in the post-communist transition, Paul Johnson presented a well developed and highly persuasive case for the development across the low income transition economies of the CIS of state managed, but World Bank supported, funded pension systems (1993). Such a proposal has both continuing and wider relevance, particularly if the ILO and the ISSA were mobilised alongside the BWIs to counterbalance the latter's tendency to discount welfare dimensions in the search for market-conforming growth.

An additional advantage of such an advisory regime would relate to its potential for the 'socially responsible' dissemination of expertise gained by the World Bank through its own international bond market ventures. As discussed above in Chapter 8, the Bank has long been active participant in global bond markets, leading to its established position as 'a market leader in bond issuance in emerging market currencies' (World Bank Website, 2000). Our proposals would simply provide the Bank with an institutionalised framework for disseminating its expertise in the innovative development and prudent management of highly profitable debt securities to DCs, albeit not, as at present, utilising this expertise largely to marginalise state pensions institutions and promote their private counterparts. For example, during 1999 the Bank issued bonds in Czech and Slovak Crowns, Polish Zloty and South African Rand and in 2000 launched bonds in Chilean and Mexican Pesos. As in the Chilean case covered above, the main target for these bonds was domestic institutional investors among which pension funds are prominent.

As outlined in the Introduction, the Bank has in recent years been increasingly open to the idea of partnerships in policy making, both with other development IOs and with DC governments. As the ILO report,

> The scope of the policy dialogue with the Bretton Woods institutions has broadened in recent years beyond the key issues of structural adjustment to include issues relating to globalization and economic growth, the relationship between economic and social development, and a variety of labour market and social issues. The main subjects of dialogue have encompassed the social and employment impact of structural adjustment policies and of globalization, labour law and wage policy issues, labour market issues, social security and pensions, enterprise development and rural credit, employment policies, gender issues and training. ... The Bretton Woods institutions have been mainly interested in seeking the ILO's views on labour market, wage policy and social safety net issues ...
>
> ILO, 1999, p.77

Inevitably, given the World Bank's overwhelming financial muscle, this emerging policy dialogue has largely been undertaken on the Bank's terms. Nevertheless, the official ILO view of these developments is largely positive. 'Sustained institutional debate has helped bring the institutions closer together and there is generally much common ground in the policy dialogue ...'. However, the ILO also stressed that '[s]ignificant differences did ... emerge, especially on policy conclusions drawn from this analysis' (ILO, 1999, p.77). Clearly, this reservation is crucial since the key test of the Bank's commitment to partnerships and to the development of a genuine policy dialogue will come at the point at which its 'inclusive model' (Beattie, 2000) is translated into specific advice and technical assistance offered to DC states. Specifically, in relation to pension reform, the Bank increasingly will be pressed to soften its entrenched anti-state predilections in response to both ILO and DC preferences. Developments in Kazakhstan - where more than half of contributors to the 'reformed' pension system remain affiliated to the State Accumulation Fund (SAF) - are instructive in this regard. As Andrews explains, with 53.1 percent of contributors and 42 percent of pension fund assets in October 2000, the SAF's contributors 'have lower incomes and/or include more individuals with income stemming in large part from the informal sector. Some of these individuals could consider their assets to be safer with the state, while other could just have less interest in participating in the system than do employees with a greater stake in the formal sector' (2000, p.28). Kazakh experience, therefore, underlines the point that distrust of the state is relative not absolute and that poor people in particular often remain more inclined to save with state institutions than with new and unfamiliar private entities.

It may be that such an encompassing and less state-antipathetic advisory regime is already emerging in the aftermath of the Asian contagion, in response to its devastating welfare consequences. Faced suddenly with acute poverty problems in previously unproblematic HPAEs, the IFIs immediately ran for cover, even suggesting the need for the inauguration of social insurance programmes (Singh and Zammit, 2000, p.1262), a policy previously regarded by the Bank as an ILO idiosyncrasy.[1] More generally, in line with the cooperative organisational arrangements described above, the IOs are increasingly moving 'from conflict to convergence' (Queisser, 2000) in their approaches to pension reform. Positively, therefore, in line with these developments, we seek to propose as our tenth and final contention that an international advisory regime for old age pension systems and related issues should be developed that is more organisationally inclusive of all the different international organisations with institutional and operational expertise in the pensions field. Operationally, this advisory regime should overtly be structured and operated to ensure that *dialogue* replaces *monologue.* In this regard we would further propose a role for international organisations in providing advice and capacity building support for pension policy reform:

- that is more modest and more circumscribed than is currently fashionable;
- that is more policy inclusive, hence less policy didactic, encompassing *all* available pension reform and restructuring options;
- that is more inclusive of all the interests, including domestic ones, that should legitimately be involved;
- and, above all, that is sensitive to key domestic requirements, and, therefore, that is also fully cognisant of relevant domestic constraints and opportunities.

The outcome of such an advisory system is an enhanced likelihood of forming a consensus among all relevant pensions policy stakeholders on the appropriate measures for addressing, in the short term, the welfare problems of the elderly and for developing, in the medium and long term, fiscally sound and sustainable systems of income provision for the old within DCs. More widely, an encompassing advisory regime would ensure a more balanced consideration of the dual roles of pension systems in contributing to both social welfare outcomes as well as economic growth in formulating policy strategies.

We feel that there is an irresistible logic to such proposals, not least given the important underlying commonalities between the pension reform 'alternatives' currently on the table. As we have sought to underline in Chapter 3, available options do not in practice involve a simple choice between public and private alternatives. Rather the choice is between forms and degrees of state and market provision. What is now crucial is increasingly to involve the states of the South on a more comprehensively inclusive basis in the design of 'their' future social protection systems, specifically acknowledging the importance of policy learning and experience sharing at the regional, or even the sub-regional, level. Here it is useful to cite the ILO's recent positive experiences with its Multidisciplinary Advisory Teams (MATs) operating on a regional basis and specifically seeking 'lessons designed from regional experience' (Fultz and Pieris, 1999, p.vii). For example as outlined in Chapter 6 in relation to the diffusion of the principle of universality in southern Africa, the experience of the Southern African Multidisciplinary Advisory Team (SAMAT) has underlined 'the benefits of regular exchanges of information and experience among Southern African countries. There are no more compelling lessons than those derived by neighbours attempting to deal with similar problems and challenges' (Fultz and Pieris, 1999, p.53). Nor, we would add, can there be a more appropriate and effective reply to the recent and earlier attempts of individual international organisations to constrain the pensions policy options available to individual states.

Notes

1. Nevertheless, the reminder provided by the Asian collapse to all those involved in pensions policy issues was timely. Inevitably, as we acknowledged in Chapter 5, the Southeast Asian NPF's performance suffered as capital markets collapsed and inflation mounted. However, if the HPAEs had not been canny enough to avoid the pensions privatisation trap, the consequences would, arguably, have been worse. Specifically, returns on private funds would have collapsed as comprehensively as those of their NPF counterparts but, potentially, with even worse consequences - widespread bankruptcy - unless, as in Chile in 1983, states stepped in to underwrite 'private provision'. In this respect it would be particularly ironic if history were to repeat itself, with the Bank highlighting the collapse of the Asian NPFs as a cautionary tale in their crusade against public management, paralleling the selective utilisation of African NPF cases in *Averting* for this purpose, highlighted above in Chapter 6.

Appendix

The various items that comprise this appendix provide additional data and illustrative material selected to illuminate and contextualise major issues and developments presented in this book.

Figure A1.1 Summary of the 1989 Washington Consensus

- **Fiscal Discipline** Budget deficits - properly measured to include provincial governments, state enterprises, and the central bank - should be small enough to be financed without recourse to the inflation tax. This size typically implies a primary surplus (that is, before adding debt service to expenditure) of several percent of GDP, as well as an operational deficit (that is, the deficit disregarding that part of the interest bill that simply compensates for inflation) of no more than about 2 percent of GDP.

- **Public-Expenditure Priorities** Expenditure should be redirected from politically sensitive areas - which typically receive more resources than their economic return can justify, such as administration, defence, indiscriminate subsidies, and white elephants - towards neglected fields with high economic returns and the potential to improve income distribution, such as primary healthcare, primary education, and infrastructure.

- **Tax Reform** Tax reform involves broadening the tax base and cutting marginal tax rates. The aim is to sharpen incentives and improve horizontal equity without lowering realised progressivity. Improved tax administration (including subjecting interest income on assets held abroad - "flight capital" - to taxation) is an important aspect of broadening the base in the Latin context.

- **Financial Liberalisation** The ultimate objective of financial liberalisation is market-determined interest rates, but experience has shown that, under conditions of a chronic lack of confidence, market-determined rates can be so high as to threaten the financial solvency of productive enterprises and government. Under that circumstance, a sensible interim objective is the

275

abolition of preferential interest rates for privileged borrowers and achievement of a moderately positive real interest rate.

- **Exchange Rates** Countries need a unified (at least for trade sanctions) exchange rate set at a level sufficiently competitive to induce a rapid growth in nontraditional exports and managed so as to ensure exporters that this competitiveness will be maintained in the future.

- **Trade Liberalisation** Quantitative trade restrictions should be rapidly replaced by tariffs, and these should be progressively reduced until a uniform low tariff in the range of 10 percent (or at most around 20 percent) is achieved. There exists, however, some disagreement about the speed with which tariffs should be reduced (with recommendations falling in a band between 3 and 10 years) and about whether it is advisable to slow down the process of trade liberalisation when macroeconomic conditions are adverse (recession and payments deficit).

- **Foreign Direct Investment** Barriers impeding the entry of foreign firms should be abolished; foreign and domestic firms should be allowed to compete on equal terms.

- **Privatisation** State enterprises should be privatised.

- **Deregulation** Governments should abolish regulations that impede the entry of new firms or that restrict competition, and then should ensure that all regulations are justified by such criteria as safety, environmental protection, or prudential supervision of financial institutions.

- **Property Rights** The legal system should provide secure property rights without excessive costs and should make such rights available to the informal sector.

Source: Williamson, 1997, pp. 58-61

Figure A1.2 Summary of the Post-Washington Consensus

- increase savings by (*inter alia*) maintaining fiscal discipline;

- reorient public expenditure toward (*inter alia*) well-directed social expenditure;

- reform the tax system by (*inter alia*) introducing an eco-sensitive land tax;

- strengthen banking supervision;

- maintain a competitive exchange rate, abandoning both floating and the use of the exchange rate as a anchor;

- pursue intraregional trade liberalisation;

- build a competitive market economy by (*inter alia*) privatising and deregulating (including the labour market);

- make well-defined property rights available to all;

- build key institutions such as independent central banks, strong budget offices, independent and incorruptible judiciaries, and agencies to sponsor productivity missions;

- increase educational spending and redirect it towards primary and secondary levels.

Source: Williamson, 1997, pp. 58-61

Table A1.1 Population Aged 60 Years or Older

Country or Area	Number (Thousands)		Percentage of Total Population		Percentage 80 Years or Older	
	1999	2050	1999	2050	1999	2050
World Total	593,111	1,969,809	10	22	11	19
More Developed Regions	228,977	375,516	19	33	16	27
Less Developed Regions	364,133	1,594,293	8	21	9	17
Least Developed Countries	30,580	180,983	5	12	7	10

Key:

- More Developed Regions comprise all regions of Europe and Northern America, Australia/New Zealand and Japan.
- Less Developed Regions comprise all regions of Africa, Asia (excluding Japan) and Latin America and the Caribbean and the regions of Melanesia, Micronesia and Polynesia.
- Least Developed Countries comprise 48 countries of which 33 are in Africa, 9 are in Asia, 1 is in Latin America and 5 are in Oceania. They are included in the less developed regions.

Source: United Nations, UNDP, Population Ageing 1999.

Table A1.2 Aged Population by Sex and Active in Labour Force

Country or Area	Population Aged 60 Years or Older		Aged Population by Sex			
	Percentage in Labour Force 1995		60 Years or Older 1999		80 Years or Older 1999	
	Men	Women	Men	Women	Men	Women
World Total	42	16	45	55	35	65
More Developed Regions	23	10	41	59	31	69
Less Developed Regions	52	20	47	53	39	61
Least Developed Countries	76	44	47	53	43	57

Key:

- More Developed Regions comprise all regions of Europe and Northern America, Australia/New Zealand and Japan.
- Less Developed Regions comprise all regions of Africa, Asia (excluding Japan) and Latin America and the Caribbean and the regions of Melanesia, Micronesia and Polynesia.
- Least Developed include 48 countries of which 33 are in Africa, 9 are in Asia, 1 is in Latin America and 5 are in Oceania. They are included in the less developed regions.

Source: United Nations, UNDP, Population Ageing 1999.

Figure A2.1 ILO Minimum Standards

As Fultz and Pieris outline,

The conventions on Social Security establish standards for the financing, benefit structure, and administration of social security schemes. In all, 30 Conventions and 15 Recommendations deal with these issues. ... The most important of these are consolidated in the Social Security Minimum Standards Convention No.102 (1952).

1999, p. 2

As defined by Social Security Minimum Standards Convention No.102 (1952), national social security systems should seek to provide the following nine benefits; namely,

- medical care,
- sickness benefit,
- maternity benefit,
- employment injury benefit,
- old age benefit,
- invalidity benefit,
- survivors' benefit,
- unemployment benefit,
- family benefit.

The satisfactory fulfilment of Convention, No.102 (1952) includes six requirements.

- First, it stipulates that protection should extend to at least half the national work force or 20 percent of residents.
- Second, it requires that benefits be provided for at least three of the nine contingencies in the ILO definition, at least one of which must be of a long-term nature (i.e., old age, disability, employment injury, or survivors benefits) or unemployment.
- Third, it calls for the cost of benefits and administration to be borne collectively by way of insurance contributions or taxation. This requirement excludes benefits which are financed exclusively by a

single employer. The portion of contributions paid by workers should not exceed 50 percent.

- Fourth, it requires that cash benefits be periodic, paid through a contingency, and set to replace a specified portion of a worker's lost wages. Exceptions are provided for minor employment-related injuries and for specific cases where the administering agency is satisfied that a lump-sum be used appropriately.

- Fifth, it establishes minimum rates of income replacement, set at 50 percent of lost wages for a worker with a family who is injured on the job, 45 percent for unemployment and maternity, and 40 percent for a married worker who retires due to old age, a worker with family who retires due to disability, or the survivors of a deceased worker.

- Finally, it requires that the government assume general responsibility for the operation of a social security scheme. In cases where it delegates this authority, worker representatives should participate in scheme management or be associated with it in a consultative capacity.

Fultz and Pieris, 1999, pp. 1-2

Figure A2.2 Swiss Chilanpore Pillared Pensions Model

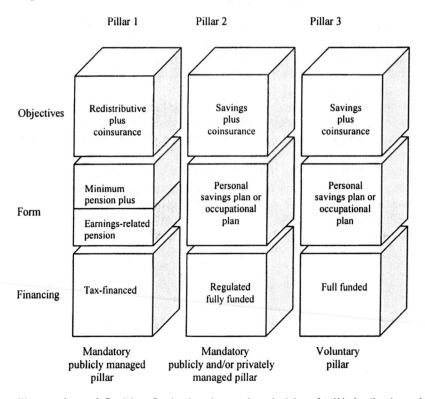

(1) a mandatory defined benefit plan based upon the principles of solidarity (i.e. it would operate on a pay-as-you-go basis) as well as the principles of proportionality, indexation and actualization and lifetime earnings. The first pillar would consist of two parts;
Part I - a minimum pension that would be fixed irrespective of salary level;
Part II - an earnings related component;
(2) a mandatory defined contribution plan with individual privately managed capitalisation accounts. A central agency would be responsible for record keeping, collecting contributions, paying pensions and sending out financial statements. The central agency could be a public body or it could be jointly owned by all the private companies that would be allowed to participate in the investment management of the pension funds;
(3) voluntary private or occupational pension schemes.

Adapted from: Vittas, 1993a, pp. 20-24

Figure A2.3 Averting the Old Age Crisis Pensions Model

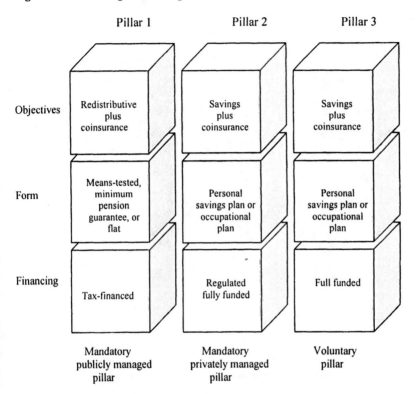

	Pillar 1	Pillar 2	Pillar 3
Objectives	Redistributive plus coinsurance	Savings plus coinsurance	Savings plus coinsurance
Form	Means-tested, minimum pension guarantee, or flat	Personal savings plan or occupational plan	Personal savings plan or occupational plan
Financing	Tax-financed	Regulated fully funded	Full funded
	Mandatory publicly managed pillar	Mandatory privately managed pillar	Voluntary pillar

(1)   a mandatory tax-financed public pillar designed to alleviate poverty;

(2)   a mandatory, funded, privately managed pillar (based on personal accounts or occupational plans) to handle people's savings;

(3)   a supplementary voluntary pillar (again based on personal saving or occupational plans) for people who want more protection.

Adapted from: World Bank, 1994, p. 15

Map A2.1 World Bank Advice on Pension Reform

Source: World Bank, http://www.worldbank.org

Countries which have received World Bank advice on pension reform

11 in Africa

Burkina Faso
Cameroon
Chad
Congo (Brazzaville)
Ghana
Guinea
Libya
Mali
Morocco
Mozambique
Togo

5 in Asia

Mongolia
Pakistan
Peoples Republic of
China
Philippines

Thailand

*17 in East and
Central Europe and
the former Soviet
Union*

Albania
Croatia
Estonia
Georgia
Hungary
Kazakhstan
Kyrgystan
Latvia
Lithuania
Macedonia FYR
Moldova
Poland
Romania
Russian Federation
Slovakia
Turkmenistan
Ukraine

16 in Latin America

Argentina
Belize
Bolivia
Brazil
Chile
Colombia
Costs Rica
El Salvador
Ecuador
Guatemala
Honduras
Mexico
Nicaragua
Panama
Peru
Uruguay

Source: World Bank,
http://www.worldbank.org

Figure A3.1 ILO Tiered Pensions Model

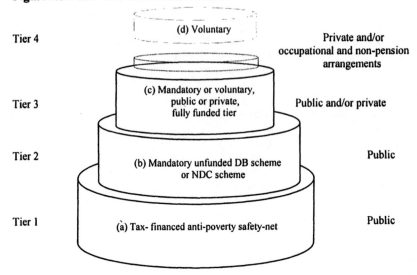

(a) a government-provided anti-poverty benefit. It provides a social safety net. It includes means tested and income tested benefits for low income elderly and flat benefits that are received based on years of residence. This tier is usually financed out of general government revenue;

(b) a mandatory unfunded defined benefit scheme or notional defined contribution scheme provided through the government social security system. This tier is the traditional pay-as-you-go social security system found in most countries. It provides social insurance for workers against some economic risks by spreading the effects of risks across the population;

(c) funded benefits provided by the government or by private sector entities. This tier could be combined with the second tier as a single partially funded plan. This tier could be mandatory or voluntary. When it is voluntary, the fourth tier can be distinguished as being composed of nonpension arrangements. While generally it is important to have a funded source of retirement income, it is not essential in all countries that the source be mandatory;

(d) a voluntary and supplementary tier. It includes private savings, voluntary occupational pension schemes, voluntary individual pension accounts, labour earnings, support from family members, and charity. In some countries, savings in the form of housing is an important aspect of retirement in the fourth tier. Housing can be used both as an investment that is liquidated in retirement and as a source of services that are paid for before retirement.

Adapted from: Turner, 1997, p. 7

Figure A3.2 The World at Six Billion

1.   World population crossed the six billion threshold on October 12, 1999.

2.   World population is projected to cross the 7 billion mark in 2013; the 8 billion mark in 2028; the 9 billion mark in 2054. World population nearly stabilises at just above 10 billion after 2200.

3.   It has taken just 12 years for the world to add this most recent billion people. This is the shortest period of time in world history for a billion people to be added.

4.   World population did not reach one billion until 1804. It took 123 years to reach 2 billion in 1927, 33 years to reach 3 billion in 1960, 14 years to reach 4 billion in 1974 and 13 years to reach 5 billion in 1987.

5.   The highest rate of world population growth (2.04 percent) took place in the late 1960s. The current rate (1995-2000) is 1.31 percent.

6.   The largest annual increase to world population (86 million) took place in the late 1980s; the current annual increase is 78 million.

7.   Of the 78 million people currently added to the world each year, 95 percent live in the less developed regions.

8.   Eighty percent of the world currently reside in the less developed regions. At the beginning of the century, 70 percent did so. By 2050, the share of the world population living in the currently less developed regions will have risen to 90 percent.

9.   The population of the world is ageing. The median age increased from 23.5 years in 1950 to 26.4 years in 1999. By 2050, the median age is projected to reach 37.8 years. The number of people in the world aged 60 years or older will also rise from the current one-of-ten persons to be two-of-nine by 2050. Currently around one-of-five persons in the developed countries are aged 60 or older; in 2050 nearly one-of-every three persons will be aged 60 or older.

10.   World life expectancy at birth is now at 65 years, having increased by a remarkable 20 years since 1950; by 2050 life expectancy is expected to exceed 76 years. However, in spite of these impressive gains, recent years have shown a devastating toll from AIDS in a number of countries. In addition, in some Eastern European countries, health has been

deteriorating and mortality, particularly among adult males, has been rising.

11. Couples in developing countries today have on average 3 children; thirty years ago they had six. More than half of all couples in developing countries now use contraception.

12. The number of persons who have moved to another country has risen to over 125 million migrants today from 75 million in 1965.

13. The world has become increasingly urban. Currently, around 46 percent of the world population lives in urban areas; the majority of the world's population will be urban by 2006.

Source: United Nations Population Division

Figure A3.3 Reprioritised World Bank Pillared Pensions Model

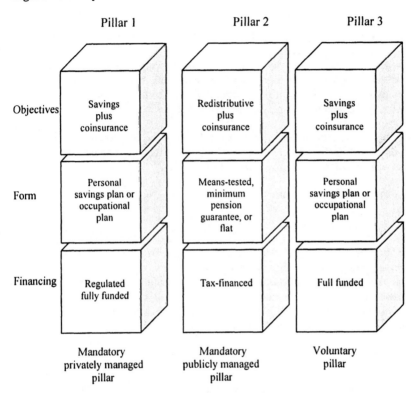

(1) a mandatory privately managed, fully funded pillar that requires people to save and manages their savings;
(2) a publicly managed, tax-financed public pillar for redistribution, to keep old people out of poverty;
(3) a voluntary pillar for people who want more savings and larger pensions.

Adapted from: James, 1995, p. 6, Chart 3

Figure A3.4 Chronology and Evolution of the ILO 'Tiers'

1992
(a) a basic minimum guaranteed (safety-net) pension, similar in scope to the present state-guaranteed minimum,
(b) a defined-benefit, earnings related pension scheme, based on a global and partially funded system rather than an individual, fully funded scheme, with employer as well as employee contributions, and combined with -
(c) a system of optional (employer-based?) complementary schemes.

If the first of the three tiers were available only for contributors, it might be necessary to add a fourth tier, basically a minimum income scheme, which would protect non-contributors (mainly in the informal sector).

Source: Gillion and Bonilla, 1992, p. 194

1993
(a) a basic tier, providing flat-rate benefits at a subsistence level on a universal or means-tested basis, funded on a pay-as-you-go basis from taxation;
(b) a mandatory, defined-benefit tier, financed mainly through contributions and operating on a partially funded basis;
(c) a voluntary complementary tier, based on individual or collective private initiative, and operating on a fully funded basis.

Source: Iyer, 1993, p. 201

1993
(a) a basic, universal, flat-rate pension provided by a compulsory public scheme;
(b) a public, and again compulsory, defined benefit (i.e. earnings-related) scheme financed on a PAYG basis from social security contributions levied as payroll taxes on both employers and employees;
(c) a voluntary, fully funded, defined-contribution scheme, whether individual or enterprise- or occupation-based, for individuals who wish to supplement the State's basic and earnings-related schemes.

Source: ILO, 1993, pp. 58-59

1995

(a) a flat-rate, possibly means-tested, basic pension, chiefly as a anti-poverty measure;

(b) a middle tier, which would comprise a compulsory, defined-benefit, PAYG social security scheme, perhaps providing benefits of a more modest scope that would have been the case if this were the only mechanism for providing for old age;

(c) the development of a third, voluntary, tier comprising personal or occupational, defined-benefit or defined-contribution schemes, operated through non-public pension funds, which would enable workers, individually or through collective bargaining, to supplement the provisions of the compulsory public social security scheme.

Source: ILO, 1993, p. 68

1997

(a) a government-provided anti-poverty benefit. It provides a social safety net. It includes means tested and income tested benefits for low income elderly and flat benefits that are received based on years of residence. This tier is usually financed out of general government revenue;

(b) a mandatory unfunded defined benefit scheme or notional defined contribution scheme provided through the government social security system. This tier is the traditional pay-as-you-go social security system found in most countries. It provides social insurance for workers against some economic risks by spreading the effects of risks across the population;

(c) funded benefits provided by the government or by private sector entities. This tier could be combined with the second tier as a single partially funded plan. This tier could be mandatory or voluntary. When it is voluntary, the fourth tier can be distinguished as being composed of nonpension arrangements. While generally it is important to have a funded source of retirement income, it is not essential in all countries that the source be mandatory;

(d) a voluntary and supplementary tier. It includes private savings, voluntary occupational pension schemes, voluntary individual pension accounts, labour earnings, support from family members, and charity. In some countries, savings in the form of housing is an important aspect of retirement in the fourth tier. Housing can be used both as an investment that is liquidated in retirement and as a source of services that are paid for before retirement.

Source: Turner, 1997, p. 7

Figure A3.5 Chronology and Evolution of the World Bank 'Pillars'

1993

(1) a mandatory defined benefit plan based upon the principles of solidarity (i.e. it would operate on a pay-as-you-go basis) as well as the principles of proportionality, indexation and actualization and lifetime earnings. The first pillar would consist of two parts;
Part I - a minimum pension that would be fixed irrespective of salary level;
Part II - an earnings related component;

(2) a mandatory defined contribution plan with individual privately managed capitalization accounts. A central agency would be responsible for record keeping, collecting contributions, paying pensions and sending out financial statements. The central agency could be a public body or it could be jointly owned by all the private companies that would be allowed to participate in the investment management of the pension funds;

(3) voluntary private or occupational pension schemes.

Source: Vittas, 1993a, pp. 20-24

1994

(1) a mandatory tax-financed public pillar designed to alleviate poverty;

(2) a mandatory, funded, privately managed pillar (based on personal accounts or occupational plans) to handle people's savings;

(3) a supplementary voluntary pillar (again based on personal saving or occupational plans) for people who want more protection.

Source: World Bank, 1994, p. 292

1995

(1) a mandatory privately managed, fully funded pillar that requires people to save and manages their savings;

(2) a publicly managed, tax-financed public pillar for redistribution, to keep old people out of poverty;

(3) a voluntary pillar for people who want more savings and larger pensions.

Source: James, 1995, p. 6

Figure A6.1 Definitions of 'Informal' and 'Underground' Economies

It is important to highlight the key features which distinguish the 'informal economy' from the 'underground economy'.

> [T]he informal sector is often confused with the parallel or underground economy. This latter notion ... is one element in a non-observed economy, and the informal sector is clearly distinguishable from the parallel or underground economy (illegal activities prohibited by their very nature, which is criminal) ... in that it consists of ordinary legal economic activities carried on illegally because they are unregistered. This non-registration is due less to a deliberate desire to evade current legislation than to the inability of States and their governments to enforce regulations which may be quite unsuited to everyday circumstances in developing countries.
>
> Charmes, 2000, p.62

A conceptual 'working definition' of the informal sector, underpinned by wide international agreement, only came into existence in 1993, when the International Conference of Labour Statisticians concluded that:

> [t]he informal sector may be broadly defined as consisting of units engaged in the production of goods or services with the primary objective of generating employment and incomes to the persons concerned. These units typically operate at a low level of organisation, with little or no division between labour and capital as factors of production and on a small scale. Labour relations - where they exist - are based mostly on casual employment, kinship or personal and social relations rather than contractual arrangements with formal guarantees.
>
> As quoted in Charmes, 2000, p.62

Table A6.1 Changes in Coverage in Selected SSA Countries

Country	Contributors/ Labour Force (1989)	Contributors/ Labour Force	% Change in Contributors/ Labour Force
Benin	n/a	4.8 (1996)	n/a
Burkina Faso	n/a	3.1 (1996)	n/a
Burundi	4.7	3.3 (1993)	-30.0
Cameroon	13.7	13.7 (1993)	0.0
Chad	1.1	1.1 (1990)	0.0
Congo (Brazzaville)	n/a	5.8 (1992)	n/a
Côte d'Ivoire	9.3	9.3 (1997)	0.0
Gabon	n/a	7.3 (1991)	n/a
Ghana	13.2	7.2 (1993)	-45.0
Guinea	n/a	1.5 (1993)	n/a
Kenya	n/a	18.0 (1995)	n/a
Madagascar	8.2	5.4 (1993)	-34.0
Mali	2.5	2.5 (1990)	0.0
Niger	2.8	1.3 (1992)	-53.0
Nigeria	n/a	1.3 (1993)	n/a
Rwanda	9.3	9.3 (1993)	0.0
Senegal	n/a	6.9 (1992)	n/a
Sudan	n/a	3.9 (1996)	n/a
Togo	n/a	6.0 (1997)	n/a
Uganda	n/a	8.2 (1994)	n/a
Zambia	13.8	10.2 (1994)	-26.0

Sources: World Bank, 1994, p. 356, Table A.4; Palacios and Pallares-Miralles, 1999

Table A8.1 Fiscal Requirements of the Chilean Reforms, 1981-1996 (% of GDP)

Year	Recognition Bonds	Pensions Expenditure on Workers Retired under the PAYG System	Total Fiscal Cost
1981	0.00	1.45	1.45
1982	0.09	1.85	1.93
1983	0.17	2.36	2.52
1984	0.22	3.22	3.43
1985	0.24	4.22	4.46
1986	0.33	3.94	4.27
1987	0.41	3.32	3.74
1988	0.42	3.40	3.82
1989	0.41	2.55	2.96
1990	0.50	3.23	3.73
1991	0.44	3.30	3.75
1992	0.49	3.10	3.59
1993	0.60	3.07	3.68
1994	0.65	2.97	3.63
1995	0.67	2.77	3.44
1996	0.69	2.60	3.29

Source: Rodriguez, 1999

Table A8.2 Chilean AFP Portfolio Diversification, 1981-1998 (% of total assets, December of each year)

| | Total Portfolio | | | | | | | | |
| | Stocks | | | Bonds and Other Fixed-Income Securities | | | | | |
Year	Chilean	Non-Chilean	Total Stocks	Government	Corporate	Non-Chilean	Total Bonds	Others*	Cash & Equivalents
1981	0.00	0.00	0.00	28.10	71.90	0.00	00.00	0.00	0.00
1982	0.00	0.00	0.00	26.00	74.00	0.00	100.00	0.00	0.00
1983	0.00	0.00	0.00	44.50	55.60	0.00	100.00	0.00	0.00
1984	0.00	0.00	0.00	42.40	57.10	0.00	99.50	0.00	0.50
1986	3.80	0.00	3.80	46.60	49.50	0.00	96.10	0.00	0.10
1987	6.20	0.00	6.20	41.40	52.00	0.00	93.40	0.00	0.40
1988	8.10	0.00	8.10	35.40	56.50	0.00	91.90	0.00	0.00
1989	10.10	0.00	10.10	41.60	48.30	0.00	89.90	0.00	0.10
1990	11.30	0.00	11.30	44.10	44.60	0.00	88.70	0.00	0.10
1991	23.80	0.00	23.80	38.30	37.70	0.00	76.00	0.00	0.10
1992	24.00	0.00	24.00	40.90	34.80	0.00	75.70	0.20	0.10
1993	31.80	0.00	31.80	39.30	27.90	0.60	67.80	0.30	0.10
1994	32.10	0.00	32.10	39.70	26.40	0.90	67.00	0.90	0.00
1995	29.40	0.00	29.40	39.40	28.40	0.20	68.00	2.60	0.10
1996	26.00	0.01	26.01	42.10	28.32	0.53	70.95	3.00	0.10
1997	23.40	0.03	23.43	39.60	32.64	1.22	73.46	3.10	0.00
1998	14.90	0.00	14.90	40.96	35.44	5.63	82.03	2.88	0.19

*Share of closed-end mutual funds

Source: Rodriguez, 1999

Bibliography

Abas, A. (1995), 'The Transformation Of a Provident Fund Into a Social Insurance Pension Scheme: Development Management Impacts In Malaysia', Dissertation MSc, Glasgow Caledonian University, Glasgow.

Adamchak, D.J. (1999), 'The Economic Condition of Elderly Zimbabweans', *The ACP-EU Courier*, no. 176, pp. 53-54.

Adjei, E.N.A. (1999), 'Pension Schemes in Africa: The National Experience of Ghana', *Social Security in Africa: New Realities*, Accra, Ghana, ISSA, 6-9 July.

Aedo, C. and Larrañaga, O. (eds) (1994), *Social Service Delivery Systems: An Agenda for Reform*, Inter-American Development Bank, Washington, D.C.

Africa Confidential (1997), 'Asian Tigers, African Lions', *African Confidential*, vol. 38, no. 20.

Africa Financing Review (1997), *Africa Financing Review*, vol. 4, no. 1.

Ageing International (1995), 'Old, Black and Poor', *Ageing International*, vol. 22, no. 4.

Agnulik, P. (1999), 'The Proposed State Second Pension', *Fiscal Studies*, vol. 20, no. 4, pp. 409-421.

Aguilar, M.I. (ed) (1998), *The Politics of Age and Gerontocracy in Africa: Ethnographies of the Past and Memories of the Present*, Africa World Press, Trenton, NJ.

Ahmad, E., Drèze, J., Hills, J. and Sen, A. (eds) (1991), *Social Security in Developing Countries*, Clarendon Press, Oxford.

Ahmad, S.E. (1993), *Poverty, Demographic Characteristics, and Public Policy in CIS Countries*, IMF, Washington, D.C.

Ainsworth, M. (1994), 'AIDS and African Development', *The World Bank Research Observer*, vol. 9, no. 2, pp. 203-240.

Allardt, E. (1999), 'Globalization and the Prospects for Democracy and the Welfare State', *WIDER, Public Lecture*, http://www.unu.edu.

Amsden, A.H. (1989), *Asia's Next Giant: South Korea and Late Industrialization*, Oxford University Press, New York.

Amsden, A.H. (1997), 'Editorial: Bringing Production Back in - Understanding Government's Economic Role in Late Industrialization', *World Development*, vol. 25, no. 4, pp. 469-480.

Amsden, A.H. and Euh, Y-D. (1993), 'South Korea's 1980s Financial Reforms: Good-bye Financial Repression (Maybe), Hello New Institutional Restraints', *World Development*, vol. 21, no. 3, pp. 379-390.

Anderson, S.J. (1990), 'The Political Economy of Japanese Saving: How Postal Savings and Public Pensions Support High Rates of Household Saving in Japan', *Journal of Japanese Studies*, vol. 16, no. 1, pp. 61-92.

Andrews, E.S. (2000), 'Kazakhstan: An Ambitious Pension Reform', *World Bank Pension Reform Primer*, World Bank, Washington, D.C., http://www.worldbank.org/pensions.

Andrews, E.S. and Rashid, M. (1996), *The Financing of Pension Systems in Central and Eastern Europe*, World Bank, Washington, D.C.

Angel, A. and Graham, C. (1995), 'Can Social Sector Reform Make Adjustment Sustainable and Equitable? Lessons from Chile and Venezuela', *Journal of Latin American Studies*, vol. 27, pp. 189-219.

Apaninai, J. (1994), 'Solomon Islands - The National Provident Fund: Providing More Benefits And Services', *International Social Security Review*, vol. 47, no. 1, pp. 79-87.

Apt, N.A. (1992), 'Ageing in the Community: Trends and Prospects in Africa', *Community Development Journal*, vol. 27, no. 2, pp. 130-139.

Apt, N.A. (1994), 'Urbanization, caring for elderly people and the changing African family: The challenge to social policy', *International Social Security Review*, vol. 47, no. 3-4, pp. 111-122.

Apt, N.A. (1996), *Coping with Old Age in a Changing Africa*, Avebury, Aldershot.

Arango, T. (1999), 'Fat fees kill potential gains for Hungarian pension funds', Central European Business Journal, http://www.ceebiz.com/hungary/4569.

Ardington, E. and Lund, F. (1995), 'Pensions and development: Social security as complementary to programmes of reconstruction and development', *Development Southern Africa*, vol. 12, no. 4, pp. 557-577.

Arenas de Mesa, A. and Bertranou, F. (1997), 'Learning from Social Security Reforms: Two Different Cases, Chile and Argentina', *World Development*, vol. 25, no. 3, pp. 329-348.

Arenas de Mesa, A. and Montecinos, V. (1999), 'The Privatization of Social Security and Women's Welfare', *Latin American Research Review*, vol. 34, no. 3, pp. 7-37.

Arestis, P. and Demetriades, P. (1997), 'Financial Development and Economic Growth: Assessing the Evidence', *The Economic Journal*, vol. 107, no. 442, pp. 783-799.

Arun, S.A. and Arun, T.G. (2000), 'Gender issues in social security policy of developing countries: Indian experience', presented at *Development Economics Study Group Annual Conference*, University of Nottingham, March 2000.

Aryeetey, E. and Steel, W.F. (1995), 'Savings Collectors and Financial Intermediation in Ghana', *Savings And Development*, vol. 19, no. 2, pp. 191-212.

Aryeetey, E., Hettige, H., Nissanke, M. and Steel, W. (1997), 'Financial Market Fragmentation and Reforms in Ghana, Malawi, Nigeria, and Tanzania', *The World Bank Economic Review*, vol. 11, no. 2, pp. 195-218.

Ascher, W. (1983), 'New development approaches and the adaptability of international agencies: the case of the World Bank', *International Organization*, vol. 37, pp. 415-439.

Asher, M.G. (1994), *Social Security in Malaysia and Singapore: Practices, Issues And Reform Directions*, Institute of Strategic and International Studies, Kuala Lumpur.

Asher, M.G. (1994), 'Options for Reforming the Existing Social Security System in Malaysia', in Corporate Planning Division (ed), *Social Security Towards 2020*, Employees' Provident Fund, Kuala Lumpur.

Asher, M.G. (1996), 'Financing Old Age In Southeast Asia: An Overview', *Southeast Asian Affairs*, vol. 9, no. 1, pp. 72-98.

Asher, M.G. (1998), 'Financing old age in Singapore: Are there lessons for the welfare states?', in T.R. Marmor and P.R. De Jong (eds), *Ageing, Social Security and Affordability*, Ashgate, Aldershot, pp. 152-202.

Asher, M.G. (1999), 'The Pension System in Singapore', *Pension Reform Primer*, World Bank, Washington, D.C., http://www.worldbank.org/pensions.

Asher, M.G. and Phang, S.Y. (1997), 'Singapore's Central Provident Fund System: Implications for Saving, Public Housing, and Social Protection', in A.E. Andersson, B. Hårsman and J.M. Quigley (eds), *Government for the Future: Unification, Fragmentation and Regionalism*, Elsevier Science, Amsterdam, pp. 245-286.

Ashurst, M. (1996), 'First World Smartcards And Third World Pensioners', *Financial Times*, 16 February, p. 4.

Ashworth, J. (2000), 'South Africa's £1bn project of steel', *The Times*, 2 August, p. 25.

Asian Development Bank (1997), 'ADB Supports Pensions Reform in Kazakhstan with US$100 Million Loan', *News Release*, No.132/97', http://208.160.72.243/news/1997/nr132%2D97.asp.

Asiaweek (1995), 'Singapore opens up: Deregulating a giant fund brings the managers in', *Asiaweek*, 17 March, p. 51.

Atje, R. and Jovanovic, B. (1993), 'Stock markets and development', *European Economic Review*, vol. 37, pp. 632-640.

Bailey, C. (1994), 'The extension of social security to small establishments and the non-wage earning population', in ISSA (ed), *Organisation and methods for social security organisations in English-speaking Africa*, Social Security Documentation, African Series, No.14, ISSA, Geneva, pp. 37-50.

Bailey, C. (1997), *An Operational Framework for Pension Reform: Coverage under social security pension schemes*, ILO, Geneva.

Bailey, C. (1999), *An Operational Framework for Pension Reform: Governance Issues*, ILO, Geneva.

Bailey, C. (1999b), 'Governance of Social Security Schemes', *Social Security in Africa: New Realities*, ISSA, 6-9 July, Accra, Ghana.

Bailey, C. and van Ginneken, W. (1998), *An Operational Framework for Pension Reform: Extending personal coverage of pensions*, ILO, Geneva.

Balakrishnan, N. (1989), 'Singapore's Sleeping Booty', *Far Eastern Economic Review*, 25 May, p. 68.

Bangura, Y. (1994), 'Economic Restructuring, Coping Strategies And Social Change: Implications For Institutional Development In Africa', *Development and Change*, vol. 25, pp. 785-827.

Bank of Botswana (1994), 'Capital Market Development and Economic Diversification in Botswana', *The Research Bulletin*, vol. 12, no. 2.

Barbone, L. and Sanchez, L-A. (2000), 'Pensions and Social Security in Sub-Saharan Africa: Issues and Options', in ISSA (ed) (2000c), *Social Security in Africa: New Realities*, Social Security Documentation No.21, ISSA, Geneva, pp. 15-70.

Barger, T.C. (1999), *Financial Institutions: Lessons of Experience*, International Finance Corporation, World Bank, Washington D.C.

Barr, N. (1994), *Labour Markets And Social Policy In Central And Eastern Europe: The Transition And Beyond*, Open University Press, Washington, D.C.

Barrientos, A. (1996), 'Pension Reform and Pension Coverage in Chile: Lessons for Other Countries', *Bulletin of American Research*, vol. 15, no. 3, pp. 309-322.

Barrientos, A. (1998), *Pension Reform in Latin America*, Ashgate, Aldershot.

Barrientos, A. (2000), 'Work, retirement, and vulnerability of older persons in Latin America: What are the lessons for pension design?', *Journal of International Development*, vol. 12, no. 4, pp. 495-506.

Basu, P.K. (1994), 'Demystifying Privatization In Developing Countries', *International Journal of Public Sector Management*, vol. 7, no. 3, pp. 44-55.

Bateman, H. and Piggott, J. (1997), 'Private Pensions in OECD Countries: Australia', in *Labour Market and Social Policy Occasional Papers No.23*, OECD, Paris.

Bateman, H. and Piggot, J. (1998), 'Mandatory Retirement Saving in Australia', *Annals of Public and Cooperative Economics*, vol. 69, no. 4, pp. 547-569.

Batty, I. (1997a), 'Defusing Polish Time Bomb', *Pensions Bulletin - Cameron McKenna*, September, pp. 14-16.

Batty, I. (1997b), 'Mandatory Pension Funds in Hungary and Poland', *Benefits and Compensation International*, November, pp. 2-7.

Beattie, A. (1999), 'Stiglitz hits at World Bank policy', *Financial Times*, 29 November, p. 9.

Beattie, A. (2000), 'Strains in bank's inclusive model', *Financial Times*, 16 June, p. 12.

Beattie, R. (1997), *An Operational Framework for Pension Reform: Reform and development of pension systems in Asia and the Pacific*, ILO, Geneva.

Beattie, R. and McGillivray, W.R. (1995), 'A Risk Strategy: Reflections On The World Bank Report Averting The Old Age Crisis', *International Social Security Review*, vol. 48, no. 3-4/95, pp. 5-22.

Becker, C.M. and Urzhumova, D.S. (1996), 'Pensions Burdens and Labor Force Participation in Kazakhstan', *World Development*, vol. 26, no. 11, pp. 2807-2103.

Bendokat, R. and Dar, A. (1999), 'A Social Protection Strategy for Togo', *Social Protection Discussion Paper No.9920*, World Bank, Washington, D.C.

Benefits and Compensation International (1992), 'New direction for crossroads of the East: Central Provident Fund, Singapore', *Benefits and Compensation International*, vol. 21, no. 2, p. 34.

Bennett, R. (1990), *Decentralisation, Local Governments, and Markets: Towards a Post-Welfare Agenda*, Clarendon Press, Oxford.

Bercusson, K. (1995), 'Singapore: A Case Study In Rapid Development', *Occasional Paper No.119*, International Monetary Fund, Washington, D.C.

Berglöf, E. (1990), 'Capital Structure as a Mechanism of Control: A Comparison of Financial Systems', in M. Aoki, B. Gustafsson and O.E. Williamson (eds), *The Firm as a Nexus of Treaties*, Sage Publications, London, pp. 237-262.

Bertrand, M., Miller, D. and Mullainathan, S. (2000), 'Public Policy and Extended Families: Evidence from South Africa', *NBER Working Paper Series 7594*, Cambridge, MA.

Bhatia, R.J. and Khatkhate, D.R. (1995), 'Financial Intermediation, Savings Mobilization, and Entrepreneurial Development: The African Experience', *IMF Staff Papers*, vol. 22, no. 1, pp. 132-158.

Bhatnagar, D.D. (1985), *Labour Welfare And Social Security Legislation In India*, Deep And Deep Publishers, New Delhi.

Bhattarai, A.K. (1989), 'Social Security Programmes in India', *International Social Security Review*, vol. 42, no. 4, pp. 479-488.

Bigsten, A. and Kayizzi-Mugerwa, S. (1995), 'Rural Sector Responses to Economic Crisis in Uganda', *Journal of International Development*, vol. 2, no. 2, pp. 181-209.

Birdsall, N., Ross, D. and Sabot, R. (1995), 'Inequality and Growth Reconsidered: Lessons from East Asia', *The World Bank Economic Review*, vol. 9, no. 3, pp. 477-508.

Bitran, E. and Sáez, R.E. (1994), 'Privatisation and regulation in Chile', in B.P. Bosworth, R. Dornbusch and R. Labán (eds), *The Chilean Economy: Policy Lessons and Challenges*, The Brookings Institute, Washington, D.C.

Blackwood, D.L. and Lynch, R.G. (1994), 'The Measurement of Inequality and Poverty: A Policy Maker's Guide to the Literature', *World Development*, vol. 22, no. 4, pp. 567-578.

Blake, D. (1995), *Pension Schemes And Pension Funds In The United Kingdom*, Clarendon Press, Oxford.

Bloomestein, H.J. (1998), 'Institutional Investors, Pension Reform and Emerging

Securities Markets', in OECD (ed), *Capital Market Development in Transition Economies: Country Experiences and Policies for the Future*, OECD, Paris.

Bloomestein, H.J. (1998b), 'Institutional Investors in the New Financial Landscape', in OECD (ed), *Institutional Investors in the New Financial Landscape*, OECD, Paris.

Bobinski, C. (1997a), 'Privatisation: EU Entry provides Spur', *Financial Times*, 26 March, p. 4.

Bobinski, C. (1997b), 'Polish Pension Reform: a New Lease of Life', *Financial Times Survey: Investing in Central and Eastern Europe*, 11 April, p. 6.

Bobinski, C. (2000), 'Pension reform faces teething troubles', *Financial Times*, 4 February, p. 31.

Boldrin, M., Dolado, J.J., Jimeno, J.F. and Peracchi, F. (1999), 'The future of pensions in Europe', *Economic Policy*, vol. 29, pp. 289-320.

Bolger, A. (2000), 'Pru digs deep on provisions', *Financial Times*, 24 February, p. 27.

Bonabebey, J-R. (1995), *Quel Avenir Pour l'Afrique? Finance et Développement*, Silex/Nouvelles du Sud, Paris.

Borish, M.S. and Noël, M. (1997), 'Privatisation in the Visegrad Countries: A Comparative Assessment', *The World Economy*, vol. 20, no. 2, pp. 199-219.

Borish, M.S., Ding, W. and Noël, M. (1996), 'On the Road to EU Accession: Financial Sector Development in Central Europe', *World Bank Discussion Paper No.345*, World Bank, Washington, D.C.

Borzutzky, S. (1991), 'The Chicago Boys, Social Security And Welfare In Chile', in J.M.H. Glennerster (ed), *The Radical Right And The Welfare State: An International Assessment*, Harvester Wheatsheaf, Hemel Hempstead, pp. 79-99.

Borzutzky, S. (1997), 'Privatizing Social Security: Relevance of the Chilean Experience', in J. Midgley and M. Sherraden (eds), *Alternatives to Social Security*, Auburn House, London, pp. 75-90.

Borzutzky, S. (1998), 'Chile: The Politics of Privatization', in M.A. Cruz-Saco and C. Mesa-Lago (eds), *Do Options Exist? The Reform of Pension and Health Care Systems in Latin America*, University of Pittsburgh Press, Pittsburgh, pp. 35-55.

Bosworth, B.P., Dornbusch, R. and Labán, R. (1994), *The Chilean Economy: Policy Lessons and Change*, The Brookings Institution, Washington, DC.

Bouman, F.J.A. (1994), 'ROSCA and ASCRA: Beyond the Financial Landscape', in F.J.A. Bouman and O. Hospes (eds), *Financial Landscapes Reconstructed: The Fine Art of Mapping Development*, Boulder, Colorado, pp. 375-394.

Bouman, F.J.A. (1995), 'ROSCA: On the Origin of the Species', *Savings and Development*, vol. 19, no. 2, pp. 117-148.

Bouman, F.J.A. and O. Hospes (eds) (1994), *Financial Landscapes Reconstructed: The Fine Art of Mapping Development*, Westview Press, Boulder, Colorado.

Bowen, S. (1996), 'Pension law starts Bolivian strike', *Financial Times*, 12 November, p. 9.

Bowie, A. (1991), *Crossing The Industrial Divide*, Columbia University Press.
Bracher-Marquez, V. and Sherraden, M.S. (1994), 'Political Change and the Welfare State: The Case of Health and Food Policies in Mexico (1970-93)', *World Development*, vol. 22, no. 9, pp. 1295-1312.
Brada, J.C. (1996), 'Privatisation Is Transition - Or Is it?', *Journal of Economic Perspectives*, vol. 10, no. 2, pp. 67-86.
Broad, R., Cavanagh, J. and Bello, W. (1994), 'Development: The Market Is Not Enough', in J. Cavanagh, D. Wysham and M. Arruda (eds), *Beyond Bretton Woods: Alternatives to the Global Economic Order*, Pluto Press, London, pp. 3-15.
Brooks, S. and James, E. (1999), 'The Political Economy of Pension Reform', *World Bank Research Conference, September 14-15*.
Brownbridge, M. and Gockel, A.F. (1996), 'The Impact of Financial Sector Policies on Banking in Ghana', *IDS Working Paper 38*, IDS, University of Sussex, Brighton.
Brownbridge, M. and Harvey, C. (1998), *Banking in Africa*, James Currey, Oxford.
Bruno, M. (1996), 'Introduction: Second-generation issues in transition', in M. Bruno and B. Pleskovic (eds), *Annual World Bank Conference on Development Economics*, World Bank, Washington, D.C., pp. 363-364.
Buckley, G. (1997), 'Microfinance in Africa: Is it Either the Problem or the Solution?', *World Development*, vol. 25, no. 7, pp. 1081-1093.
Bujra, J. (1999), 'Intergenerational Deadlock? Youth and their Elders Face the AIDS Crisis in Tanzania', paper presented at *The Intergenerational Bargain, DSA Annual Conference*, University of Bath.
Burnside, C. and Dollar, D. (1997), 'Aid Spurs Growth - in a Sound Policy Environment', *Finance and Development*, vol. 34, no. 4, pp. 4-7.
Bushon, R.B. (1994), *The Employees' Provident Fund: An Overview*, Corporate Planning Division, EPF, Kuala Lumpur.
Butare, T. (1998), *Secteurs Traditionnel et Moderne dans un Processus de Developpement*, INU Press, Geneva.
Butler, E., Asher, M.G. and Borden, K. (1996), *Singapore v. Chile: Competing Models for Welfare Reform*, Adam Smith Institute, London.
Caisse de Dépôt et Placement du Québec (1998), 'A Tradition of Boldness, Caution and Expertise: The Makings of a Bright Future', *Highlights 1998*.
Calamitsis, E.A. (1999), 'Adjustment and Growth in Sub-Saharan Africa: The Unfinished Agenda', *Finance and Development*, vol. 36, no. 1, http://www.imf.org.
Callier, P. (1991), 'Financial Systems and Development in Africa', *Economic Development Institute of the World Bank*, World Bank, Washington, D.C.
Camdessus, M. (1998), 'Worldwide Crisis in the Welfare State: What next in the Context of Globalisation', Address given to Observatoire Chrétien des Réalités Economiques, IMF, 15 October, http://www.imf.org.
Caprio, G. and Levine, R. (1994), 'Reforming Finance in Transitional Socialist

Economies', *The World Bank Research Observer*, vol. 9, no. 1, pp. 1-25.

Carnegie Group (1997), 'Polish pensions - ripe for reform', *Newsletter* (London).

Carter, M.R. and May, J. (1999), 'Poverty, Livelihood and Class in Rural South Africa', *World Development*, vol. 27, no. 1, pp. 1-20.

Case, A. and Deaton, A. (1998), 'Large Cash Transfers to the Elderly in South Africa', *The Economic Journal*, vol. 108, no. 450, September, pp. 1330-1361.

Castañeda, T. (1992), *Combating Poverty: Innovative Social Reforms In Chile During The 1980s*, ICS Press, San Francisco.

Centeno, M.A. and Maxfield, S. (1992), 'The Marriage of Finance and Order: Changes in the Mexican Political Elite', *Journal of Latin American Studies*, vol. 24, no. 1, pp. 57-85.

Chand, S.K. and Jaeger, A. (1996), *Ageing Populations and Public Pension Schemes*, International Monetary Fund, Washington, D.C.

Charlton, R. (1993), 'External Debt, Economic Success and Economic Failure: State Autonomy, Africa and the NICs', in S.P. Riley (ed), *The Politics of Global Debt*, Macmillan Press, Basingstoke, pp. 168-188.

Charlton, R. (2000), 'Gender and Social Insurance: Towards Social Insecurity for Women?', *International Union Rights*, vol. 7, no. 4, December, pp. 8-9.

Charlton, R. and Donald, D. (1995), 'Bringing the Economy Back In: Reconsidering the Autonomy of the Developmental State', *Scandinavian Journal of Development Alternatives*, vol. 14, no. 1-2, pp. 55-84.

Charlton, R. and McKinnon, R. (2000), 'Beyond Mandatory Privatisation: Pensions Policy Options for Developing Countries', *Journal of International Development*, vol. 12, no. 4, pp. 483-494.

Charlton, R., McKinnon, R. and Konopielko, Ł. (1998), 'Pensions Reform, Privatisation and Restructuring in the Transition: Unfinished Business or Inappropriate Agendas?', *Europe-Asia Studies*, vol. 50, no. 8, pp. 1413-1436.

Charlton, R., McKinnon, R. and Konopielko, Ł. (2001), 'Pensions Reform and Privatisation in CEE: Opportunities Lost', in F. Columbus (ed), *Central and Eastern Europe in Transition*, vol. 4, Nova Publishing, New York, forthcoming.

Charlton, R., McKinnon, R. and Munro, H.T. (1997), 'Exploring The Future For Pensions Pillarisation', *Futures*, vol. 29, no. 2, pp. 159-176.

Charmes, J. (1999), 'Evaluating the extent of non-registration - do we accept the challenge?', *The ACP-EC Courier*, no. 178, December 1999-January 2000, pp. 62-64.

Chau, L.C. (1988), 'Symposium On Central Provident Fund', in L.C. Chau *et al.*, (ed), *Hong Kong Economics Papers No.18*, pp. 57-85.

Chen, R. and Wong, K.A. (1998), 'The Adequacy of the CPF Account for Retirement Benefits in Singapore', *Singapore International Insurance and Actuarial Journal*, vol. 2, no. 1, pp. 121-138.

Chen, R., Wong, K.A. and Chiang, M.Y. (1997), 'Singaporean's knowledge and attitudes towards the central provident fund', *Singapore Management Review*, vol. 19, no. 2, pp. 1-16.

Cheung, P. and Vasoo, S. (1992), 'Ageing Populations In Singapore', in D.R. Phillips (ed), *Ageing In East And Southeast Asia*, Edward Arnold, London.

Chiarelli, C.A.G. (1976), 'Social Security for Rural Workers in Brazil', *International Labour Review*, vol. 113, no. 2, pp. 159-169.

Choe, C. and Moosa, I.A. (1999), 'Financial System and Economic Growth: The Korean Experience', *World Development*, vol. 27, no. 6, pp. 1069-1082.

Chote, R. (1999), 'World Bank sets out plans for global code for social policy', *Financial Times*, 22 April, p. 4.

Chu, K.Y. and Gupta, S. (1996), 'Social Protection in Transition Countries: Emerging Issues', *MOCT-MOST: Economic Policy in Transitional Economies*, vol. 6, pp. 107-123.

Chu, K.Y. and Gupta, S. (eds) (1998a), *Social Safety Nets: Issues and Recent Experience*, IMF, Washington, D.C.

Chu, K.Y. and Gupta, S. (1998b), 'Social Protection in Transition Countries: Emerging Issues', in K.Y. Chu and S. Gupta (eds), *Social Safety Nets: Issues and Recent Experience*, IMF, Washington, D.C., pp. 94-113.

Chvátal, M. (1999), 'Voluntary Funds - What's gone wrong?', *Employee Benefits International*, March, pp. 6-7.

Cichon, M. (1999), 'Notional defined-contribution schemes: Old wine in new bottles?', *International Social Security Review*, vol. 52, no. 4, pp. 87-105.

Claessens, S. (1993), 'Alternative Forms of External Finance: A Survey', *The World Bank Research Observer*, vol. 8, no. 1, pp. 91-117.

Claessens, S. (1995), 'The Emergence of Equity Investment in Developing Countries: Overview', *World Bank Economic Review*, vol. 9, no. 1, pp. 1-17.

Claessens, S. and Glaessner, T. (1997), *Are Financial Sector Weaknesses Undermining the East Asian Miracle*, World Bank, Washington, D.C.

Claessens, S., Dooley, M.P. and Warner, A. (1995), 'Portfolio Capital Flows: Hot or Cold?', *World Bank Economic Review*, vol. 9, no. 1, pp. 153-174.

Clare, G. (1997), 'The Regulatory Framework for Pension Funds in Europe', *Benefits & Compensation International*, vol. 26, no. 10, pp. 21-28.

Clements, P. (1993), 'An Approach to Poverty Alleviation for Large International Development Agencies', *World Development*, vol. 21, no. 10, pp. 1633-1646.

Clover, C. (1999), 'Pension scheme could pay dividends', *Financial Times: Kazakhstan Survey*, p. 2.

Cockburn, C. (1980), 'The Role Of Social Security In Development', *International Social Security Review*, vol. 3, no. 4, pp. 337-358.

Collier, P. and Gunning, J.W. (1999a), 'The IMF's Role in Structural Adjustment', *The Economic Journal*, vol. 109, no. 504, pp. 634-651.

Collier, P. and Gunning, J.W. (1999b), 'Explaining African Economic Performance', *Journal of Economic Literature*, vol. 37, no. 1, pp. 64-111.

Collier, P. and Gunning, J.W. (1999c), 'Why Has Africa Grown Slowly?', *Journal of Economic Perspectives*, vol. 13, no. 3, pp. 3-22.

Collier, P. and Mayer, C. (1999), 'The Assessment: Financial Liberalization, Financial Systems, and Economic Growth', *Oxford Review of Economic Policy*, vol. 5, no. 4, pp. 1-12.

Collier, D. and Messick, R.E. (1975), 'Prerequisites versus diffusion: Testing alternative explanations of social security adoption', *American Political Science Review 69*, pp. 1299-1355.

Cooke, A. (1992), 'Profile on The Gambia: Shining light in African social security', *Benefits & Compensation International*, May, p. 10.

Cooke, K. (1995), 'Malaysia Unveils Capital Market Reforms', *Financial Times*, 23 June, p. 8.

Cooke, K. (1997), 'Malaysia Unveils Capital Market Reforms', *Financial Times*, 24 June, p.8.

Corkery, J., Daddah, T.O., O'Nuallain, C. and Land, T. (1998), *Management of Public Service Reform: A Comparative Review of Experiences in the Management of Programmes of Reform of the Administrative Arm of Central Government*, IOS Press/IIAS, Amsterdam.

Cornia, G.A. (1999), 'Social Funds in Stabilization and Adjustment Programmes', *UNU/WIDER, Research for Action*, no. 48.

Cornia, G.A., Honikka, J., Paniccià, R. and Popov, V. (1996), *Long-Term Growth and Welfare in Transitional Economies: The Impact of Demographic, Investment and Social Policy Changes*, World Institute for Development Economics Research, Helsinki.

Costabal, M. (1981), 'Efectos economicos de la reforma previsional', *Gestion*, VI: 64, 64.

Coudouel, A., Marnie, S. and Micklewright, J. (1998), 'Targetting Social Assistance in a Transition Economy: The Mahallas in Uzbekistan', *Innocenti Occasional Papers, Economic and Social Policy Series 63*, UNICEF, Florence.

Cox, D. and Jimenez, E. (1992), 'Social Security and Private Transfers in Developing Countries: The Case of Peru', *The World Bank Economic Review*, vol. 6, no. 1, pp. 155-169.

CPF Study Group (1986), 'Report Of The Central Provident Fund Study Group', *The Singaporean Economic Review*, vol. 31, no. 1, pp. 1-103.

CPP (2000), 'Canada Pension Plan Investment Board', *CPP*, http://www.cppib.ca/FAQs/faqs.htm.

Cramer, C. and Pontara, N. (1998), 'Rural poverty and poverty alleviation in Mozambique: what's missing from the debate?', *The Journal of Modern African Studies*, vol. 36, no. 1, pp. 101-138.

Cruz-Saco, M.A. and Mesa-Lago, C. (1998), 'Do Options Exist? The Reform of Pension and Health Care Systems in Latin America', University of Pittsburgh Press, Pittsburgh.

Cutright, P. (1965), 'Political Structure, Economic Development, and National Social Security Programs', *American Journal of Sociology*, vol. 70, no. 5, pp. 537-550.

Czúcz, O. (1996), 'The Resurgence of Poverty and Struggle Against the Exclusion: A New Challenge for Social Security? Some Hungarian Experiences', in, *Adapting to new economies and social realities: What challenges, opportunities and new tasks for social security?*, International Social Security Association/European Commission - DG V, March, Aarhus, Denmark.

Dangana, M.A. (1992), *Adapting The Legal And Administrative Structures Of Provident Funds To Achieve Optimum Efficiency*, ISSA, Geneva.

Davis, E.P. (1993a), 'The Structure, Regulation and Performance of Pension Funds in Nine Industrial Countries', *Policy Research Working Paper, Financial Sector Development Department*, WPS 1229, World Bank, Washington, D.C.

Davis, E.P. (1993b), 'The Development of Pension Funds: A Forthcoming Financial Revolution for Continental Europe', in R. O'Brien (ed), *Finance and the International Economy 7, the Amex Essay Awards 1993*, Oxford University Press, Oxford, pp. 109-126.

Davis, E.P. (1995a), *Pension Funds: Retirement Income And Capital Markets - An International Perspective*, Clarendon Press, Oxford.

Davis, E.P. (1995b), 'The State of Public Pensions in the OECD', *Public Policy*, September, pp. 3-8.

Davis, E.P. (1995c), 'International Investment of Pension Funds in Europe: Scope and Implications for International Financial Stability', *Finanzmarkt und Portfolio Management*, vol. 9, no. 2, pp. 162-186.

Davis, E.P. (1997a), *Public Pensions, Pension Reform and Fiscal Policy*, European Monetary Institute, Frankurt am Main.

Davis, E.P. (1997b), 'The Reform of Retirement Income Provision in the EU', *The Pensions Institute, Discussion Paper PI-9708*, Birkbeck College, University of London, London.

Davis, E.P. (1999), *Investment of Mandatory Funded Pension Schemes*, The Pensions Institute, Birkbeck College, University of London, London.

Dawson, I. (2000), 'Poland: Funds that are flying', *Euromoney*, January, pp. 63-68.

Daykin, C.D. and Lewis, D. (1999), 'A Crisis of Longer Life - Reforming Pension Systems', *mimeo*.

Deacon, B. with Hulse, M. and Stubbs, P. (1997), *Global Social Policy: International Organisations and the Future of Welfare*, Sage Publications, London.

Deerpalsing, N. (1999), 'Pension Schemes in Africa: The National Experience of Mauritius', *Social Security in Africa: New Realities*, 6-9 July, ISSA, Accra, Ghana.

de Gregorio, J. and Guidotti, P.E. (1995), 'Financial Development and Economic Growth', *World Development*, vol. 23, no. 3, pp. 433-448.

Demery, L. and Squire, L. (1996), 'Macroeconomic Adjustment and Poverty in Africa: An Emerging Picture', *The World Bank Research Observer*, vol. 11, no. 1, pp. 39-59.

Demirgüç-Kunt, A. and Levine, R. (1996), 'Stock Markets, Corporate Finance, and

Economic Growth: An Overview', *The World Bank Economic Review*, vol. 10, no. 2, pp. 223-239.

Demirgüç-Kunt, A. and Schwarz, A. (1996), 'A Reform Proposal for Costa Rica's Pension System', *Finance and Development*, September, pp. 44-46.

De Neuborg, C. and Weigand, C. (2000), 'Social Policy as Social Risk Management', paper presented at ISSA, *The Year 2000 International Research Conference on Social Security: Social Security in the Global Village*, Helsinki.

Derricourt, N. and Miller, C. (1992), 'Editorial Introduction: Empowering Older People - An Urgent Task for Community Development in an Ageing World', *Community Development Journal*, vol. 27, no. 2, pp. 117-121.

Deutsch, A. (1997a), 'Hungary's "In Vivo" Pension Reform Experience', *Transition*, vol. 8, no. 6, pp. 19-20.

Deutsch, A. (1997b), 'Pension Reform for Beginners: The Hungarian Case', *World Economic Affairs*, Autumn, pp. 53-58.

Deutsch, A. and Zowall, H. (1988), 'Compulsory Savings And Taxes In Singapore', *Paper no.65*, ASEAN Economic Research Unit (ed), Institute Of Southeast Asian Studies.

Devereux, S. (1999), 'Making Less Last Longer: Informal Safety Nets in Malawi', *IDS Discussion Paper 373*, University of Sussex, Brighton.

Diamond, P. and Valdés-Prieto, S. (1994), 'Social Security Reforms', in B. Bosworth, R. Dornbusch and R. Laban (eds), *The Chilean Economy*, The Brookings Institution, Washington, D.C.

Dickie, M., Kynge, J., Jacob, R. and Nakamoto, M. (2000), 'Stocks may be hit by volatility', *Financial Times*, 20 March, p. 8.

Dixon, H. (1997), 'Controversy: Finance and Development', *The Economic Journal*, vol. 107, no. 442, pp. 752-753.

Dixon, J. (1982), 'Provident Funds In The Third World: A Cross-National Review', *Public Administration And Development*, vol. 2, pp. 325-344.

Dixon, J. (1983), 'Provident Funds: Their Nature And Performance', in ILO (ed), *Social Security: Principles And Practice*, International Labour Office/FNPF, Geneva, pp. 110-126.

Dixon, J. (1989a), 'A Comparative Study on Provident Funds: Their Present and Future Explored', *International And Comparative Social Welfare*, vol. 5, no. 2, pp. 1-28.

Dixon, J. (1989b), *National Provident Funds: The Enfant Terrible of Social Security*, International Fellowship for Social and Economic Development Inc., Canberra, Australia.

Done, K. (1998a), 'Facing hard times, great expectations', *Financial Times Survey: Slovenia*, 18 May, p. 3.

Done, K. (1998b), 'Reformers bite the bullet', *Financial Times, Survey: Croatian Finance and Investment*, 14 December, p. 2.

Dornbusch, R. and Reynoso, A. (1989), 'Financial Factors in Economic Development', *American Economic Review*, vol. 79, no. 2, pp. 204-209.

Drake, P.J. (1969), *Financial Development In Malaya And Singapore*, Australian National University Press, Canberra.

Drèze, J. and Sen, A. (1989), *Hunger and Public Action*, Clarendon Press, Oxford.

Drèze, J. and Sen, A. (1989b), *Public Action For Social Security: Foundations And Strategy, no.20*, S.T.I.C.E.R.D, London.

Duffield, M. (1992), 'The Emergence Of A Two-Tiered Welfare In Africa: Marginalisation or an Opportunity For Reform?', *Public Administration And Development*, vol. 12, no. 2, pp. 139-154.

Dugger, W.M. (1999), 'Old Age Is an Institution', *Review of Social Economy*, vol. 57, no. 1, pp. 84-98.

Dunne, N. (1999), 'Knives out in Washington for a free spirit', *Financial Times*, 25 November, p. 13.

EBRD (1996a), *Transition Report 1996: Infrastructure and Savings*, EBRD, London.

EBRD (1996b), *Transition Report Update - April 1996*, EBRD, London.

EBRD (1997), *Transition Report 1997: Enterprise Performance and Growth*, EBRD, London.

EBRD (1998), *Transition Report 1998: Financial Sector in Transition*, EBRD, London.

EBRD (1999), *Transition Report 1999: Ten Years of Transition*, EBRD, London.

EBRD (2000), *Transition Report Update - May 2000*, EBRD, London.

EC (1995), *Social Protection in the Member States of the European Union 1994*, Office for Official Publications of the European Community, Luxembourg.

EC (1996), *Social Protection in the Member States of the European Union 1995*, Office for Official Publications of the European Community, Luxembourg.

EC (1997a), *Agenda 2000: For a Stronger and Wider Union, 1*, EC, Brussels.

EC (1997b), 'Economic Situation and Economic Reform in Central and Eastern Europe', *European Economy, Supplement C*, September, Brussels.

EC (1998a), 'Modernising and Improving Social Protection in the European Union', *Communication from the Commission*, 27 January, http://europa.eu.int.

EC (1998b), 'European Economy', *Supplement C, Economic Reform Monitor*, EC, Brussels.

EC (1999), 'Supplementary Pensions in the Single Market: A Green Paper', http://europa.eu.int.

Echeverri-Gent, J. (1988), 'Guaranteed Employment in an Indian State: The Maharashtra Experience', *Asian Survey*, vol. 28, no. 12, pp. 1294-1310.

Echeverri-Gent, J. (1992), 'Public Participation and Poverty Alleviation: The Experience of Reform Communists in India's West Bengal', *World Development*, vol. 20, no. 10, pp. 1401-1422.

Economic Bulletin (2000), 'Introduction of a Funded Component of Old-Age Provision Reduces Economic Growth', *Economic Bulletin*, vol. 37, no. 1, pp. 27-32.

Economist (1994), 'Czech Pensions - Fond of Funds', *The Economist*, 22 October,

p. 122.

Economist (1996), 'Smelling of Moses: Fiscal providence, Singapore style', *The Economist*, 13 January, pp. 63-64.

Economist (1997), 'Business in Eastern Europe Survey - Money Talks', *The Economist*, 22 November, pp. 19-23.

Economist (1997), 'Pension promises', *The Economist*, 22 November, p. 98.

Economist (1999a), 'Latin lessons on pensions', *The Economist*, 12 June, p. 119.

Economist (1999b), 'UN Development Programme: Staying On', *The Economist*, 10 July, p. 66.

Economist (1999c), 'Helping the poorest', *The Economist*, 14 August, pp. 11-12.

Economist (1999c), 'Orphans of the virus', *The Economist*, 14 August, p. 47.

Economist (1999d), 'Sick patients, warring doctors', *The Economist*, 18 September, pp. 113-114.

Economist (2000a), 'Saving society', *The Economist*, 23 February, p. 111.

Economist (2000b), 'Easing Brazil's pensions burden', *The Economist*, 25 March, pp. 67-68.

Economist (2000c), 'Argentine Survey: The limits to management', *The Economist*, 6 May, p. 7.

Economist (2000d), 'The hopeless continent', *The Economist*, 13-19 May.

Economist (2000e), 'Trade before the Tariffs', *The Economist*, 8-14 January, p. 98.

Eddy, K. (1998), 'Victims of its success', *Financial Times Survey: Hungary*, 7 December, p. 2.

Edwards, C.T. (1970), *Public Finances In Malaya And Singapore*, Australian National University Press, Canberra.

Edwards, S. (1990), 'The Sequencing of Economic Reform: Analytical Issues and Lessons from Latin American Experiences', *The World Economy*, vol. 13, no. 1, pp. 1-14.

Edwards, S. and Edwards, A.C. (2000), 'Economic reforms and labour markets: policy issues and lessons from Chile', *Economic Policy*, vol. 30, April, pp. 183-229.

Eggerstedt, H. and Sonntag, H. (1996), *Pension Systems at the crossroads: Prospects for fully funded pension systems in Eastern Europe*, Deutsche Bank Research, Frankfurt am Main, Germany.

Eichengreen, B. (1995), 'Financing Infrastructure in Developing Countries: Lessons from the railway age', *The World Bank Research Observer*, vol. 10, no. 1, pp. 75-91.

EISS (1994), *The Nordic Model Of Social Security In A European Perspective*, ACCO, Leuven.

Eldemire-Shearer, D. (1999), 'Change, Family Life, Coping Strategies and Seniors', *The Ageing and Development Report: Poverty, Independence and the World's Older People*, Earthscan Publications, London, pp. 98-107.

Elson, D. and Catagay, N. (2000), 'The Social Content of Macroeconomic Policies', *World Development*, vol. 28, no. 7, pp. 1347-1364.

Emmerij, L. (ed) (1997), *Economic and Social Development into the XXI Century*, Inter-American Development Bank, Washington, D.C.

Eng, D.C.K. (1994), 'Emerging Demographic Trends In Malaysia And Their Socio-Economic Implications', in Corporate Planning Division (ed), *Social Security Towards 2020: Workshop On Social Security, Paper no.2*, Corporate Planning Division, EPF, Kuala Lumpur.

EPF Corporate Planning Division (1994), *Social Security Towards 2020*, Corporate Planning Division EPF, Kuala Lumpur.

Erinosho, O. (1994), 'African Welfare Systems In Perspective', *International Social Science Journal*, no. 140, pp. 247-255.

Ermisch, J.F. and Huff, W.G. (1999), 'Hypergrowth in an East Asian NIC: Public Policy and Capital Accumulation in Singapore', *World Development*, vol. 27, no. 1, pp. 21-38.

Ernst and Young and the Old Age Pension Technical Implementation Team (1998), *Overview of a Proposed Strategy for: Social Benefit Policy Development and Social Benefit Delivery and Administration in the Republic of Botswana*, Government Printer, Gaborone, Botswana.

Espina, A. (1996), 'Reform of pension schemes in the OECD countries', *International Labour Review*, vol. 135, no. 2, pp. 181-206.

Esping-Andersen, G. (1994), 'After The Golden Age: The Future Of The Welfare State In The New Global Order', *Occasional Paper no.7, World Summit For Social Development*, UNRISD United Nations Research Institute, Geneva.

Evans, R. (1999), 'Growing old in Africa', *The ACP-EU Courier*, no. 176, pp. 40-42.

Everaert, L., Feyzioglu, T., Horváth, B., Stella, P., Cangiano, M. and Doughty, A. (1999), *Bulgaria: Recent Economic Developments and Statistical Appendix*, IMF, Washington, D.C.

Expenditure Policy Division (1998), 'Social Dimensions of the IMF's Policy Dialogue', in K.Y. Chu, and S. Gupta (eds), *Social Safety Nets: Issues and Recent Experience*, IMF, Washington, D.C.

FAO (1995), *Safeguarding Deposits: Learning from Experience*, FAO, Rome.

Fares, C. (1992), 'Le Regime d'Assurance Vieillesse dans Douze Pays d'Afrique Lies à la France Par Une Convention de Securité Sociale: Benin, Cameroun, Cap-Vert, Côte-d'Ivoire, Gabon, Madagascar, Mali, Mauritanie, Niger, Sénégal et Togo', *Bulletin de Liaison et d'Information*, no. 3/4, pp. 7, 50-55.

Faulkner, K.A. and Jackson, B.S. (1994), 'India Enters A New Era', *Benefits And Compensation International*, June 1994, pp. 8-12.

Fazio, H. and Riesco, M. (1997), 'The Chilean Pension Fund Associations', *New Left Review*, May/June, pp. 90-100.

Federation of Social Insurance Offices (1998), 'The Future of Social Security', *The Stockholm Conference*, 29 June-1 July, FSIO, Stockholm.

Felix, D. (1994), 'International capital mobility and Third World development: Compatible marriage or troubled relationship?', *Policy Sciences*, vol. 27, no. 4, pp. 365-394.

Ferreira, M. (1999), 'The Generosity and Universality of South Africa's Social Pension System', *The ACP-EU Courier*, no. 176, pp. 55-56.

Ferreira, M., Lund, F. and Moller, V. (1995), 'Status Report from South Africa', *Ageing International*, no. 12, pp. 16-20.

Ffrench-Davis, R. and Resien, H. (eds) (1998), *Capital Flows and Investment Performance: Lessons from Latin America*, OECD, Paris.

Fidler, S. (1997), 'Emerging Markets', *Financial Times*, 8 September, p. 15.

Fidler, S. (1998), 'Private pensions boost for savings', *Financial Times Survey: Latin American Finance*, 12 March, p. 4.

Fidler, S. (1999), 'IMF urged to raise private sector capital', *Financial Times*, 10 October, p. 5.

Fidler, S. (2000), 'Bank rethink urged on pension funds', *Financial Times*, 6 April, p. 10.

Field, F. (1995), *Making Welfare Work*, Institute for Community Studies, London.

Filatotchev, I. (1997), 'Review Article - Privatisation and Corporate Governance in Transitional Economies', *The World Economy*, vol. 20, no. 4, pp. 497-510.

Financial Times (1997), 'Poland unveils cabinet posts', 30 October, p. 2.

Fine, B. (1999), 'The Development State Is Dead - Long Live Social Capital?', *Development and Change*, vol. 30, pp. 1-19.

Fischer, S. (1990), 'Comments: What Washington Means by Policy Reform', in J. Williamson (ed), *Latin American Adjustment: How Much Has Happened?*, IIE, Washington, D.C, pp. 25-28.

Fischer, B. (1995), 'Foreign Portfolio Equity Investment in Emerging Markets: A Panacea for Economic Development?', *Savings and Development*, vol. 19, no. 2, pp. 149-173.

Fischer, S. (1996), 'Second-generation issues in transition: Stabilisation and growth', in M. Bruno and B. Pleskovic (eds), *Annual World Bank Conference of Development Economics, 1995*, World Bank, Washington, D.C., pp. 364-367.

Fischer, S. and Hernández-Catá, E. (1998), *Africa: Is this the turning point?*, IMF Paper on Policy Analysis, Washington, D.C.

Fletcher, L.P. (1976), 'The Provident Fund Approach To Social Security In The Eastern Caribbean', *Journal of Social Policy*, vol. 5, no. 1, pp. 1-17.

Forss, M., Kalimo, E. and Purola, T. (2000), 'Globalisation and the Concept of Insurance', paper presented at ISSA, *The Year 2000 International Research Conference on Social Security: Social Security in the Global Village*, Helsinki.

Fox, L. (1994), 'Old-Age Security in Transitional Economies', in *Policy Research Working Paper 1257*, World Bank, Washington, D.C.

Fox, L. (1995), 'Can Eastern Europe's Old-Age Crisis Be Fixed', *Finance and Development*, vol. 32, no. 4, pp. 34-37.

Frieden, J.A. (1991), 'Invested Interests: The Politics of National Economic Policies in a World of Global Finance', *International Organization*, vol. 45, no. 4, pp. 425-451.

Fry, M.J. (1989), 'Financial Development: Theories and Recent Experience', *Oxford Review of Economic Policy*, vol. 5, no. 4, pp. 13-28.

Fry, M.J. (1997), 'In Favour of Financial Liberalisation', *The Economic Journal*, vol. 107, no. 442, pp. 754-770.

Frydman, R. and Rapaczynski, A. (1994), *Privatisation in Eastern Europe: Is the State Withering Away*, CEU, London.

Frydman, R., Gray, C.W. and Rapaczynski, A. (1996a), *Corporate Governance in Central Europe and Russia: Banks, Funds and Foreign Investors*, CEU, London.

Frydman, R., Gray, C.W. and Rapaczynski, A. (1996b), *Corporate Governance in Central Europe and Russia: Insiders and the State*, CEU, London.

Fuchs, M. (1988), 'Social Security in Third World Countries', in F. von Benda-Beckmann, K. von Benda-Beckmann, E. Casino, F. Hirtz, G.R. Woodman and H.F. Zacher (eds), *Between Kinship and the State: Social Security Law in Developing Countries*, Foris Publications, Dordrecht, pp. 39-51.

Fultz, E. (1997), 'Social security in the 1990s: An analysis of international social security trends and their implications for English-speaking Africa', *Sub-Regional Seminar on Social Protection Reform Strategies for English-Speaking Africa*, Harare, 21-25 April, ILO, Geneva.

Fultz, E. and Pieris, B. (1997), 'The Social Protection of Migrant Workers in South Africa', *ILO/SAMAT Policy Paper no.3*, ILO/SAMAT, Harare, Zimbabwe.

Fultz, E. and Pieris, B. (1999), 'Social Security Schemes in Southern Africa: An Overview and Proposals for Future Development', *ILO/SAMAT Discussion Paper no.11*, ILO/SAMAT, Harare, Zimbabwe.

Ganapathi, A.L. (1992), 'National Strategies for the Extension of Social Security Protection to the Entire Population: The Case of India', *Asian News Sheet*, vol. 22, no. 4, pp. 30-33.

Garber, P, (1996), 'Managing risks to financial markets from volatile capital flows: the role of prudential regulation', *International Journal of Finance and Economics*, Vol. 1, pp.183-195.

Gaye, B.S.B. (1994), *Management Accountability, Transparency And Control Measures Designed To Achieve Optimum Cost-Effectiveness And Compliance*, International Social Security Association, ISSA/PF/XIV/GAMBIA/94/2.

Geneva Association (1995-2000), *The Four Pillars*, Research Programme on Social Security, Insurance, Savings and Employment, Geneva.

George, S. and Sabelli, F. (1994), *Credits sans Frontiers: La religion seculaire de la Banque mondiale*, La Decouverte/Essias, Paris.

Gerdes, V. (1971), 'African Provident Funds', *Industrial And Labour Relations Review*, vol. 24, no. 4, pp. 572-587.

Gerdes, V. (1975), 'Precursors of Modern Social Security in Indigenous African Institutions', *The Journal of Modern African Studies*, vol. 13, no. 2, pp. 209-228.

Gerschenkron, A. (1962), *Economic Backwardness in Historical Perspective: a book of essays*, Belknap Press of Harvard University Press, Cambridge.

Gertler, P.J. (1998), 'On the Road to Social Health Insurance: the Asian Experience', *World Development*, vol. 26, no. 4, pp. 717-732.

Gesell, R., Müller, K. and Süß, D. (1999), 'Social Security Reform, Privatisation, and the Promise of Uwlaszczenie: An analysis of competing proposals', in J. Schroeder (ed), *Proceedings of Lubniewice '98: From Plan to Market: Selected Problems of the Transition*, UNI-DRUK, Poznan.

Ghaffar, R.A. (2000), 'Pensions funds and capital market development', *Social Security Challenges in Asia and the Pacific, Social Security Documentation, no.25*, ISSA, Geneva, pp. 93-107.

Ghilarducci, T. and Liébana, P.L. (2000), 'Unions's Role in Argentine and Chilean Pension Reform', *World Development*, vol. 28, no. 4, pp. 753-762.

Gilbert, N. and Moon, A. (1988), 'Analysing Welfare Effort: An Appraisal Of Comparative Methods', *Journal Of Policy Analysis And Management*, vol. 7, no. 2, pp. 326-340.

Gilbert, C., Powell, A. and Vines, D. (1999), 'Positioning the World Bank', *The Economic Journal*, vol. 109, no. 459, pp. 598-633.

Gillion, C. (1997), *An operational framework for pension reform: Overview*, ILO, Geneva.

Gillion, C. (1999), *The development and reform of social security pensions: The approach of the International Labour Office, Executive Summary for Social Security Pensions: Development and Reform*, ILO, Geneva.

Gillion, C. (2000), 'The development and reform of social security pensions: The approach of the International Labour Office', *International Social Security Review*, vol. 53, no. 1, pp. 35-63.

Gillion, C. and Bonilla, A. (1992), 'Analysis Of A National Private Pension Scheme: The Case Of Chile', *International Labour Review*, vol. 131, no. 2, pp. 171-195.

Gillion, C., Turner, J., Bailey, C. and Latulippe, D. (2000), *Social Security Pensions: Development and Reform*, ILO, Geneva.

Glover, C. (1999), 'Pension scheme could pay dividends', *Financial Times Survey: Kazakhstan*, 1 July, p. 2.

Gobin, M. (1977), 'The Role Of Social Security In The Development Of The Caribbean Territories', *International Social Security Review*, vol. 30, no. 1, pp. 9-20.

Godfrey, V.N. (1974), 'A Broader Role For National Provident Funds: The Zambian Experience', *International Labour Review*, vol. 30, pp. 137-152.

Goldstein, M., Folkerts-Landau, D., El-Erian, M., Fries, S. and Rojas-Suarez, L. (1992), 'International Capital Markets: Developments, Prospects, and Policy Issues', *World Economic and Financial Surveys*, IMF, Washington, D.C.

Golinowska, S. (1997), 'Reforma systemu Emerytalno-Rentowego', *CASE Report 6*, Warsaw.

Golub, S.S. (1997), 'Are International Labor Standards Needed to Prevent Social

Dumping', *Finance and Development*, vol. 34, no. 4, pp. 20-25.

Goodman, R., White, G. and Kwon, H-J. (1998), *Welfare Orientalism and the State*, Routledge, London.

Gopinath, P. (1994), cited in 'The ILO and Bretton Woods: A Common Vision', *International Labour Review*, vol. 133, no. 5-6, pp. 695-713.

Gore, C. (2000), 'The Rise and Fall of the Washington Consensus as a Paradigm for Developing Countries', *World Development*, vol. 28, no. 5, pp. 789-804.

Gorman, M. (1999), 'HelpAge International: working to correct a misleading image', *The ACP-EU Courier*, no. 176, pp. 60-61.

Gorman, M. (1999b), 'Development and the Rights of Older People', *The Ageing & Development Report: Poverty, Independence and the World's Older People*, Earthscan Publications, London, pp. 3-21.

Grabel, I. (1995), 'Speculation-led economic development: a post-Keynesian interpretation of financial liberalization programmes in the Third World', *International Review of Applied Economics*, vol. 9, no. 2, pp. 127-149.

Grabel, I. (1996), 'Stock Markets, Rentier Interest, and the Current Mexican Crisis', *Journal of Economic Issues*, vol. 30, no. 2, pp. 443-461.

Grabel, I. (1996), 'Marketing the Third World: The Contradictions of Portfolio Investment in the Global Economy', *World Development*, vol. 24, no. 11, pp. 1761-1776.

Grabel, I. (1997), 'Savings, Investment, and Functional Efficiency: A Comparative Examination of National Financial Complexes', in R. Pollin (ed), *The Macroeconomics of Saving, Finance and Investment*, The University of Michigan Press, Ann Arbor, pp. 251-297.

Gramlich, E.M. (1996), 'Different Approaches for Dealing with Social Security', *The American Economic Review*, vol. 86, no. 2, pp. 358-377.

Greskovits, B. (1995), 'Demagogic Populism In Eastern Europe', *Telos*, no. 102, pp. 91-106.

Griffith-Jones, S., Cailloux, J. and Pfaffenzeller, S. (1998), *The East Asian Financial Crisis: A Reflection on its Causes, Consequences and Policy Implications*, IDS Discussion Paper 367, IDS, University of Sussex, Brighton.

Grown, C., Elson, D. and Catagay, N. (2000), 'Introduction: Growth, Trade, Finance and Gender Inequality', *World Development*, vol. 28, no. 7, pp. 1145-1156.

Gruat, J-V. (1990), 'Social Security Schemes In Africa', *International Labour Review*, vol. 129, no. 4, pp. 405-421.

Gruat, J-V. (1996), 'Improving the Administrative Systems of Social Security Institutions', *12th African Regional Conference of the ISSA*, Libreville, Gabon.

Gruat, J-V. (1997a), *An Operational Framework for Pension Reform: Adequacy and social security principles in pension reform*, ILO, Geneva.

Gruat, J-V. (1997b), 'Social Security Principles in Pension Reform', *International Conference on Problems of Developing and Reforming Social Security Schemes*, ISSA, AOPF, Alma-Ata, Kazakhstan.

Gruber, J. and Wise, D.A. (1999), *Social Security and Retirement around the World*, The University of Chicago Press, Chicago.

Grunberg, I. (1998), 'Double Jeopardy: Globalization, Liberalization and the Fiscal Squeeze', *World Development*, vol. 26, no. 4, pp. 591-605.

Guhan, S. (1992), 'Social Security in India', in B. Harriss *et al.* (eds), *Poverty in India: Research and Policy*, OUP, Bombay, pp. 282-298.

Guhan, S. (1994), 'Social Security Options For Developing Countries', *International Labour Review*, vol. 133, no. 1, pp. 35-53.

Gupta, S. and Hagemann, R. (1998), 'Social Protection During Russia's Economic Transformation', in K.Y. Chu and S. Gupta (eds), *Social Safety Nets: Issues and Recent Experience*, IMF, Washington, D.C., pp. 216-224.

Gustafsson, B. and Makonnen, N. (1994), 'The Importance of Remittances for the Level and Distribution of Economic Well-Being in Lesotho', *Journal of International Development*, vol. 6, no. 4, pp. 373-398.

Habibullah, M. S. (1999), 'Financial Development and Economic Growth in Asian Countries: Testing the Financial-Led Growth Hypothesis', *Savings and Development*, vol. 23, no. 3, pp. 279-290.

Hadjimichael, M.T., Ghura, D., Muhleisen, M., Nord, R. and Uçer, E.M. (1995), *Sub-Saharan Africa: Growth, Savings and Investment, 1986-93*, International Monetary Fund, Washington, D.C.

Hale, D. (1999), 'US cycle theory', *Financial Times*, 17 February, p. 20.

Hammer, L.C., Pyatt, G. and White, H. (1999), 'What do the World Bank's Poverty Assessments teach us about Poverty in Sub-Saharan Africa?', *Development and Change*, vol. 30, pp. 795-823.

Hanson, P. (1997), 'What Sort of Capitalism is Developing in Russia?', *Communist Economies and Economic Transformation*, vol. 9, no. 1, pp. 27-42.

Harmes, A. (1998), 'Investment Civilisation: Mutual Funds and the Cultural Underpinnings of Neoliberal Financial Orthodoxy', *Annual Meeting of the British International Studies Association*, University of Sussex, Brighton.

Harmes, A. (1998), 'Institutional investors and the reproduction of neoliberalism', *Review of International Political Economy*, vol. 5, no. 1, pp. 92-121.

Harris, E. (1999), 'Impact of the Asian Crisis on Sub-Saharan Africa', *Finance and Development*, vol. 36, no. 1, http://www.imf.org.

Harris, R.D.F. (1997), 'Stock markets and development: A re-assessment', *European Economic Review*, vol. 41, pp. 139-146.

Harrison, D. (1998), *Global Pension Strategies*, FT Business Limited, London.

Harriss, B., Guhan, S. and Cassen, R. H. (1992), *Poverty in India: Research and Policy*, OUP, Bombay.

Hassan, F.M.A. and Peters, R.K., Jr. (1996), 'The Structure of Incomes and Social Protection during the Transition: The Case of Bulgaria', *Europe-Asia Studies*, vol. 48, no. 4, pp. 629-646.

Hauser, R. (1995), 'Problems of the German Welfare State After Unification', *Oxford Review of Economic Policy*, vol. 11, no. 3, pp. 44-58.

Hausmann, R. and Reisen, H. (eds) (1997), *Promoting Savings in Latin America*, IDB/OECD, Paris.

Heinrich, G. (1997), 'Pension Reform in Central and Eastern Europe: Yet Another Transition...?', *CERT Discussion Paper, 97/5*, Edinburgh.

Helbling, C. (1991), *Les Institutions de Prevoyance et la LPP*, Haupt, Bern.

Helleiner, E. (1994), 'Editorial: The world of money: The Political economy of international capital mobility', *Policy Sciences*, vol. 27, no. 4, pp. 295-298.

Heller, P.S. (1998), 'Rethinking Public Pension Reform Initiatives', *IMF Working Paper WPS/98/61*, Washington, D.C.

Hellinger, D. and Hamond, R. (1994), 'Debunking the Myth', *Africa Report*, Nov-Dec, pp. 52-55.

HelpAge International (1998), 'Ageing: the forgotten development issue', no. 1, *Ageing & Development*, pp. 1-3.

HelpAge International (1999), 'Pensions in Crisis', *Ageing & Development*, no. 3, p. 4.

HelpAge International (1999b), 'Pressure on pensions in South Africa', no. 4, *Ageing and Development*, p. 5.

HelpAge International (1999c), 'Making ends meet in Tanzania', no. 4, *Ageing and Development*, p. 5.

HelpAge International (1999d), *The Ageing and Development Report: Poverty, Independence & the World's Older People*, Earthscan Publications, London.

HelpAge International (2000), 'Research Update', *Ageing and Development*, no. 6, July, Earthscan Publications, London, p. 12.

HelpAge International (2000b), *Ageing Issues in Africa*, HelpAge International, African Regional Development Centre, Nairobi, Kenya.

HelpAge International (2000c), 'Fighting for the rights of older people', *Ageing and Development*, no. 6, p. 8.

Hemming, R. (1999), 'Should Public Pensions Be Funded?', *International Social Security Review*, vol. 52, no. 2, pp. 3-29.

Henderson, J. (1999), 'Uneven crises: institutional foundations of East Asian economic turmoil', *Economy and Society*, vol. 28, no. 1, pp. 327-368.

Hensley, M.L. and White, E.P. (1993), 'The Privatisation Experience in Malaysia: Integrating Build-Operate-Own and Build-Operate-Transfer Techniques within the National Privatisation Strategy', *Columbia Journal of World Business*, vol. 28, no. 1, p. 70-82.

Hepp, S. (1998), 'Mandatory Occupational Pension Schemes in Switzerland: The First Ten Years', *Annals of Public and Cooperative Economics*, vol. 69, no. 4, pp. 533-545.

Hernández-Catá, E. (1999), 'Sub-Saharan Africa: Economic Policy and Outlook for Growth', *Finance and Development*, vol. 36, no. 1, http://www.imf.org.

Herring, R.J. and Edwards, R.M. (1983), 'Guaranteeing Employment to the Rural Poor: Social Functions and Class Interests in the Employment Guarantee Scheme in Western India', *World Development*, vol. 11, no. 7, pp. 575-592.

Hervo-Akendengué, A. (1972), 'Social Security as an Instrument in Economic and Social Development of African Countries', *International Social Security Review*, vol. 25, no. 3, pp. 177-214.

Herzberg, N. (2000), 'L'Afrique minée par l'épidémie de sida', *Le Monde Dossiers & Documents*, no. 287, p. 3.

Heslop, A. (1996), *Participatory Needs Assessment with Older People in Clermont Township, Durban, South Africa*, HelpAge International, London.

Heslop, A. (1999), 'Poverty and Livelihoods in an Ageing World', *The Ageing & Development Report: Poverty, Independence and the World's Older People*, Earthscan Publications, London, pp. 22-32.

Heslop, A. (1999b), 'Ageing and Development', *Working Paper 3*, Social Development Department, DFID, London.

Hicks, J.R. (1959), *Essays In World Economics*, Clarendon Press, Oxford.

Hiebert, M. (1995), 'Park It Here: Mutual Funds Vie For Singapore's Cash Hoard', *Far East Economic Review*, 23 November, p. 63.

Hills, J. (1995), 'Funding the Welfare State', *Oxford Review of Economic Policy*, vol. 11, no. 3, pp. 27-43.

Hoddinott, J. (1992), 'Rotten Kids or Manipulative Parents: Are Children Old Age Security in Western Kenya?', *Economic Development and Cultural Change*, vol. 40, no. 3, pp. 545-565.

Holberton, S. (1995), 'HK Pension Plan Scrapped', *Financial Times*, 30 January, p. 6.

Holzmann, R. (1991), 'The provision of complementary pensions: Objectives, forms and constraints', *International Social Security Review*, vol. 44, no. 1, pp. 75-93.

Holzmann, R. (1994), 'Funded and Private Pensions for Eastern European Countries in Transition?', *Revista de Análisis Económico*, vol. 9, no. 1, pp. 183-210.

Holzmann, R. (1997a), *Pension Reform in Central and Eastern Europe: Necessity, Approaches and Open Questions*, University of Saarland, Saarbrücken.

Holzmann, R. (1997b), 'Pension Reform, Financial Market Development, and Economic Growth: Preliminary Evidence from Chile', *IMF Staff Papers*, vol. 44, no. 2, pp. 149-178.

Holzmann, R. (1997c), *Fiscal Alternatives of Moving from Unfunded to Funded Pensions*, OECD Development Centre, Technical Papers no. 126, OECD, Paris.

Holzmann, R. (1999), 'The World Bank and Global Pension Reform - Realities not Myths', *European Pension News*, November, http://www.worldbank.org.

Holzmann, R. (2000), 'The World Bank approach to pension reform', *International Social Security Review*, vol. 53, no. 1, pp. 11-34.

Holzmann, R. and Jørgensen, S. (1999), 'Social Protection as Social Risk Management: Conceptual Underpinnings for the Social Protection Sector Strategy Paper', *Journal of International Development*, vol. 11, no. 7, pp. 1005-1027.

Holzmann, R. and Jørgensen, S. (2000), 'Social Risk Management: A new conceptual framework for social protection, and beyond', *Social Protection Discussion Paper no.6*, World Bank, Washington, D.C.

Holzmann, R. and Stiglitz, J.E. (2001), *New Ideas About Old Age Social Security: Toward Sustainable Pension Systems in the 21ˢᵗ Century*, World Bank, Washington, D.C.

Holzmann, R., MacArthur, I.W. and Sin, Y. (2000), 'Pension Systems in East Asia and the Pacific: Challenges and Opportunities', *Social Protection Discussion Paper no.0014*, World Bank, Washington, D.C.

Hope-Kempe, R. (1997), *African Political Economy: Contemporary Issues in Development*, M.E. Sharpe, London.

Howell, M. (1999), 'Asia's 'Victorian' Financial Crisis', *IDS Bulletin: East Asia: What Happened to the Development Miracle?*, pp. 56-73.

Hu, Z-L. (1998), 'Social Protection, Labour Market Rigidity, and Enterprise Restructuring in China', in K.Y. Chu and S. Gupta (eds), *Social Safety Nets: Issues and Recent Experience*, IMF, Washington, D.C., pp. 129-146.

Huber, E. (1996), 'Options for Social Policy in Latin America: Neoliberal versus Social Democratic Models', in G. Esping-Andresen (ed), *Welfare States in Transition*, Sage Publications and UNRISD, London, pp. 141-191.

Huff, W.G. (1995), 'The Developmental State, Government, And Singapore's Economic Development Since 1960', *World Development*, vol. 23, no. 8, pp. 1421-1438.

Huff, W.G. (1995), 'What is the Singapore model of economic development?', *Cambridge Journal of Economics*, vol. 19, no. 6, pp. 735-759.

Hutton, W. (1996), 'Forget Austerity Era - Britain's Rich', *The Guardian*, 16 October, p. 15.

IBIS (2000), 'Singapore: Tax Relief for Personal Pension Funds Promised for this Year', *IBIS Report*, April, Chicago, IL.

IDS Bulletin (1995), 'Special Issue: Fifty Years On: The UN and Economic and Social Development', *IDS Bulletin*, vol. 26, no. 4.

IFC (1998), *Emerging Capital Market Factbook 1998*, IFC, Washington, D.C.

Iglesias, A. and Palaçios, R.J. (2000), 'Managing public pension reserves: Part I: Evidence from the international experience', in World Bank (ed), *Pension Primer*, Washington, D.C., http://www.worldbank.org/pensions.

IIF (1999), 'Capital Flows to Emerging Market Economies', *Press Release*, Institute of International Finance Inc, 27 January, p. 1.

Iliffe, J. (1987), *The African Poor: A History*, Cambridge UP, Cambridge.

ILO (1944), *ILO Constitution, Annex, The Declaration of Philadelphia*, http://www.ilo.org.

ILO (1955), 'Reports And Inquiries: The Colombo Plan', *International Labour Review*, vol. 71, pp. 498-515.

ILO (1961), 'Social Security in Africa South of the Sahara', *International Labour Review*, vol. 84, no. 3, pp. 144-171.

ILO (1977), 'Improvement and Harmonisation of Social Security Systems in Africa: Report 2', *Fifth African Regional Conference, Abidjan*, ILO, Geneva.

ILO (1980), *Report to the Government of the Republic of Botswana on Social Security Policy*, ILO, Geneva.

ILO (1983), *Social Security: Principles And Practice*, ILO/ FNPF, Geneva.

ILO (1987), *L'investissement des fonds de la sécurité sociale dans les pays en développement*, ILO, Geneva.

ILO (1989), *From Pyramid to Pillar: Population Change and Social Security in Europe*, ILO, Geneva.

ILO (1992), *Swaziland/ Report On The Actuarial Study For The Development Of A National Pension Scheme: Project Findings And Recommendations*, ILO, Geneva.

ILO (1993), *Social Insurance And Social Protection*, ILO, Geneva.

ILO (1993b), *World Labour Report 1993*, ILO, Geneva.

ILO (1994a), *Uganda/ Background Information On Social Security*, ILO, Geneva.

ILO (1994b), *Swaziland/ Draft Legislation Development Of A National Pension Scheme: Project Report*, ILO, Geneva.

ILO (1994c), 'Report of the Director General, Eighth African Regional Conference, Mauritius', ILO, Geneva.

ILO (1994d), 'The impact of structural adjustment programmes on social security in African - the ILO perspective', in ISSA (ed), *The impact of structural adjustment programmes on social security in African countries, African Series No.15*, ISSA, Geneva, pp. 93-101.

ILO (1995a), *Report Of The Director General, Fifth European Regional Conference, Warsaw*, ILO, Geneva.

ILO (1995b), *Press Release: Europe's Social Protection Systems Under Increasing Strain: Problems Are Most Acute In The East*, ILO, Geneva.

ILO (1997a), *Social Security Financing*, ILO, Geneva.

ILO (1997b), *Pension Schemes*, ILO, Geneva.

ILO (1997c), *Republic of Botswana: Review of Social Protection, ILO/TF/Botswana/R.4*, ILO, Geneva.

ILO (1999), *The role of the ILO in technical cooperation, Report VI, International Labour Conference, 87th Session*, ILO, Geneva.

ILO (1999b), *Decent Work: Report of the Director General, 87th International Labour Conference*, ILO, Geneva.

ILO (1999c), *Report of the Director General, Decent Work and Protection for all in Africa*, Ninth African Regional Meeting, Abidjan, ILO, Geneva.

ILO (2000), *World Labour Report 2000: Income security and social protection in a changing world*, ILO, Geneva.

IMF (1994), 'IMF Holds Seminar on Public Pension Reform', *IMF Survey*, 26 September, p. 303.

IMF (1995a), *World Economic Outlook*, IMF, Washington, D.C.

IMF (1995b), *South Africa - Selected Economic Issues*, IMF, Washington, D.C.

IMF (1997), 'Namibia - Recent Economic Developments', *IMF Staff Country Reports no.97/119*, pp. 20-21, http://www.imf.org.

IMF Research Department Staff (1997), 'Capital Flow Sustainability and Speculative Currency Attacks', *Finance and Development*, vol. 34, no. 4, pp. 8-11.

IMF (1998), 'Republic of Kazakhstan - Recent Economic Developments', *IMF Staff Country Reports*, August, http://www.imf.org.

Impavido, G. (1997), 'Pension Reform and the Development of Pension Funds and Stock Markets in Eastern Europe', *MOCT-MOST: Economic Policy in Transitional Economies*, vol. 3, no. 7, pp. 101-135.

Interben (1996), 'China: Economic Planning, Social Insurance', *Interben: The World Of International Benefits*, August, pp. 17-18.

ISSA (1975), 'Transformation of Provident Funds into Pension Schemes', *International Social Security Review*, vol. 28, no. 3, pp. 276-289.

ISSA (1981), 'The Committee on Provident Funds', *International Social Security Review*, vol. 34, no. 1, pp. 108-112.

ISSA (1987), 'Conjugating Public and Private: The Case of Pensions', *Studies and Research No.24*, International Social Security Association, Geneva.

ISSA (1990), 'Social Security In Malaysia', *Asian News sheet*, vol. 20, no. 3, pp. 18-20.

ISSA (1992), 'Implications for social security of structural adjustment policies: The Leo Wildmann Symposium', *International Social Security Review*, vol. 45, no. 2.

ISSA (1993a), 'The Financing Of Social Insurance In Central And Eastern Europe', *Social Security Documentation, European Series, no.20*, ISSA, Geneva.

ISSA (1993b), 'The Implications for Social Security of Structural Adjustment Policies', *Studies and Research, no.34*, ISSA, Geneva.

ISSA (1994a), *Restructuring Social Security In Central And Eastern Europe: A Guide To Recent Developments, Policy Issues And Options*, ISSA, Geneva.

ISSA (1994b), 'The Impact of Structural Adjustment Programmes on Social Security in African Countries', *Social Security Documentation, African Series no.15*, ISSA, Geneva.

ISSA (1994c), *Organisation and methods for social security organisations in English-speaking Africa*, ISSA, Geneva.

ISSA (1995a), 'Social Security In The Caribbean: Bahamas, Barbados, Belize, British Virgin Islands, Saint Kitts, Saint Lucia, Trinidad', *International Social Security Review*, vol. 95, no. 2, pp. 73-116.

ISSA (1995b), 'Nepal: Employees' Provident Fund (EPF)', *Asia And Pacific News Sheet*, ISSA.

ISSA (1995c), 'Singapore: Central Provident Fund: Progress During 1994', *Asia And Pacific News Sheet*, ISSA, pp. 19-23.

ISSA (1995d), 'Towards A Comprehensive And Integrated Social Security System In India', *Asia And Pacific News Sheet*, ISSA, pp. 24-28.

ISSA (1995e), 'Social Security Tomorrow: Permanence And Change', *Studies And Research no.36*, ISSA, Geneva.

ISSA (1995f), 'Pensions de retraite en Afrique francophone', *Série Africaine no.16*, ISSA, Geneva.

ISSA (1997), 'Introduction of individual pension accounts', *Trends in Social Security*, ISSA, Geneva, p. 13.

ISSA (1998a), 'Tajikistan', *Trends in Social Security*, no. 1, pp. 9-12.

ISSA (1998b), *Trends in Social Security*, no. 3, pp. 9-12.

ISSA (1998c), 'Social Security Issues in English-speaking African Countries', in *African Series no.19*, ISSA, Abidjan.

ISSA (1998d), 'Problèmes et perspectives de la sécurité sociale dans les pays francophone d'Afrique', *Série Africaine no.20*, ISSA, Abidjan.

ISSA (1998e), 'The defence of social security', *African Series no.18*, ISSA, Abidjan.

ISSA (1998f), *Permanent Committee on Old Age, Invalidity and Survivors' Insurance*, 26th General Assembly, Marrakech, 25-31 *October 1999*.

ISSA (1998g), *Programme and Budget for the Triennium 1999-2001*, 26th General Assembly, Marrakech, 25-31 October 1998.

ISSA (1998h), 'Recent developments in old-age, invalidity and survivor's insurance', *Permanent Committee on Old-age, Invalidity and Survivor's Insurance*, 26th General Assembly, Marrakech, October.

ISSA (1999a), 'Singapore: Cut in employer contributions to mandatory provident fund', *Trends in Social Security*, no. 1, p. 12.

ISSA (1999b), 'Cote d'Ivoire: Introduction of complementary retirement insurance being discussed', *Trends in Social Security*, no. 2, p. 4.

ISSA (1999c), 'Sixteenth Meeting of the Committee (on Provident Funds), Marrakech, Morocco', ISSA, Manila.

ISSA (1999d), *ISSA Bulletin*, no. 13, p. 4.

ISSA (1999e), 'Kenya', *African News Sheet*, no. 20, p. 7.

ISSA (1999f), 'Nicaragua', *Trends in Social Security*, no. 4, p. 7.

ISSA (2000a), 'Macedonia', *Trends in Social Security*, no. 2, p. 18.

ISSA (2000b), 'Chile' and 'Venezuela', *Trends in Social Security*, no. 3, pp. 5-7.

ISSA (ed) (2000c), *Social Security in Africa: New Realities*, Social Security Documentation no.21, ISSA, Geneva.

ISSR (1996), 'Developments and Trends in Social Security 1993-1995: Countries in Economic Transition', *International Social Security Review*, vol. 49, no. 2, pp. 49-60.

Iyer, S.N. (1993a), 'Pension Reform in Developing Countries', *International Labour Review*, vol. 132, no. 2, pp. 187-207.

Iyer, S.N. (1993b), 'Principles of Social Insurance Financing with Special Emphasis on the Present Situation of Central and Eastern Europe', in ISSA (ed), *The Financing of Social Insurance in Central and Eastern Europe, European Series, no.20*, ISSA, Geneva, pp. 53-61.

Jain, S. (1997), 'Feasibility study on area-based pilot projects in Anand (Gujarat) and Nizamabad (Andhra Pradesh)', in W. van Ginneken (ed), *Social Security for the Informal Sector, Issues in Social Protection Discussion Paper no.5*, ILO, Geneva.

James, E. (1995), 'Averting The Old Age Crisis', *Finance And Development*, June 1995, pp. 4-7.

James, E. (1997), *New Systems for Old Age Security*, World Bank, Washington, D.C.

James, E. (1998a), 'The Political Economy of Social Security Reform: A Cross-Country Review', *Annals of Public and Cooperative Economics*, vol. 69, no. 4, pp. 451-482.

James, E. (1998b), 'New Models for Old Age Security: Experiments, Evidence, and Unanswered Questions', *The World Bank Research Observer*, vol. 13, no. 2, pp. 271-301.

Jamieson, B. (1996), 'The Chile Factor', *Pensions World*, March 1996, pp. 23-26.

Jayansankaran, S. (1995), 'Privatisation Pioneer', *Far Eastern Economic Review*, 19 January 1995, pp. 42-44.

Jefferis, K.R. and Kelly, T.F. (1999), 'Botswana: Poverty Amid Plenty', *Oxford Development Studies*, vol. 27, no. 2, pp. 211-231.

Jenkins, G. (1992), 'Privatisation And Pension Reform In Transition Economies', *Public Finance*, vol. 47, no. Public Finance In A World In Transition, pp. 141-151.

Jenkins, M. (1981), 'Social Security Trends In The English-Speaking Caribbean', *International Labour Review*, vol. 120, no. 5, pp. 631-643.

Jenkins, M. (1992), 'Problems and Issues Related to Extending Social Security Protection to the Entire Population: An Overview', *Asian News Sheet*, vol. 22, no. 4, pp. 25-29.

Jenkins, M. (1993), 'Extending social security protection to the entire population: Problems and issues', *International Social Security Review*, vol. 46, no. 2/93, pp. 3-20.

Jensen, R. (1997), *Public transfers, private transfers and the 'crowding out' hypothesis: theory and evidence from South Africa*, Department of Economics, Princeton University, *mimeo.*

Jessup, P. and Bochnak, M. (1992), 'A Case for a U.S. Postal Savings System', *Challenge*, Nov-Dec, pp. 57-59.

Johnson, P. (1993), *A Rationale and Design for a Funded System for the Low-Income Transition Economies of the CIS*, London School of Economics, London.

Johnson, P. (1996), 'The Anatomy of the 'Old Age Crisis', in P. Lloyd-Sherlock and P. Johnson (eds), *Ageing and Society: Global Comparisons*, S.T.I.C.E.R.D, London, pp. 5-18.

Johnson, P. (1998), 'The Reform of Pensions in the UK', *Annals of Public and Cooperative Economics*, vol. 69, no. 4, pp. 517-532.

Jomo, K.S. (1995), 'Privatizing Malaysia: Rents, Rhetoric, Realities', Westview Press, Oxford.

Jomo, K.S. (1998), 'Financial Liberalization, Crises, and Malaysian Policy Responses', *World Development*, vol. 26, no. 8, pp. 1563-1574.

Jonczyk, J. (1993), 'Problems of Social Insurance in Poland and Other Participating Countries of Central and Eastern Europe Arising from the Transition from a Centrally-planned to a Market Economy', in ISSA (ed), *The Financing Of Social Insurance in Central And Eastern Europe*, International Social Security Association, Geneva, pp. 3-38.

Jonczyk, J. (1994), 'Transformation of Social Protection Systems in Central and Eastern Europe', in ISSA (ed), *Restructuring Social Security in Central and Eastern Europe*, ISSA, Geneva, pp. 3-12.

Jordan, R. (1999), 'The guide', *The Guardian, G2* (London), 7 December, p. 24.

Jørgensen, S.L. and Van Domelen, J. (1999), 'Helping the Poor Manage Risk Better: The Role of Social Funds', paper presented at IADB Conference on Social Protection and Poverty Reduction, February 4-5, Washington, D.C.

Joshi, M. (1972), 'The Role Of Contractual Savings', *Finance and Development*, vol. 9, no. 4, pp. 43-48.

Justaert, M. (1995), 'The mutual benefit movement as a basis for the organisation of social security for the self-employed in developing countries', *ISSA Permanent Committee on Mutual Benefit, 25th General Assembly, Nusa Dua*, ISSA, Geneva.

Jütting, J. (2000), 'Social security systems in low-income countries: Concepts, constraints and the need for cooperation', *International Social Security Review*, vol. 53, no. 4, pp. 3-24.

Kabaj, M. and Kowalik, T. (1995), 'Who is Responsible for Postcommunist Successes in Eastern Europe?', *Transition*, vol. 6, no. 7-8, pp. 1-2.

Kalderén, L. (1998), 'The Role of the Government in the Development of the Securities Markets', in OECD (ed), *Capital Market Development in Transition Economies: Country Experiences and Policies for the Future*, OECD, Paris.

Kandiah, M. (1992), 'The National and Social Welfare Policy', in C.K. Sin and I.M. Salleh (eds), *Caring Society: Emerging Issues and Future Directions*, Institute of Strategic and International Studies, Kuala Lumpur.

Kandiyoti, D. (1999), 'Poverty in Transition: An Ethnographic Critique of Household Surveys in Post-Soviet Central Asia', *Development and Change*, vol. 30, pp. 499-524.

Kane, C. and Palaçios, R. (1996), 'The Implicit Pension Debt', *Finance And Development*, vol. 33, no. 2, pp. 36-38.

Karpinska, N. (1999), 'Before signing clients this week, fund rethink fees', *Central European Business Journal*, http://www.ceebiz/ poland/4948.

Kaseke, E. (1988), 'Social Security In Zimbabwe', *Journal Of Social Development In Africa*, vol. 3, no. 1, pp. 5-19.

Kaseke, E. (1999), 'Social security and the elderly: the African experience', *The*

ACP-EU Courier, no. 176, pp. 50-52.

Kasente, D. (2000), 'Gender and Social Security Reform in Africa', *International Social Security Review*, vol. 53, no. 3, pp. 27-41.

Katembwe, A. (1994), *Objectives Of Provident Funds in The Context Of National Social Protection And Assessment Of Their Achievements*, International Social Security Association, ISSA/PF/XIV/Gambia/94/3.

Kaufmann, O. (1994), 'Legal problems relating to Social Security in African Countries', *Social Security in Africa: Proceedings of the International Conference, Berlin, November 1993*, German Foundation for International Development (DSE).

Kaushik, R.S. (1997), 'Challenges and Opportunities for Pension Schemes in Asia and the Pacific: The Experience of the Employees' Provident Fund of India', in ISSA (ed), *Eleventh Regional Conference for Asia and the Pacific*, ISSA, Manila.

Kay, S.J. (1999), 'Unexpected Privatizations: Politics and Social Security Reform in the Southern Cone', *Comparative Politics*, vol. 31, no. 4, pp. 403-422.

Kenny, C.J. and Moss, T.J. (1998), 'Stock Markets in Africa: Emerging Lions or White Elephants?', *World Development*, vol. 26, no. 5, pp. 829-843.

Kibazo, J. (1997), 'Brake put on sub-Sahara', *Financial Times*, 13 October, p. 34.

Killick, T. (1995), 'Flexibility and Economic Progress', *World Development*, vol. 23, no. 5, pp. 721-734.

Killick, T. (1995), 'Structural Adjustment and Poverty Alleviation: An Interpretative Survey', *Development and Change*, vol. 26, no. 2, pp. 305-331.

Killick, T. with Guantilaka, R. and Marr, A. (1998), *Aid and the Political Economy of Policy Change*, Routledge, London.

Kimuyu, P.K. (1999), 'Rotating Saving and Credit Associations in Rural East Africa', *World Development*, vol. 27, no. 7, pp. 1299-1308.

Klau, M. (1998), 'Exchange Rate Regimes and Inflation and Output in sub-Saharan Countries', *BIS Working Papers*, no.53, Basle.

Klitgaard, R. (1997), 'Unanticipated Consequences in Anti-Poverty Programs', *World Development*, vol. 25, no. 12, pp. 1963-1972.

Knight, M. (1998), *Developing Countries and the Globalization of Financial Markets*, IMF, Washington, D.C.

Knight, M. (1999), 'Developing and Transition Countries Confront Financial Globalization', *Finance and Development*, vol. 36, no. 2, http://www.imf.org.

Kochanowicz, J. (1993), 'The Disappearing State: Poland's Three Years of Transition', *Social Research*, vol. 60, no. 4, p. 822.

Kochar, A. (1999), 'Evaluating Familial Support for the Elderly: The Intrahousehold Allocation of Medical Expenditures in Rural Pakistan', *Economic Development and Cultural Change*, vol. 47, no. 3, pp. 621-656.

Konopielko, Ł. (1997), 'Polish Banking Sector on its Way to the European Union', *Proceedings of the Third Annual Conference on Central and East Europe in a Global Context, CREEB*, Buckinghamshire Business School, UK.

Konopielko, Ł. (1999), 'Polish Pension Reform and Corporate Governance Issues', *Law in Transition*, Autumn, pp. 56-60.

Konrad, K.A. (1995), 'Social security and strategic *inter-vivos* transfers of social capital', *Journal of Population Economics*, vol. 8, no. 3, pp. 315-326.

Kopits, G. (1992), 'Social Security', in V. Tanzi (ed), *Fiscal Policies In Economies In Transition, Part iii*, International Monetary Fund, Washington, D.C.

Kornai, J. (1992), 'The Postsocialist Transition and the State: Reflections in the Light of Hungarian Fiscal Problems', *American Economic Review*, vol. 82, no. 2, pp. 1-21.

Kornai, J. (1997a), 'Editorial: Reforming the Welfare State in Postsocialist Societies', *World Development*, vol. 25, no. 8, pp. 1183-1186.

Kornai, J. (1997b), 'The Reform of the Welfare State and Public Opinion', *American Economic Review*, vol. 87, no. 2, pp. 339-343.

Kow, C.A. (1990), 'Current Problems And Issues Encountered By Provident Fund Schemes In Asia And The Pacific - The Malaysian Experience', *Asian News Sheet*, vol. 20, no. 3, pp. 27-31.

Krol, J. (1995/6), 'Private Retirement Provision in Poland', *East-West Review of Social Policy*, vol. 1, no. 1, pp. 3-14.

Ksiezopolski, M. (1993), 'Social Policy In Poland In The Period Of Political And Economic Transition: Challenges And Dilemmas', *Journal Of European Social Policy*, vol. 3, no. 3, pp. 177-194.

Kuczynski, P-P. (1999), 'Privatization and the Private Sector', *World Development*, vol. 27, no. 1, pp. 215-224.

Kudat, A. and Youssef, N.H. (1999), *Older People in Transition Economies: An Overview of their Plight in Europe, Central Asia Region*, UN, Geneva.

Kuhelj, J. (1992), *Pension And Disability Insurance In The Republic Of Slovenia*, The Institute For Pension And Disability Insurance Of Slovenia, Ljubljana.

Kumar, S.V. (1998), 'Reponses to the issues of ageing: The Indian scenario', *BOLD*, vol. 8, no. 3, pp. 7-26.

Kuper, S.K.H. (1944), 'Voluntary Associations In An Urban Township', *African Studies*, vol. 3, pp. 179-186.

Kwon, H-J. (1997), 'Beyond European Welfare Regimes: Comparative Perspectives on East Asian Welfare Systems', *Journal of Social Policy*, vol. 26, no. 4, pp. 467-484.

Kwon, H-J. (1999), 'Inadequate Policy or Operational Failure? The Potential Crisis of the Korean National Pension Programme', *Social Policy and Administration*, vol. 33, no. 1, pp. 20-38.

Kwon, H-J. (1999), 'East Asian Welfare States in Transition: Challenges and Opportunities', *IDS Bulletin*, vol. 30, no. 4, pp. 82-93.

Kynge, J. (1997), 'Government bond debut by Malaysia', *Financial Times*, 18 September, p.40.

Kynge, J. (1997a), 'Malaysia lifts shares curb and delays building plans', *Financial Times*, 5 September, p. 1.

Kynge, J. (1999), 'China may stick with Keynesian path of economic expansion', *Financial Times*, 7 April, p. 4.

Kynge, J. (2000), 'China's pension system 'in crisis'', *Financial Times*, 10 April, p. 10.

Laczko, F. (1994), *Older People in Eastern and Central Europe: The Price of Transition to a Market Economy*, HelpAge International, London.

Latulippe, D. (1997), *An Operational Framework for Pension Reform: Comprehensive quantitative modelling for a better pension strategy*, ILO, Geneva.

Lavelle, K.C. (1999), 'International financial institutions and emerging capital markets in Africa', *Review of International Political Economy*, vol. 6, no. 2, pp. 200-224.

Leapman, B. (2000), 'Ministers want trendy name for pensioners', *Evening Standard* (London), 29 March, p. 4.

Leckie, S. (1999), *Pension Funds in China*, ISI Publications, Hong Kong.

Ledgerwood, J. (1999), *Microfinance Handbook: An Institutional and Financial Perspective*, World Bank, Washington, D.C.

Lee, O.L. (2000), 'Retirement under the social security system of Singapore', *Insurance Research and Practice*, vol. 15, no. 1, pp. 40-44.

Legrand, T.K. (1995), 'The Determinants of Men's Retirement Behaviour in Brazil', *The Journal of Development Studies*, vol. 31, no. 5, pp. 673-701.

Lennox, C. (1998), 'Botswana lays the foundation for a social security system', *Social Security Bulletin*, vol. 61, no. 2, pp. 41-42.

Le Roux, P. (1995), 'Poverty and Social Policies: Some Critical Policy Choices for South Africa', *Report of the Committee on Strategy and Policy Review of Retirement Pensions*, Government of South Africa.

Leung, J.C.B. and Wong, H.S.W. (1999), 'The Emergence of a Community-based Social Assistance Programme in Urban China', *Social Policy and Administration*, vol. 33, no. 1, pp. 39-54.

Levine, R. (1997), 'Financial Development and Economic Growth: Views and Agenda', *Journal of Economic Literature*, vol. 35, no. 2, June, pp. 688-726.

Lewis, P. and Stein, H. (1997), 'Shifting Fortunes: The Political Economy of Financial Liberalization in Nigeria', *World Development*, vol. 25, no. 1, pp. 5-22.

Lex Comment (1996), 'Chile Pension', *Financial Times*, 12 January, p. 19.

Lipton, M. (1997), 'Editorial: Poverty - Are There Holes in the Consensus', *World Development*, vol. 25, no. 7, pp. 1003-1007.

Lloyd-Sherlock, P. (1997), *Old Age and Urban Poverty in the Developing World: The Shanty Towns of Buenos Aires*, Macmillan Press, Basingstoke.

Lloyd-Sherlock, P. (1999), 'Income security for poor older people in developing countries', *The ACP-EU Courier*, no. 176, pp. 448-450.

Lloyd-Sherlock, P. (2000), 'Failing the Needy: Public Social Spending in Latin America', *Journal of International Development*, vol. 12, no. 1, pp. 101-120.

Lloyd-Sherlock, P. (2000), 'Old Age and Poverty in Developing Countries: New Policy Challenges', *World Development*, vol. 18, no. 12, pp. 2157-2168.

Lloyd-Sherlock, P. and Johnson, P. (1996), 'Ageing and Social Policy: Global Comparisons', S.T.I.C.E.R.D, London.

Lodahl, M. (1999), 'Old-age Pensions in Russia: More Subsistence Benefit than Social Insurance', *Economic Bulletin*, vol. 36, no. 12, pp. 17-22.

Loh, C. and Veall, M.R. (1985), 'A Note On Social Security And Private Savings In Singapore', *Public Finance/Finances Publiques*, vol. 40, no. 2, pp. 299-303.

Long, M. (1991), 'Financial Systems and Development', in P. Callier (ed), *Financial Systems and Development in Africa*, EDI, Washington, D.C., pp. 159-172.

Loyd, L.K. (1986), 'The Development Of Computer Systems In The Administration Of Social Security: The Malaysian Experience', *International Social Security Review*, vol. 39, no. 1, pp. 24-37.

Lucas, R.E.B. and Stark, O. (1985), 'Motivations to Remit: Evidence from Botswana', *Journal of Political Economy*, vol. 93, no. 5, pp. 901-918.

Luce, E. (1999), 'Intercity rivalry intensifies', *Financial Times Survey: Asian Financial Markets*, 30 April, p. 4.

Luce, E. (1999b), 'ADB boosts Singapore's bond hopes', *Financial Times*, 9 March, p.36.

Luce, E. and Blitz, J. (1999), 'Italy may securitise social security arrears', *Financial Times*, 22 April, p. 1.

Lukaukus, A. (1999), 'Managing mobile capital: recent scholarships on the political economy of international finance', *Review of International Political Economy*, vol. 6, no. 2, pp. 262-287.

Lund, F. (1993), 'State social benefits in South Africa', *International Social Security Review*, vol. 46, no. 1, pp. 5-25.

Lund, F. and Srinivas, S. (2000), *Learning from Experience: A gendered approach to social protection for workers in the informal economy*, ILO, Turin.

MacKenzie, G.A., Gerson, P. and Cuevas, A. (1997), 'Can Public Pensions Reform Increase Saving?', *Finance and Development*, vol. 34, no. 4, pp. 46-49.

MacPherson, S. (1988), 'Social Security and Social Assistance in Developing Countries', in M.T. Meulders-Klein and J. Ekelaar (eds), *Family, State and Individual Economic Security, vol.2*, E. Story-Scientia, Brussels, pp. 583-912.

Mantel, J. (2000), *Demographics and the Funded Pension System: Ageing Population, Mature Pension Funds and Negative Cash Flows*, Merrill Lynch Report, London, UK.

Mark, I. (1996), 'Chile's Private Pension Funds: Fêted Abroad, Maligned At Home', *Financial Times*, 18 January, p. 6.

Marsh, V. (1997), 'Hungary spreads the pension load', *Financial Times*, 22 January, p. 2.

Marsh, V. (1998), 'Retirement mooted for scheme', *Financial Times Survey: Slovenia*, 18 May, p. 3.

Marsland, D. 1992), 'The Roots and Consequences Of Paternalistic Collectivism: Beveridge and his influence', *Social Policy And Administration*, vol. 26, no. 2, pp. 144-150.

Matesova, J. (1996), 'Second-generation Issues in Transition: Mass Privatisation and Restructuring', in M. Bruno and B. Pleskovic (eds), *Annual World Bank Conference on Development Economics, 1995*, World Bank, Washington, D.C., pp. 367-373.

McDonald, C., Schiller, C. and Ueda, K. (1999), *Income Distribution, Informal Safety Nets, and Social Expenditures in Uganda*, IMF, Washington, D.C.

McGillivray, W.R. (1983), 'Social Security Protection In The Developing Countries Of The South Pacific', in ILO (ed), *Social Security: Principles And Practices*, International Labour Office /FPNF, Geneva.

McGillivray, W.R. (1997), *An Operational Framework for Pension Reform: Retirement System Risks*, ILO, Geneva.

McGregor, R. (2000), 'China to set up pensions fund', *Financial Times*, 27 September, p. 12.

McKinnon, R. (1996), 'The Public Management Of National Provident Funds For State-led Development: The Case Of Malaysia's Employees' Provident Fund', *The International Journal Of Public Sector Management*, vol. 9, no. 1, pp. 44-60.

McKinnon, R. (2000), 'Social Insurance as Social Partnership', *International Union Rights*, vol. 7, no. 4, December, pp. 3-5.

McKinnon, R. and Charlton, R. (1998), 'Hipokrye: czy vczniowie? (Pension Reform as Paradox, Irony and Hypocrisy: Uncomfortable Eastern Lessons for the EU)', *Asekuracja and Re, Warsaw*, May, pp. 40-42.

McKinnon, R. and Charlton, R. (2000), 'Reaffirming Public-Private Partnerships in Retirement Pension Provision', *International Journal of Public Sector Management*, vol. 13, no. 2, pp. 153-168.

McKinnon, R. and Charlton, R. (2001), 'Defending Partnership in Pensions Provision', *International Union Rights*, forthcoming.

McKinnon, R., Charlton, R. and Konopielko, Ł. (1999a), 'Non-State Pension Funds: Private Sector Developments in Transition Economies', *Faculty of Business Working Paper no.17*, Glasgow Caledonian University.

McKinnon, R., Charlton, R. and Konopielko, Ł. (1999b), 'The Emergence of Contractual Savings Sectors in Transition Economies: Business and Policy in the Rise of the Non-State Pension Fund', *Journal of European Financial Services*, vol. 3, no. 3, pp. 24-47.

McKinnon, R., Charlton, R. and Munro, H.T. (1997), 'The National Provident Fund Model: An analytical and evaluative reassessment', *International Social Security Review*, vol. 50, no. 2, pp. 43-61.

McKinnon, R.I. (1989), 'Financial Liberalization and Economic Development: a Reassessment of Interest-Rate Policies in Asia and Latin America', *Oxford Review of Economic Policy*, vol. 5, no. 4, pp. 29-54.

McNulty, S. (1998), 'Singapore to loosen finance grip', *Financial Times*, 3 February, p. 4.

Meadows, P. (1996), *Working Out - or Working In?: Contributions to the Debate on the Future of Work*, Joseph Rowntree Foundation, York.

Mehrotra, S. and Jolly, R. (1998), *Development with a Human Face: Experiences in Social Achievement and Economic Growth*, Clarendon Press, Oxford.

Meller, P. (1989), 'Criticisms and suggestions on the cross-conditionality of the IMF and the World Bank', *CEPAL Review*, no. 37, pp. 65-78.

Meller, P. (1990), 'Comments: What Washington Means by Policy Reform', in J. Williamson (ed), *Latin American Adjustment: How much has happened?*, IIE, Washington, D.C., pp. 54-85.

Mesa-Lago, C. (1986), 'Social Security And Development In Latin America', *CEPAL Review*, pp. 135-150.

Mesa-Lago, C. (1989), *Ascent To Bankruptcy*, University Of Pittsburgh, Pittsburgh.

Mesa-Lago, C. (1991a), *Social Security And Prospects For Equity In Latin America*, The World Bank, Washington, D.C.

Mesa-Lago, C. (1991b), *Portfolio Performance Of Selected Social Security Institutions In Latin America*, The World Bank, Washington, D.C.

Mesa-Lago, C. (1996), 'Pension System Reforms in Latin America: the Position of the International Organisations', *CEPAL Review*, no. 60, pp. 73-98.

Mesa-Lago, C. (1997), 'Social Welfare Reform in the Context of Economic-Political Liberalization: Latin American Cases', *World Development*, vol. 25, no. 4, pp. 497-517.

Mesa-Lago, C. and Pérez-López, J. (1999), 'Cuba's Economy: Twilight of an era', *Transition*, vol. 10, no. 2, pp. 22-25.

Messkoub, M. (1999), 'Crisis of Ageing in Less Developed Countries: Too Much Consumption or Too Little Production?', *Development and Change*, vol. 30, pp. 217-235.

Midgley, J. (1984a), *Social Security, Inequality And The Third World*, John Wiley And Sons, London.

Midgley, J. (1984b), 'Social assistance: An alternative form of social protection in developing countries', *International Social Security Review*, vol. 37, no. 3, pp. 247-264.

Midgley, J. (1996), 'Introduction: Social Work and Economic Development', *International Social Work*, vol. 39, no. Special Issue, pp. 5-12.

Midgley, J. and Sherraden, M. (eds) (1997), *Alternatives to Social Security: An International Enquiry*, Auburn House, London.

Mikhalev, V. (1996), 'Social Security in Russia under Economic Transformation', *Europe-Asia Studies*, vol. 48, no. 1, pp. 5-25.

Milburn-Pyle, P. (1991), 'Retirement Provision In The New South Africa', *Benefits And Compensation International*, November 1991, pp. 8-14.

Miles, D. and Timmerman, A. (1999), 'Risk sharing and transition costs in the reform of pension systems in Europe', *Economic Policy*, vol. 29, pp. 253-286.

Millar, J. (1997), 'The Importance of Initial Conditions in Economic Transitions: An Evaluation of Economic Reform Progress in Russia', *Journal of Socio-Economics*, vol. 26, no. 4, pp. 359-381.

Mingat, A. (1998), 'The Strategy Used by High-performing Asian Economies in Education: Some Lessons for Developing Countries', *World Development*, vol. 26, no. 4, pp. 695-715.

Ministry of Finance and Development Planning (2000), *Annual Economic Report 2000*, Government Printer, Gaborone, Botswana.

Mistry, P.S. (1999), 'Commentary: Mauritius - quo vadis?', *African Affairs*, vol. 98, no. 393, pp. 551-569.

Mitchell, O. (1998), *Building an Environment for Pension Reform in Developing Countries*, Human Development Network, Social Protection Group, World Bank, Washington, D.C.

Mitchell-Weaver, C. and Manning, B., (1991-92), 'Public-Private Partnerships in Third World Development: A Conceptual Overview', *Studies in Comparative International Development*, vol. 26, no. 4, pp. 45-67.

Miurin, P. and Sommariva, A. (1993), 'The financial reforms in Central and Eastern European countries and in China', *Journal of Banking and Finance*, vol. 17, no. 5, pp. 883-911.

Mkandawire, T. (1999), 'The Political Economy of Financial Reform in Africa', *Journal of International Development*, vol. 11, no. 3, pp. 321-342.

Mkulo, M.H.M. (1992), *Adapting The Legal And Administrative Structures Of Provident Funds To Achieve Optimum Efficiency*, International Social Security Association, ISSA/PFXIII/1-TANZANIA; ISSA/GA/XXIV/3/PF/1.

Mkulo, M.H.M. (1994), 'The impact of structural adjustment programmes on social security in eastern and southern African countries', in ISSA (ed), *The impact of structural adjustment programmes on social security in African countries, Social Security Documentation, African Series, no.15*, ISSA, Geneva, pp. 1-12.

MOBAA (1999), *Mauritius: Business Guide 1999-2000*, MOBAA, Port Louis.

Mohamed, S. (1992), 'Financing Of Social And Pensions In Malaysia: Some Options', in C.K. Sin and I.M. Salleh (eds), *Caring Society: Emerging Issues And Future Directions*, Institute For Strategic And International Studies, Kuala Lumpur, pp. 391-440.

Montagnon, P. (1998), 'New Zealand's 'grey power' starts to flex its muscles', *Financial Times*, 2 November, p. 7.

Morande, F. (1990), 'Chile: Recent Past, Prospects, and Challenges', in F.D. McCarthy (ed), *Problems of Developing Countries in the 1990s*, Vol. II Country Studies, World Bank, Washington, D.C., pp. 8-36.

Morrissey, D. (1999), 'An Ageing World', *The ACP-EU Courier*, no. 176, pp. 38-39.

Moser, C. (1998), 'The Asset Vulnerability Framework: Reassessing Urban Reduction Strategies', *World Development*, vol. 26, no. 1, pp. 1-19.

Moss, T.J. (2000), 'The Political Economy of Global Portfolio Investment and Financial Sector Development in Africa: An Examination of the Determinants and Consequences of African Stock Exchanges, with special reference to Ghana', *Ph.D. Thesis*, Department of Political Studies, SOAS, University of London.

Mouton, P. (1975), *Social Security in Africa: Trends, Problems and Prospects*, ILO, Geneva.

Mouton, P. and Yahiel, M. (1997), 'Les Pays d'Europe Centrale et Orientale Face à la Réforme des Systèmes de Retraite', *Retraite et Société*, no. 18, pp. 34-48.

MTI Hungarian Press Agency (1998a), 'Over one quarter of employees belong to private pension funds', *MTI Weekly Bulletin*, no. 44, pp. 13-14.

MTI Hungarian Press Agency (1998b), 'Pension', *MTI Reports*, pp. 1-2.

Muhammad, R.A.K. (1992), 'Administrative Reforms and Bureaucratic Modernisation in the Malaysian Public Sector', in, Proceedings of a Commonwealth Roundtable, *The Changing Role of Government: Administrative Structures and Reforms*, Sydney, Australia, Commonwealth Secretariat, London.

Muindi, S.W. (1994), *The Effects of Inflation On Provident Funds*, International Social Security Association, Geneva.

Mullan, P. (2000), *The Imaginary Time Bomb: Why an Ageing Population is not a Social Problem*, I.B. Tauris, London.

Müller, K. (1999), 'Pension Reform Paths in Comparison', *Czech Sociological Review*, vol. 7, no. 1, pp. 51-66.

Müller, K. (2000a), *The Political Economy of Pension Reform in Central-Eastern Europe*, Edward Elgar, Cheltenham.

Müller, K. (2000b), 'Pension privatisation in Latin America', *Journal of International Development*, vol. 12, no. 4, pp. 507-518.

Müller, K. (2000c), 'Les pays en transition: la reforme des retraites, dix ans après', *Retraite et Société (Paris)*, no. 29, March, pp. 21-37.

Müller, K., Ryll, A. and Wagener, H.J. (1999), *Transformation of Social Security: Pensions in Central-Eastern Europe*, Physica-Verlag, Heidelberg.

Mulligan, M. (1999a), 'Chile set to cut rates again as activity falls', *Financial Times*, 23 February, p. 7.

Mulligan, M. (1999b), 'Cash-rich pension funds go shopping overseas', *Financial Times*, 27 July, p. 30.

Mulozi, S.L. (1994), 'The extension of social security to the non-wage earning population', in ISSA (ed), *Organisation and methods for social security organisations in English-speaking Africa, Social Security Documentation, African Series, no.14*, ISSA, Geneva, pp. 29-36.

Muncey, S. (1994), 'Providence Overseas - Singapore, Hong Kong, Malaysia, Thailand, Indonesia, Korea, Philippines', *Pensions World*, vol. 23, no. 3, pp. 27-29.

Mundle, S. (1998a), 'Introduction to Special Section of World Development on

Financing Human Development', *World Development*, vol. 26, no. 4, pp. 657-658.

Mundle, S. (1998b), 'Financing Human Development: Some Lessons from Advanced Asian Countries', *World Development*, vol. 26, no. 4, pp. 659-672.

Munro, A.R. and Snyman, A.M. (1995), 'The Life Insurance Industry in South Africa', *The Geneva Papers on Risk and Insurance*, vol. 20, no. 75, pp. 127-140.

Munro, H.T. (1989), 'The Fourth Pillar', *Pensions World*, vol. 18, no. 2, pp. 107-112.

Munro, W., Padayachee, V., Lund, F. and Valodia, I. (1999), 'The State in A Changing World: Plus ça Change? Reflections from the South on the World Bank's 1997 World Development Report', *Journal of International Development*, vol. 11, no. 1, pp. 75-91.

Murinde, V. and Eng, F.S.H. (1994), 'Financial development and economic growth in Singapore: demand-following or supply-leading?', *Applied Financial Economics*, vol. 4, pp. 391-404.

Murray, M.N. (1992), 'Social Insurance in Developing Countries: Are There Net Benefits to Program Participation?', *The Journal of Developing Areas*, vol. 26, no. 2, pp. 193-212.

Murrel, P. (1996), 'How Far Has the Transition Progressed?', *The Journal of Economic Perspectives*, vol. 10, no. 2, pp. 25-44.

Myers, R.J. (1993), *Social Security*, Pensions Research Council And University Of Pennsylvania, Pennsylvania.

Nair, S.B. and Tracy, M.B. (1989), 'Pensions for women in the Third World: A Case Study of Kerala, India', *International Journal of Contemporary Sociology*, vol. 26, no. 3-4, pp. 175-187.

Nakamae, N. (2000), 'Japanese financial institutions eye the post office's huge savings honeypot', *Financial Times*, 21 January, p. 10.

Narayan, D. and Pritchett, L. (1999), 'Cents and Sociability: Household Income and Social Capital in Rural Tanzania', *Economic Development and Cultural Change*, vol. 47, no. 4, pp. 871-897.

Ndulu, B.J. and O'Connell, S.A. (1999), 'Governance and Growth in Sub-Saharan Africa', *Journal of Economic Perspectives*, vol. 13, no. 3, pp. 41-66.

Negara, B. (1979), *Money And Banking In Malaysia*, Tien Wah Press, Kuala Lumpur.

Nigh, J.O. and Wever, E.M. (1996), 'The Drive to Privatize', *Emphasis*, no. 2, pp. 2-5.

Nikonoff, J. (1999), *La Comédie des Fonds de Pension*, Arléa, Paris.

NSSF (1998), 'From a provident fund to a social insurance scheme', *Quarterly Journal of NSSF* (Tanzania), p. 4.

Nunberg, B. (1990), 'Public Sector Management Issues in Structural Adjustment Lending', *World Bank Discussion Papers 99*, World Bank, Washington, D.C.

OASIS (1999), 'Interim Report', *Old Age Social and Income Support - Project*

Oasis, http://www.oasis-india.org.

O'Donnell, P. (1999), 'Social Protection as a productive factor: Bulgaria', *Consensus*, no.5.

OECD (1997), *Economic Outlook, 61*, OECD, London.

OECD (1998), *Maintaining Prosperity in an Ageing Society*, OECD, Paris.

OECD (1999a), 'DAC Annual Report: 'Stay the Course' through the Financial Crisis', News Release, http://www.oecd.org/news_and_events/release/nw99-10a.htm.

OECD (1999b), 'Maintaining prosperity in an Ageing society', *OECD Policy Brief*, October, pp. 1-8.

OECD (ed) (1998), 'Institutional Investors in the New Financial Landscape', OECD, Paris.

Okatcha, K. (1999), 'Old Aids: the impact of AIDS on older people', *The ACP-EU Courier*, no. 176, pp. 62-65.

Olivier, M. *et al.* (1999), *Social Insurance and Social Assistance: Towards a Coherent Approach*, A Report to the Department of Welfare, South Africa, CICLA/FES.

Onis, Z. (1995), 'The Limits Of Neoliberalism', *Journal Of Economics Issues*, vol. 29, no. 1, pp. 97-119.

OPSSR (1997a), *Polish Pension Reform Package: Part One*, Office of the Plenipotentiary for Social Security Reform, Warsaw.

OPSSR (1997b), *Security Through Diversity: Reform of the Pension System in Poland*, Office of the Plenipotentiary for Social Security Reform, Warsaw.

Orenstein, M. (1999), *A Political-Institutional Analysis of Pension Reform in the Postcommunist Countries*, Syracuse, NY, *mimeo*.

Orlik, T. (1998), 'Fundusze a perspecktywy bankowosci inwestycyjnej', *Bank*, vol. 1, no. 64, pp. 57-61.

Orszag, P.R. and Stiglitz, J.E. (1999), 'Rethinking Pension Reform: Ten Myths About Social Security Systems', conference paper presented at *New Ideas About Old Age Security*, September 14-15, The World Bank, Washington, D.C.

Ostrovsky, A. (1999), 'Baby boomers boost bond market', *Financial Times*, 12 February, p. 9.

Ott, M. (1997), 'Capital Market Implications of Pension and Social Insurance Reform in the NIS', *Barents Group Contract 4305-001*, Washington, D.C.

Ouattara, A. D. (1999), 'An Agenda for the 21st Century', *Finance and Development*, vol. 36, no. 1, http://www.imf.org.

Outreville, J. (1994), 'Life Insurance in Developing Countries: A Cross-Country Analysis', in , *UNCTAD/OSG Discussion Paper no.93*, UNCTAD, Geneva.

Palaçios, R. and Pallarès-Miralles, M. (2000), *International Patterns of Pension Provision*, Pensions Primer Paper, World Bank, Washington, D.C., http://www.worldbank.org/pensions.

Paltsev, S. (1999), 'Kyrgystan Pension System in Transition', draft background paper for Asian Development Bank Pension Reform Technical Project (TA

Project no.2963-KGZ), University of Colorado.

Parrott, A.L. (1968), 'Problems Arising From The Transition From Provident Funds to Pension Schemes', *International Social Security Review*, vol. 21, no. 4, pp. 530-557.

Parrott, A.L. (1985), *The Iron Road To Social Security*, The Book Guild, Sussex, Brighton.

Patrick, H.T. (1972), 'Economic Development and Economic Growth in Underdeveloped Countries: Reply', *Economic Development and Cultural Change*, vol. 20, no. 2, pp. 326-329.

Paukert, F. and Robinson, D. (1992), *Incomes Policies in the Wider Context: Wage, Price and Fiscal Initiatives in Developing Countries*, ILO, Geneva.

Paulson, J.A. and McAndrews, J. (1998), 'Financial Services for the Urban Poor: South Africa's E Plan', *World Bank Working Paper 2016*, Washington, D.C.

Pauly, L.W. (1994), 'National financial structures, capital mobility, and international economic rules: The normative consequences of East Asian, European, and American distinctiveness', *Policy Sciences*, vol. 27, no. 4, pp. 343-363.

Pauly, L.W. (1999), 'Good governance and bad policy: the perils of international organisational overextension', *Revue of International Political Economy*, vol. 6, no. 4, pp. 401-424.

Pedersen, P.O. and McCormick, D. (1999), 'African business systems in a globalising world', *The Journal of Modern African Studies*, vol. 37, no. 1, pp. 109-135.

Pender, J. (2000), 'From "Structural Adjustment" to "Comprehensive Development Framework": Conditionality Transformed', paper presented at the *African Studies Association of the UK Biennial Conference, Africa: Past, Present and Future*, 11-13 September, Trinity College, Cambridge.

Peng, I. (1995), 'Comparative Welfare Regimes: The East Asian States', *Social Science Japan*, August, pp. 14-15.

Perrin, G. (1985), 'The Recognition Of The Right To Social Protection As A Human Right', *Labour And Society*, vol. 10, no. 2, pp. 239-257.

PERTA (1996), *Privatizing Pensions: Labor's Stake in 6 European Nations*, PERTA program, Rome.

Phirinyane, D. (1999), 'Gov't plans consolidated welfare policy', *Botswana Daily News*, September 3, no.166, p. 1.

Pilch, M. and Wood, V. (1979), *Pension Schemes: A Guide To Principles And Practices*, Gower Press, London.

Piñera, J. (1995), 'Empowering Workers: The Privatization of Social Security in Chile', *Cato Journal*, vol. 15, no. 2-3, cited in http://www.pensionreform.org.

Pollin, R. (ed) (1997), *The Macro-economics of Saving, Finance and Investment*, The University of Michigan Press, Ann Arbor.

Popiel, P.A. (1994), *Financial Systems in Sub-Saharan Africa: A Comparative Study*, World Bank, Washington, D.C.

Porter, M.E. (1990), *The Competitive Advantage of Nations*, Macmillan, Basingstoke.

Porter, R.C. (1966), 'The Promotion of the 'Banking Habit' and Economic Development', *The Journal of Development Studies*, vol. 2, no. 4, pp. 346-366.

Powell, A. (1989), 'The Management of Risk in Developing Country Finance', *Oxford Review of Economic Policy*, vol. 5, no. 4, pp. 69-87.

Praetorius, B. (1999), 'South African Economic Policy on the Horns of a Dilemma', *Economic Bulletin*, vol. 36, no. 10, pp. 23-28.

Purwoko, N. (1996), 'Indonesian social security in transition: An empirical analysis', *International Social Security Review*, vol. 49, no. 1, pp. 51-71.

Quadagno, J. (1987), 'Theories of the Welfare State', *Annual Review of Sociology*, vol. 13, pp. 109-128.

Queisser, M. (1991), 'Social Security Systems In South East Asia - Indonesia, Philippines And Singapore', *International Social Security Review*, vol. 44, no. 1-2, pp. 121-135.

Queisser, M. (1995), 'Chile And Beyond: The Second Generation Pension Reforms In Latin America', *International Social Security Review*, vol. 48, no. 3-4/95, pp. 23-40.

Queisser, M. (1998), *The Second-Generation Pension Reforms in Latin America*, OECD, Paris.

Queisser, M. (1999), *Pension Reform: Lessons from Latin America*, OECD, Paris.

Queisser, M. (2000), 'Pension reform and international organizations: From conflict to convergence', *International Social Security Review*, vol. 53, no. 2, pp. 31-46.

Queisser, M. and Vittas, D. (2000), 'The Swiss Multi-Pillar Pension System: Triumph of Common Sense?', WPS 2416, World Bank, Washington, D.C.

Queisser, M., Bailey, C. and Woodall, J. (1997), *Reforming Pensions in Zambia: An Analysis of Existing Schemes and Options for Reform*, World Bank, Washington, D.C.

Radha-Devi, D. (1998), 'The Aged in Africa: A Situation Analysis', *BOLD*, vol. 8, no. 2, pp. 2-14.

Rahman, H. (2000), 'Poor senior citizens', *The News* (Pakistan), 16 December, p. 6.

Rajnes, D.M. (1995), 'Financing Old-Age Pensions: The Challenge to Public Provision in Central and Eastern Europe', in K. Stephenson (ed), *Social Security: Time for a Change*, Jai Press, Greenwich, Connecticut, pp. 105-123.

Ramesh, M. (1992), 'Social Security In Singapore: Redrawing The Public-Private Boundary', *Asian Survey*, vol. 32, no. 12, pp. 1093-1108.

Ramesh, M. (1993), 'Social Security In Singapore: The State And The Changing Social And Political Circumstances', *Journal of Commonwealth and Comparative Politics*, vol. 31, no. 3, pp. 111-121.

Ramonet, I. (1999), 'Social-conformisme', *Le Monde Diplomatique* (Paris), April, p. 1.

Ranis, G. (1995), 'Another Look at the East Asian Miracle', *The World Bank*

Economic Review, vol. 9, no. 3, pp. 509-534.

Rao, M.G. (1998), 'Accomodating Public Expenditure Policies: the Case of Fast Growing Asian Economies', *World Development*, vol. 26, no. 4, pp. 683.

Rao, M.G. and Das-Gupta, A. (1995), 'Intergovernmental transfers and poverty alleviation', *Environment and Planning*, vol. 13, no. 1, pp. 1-23.

Reisen, H. (1997), 'Liberalizing Foreign Investments by Pension Funds: Positive and Normative Aspects', *World Development*, vol. 25, no. 7, pp. 1173-1182.

Reisen, H. (1999), *After the Great Asian Slump: Towards a Coherent Approach to Global Capital Flows*, OECD, Paris.

Reisen, H. and Williamson, J. (1994), *Pension Funds, Capital Controls and Macroeconomic Stability*, OECD, Paris.

Republic of Slovenia (1996), *Starting Points for the Reform of the Pension and Disability Insurance System*, Ministry of Labour, Family and Social Affairs, Ljubljana.

Republic of Slovenia (1997), *White Paper on Pension Reform and Disability Insurance system - Proposal*, Ministry of Labour, Family and Social Affairs, Ljubljana.

Reviglio, F. (1967a), *Social Security: A Means Of Savings Mobilisation For Economic Development*, International Monetary Fund, Washington, D.C.

Reviglio, F. (1967b), *The Social Security Sector And Its Financing In Developing Countries*, IMF, Washington, D.C.

Ribe, F. (1994), 'Funded Social Security Systems: A Review of Issues in Four East Asian Countries', *Revista de Análisis Económico*, vol. 9, no. 1, pp. 169-182.

Riboud, M. and Chu, H. (1997), *Pension Reform, Growth, and the Labour Market in Ukraine*, World Bank, Washington, D.C.

Ridding, J. (1996), 'A Dip In The Tempting Pool', *Financial Times*, 20 May, p. 16.

Ridding, J. (1997), 'HK pension plan hangs in the balance', *Financial Times*, 13 February, p. 6.

Riedinger, J.M. (1994), 'Innovation in Rural Finance: Indonesia's Badan Kredit Kecamatan Program', *World Development*, vol. 22, no. 3, pp. 301-313.

Riley, B. (1996), 'Pension Fund Investment', *Financial Time Survey*, 2 May, pp. 1-7.

Riley, B. (1999a), 'Misery of the Meldrews', *Financial Times: Money*, 13-14 February, p. 1.

Riley, B. (1999b), 'Managers relish the tick of the time bomb', *Financial Times*, 21 May, p.1

Riley, S.P. (1998), 'The Political Economy of Anti-Corruption Strategies in Africa', in M. Robinson (ed), *Corruption and Development*, Frank Cass, London.

Risseeuw, C. (2000), 'Aging: A Gendered Policy Concern in the South and the North', *Asian Journal of Women's Studies*, vol. 16, no. 2, pp. 11-49.

Ritter, G.A. (1983), *Social Welfare in Germany and Britain*, Berg, Leamington Spa.

Robinson, A. (1997), 'Foreign investment spurs growth in Poland', *Financial Time*,

Survey: Poland, 26 March, p. 2.

Robinson, M. (1998), 'Corruption and Development: An Introduction', in M. Robinson (ed), *Corruption and Development*, Frank Cass, London, pp. 1-14.

Rocha, R. and Palaçios, R. (1996), 'The Hungarian Pension System in Transition: *mimeo*'.

Rodriguez, L.J. (1999), 'Chile's Private Pension System at 18: Its Current State and Future Challenges', *The Cato Project on Social Security Privatization*, 30 July, pp. 1-23.

Rodrik, D. (1995), 'Getting interventions right: how South Korea and Taiwan grew rich', *Economic Policy*, no. 20, pp. 55-107.

Rodrik, D. (1997), 'Trade, Social Insurance, and the Limits to Globalization', *NBER Working Paper Series*, no. 5905, Cambridge, MA.

Roduit, G. (1993), 'Switzerland: Compulsory And Voluntary Complementary Pension Schemes', *International Social Security Review*, vol. 46, no. 4, pp. 75-81.

Rohrlich, G.F. (1968), 'Social security and economic development: The evaluation of program needs at successive stages of development', in E.M. Kassalow (ed), *The Role of Social Security in Economic Development*, Government Printing Office, Washington, D.C.

Rössler, N. (1996), 'Eastern Europe: How Supplementary Retirement Provision Fits into the New Philosophy', *Benefits and Compensation International*, April, pp. 15-19.

Rowat, M.D. (1999), 'The Emerging Role of the State in Latin America', *Public Management*, vol. 1, no. 2, pp. 261-287.

Ruf-Fiedler, O. (1997), *Russia Report 1997: Insurance market survey with emphasis on life business*, SwissRe, Zurich.

Rutherford, S. (1998), 'The Savings of the Poor: Improving Financial Services in Bangladesh', *Journal of International Development*, vol. 10, no. 1, pp. 1-16.

Rutkowski, M. (1998), 'A New Generation of Pension Reforms Conquers the East - A Taxonomy in Transition Economies', *Transition*, vol. 9, no. 4, pp. 16-19.

Ryba, M. (1998), *The Role of the International Labour Organization and the World Bank with pension reforms in Africa (Working Document)*, ILO Area Office in Kinshasa, Kinshasa.

Rys, V. (1964), 'The sociology of social security', *The Bulletin of the International Social Security Association*, vol. 23, no. 1, pp. 3-34.

Rys, V. (1993), 'Social Security Reform in Central Europe: Issues and Strategies', *Journal of European Social Policy*, vol. 3, no. 3, pp. 158-176.

Sachs, J. (1999), 'Sachs on Development: Helping the world's poorest', *The Economist*, 14 August, pp. 16-22.

Sagner, A. and Mtati, R.Z. (1999), 'Politics of Pension Sharing in Urban South Africa', *Ageing and Society*, no. 19, pp. 393-416.

Salleh, I.M. and Meyanathan, S.D. (1993), *Malaysia: Growth, Equity and Structural Transformation*, World Bank, Washington, D.C.

Sandilands, R.J. (1992), 'Savings, Investment And Housing In Singapore's Growth, 1965-90', *Savings And Development*, vol. 16, no. 2, pp. 119-143.

Santamaria, M. (1992), 'Privatising Social Security: The Chilean Case', *Colombia Journal Of World Business*, vol. 27, no. 1, pp. 38-51.

Sauerborn, R., Berman, P. and Nougtara, A. (1996), 'Age bias, but no gender bias, in the intra-household resource allocation for health care in rural Burkina Faso', *Health Transition Review*, vol. 6, pp. 131-145.

Schatz, S.P. (1994), 'Structural Adjustment in Africa: a Failing Grade So Far', *The Journal of Modern African Studies*, vol. 32, no. 4, pp. 679-692.

Schiffman, H.N. (1993), 'The role of banks in financial restructuring in countries of the former Soviet Union', *Journal of Banking and Finance*, vol. 17, no. 5, pp. 1059-1072.

Schlosstein, S. (1991), *Asia's New Little Dragons: The Dynamic Emergence of Indonesia, Thailand and Malaysia*, Contemporary Books, New York.

Schmähl, W. (1992), 'Transformation and Integration of Public Pension Schemes - Lessons from the Process of Unification', *Public Finance*, vol. 47, no. Supplement, pp. 34-56.

Schmähl, W. (1998), 'Fundamental decisions for the reform of pension programmes', in *26th General Assembly, 3rd Leo Wildmann Symposium, Creating consensus: Process and choice in social security reform*, ISSA, Marrakech.

Schmidt, R.H. and Tyrell, M. (1997), 'Financial Systems, Corporate Finance and Corporate Governance', *European Financial Management*, vol. 3, no. 3, pp. 333-361.

Schmidt, S. (1995), 'Social security in developing countries: basic tenets and fields of state intervention', *International Social Work*, vol. 38, pp. 7-26.

Schmidt-Hebbel, K., Servén, L. and Solimano, A. (1996), 'Saving and Investment: Paradigms, Puzzles, Policies', *The World Bank Research Observer*, vol. 11, no. 1, pp. 87-117.

Schreider, G. and Sharma, M. (1999), 'Impact of Finance on Poverty Reduction and Social Capital Formation: A Review and Synthesis of Empirical Evidence', *Savings and Development*, vol. 23, no. 1, pp. 67-92.

Schulz, J.H. (1999), 'Economic Security in Old Age: A Family-Government Partnership', *The Ageing and Development Report: Poverty, Independence and the World's Older People*, Earthscan Publications, London, pp. 82-97.

Schulze, G. and Ursprung, H.W. (1999), 'Globalisation of the Economy and the Nation State', *The World Economy*, vol. 22, no. 3, pp. 295-352.

Searjeant, G. (1996), 'State pension is touchstone for the Utilitarian Party', *The Times*, 3 October, p. 29.

Secondi, G. (1997), 'Private Monetary Transfers in Rural China: Are Families Altruistic?', *The Journal of Development Studies*, vol. 33, no. 4, pp. 487-511.

Sen, A. (1998), 'Human Development and Financial Conservatism', *World Development*, vol. 26, no. 4, pp. 733-742.

Sender, J. (1999), 'Africa's Economic Performance: Limitations of the Current Consensus', *Journal of Economic Perspectives*, vol. 13, no. 3, pp. 89-114.

Seshamani, V. and Kaunga, E. (1999) 'Zambia', in W. van der Geest and R. van der Hoeven (eds), *Adjustment Employment and Missing Institutions in Africa: The Experience in Eastern and Southern Africa*, ILO, Geneva.

Shaw, J. (1999), 'A World Bank Intervention in the Sri Lankan Welfare Sector: The National Development Trust Fund', *World Development*, vol. 27, no. 5, pp. 825-838.

Sherraden, M. (1995), 'Social Policy in Latin America: Questions of Growth, Equality, and Political Freedom', *Latin American Research Review*, vol. 30, no. 1, pp. 176-190.

Sherraden, M. (1997), 'Provident Funds and Social Protection: The Case of Singapore', in J. Midgley and M. Sherraden (eds), *Alternatives to Social Security: An International Enquiry*, Auburn House, London, pp. 33-60.

Shome, P. (1977), 'The Role of Contractual Savings Institutions: A Preliminary Survey', *Studies in Domestic Finance no.52*, Public and Private Finance Division, World Bank, Washington, D.C.

Shome, P. and Saito, K.W. (1973), 'The Impact Of Contractual Savings On Resource Mobilisation And Allocation: The Experience Of Malaysia', *Malayan Economic Review*, no. 23, pp. 54-72.

Shome, P. and Saito, K.A. (1980), *Social Security Institutions And Capital Creation: Singapore, The Philippines, India And Sri Lanka*, Sritua Arief Associates, Kuala Lumpur.

Simonovits, A. (2000), 'Partial privatization of a pension system: Lessons from Hungary', *Journal of International Development*, vol. 12, no. 4, pp. 519-529.

Sin, L.Y. (1985), 'Central Provident Fund, Insurance And Economic Security: The Case Of Singapore', *The Southeast Asian Economic Review*, vol. 6, no. 2, pp. 77-94.

Singh, A. (1993), 'The Stock Market and Economic Development: Should Developing Countries Encourage Stock Markets?', *UNCTAD Review*, pp. 1-28.

Singh, A. (1995), 'Pension Reform, The Stock Market, Capital Formation and Economic Growth: A Critical Commentary on the World Bank's Proposals', *CEPA, Working Paper*, no. 2, pp. 1-32.

Singh, A. (1997), 'Portfolio Equity Flows and Stock Markets in Financial Liberalization', *Development*, vol. 40, no. 3, pp. 22-29.

Singh, A. (1999), 'Should Africa Promote Stock Market Capitalism', *Journal of International Development*, vol. 11, no. 3, pp. 343-365.

Singh, A. and Weisse, B.A. (1998), 'Emerging Stock Markets, Portfolio Capital Flows and Long-Term Economic Growth: Micro and Macroeconomic Perspectives', *World Development*, vol. 26, no. 4, pp. 607-622.

Singh, A. and Zammit, A. (2000), 'International Capital Flows: Identifying the Gender Dimension', *World Development*, vol. 28, no. 7, pp. 1249-1268.

Singh, P. (1997), *Social Security Systems in Developing Countries: Asia, Africa and South America*, Friedrich Ebert Stiftung, New Delhi.

Singh, P. (2000), 'India decides to open State-dominated pension system to the private sector', *Global Pensions*, April, pp.31-32.

Sinn, H-W. (1992), 'Privatisation in East Germany', *Public Finance*, vol. 47, Supplement, pp. 152-171.

Skocpol, T. and Amenta, E. (1986), 'States and Social Policies', *Annual Review of Social Policy*, vol. 12, pp. 131-57.

Snavely, K. (1996), 'The Welfare State and the Emerging Non-profit Sector in Bulgaria', *Europe-Asia Studies*, vol. 48, no. 4, pp. 647-662.

Spalding, R.J. (1980), 'Welfare Policymaking: Theoretical Implications of a Mexican Case Study', *Comparative Politics*, vol. 12, no. 4, pp. 419-438.

SSA (1997), *Social Security Programs Throughout the World*, Social Security Administration, Washington, D.C.

SSA (1999), *Social Security Programs Throughout the World*, SSA, Washington, D.C.

Stack, M. (1967), 'Forty Years in the Service of Social Security', *International Social Security Review*, vol. 20, no. 1, pp. 3-41.

Standing, G. (1996), 'Social Protection in Central and Eastern Europe: a Tale of Slipping Anchors and Torn Safety nets', in G. Esping-Andersen (ed), *Welfare States in Transition: National Adaptions in Global Economies*, Sage Publications/UNRISD, London, pp. 225-255.

Standing, G. (1999a), *Global Labour Flexibility: Seeking Distributive Justice*, Macmillan Press, London.

Standing, G. (1999b), 'New Development Paradigm or Third Wayism? A Critique of a World Bank Rethink', *mimeo*.

Standing, G. (2000), 'Brave New Worlds? A Critique of Stiglitz's World Bank Rethink', *Development and Change*, vol. 31, no. 4, pp.737-763.

Standing, G., Sender, J. and Weeks, J. (1996), *Restructuring the Labour Market: The South African Challenge*, ILO, Geneva.

Stanovik, T. and Kukar, S. (1995), 'The Pension System in Slovenia: Past Developments and Future Prospects', *International Social Security Review*, vol. 48, no. 1, pp. 35-44.

Stein, C. and Kalache, A. (1999), 'Ageing and Health', *The ACP-EU Courier*, no. 176, pp. 43-45.

Steinherr, A. (1993), 'An innovatory package for financial sector reforms in Eastern European countries', *Journal of Banking and Finance*, vol. 17, no. 5, pp. 1033-1057.

Stern, D. (2000), 'Oil poses new dependency risk', *Financial Times Survey: Kazakhstan*, 11 December, p. 2.

Stern, N.H. and Lankes, H.P. (1998), 'Making the most of markets: The role of IFIs', *Cahiers Papers EIB*, vol. 3, no. 2, pp. 103-114.

Stiglitz, J.E. (1989), 'Financial Markets and Development', *Oxford Review of Economic Policy*, vol. 5, no. 4, pp. 55-67.

Stiglitz, J.E. (1993), 'The Role of the State in Financial Markets', in M. Bruno and B. Pleskovic (eds), *Proceedings of the World Bank Annual Conference on Development Economics 1993*, World Bank, Washington, D.C., pp. 19-52.

Stiglitz, J.E. (1996), 'Some Lessons from the East Asian Miracle', *The World Bank Research Observer*, vol. 11, no. 2, pp. 151-177.

Stiglitz, J.E. (1998), 'More Instruments and Broader Goals: Moving Toward the Post-Washington Consensus', in *WIDER Annual Lectures 2*, UNU/WIDER, Helsinki.

Stiglitz, J.E. (1998), 'Towards a New Paradigm for Development: Strategies, Policies, and Processes', *Prebisch Lecture*, UNCTAD, Geneva, UNCTAD.

Stiglitz, J.E. (1998), 'The Role of the Financial System in Development', presented at the *Fourth Annual Bank Conference on Development in Latin America and the Caribbean (LAC ABCDE)*, World Bank, http://www.worldbank.org.

Stiglitz, J.E. (1998), 'Redefining the Role of the State: What should it do? Should it Do it? And How should these decisions be made?', *speech marking the tenth anniversary of MITI Research Institute*, Tokyo, Japan, World Bank, http://www.worldbank.org.

Stiglitz, J.E. (1999), 'The World Bank at the Millennium', *The Economic Journal*, vol. 109, no. 459, pp. 577-597.

Stiglitz, J.E. and Uy, M. (1996), 'Financial Markets, Public Policy, and the East Asian Miracle', *The World Bank Research Observer*, vol. 11, no. 2, pp. 249-275.

Strang, D. and Chang, P.M.Y. (1993), 'The International Labour Organisation and the Welfare State: Institutional Effects on National Welfare Spending', *International Organization*, vol. 47, no. 2, pp. 235-262.

Strang, D. and Meyer, J.W. (1993), 'Institutional conditions for diffusion', *Theory and Society*, vol. 22, no. 4, pp. 487-511.

Street, A. (1988), 'Benefits In Singapore: The Central Provident Fund', *Benefits And Compensation International*, pp. 19-23.

Subbarao, K. (1998), *Namibia's Social Safety Net: Issues and Options for Reform, Policy Research Working Paper 1996*, World Bank, Washington, D.C.

Suh, S. and Shameen, A. (1997), 'Markets Ablaze', *Asiaweek*, 27 March, pp. 54-63.

Sundén, A. (1998), 'The Swedish NDC Pension Reform', *Annals of Public and Cooperative Economics*, vol. 69, no. 4, pp. 571-583.

Svejnar, S. (1996), 'Pensions in the former Soviet Bloc: Problems and Solutions', *Working Paper 14, The William Davidson Institute, University of Michigan Business School*, Michigan.

SwissRe (1998a), 'Eastern Europe: social security reforms bring change to life and health', *Sigma*, no. 1, pp. 36-41.

SwissRe (1998b), 'Insurance industry in Central and Eastern Europe: Increasing competition - different prospects for growth', *Sigma*, no. 7.

SwissRe (1999), 'World Insurance in 1997: Booming life business, but stagnating non-life business', *Sigma*, no. 3.

SwissRe (2000), 'Emerging markets: the insurance industry in the face of globalisation', *Sigma*, no. 4.

Szeftel, M. (1998), 'Misunderstanding African Politics: Corruption and the Governance Agenda', *Review of African Political Economy*, vol. 76, no. 25, pp. 221-240.

Szegö, G. (1993), 'Introduction', *Journal of Banking and Finance*, vol. 17, no. 5, pp. 773-784.

Tamburi, G. (1969), 'The ILO and Social Security: The Challenge of Technical Co-operation', *International Social Security Review*, vol. 22, no. 4, pp. 480-491.

Tamburi, G. (1992), 'Misunderstanding Pension Privatisation: The Case Against The Do-It-Yourself Pension Kits', *Benefits And Compensation International*, March 1992, pp. 2-8.

Tamburi, G. (1997), 'Increased Private Participation in Retirement Pension Provision Trends and Policies', *Report prepared for the OECD Insurance Committee*, September 1997.

Tamburi, G. (1999), 'Motivation, purpose and processes in pension reform', *International Social Security Review*, vol. 52, no. 3/99, pp. 15-44.

Tamburi, G. and Mouton, P. (1987), 'The uncertain frontier between private and public pension schemes', pp. 29-43; in ISSA, *Conjugating Public and Private: The Case of Pensions*, ISSA, Studies and Research No.24, Geneva.

Tang, K-L. (1996), 'The determinants of social security in developing countries: a comparative analysis', *International Social Work*, vol. 39, no. 4, pp. 377-393.

Tanzi, V. (1999), 'Transition and the Changing Role of Government', *Finance & Development*, vol. 36, no. 2, http://www.imf.org.

Targett, S. (2000), 'Pension funds urged to invest in third world', *Financial Times*, 15 March, p. 5.

Taylor, L. (1997), 'Editorial: The Revival of the Liberal Creed - the IMF and the World Bank in a Globalized Economy', *World Development*, vol. 25, no. 2, pp. 145-152.

Taylor, P. (2000), 'Co-ordination in the UN System: The Reform Process in the Economic and Social Organizations of the UN', in D. Robinson, T. Hewitt and J. Harriss (eds), *Managing Development: Understanding Inter-Organizational Relationships*, Sage Publication and The Open University, London, pp. 193-213.

Taylor, R. (1996), 'Bigger role for governments will be in fashion next year', *Financial Times*, 28 June, p. 4.

Taylor-Gooby, P. (1999), 'Policy Change at a Time of Retrenchment: Recent Pension Reform in France, Germany, Italy and the UK', *Social Policy and Administration*, vol. 33, no. 1, pp. 1-19.

Teo, P. (1994), 'The National Policy On Elderly People In Singapore', *Ageing and Society*, vol. 14, pp. 405-427.

Thakor, A.V. (1996), 'The design of financial systems: An overview', *Journal of Banking and Finance*, no. 20, pp. 917-948.

Thérin, F. (2000), 'L'Afrique du Sud minée par le sida', *L'Express* (Paris), *25 May*, p. 28.

Thießen, U. (1998), 'Reform of Taxation and Social Security Systems in the CIS Countries: The Case of Ukraine', *Economic Bulletin*, vol. 35, no. 1, pp. 31-36.

Thompson, L.H. (1996), 'Private and public aspects of pension management', *Asia and Pacific News Sheet*, vol. 26, no. 3, pp. 18-25.

Thompson, L. (1998), *Older and Wiser: The Economics of Public Pensions*, The Urban Institute Press, Washington, D.C.

Thorne-Erasmus, J. (1998), 'Progress towards poverty reduction in South Africa', *paper presented at the 1998 Development Studies Association Conference*, University of Bradford, 9-11 September, Bradford.

Thornhill, J. (1998), 'Flemings aims to hit right note in Russian mutual fund sector', *Financial Times*, 1 July, p. 32.

Thornton, J. (1996), 'Financial deepening and economic growth in developing economics', *Applied Economic Letters*, vol. 3, no. 4, pp. 243-246.

Tout, K. (1992), 'Does Third Age plus Third World Equal Third Class', *Community Development Journal*, vol. 27, no. 2, pp. 122-129.

Toye, J. and Moore, M. (1998), 'Taxation, Corruption and Reform', in M. Robinson (ed), *Corruption and Development*, Frank Cass, London, pp. 60-84.

Trejos, J.D. *et al.* (1994), 'Enhancing Social Services in Costa Rica', in C. Aedo and O. Larrañaga (eds), *Social Service Delivery Systems: An Agenda for Reform*, Inter-American Development Bank, Washington, D.C.

Tribe, M. (1975), 'Social Security Systems in Developing Countries', *Department of Political Economy, Glasgow University, mimeo*.

Tribe, M. (1976a), 'The Household Economy and Social Security Policy: With particular reference to Africa South of the Sahara', *International Journal of Social Economics*, vol. 3, no. 3, pp. 179-197.

Tribe, M. (1976b), 'African Social Security - A Comment', *Journal of Modern African Studies*, vol. 14, no. 3, pp. 514-516.

Tribe, M. (1978), 'Social Security in an African Context', in T. Younis (ed), *Public Administration and the Dynamics of Change, Seminar Papers 1977-78*, Glasgow College of Technology, Glasgow.

Troisi, J. (1998), 'Meeting the Challenges of Ageing in India', *BOLD*, vol. 8, no. 3, pp. 4-6.

Turner, J. (1997), *An Operational Framework for Pension Reform: Retirement income systems for different economic, demographic and political environments*, ILO, Geneva.

Turner, J. and Korczyk, S. (1997), *An Operational Framework for Pension Reform: Design issues for defined benefit and defined contribution plans*, ILO, Geneva.

Turner, M. (1999), 'One man's dream to unite Africa', *Financial Times*, 29 November, p. 29.

UNCTAD (2000), *Capital Flows and Growth in Africa*, UN, Geneva.

UNCTAD (2000b), The Least Developed Countries 2000 Report Aid, Private Capital Flows and External Debt: The Challenge of Financing Development in the LDCs, UN, Geneva.

UNDP (1997), *Human Development Report 1997*, OUP, New York.

UNDP (1999), *Human Development Report 1999*, OUP, New York.

UNECA (1997), *Economic and Social Survey of Africa 1995-1996*, UNECA, Geneva.

United Nations (1986), *Developmental Social Welfare: A Global Survey Of Issues And Priorities Since 1968*, United Nations, New York.

Valdés-Prieto, S. (ed) (1997), *The Economics of Pensions: Principles, Policies and International Experience*, Cambridge University Press, Cambridge.

Valticos, N. (1969), 'Fifty Years of Standard Setting', *International Labour Review*, vol. 100, pp. 201-237.

van de Laar, A. (1980), *The World Bank and the Poor*, Martinus Nijhoff Publishing, Boston.

van de Walle, N. (1999), 'Aid's Crisis of Legitimacy: current proposals and future prospects', *African Affairs*, vol. 98, no. 392, pp. 337-352.

van de Walle, D. and Nead, K. (eds) (1995), *Public Spending and the Poor*, The John Hopkins University Press, Baltimore, Maryland.

van den Brink, R. and Chavas, J.P. (1997), 'The Microeconomics of an Indigenous African Institution: The Rotating Savings and Credit Associations', *Economic Development and Cultural Change*, vol. 45, no. 4, pp. 745-772.

van der Geest, W. and van der Hoeven, R. (eds) (1999), *Adjustment Employment and Missing Institutions in Africa: The Experience in Eastern and Southern Africa*, ILO, Geneva.

van Ginneken, W. (1996), *Social security for the informal sector: Issues, options and tasks ahead*, Working Paper: Promoting Interdepartmental Project on the Urban Informal Sector (1994/95), ILO, Geneva.

van Ginneken, W. (ed) (1997), 'Social Security for the Informal Sector: Investigating the feasibility of pilot projects in Benin, India, El Salvador and Tanzania', *Issues in Social Protection Discussion Paper 5*, ILO, Geneva.

van Ginneken, W. (ed) (1999a), 'Social security for the excluded majority: Case studies of developing countries', ILO, Geneva.

van Ginniken, W. (1999b), 'Social Security for the informal sector: A new challenge for the developing countries', *International Social Security Review*, vol. 52, no. 1, pp. 49-69.

Vatter, H.G. and Walker, J.F. (1998), 'Support for Baby-Boom Retirees - Not to worry', *Journal of Economic Issues*, vol. 32, no. 1, pp. 79-86.

Verbon, H. (1988), *The Evolution Of Public Pension Schemes*, Springer-Verlag, Berlin.

Vilas, C.M. (1996), 'Neoliberal Social Policy: Managing Poverty (Somehow)', *NACLA Report on the Americas*, vol. 29, no. 6, pp. 16-25.

Villacorta, L. (1994), 'Social Security In Asia And The Pacific: Current Provision,

Recent Changes And Future Trends', in EPF Corporate Planning Division (ed), *Workshop On Social Security*, Corporate Planning Division, EPF, Kuala Lumpur.

Vittas, D. (1992), 'Contractual Savings And Emerging Securities Markets', *Working Paper, Country Economic Series, WPS858*, The World Bank, Washington, D.C.

Vittas, D. (1993a), 'Swiss-Chilanpore: The Way Forward For Pension Reform? Switzerland, Singapore And Chile', *World Bank, Working Paper, WPS 1093*, The World Bank, Washington, D.C.

Vittas, D. (1993b), 'Options For Pension Reform In Tunisia', *Policy Research Working Papers Financial Sector Development Department WPS 1154*, The World Bank, Washington, D.C.

Vittas, D. (1993c). 'The Simple(r) Algebra Of Pension Plans', *Policy Research Working Papers Financial Sector Development Department WPS 1145*, The World Bank, Washington, D.C.

Vittas, D. (1995), 'Sequencing Social Security, Pension, and Insurance Reforms', *Working Paper Series 1531*, World Bank, Washington, D.C.

Vittas, D. (1996), 'Private Pension Funds in Hungary: Early Performance and Regulatory Issues', *Policy Research Working Paper 1638*, World Bank, Washington, D.C.

Vittas, D. (1997a), 'The Argentine Pension Reform and its Relevance for Eastern Europe', *Policy Research Working Paper 1819*, World Bank, Washington, D.C.

Vittas, D. (1997b), 'Private Pension Funds in Argentina's New Integrated Pension System', *Policy Research Working Papers 1820*, World Bank, Washington, D.C.

Vittas, D. (1998a), 'Regulatory Controversies of Private Pension Funds', *Policy Research Working Paper 1893*, World Bank, Washington, D.C.

Vittas, D. (1998b), 'The Role of Non-Bank Financial Intermediaries (with Particular Reference to Egypt)', *Policy Research Working Paper 1892*, World Bank, Washington, D.C.

Vittas, D. (1998c), 'Institutional Investors and Securities Markets: Which Comes First?', *ABCD LAC Conference*, San Salvador, El Salvador, Development Research Group, The World Bank, Washington, D.C.

Vittas, D. (2000), 'Pension Reform and Capital Market Development: "Feasibility" and "Impact" Preconditions', *WPS 2414*, World Bank, Washington, D.C.

Vittas, D. and Cho, Y.C. (1996), 'Credit Policies: Lessons from Japan and Korea', *The World Bank Research Observer*, vol. 11, no. 2, pp. 277-298.

Vittas, D. and Iglesias, A. (1992), 'The Rationale and Performance of Personal Savings Plans in Chile', *Working Paper, Country Economics Department, WPS867*, The World Bank, Washington, D.C.

Vittas, D. and Kawaura, A. (1994), 'Policy-based Finance and Financial Sector Development in Japan', *Financial Sector Development Department, World Bank, draft*.

Vittas, D. and Michelitsch, R. (1996), 'The Potential Role of Pension Funds: Lessons from OECD and Developing Countries', in R. Frydman, C.W. Gray and A. Rapacynski (eds), *Corporate Governance in Central Europe and Russia: Banks, Funds and Investors*, CEU, London, pp. 242-292.

Vittas, D. and Skully, M. (1991), 'Overview Of Contractual Savings Institutions', *Policy Research And External Affairs Working Papers Financial Policy And Systems WPS 605*, The World Bank, Washington, DC.

Vivian, J. (1994), *Social Safety Nets And Adjustment In Developing Countries, Occasional Paper no.1*, World Summit For Social Development, UNRISD, Geneva.

Voirin, M. (1994), 'Social Security in Central and Eastern Europe: Continuity and Change', in ISSA (ed), *Restructuring Social Security in Central and Eastern Europe: A Guide to Recent Developments, Policy Issues and Options*, ISSA, Geneva, pp. 184-185.

von Benda-Beckman, F., Gsänger, H. and Midgley, J. (1997), 'Indigenous Support and Social Security: Lessons from Kenya', in J. Midgley and M. Sherraden (eds), *Alternatives to Social Security*, Auburn House, London, pp. 105-120.

von Pischke, J.D. (1994), 'Structuring Credit to Manage Real Risks', in F.J.A. Bouman and O. Hospes (eds), *Financial Landscapes Reconstructed: The Fine Art of Mapping Development*, Boulder, Colorado, Westview Press.

Wade, R. (1985), 'East Asian Financial Systems as a Challenge to Economics: Lessons from Taiwan', *California Management Review*, vol. 27, no. 4, pp. 106-127.

Wade, R. (1994), 'Selective Industrial Policies in East Asia: is the East Asian Miracle right?', in A. Fishlow *et al.* (ed), *Miracle of Design ? Lessons from the East Asian Experience*, Overseas Development Council, Washington, D.C.

Wade, R. (1996), 'Globalisation and its Limits: Reports of the Death of the National Economy are Greatly Exaggerated', in S. Berger and R. Dore (eds), *National Diversity and Global Capitalism*, Cornell University Press, Ithaca, pp.60-88.

Wadhawan, S.K. (1969), 'Employees' Provident Fund Scheme - Development And Future Plans', *International Social Security Review*, vol. 22, no. 2, pp. 251-257.

Wagner, G.C., Kirner, E., Leinert, J. and Meinhardt, V. (1999), 'Fully Funded Insurance: No Panacea for Social Security for the Elderly', *Economic Bulletin*, vol. 36, no. 1, pp. 37-44.

Wagstyl, S. and Anderson, R. (1998), 'Czechs feel cheated as they go to the polls', *Financial Times*, 19 June, p. 4.

Wallich, C. (1983), 'Savings mobilization through social security: The experience of Chile through 1916-77', *Staff Working Papers 553*, World Bank, Washington, D.C.

Waterman, M. (1987), 'Changing Times In Zimbabwe', *Benefits And Compensation International*, vol. 16, no. 11, pp. 24-28.

Weyland, K. (1996), 'How Much Political Power do Economic Forces Have?

Conflicts Over Social Insurance Reform in Brazil', *Journal Public Policy*, vol. 16, no. 1, pp. 59-84.

White, G. (1998), 'China: towards an East Asian model?', in R. Goodman, R. White and H-J. Kwon (eds), *Welfare Orientalism and the State*, Routledge, London, pp.175-198.

Whitehead, A. and Lockwood, M. (1999), 'Gendering Poverty: A Review of Six World Bank African Poverty Assessments', *Development and Change*, vol. 30, no. 3, pp. 525-555.

Whiteside, N. (1996), 'Creating The Welfare State In Britain', *Journal Of Social Policy*, vol. 25, no. 1, pp. 83-103.

Williams, D. and Young, T. (1994), 'Governance, the World Bank and Liberal Theory', *Political Studies*, vol. 42, pp. 84-100.

Williams, F. (1998), 'ILO feels its age as it tries to keep up with a changing world', *Financial Times*, 2 June, p. 6.

Williamson, J. (1990), '*Latin American Adjustment: How much has happened?*', IIE, Washington, D.C.

Williamson, J. (1994), 'The Political Economy of Policy Reform', Institute for International Economics, Washington, D.C.

Williamson, J. (1997), 'Washington Consensus Revisited', in L. Emmerij (ed), *Economic and Social Development into the XXI Century*, Inter-American Development Bank, Washington, D.C.

Williamson, J. (1997b), 'Should Women Support the Privatization of Social Security?', *Challenge*, vol. 40, no. 4., July-August, pp. 97-108.

Williamson, J.B. and Pampel, F.C. (1993), *Old-Age Security in Comparative Perspective*, Oxford University Press, Oxford.

Wilson, A.O. (1999), 'Targeted medical services for older Africans - a new imperative', *The ACP-EU Courier*, no. 176, pp. 46-47.

Wolf, M. (1999), 'Caught in the transition trap', *Financial Times*, 30 June, p. 23.

Wolfensohn, J. and Stiglitz, J.E. (1999), 'Growth is not enough', *Financial Times*, 22 September, p. 22.

Wolffe, R. (1999), 'Chief economist at World Bank quits', *Financial Times*, 25 November, p. 13.

Wong, C.K. and Lee, N.S.P. (2000), 'Popular Belief in State Intervention for Social Protection in China', *Journal of Social Policy*, vol. 29, no. 1, pp. 109-116.

Wong, J. (1994), 'The Social Dimension of Singapore's Economic Restructuring', in UN (ed), *Social Costs of Economic Restructuring in Asia and the Pacific, Development Papers no.15*, UN, Bangkok.

World Bank (1987), *Chile: Adjustment and Recovery, Report no. 6276*, World Bank, Washington, D.C.

World Bank (1989), *Malaysia: Matching Risks and Rewards in a Mixed Economy*, World Bank, Washington, D.C.

World Bank (1989), *World Development Report 1989*, World Bank, Washington, D.C.

World Bank (1990), *Mexico: Contractual Savings Report vol. I and II*, World Bank, Washington, D.C.

World Bank (1990), *World Development Report 1990*, World Bank, Washington, D.C.

World Bank (1993), *The East Asian Miracle: Economic Growth And Public Policy*, Oxford University Press, Oxford.

World Bank (1994), *Averting The Old Age Crisis: Policies to Protect the Old and Promote Growth*, Oxford University Press, Oxford.

World Bank (1994b), *Adjustment in Africa*, World Bank, Washington, D.C.

World Bank (1995), *Bureaucrats in Business: The Economics and Politics of Government Ownership*, OUP, Oxford.

World Bank (1996), *World Development Report 1996: From Plan to Market*, The World Bank, Washington, D.C.

World Bank (1997a), *Private Capital Flows to Developing Countries: The Road to Financial Integration*, OUP, Washington, D.C.

World Bank (1997b), 'The Commission's Report Card', *Transition*, August, pp. 5-7.

World Bank (1997c), *World Bank Development Report 1997: The State in a Changing World*, World Bank, Washington, D.C.

World Bank (1997d), 'China Engaged: Integration with the Global Economy', *China 2020*, World Bank, Washington, D.C.

World Bank (1998), 'Press Release: World Bank to Support Pension Reform in Hungary', http://www.worldbank.org/html/extme/ press.html, site accessed: 27 January 1998.

World Bank (1998b), 'World Bank Lending Rises in Fiscal 1998', *Press Release*, no. 99/1884/S, 15 July 1998, http://www.worldbank.org; site accessed: 8 December 2000.

World Bank (1999a), '1999 Global Development Finance Report', http://www.worldbank.org/prospects/gdf99/chap4.pdf.

World Bank (1999b), *World Bank Development Report: Knowledge for Development*, World Bank, Washington, D.C.

World Bank (1999c), 'Development Dividend of Good Governance', *Transition*, vol. 10, no. 5, p. 3.

World Bank (1999d), 'What is Social Protection?', *Social Protection Overview*; http://www.worldbank.org: site accessed: 5 November 1999.

World Bank (2000), *World Bank Development Report 2000/2001: Attacking Poverty*, World Bank, Washington, D.C.

World Bank (2001), *Social Protection Sector Strategy: From Safety Net to Springboard*, World Bank, Washington, D.C.

World of Information (1995), *Africa Review 1995: The Economic and Business Review*, Kogan Page Ltd, Woking, UK.

Wuyts, M. (1996), 'Foreign Aid, Structural Adjustment, and Public Management: The Mozambican Experience', *Development and Change*, vol. 27, no. 4, pp. 717-749.

Yadava, K.N.S., Yadava, S.S. and Sharma, C.L.N. (1996), 'Socioeconomic Factors and Behavioural Problems of the Elderly Population: A Study of Rural Areas of Uttar Pradesh', *Ageing and Society*, vol. 16, no. 5, pp. 525-542.

Yanagihara, T. (1994), 'Anything new in the Miracle Report? Yes and No', *World Development*, vol. 22, no. 4.

Yaron, J. and Benjamin, M. (1997), 'Developing Rural Financial Markets', *Finance and Development*, vol. 34, no. 4, pp. 40-43.

Yee, L.D.S. (1983), 'Provident Funds: Observations Based On Experience In Fiji', in ILO (ed), *Social Security: Principles And Practices*, International Labour Office/FNPF, Geneva, pp. 127-136.

Yee, L.D.S. (1994), 'Provident Funds And Investment In Developing Countries In The Pacific', *International Social Security Review*, vol. 47, no. 1, pp. 55-72.

Yi, L. (1994), 'Social Security Reform In China Reviewed', *Benefits And Compensation International*, April 1992, pp. 2-8.

Yi, P.L. (1997), *Pension System Reform in China*, Sedgwick Noble Lowndes, Croydon.

Young, T. (1995), 'A Project to be Realised: Global Liberalism and Contemporary Africa', *Journal of International Studies*, vol. 24, no. 3, pp. 527-546.

Zuckerman, E. (1989), 'Adjustment Programs and Social Welfare', *World Bank Discussion Papers 44*, World Bank, Washington, D.C.

Zuckerman, E. and de Kadt, E. (1997), *The Public-Private Mix in Social Services: Health Care and Education in Chile, Costa Rica and Venezuela*, IADB, Washington, D.C.

Index